P9-DOG-163

BOOKS BY MICHAEL BESCHLOSS

Reaching for Glory: Lyndon Johnson's Secret White House Tapes, 1964–1965 (2001)

Taking Charge: The Johnson White House Tapes, 1963–1964 (1997)

The Crisis Years: Kennedy and Khrushchev, 1960–1963 (1991)

Mayday: Eisenhower, Khrushchev and the U-2 Affair (1986)

Kennedy and Roosevelt: The Uneasy Alliance (1980)

At the Highest Levels: The Inside Story of the End of the Cold War (1993)
(with Strobe Talbott)

Michael Beschloss

ROOSEVELT, TRUMAN AND THE DESTRUCTION OF HITLER'S GERMANY, 1941–1945

THE CONQUERORS

Simon & Schuster NEW YORK LONDON TORONTO SYDNEY SINGAPORE

SIMON & SCHUSTER
Rockefeller Center
1230 Avenue of the Americas, New York, NY 10020

For information regarding special discounts for bulk purchases,
please contact Simon & Schuster Special Sales at
1-800-456-6798 or business@simonandschuster.com

Maps by Jeffrey L. Ward, Inc.

Manufactured in the United States of America

1 3 5 7 9 10 8 6 4 2

Library of Congress Cataloging-in-Publication Data
Beschloss, Michael R.
The conquerors : Roosevelt, Truman and the destruction of Hitler's Germany,
1941–1945 / Michael Beschloss.
p. cm.
Includes bibliographical references and index.
1. Roosevelt, Franklin D. (Franklin Delano), 1882–1945. 2. Truman, Harry S., 1884–1972.
3. World War, 1939–1945—Germany. 4. Reconstruction (1939–1951)—Germany.
5. World War, 1939–1945—Diplomatic history. 6. United States—Foreign relations—1933–1945.
7. United States—Politics and government—1933–1945.
8. Morgenthau, Henry, 1891–1967. I. Title.
E807 .B46 2002
940.53'144'0943—dc21 2002030331

ISBN 0-684-81027-1

Credits for the photograph section are listed following the index.

For Afsaneh

PREFACE

THIS BOOK TELLS THE STORY of an important American success. During World War II, many Americans grimly expected that, even if the Allies won the war, the world would someday have to cope again with a raging, militaristic Germany under some future version of Adolf Hitler.[1] Instead, almost sixty years after VE-Day, Germany is democratic and peaceful.

The Conquerors argues that this success owes much to the wartime leadership of Franklin Roosevelt—and that of Harry Truman, during the four months after FDR's death. This book shows that while Roosevelt and then Truman fought the European war and bargained with their allies, Winston Churchill and Joseph Stalin, they had a larger aim than merely defeating the Nazis. They were determined that, after victory, the German system that had produced Hitler and his depraved movement should be so transformed that Germany could never again threaten the world.

As this volume demonstrates, during World War II neither Roosevelt nor Truman dealt flawlessly with the problems of Germany. In his self-assured private monologues about the German national character, FDR did not mention the Holocaust. Shockingly disengaged from the struggle to rescue Jewish refugees from Hitler, he made no serious effort to explore whether

1. Americans were asked in an April 1944 survey, "Assuming that Germany loses the war, do you think she will start as soon as possible preparing for another war?" Sixty percent said yes.

bombing the death camps might save many lives. During the last year of the war, sagging from an illness that he concealed from the public, Roosevelt was no longer able, as he once had, to balance a hundred different personalities and issues, which made him increasingly prone to mistakes. As for Truman, he suffered from having to carry out FDR's private intentions for postwar Germany without Roosevelt having ever bothered to tell him at length what they were.

The Conquerors shows above all, however, that, while heroically leading the fight against the Nazis, FDR and Truman also helped to lay the groundwork for postwar Germans to spare themselves and the world a future Adolf Hitler. Along with vanquishing the imperial Japanese, leading Japan toward democracy and thwarting the Soviet Union, this was one of America's great twentieth-century international achievements.

This book draws on relevant Soviet, British and German documents, but it concentrates on the American part of the story, especially the largely hidden role of FDR's closest friend in the Cabinet, Secretary of the Treasury Henry Morgenthau, Jr. The book shows how Morgenthau's horror on learning of the Holocaust compelled him to jeopardize his friendship with the President by demanding that he work harder to save Jews. Then, "obsessed" by Germany, he lobbied Roosevelt to support his draconian plan to destroy postwar Germany's factories and mines and let the defeated Germans "stew in their own juice." As the book shows, FDR's determination to change postwar Germany moved him to endorse much of Morgenthau's plan and pressure a reluctant Churchill to do the same. At one moment of irritation the President blurted out that male Germans should be "castrated."

In the end, however, Roosevelt knew that, while born out of justifiable anger at the Nazis and dread of a revived postwar Germany, Morgenthau's plan would violate old American traditions of magnanimity—and that, by fueling German resentment, it might create the conditions for another Hitler. History now shows that by destroying a barrier to Soviet power and alienating the Germans from Britain and America, the plan could have also opened the way for the Soviet Union to dominate postwar Europe. As this book relates, by the end of his life, Roosevelt had arrived at a different design, adopted in its essentials by Truman, that managed to thwart whatever menacing ambitions the Soviets had for Europe—and give postwar Germans the chance to prove themselves.

I started work on *The Conquerors* in 1992, soon after East and West Germany were merged. I researched and wrote for four years, then set the nearly completed manuscript aside to await the release of number of previously closed American, British and Soviet archives—and to write two volumes of a trilogy on Lyndon Johnson's White House tapes. Fortified with thousands of newly opened documents, I completed the book in 2001 and 2002.

The additional time provided not only previously unrevealed information but also hindsight. Had I written and published this book shortly after Germany was unified, I might have felt compelled to be more tentative in writing about whether its democratic experiment had succeeded. But after more than a decade of democracy in that once tragic country, it is easier to arrive at a more lasting verdict on how two American Presidents helped to make it possible.

—Michael Beschloss
Washington, D.C.
August 2002

CONTENTS

"We come as conquerors, but not as oppressors."

—General Dwight Eisenhower to the German people
as Allied forces entered Germany, November 1944

"The success of this occupation can only be judged fifty years from now. If the Germans at that time have a stable, prosperous democracy, then we shall have succeeded."

—Eisenhower in Frankfurt, October 1945

The Conquerors

CHAPTER ONE

The Plot to Murder Hitler

HAD THE PLOTTERS BEEN MORE DEFT, Thursday, July 20, 1944, would have been Adolf Hitler's last day on earth.

Six weeks after D-Day, the United States, Great Britain and their allies had landed a million men in France. The Red Army was marching westward. When Hitler's generals proposed retreat behind more defensible lines, the Führer had shaken his head, crying, "Victory or death!"

Now Hitler was burrowed in at the Wolf's Lair, his field headquarters near Rastenburg, in a melancholy, dank East Prussian forest. At noon, in a log barracks, he listened to a gloomy report from one of his army chiefs about Germany's retreat on the Eastern front. In the steamy room, Hitler took off the eyeglasses he vainly refused to use in public and mopped his forehead with a handkerchief. SS men and stenographers stood around the massive, long oak table like nervous cats. Maps were unfurled. Hitler leaned over them and squinted through a magnifying glass, grimacing at the bad news.

Into the room strode a thirty-seven-year-old officer named Claus von Stauffenberg. He was a Bavarian nobleman, with blond hair and sharp cheekbones, who had lost an eye and seven fingers to an Allied mine in Tunisia while fighting for Germany. Unknown to the Führer or the other two dozen people in the chamber, Stauffenberg was part of a secret, loosely rigged anti-Hitler conspiracy that included military officers, diplomats, businessmen, pastors, intellectuals, landed gentry.

Some wanted historians of the future to record that not all Germans were Nazis. Some simply wanted to spare their nation the full brunt of conquest by the Soviet, American and British armies. Still others were unsettled by Hitler's war against the Jews. For years, the plotters had tried to kill Hitler with rifles and explosives, but the Führer had always survived.

Disgusted by what he heard about Nazi brutality in Russia, Stauffenberg had taught himself how to use his remaining three fingers to set off a bomb. By luck, in July 1944, he was summoned to the Wolf's Lair to help brief Hitler about the Eastern front. When Stauffenberg entered the room, the Führer shook his hand, stared at him appraisingly, then returned to his maps.

Inside Stauffenberg's briefcase, swaddled in a shirt, was a ticking time bomb. While the Army chief droned on, Stauffenberg put the briefcase under the table. Leaving his hat and belt behind, as if he were stepping out for a moment, Stauffenberg walked out of the room and left the barracks.

About a quarter to one came a loud boom and swirl of blue-yellow flame, followed by black smoke.

Outside the barracks, Stauffenberg saw men carry out a stretcher on which lay a body shrouded by what seemed to be Hitler's cloak. Rushing to his car for a getaway flight to Berlin, he presumed that Adolf Hitler was no more. Stauffenberg hoped that next would come a public declaration of Hitler's assassination, an Army revolt and establishment of an anti-Nazi government in Berlin.

But when he arrived at General Staff headquarters on Bendler Street, there was only disarray. Fellow plotters were not convinced that Hitler had been killed. Aghast, Stauffenberg cried, "I myself saw Hitler carried out dead!"

But he was wrong. Striving for a better view of the maps, one of the Führer's aides had pushed the briefcase behind one of the table's massive supports, protecting Hitler from certain death. Stauffenberg and his adjutant, Werner von Haeften, a collaborator, had felt too rushed to put a second bomb in the briefcase. Had they done so, Hitler would have certainly been killed.

Instead, when the smoke cleared Hitler was still standing. With bloodshot eyes staring out from a soot-blackened face, he tamped down flame from his trousers. His hair stood out in spikes. His ruptured eardrums were bleeding. His right arm dangled numb at his side.

A weeping Field Marshal Wilhelm Keitel threw his arms around Hitler: "My Führer, you're alive! You're alive!"

After donning a fresh uniform, seemingly exhilarated by his survival, Hitler was almost merry. "Once again everything turned out well for me!" he chortled to his secretaries. "More proof that fate has selected me for my mission!" That afternoon he showed his scorched clothes to the visiting ousted Italian dictator Benito Mussolini: "Look at my uniform! Look at my burns!" Hitler had the uniform sent to his mistress, Eva Braun, for safekeeping as proof of his historical destiny.

When generals telephoned from the far reaches of the German Reich to learn whether, as some had heard, Hitler was dead, the Führer was furious that they should even raise the question. With froth on his lips, he shouted, "Traitors in the bosom of their own people deserve the most ignominious of deaths. . . . Exterminate them! . . . I'll put their wives and children into concentration camps and show them no mercy!" He even confronted his Alsatian dog: "Look me in the eyes, Blondi! Are you also a traitor like the generals of my staff?"

It did not take Hitler's men long to discover who was behind the plot. In Berlin, Stauffenberg and three fellow plotters were arrested. A five-minute trial, "in the name of the Führer," found them guilty of treason. In a shadowy courtyard, they were hauled before a firing squad.

Just before his execution, remembering his country before Hitler, Stauffenberg cried out, "Long live eternal Germany!"

AN HOUR AFTER MIDNIGHT on Friday, July 21, Berlin time, Hitler spoke by radio from the Wolf's Lair.[1] After a burst of military music, he declared, "Fellow members of the German race!" An "extremely small clique of ambitious, unscrupulous and foolish, criminally stupid officers" had plotted to kill him and the German high command—"a crime that has no equal in German history."

1. The broadcast was so late because Hitler's men had to summon the radio crew, who were swimming in the Baltic.

The plotters had "no bond and nothing in common with the German people." He was "entirely unhurt, apart from minor grazes, bruises or burns." Failure of the plot was "a clear sign from Providence that I must carry on with my work."

Hitler had come to power claiming that Germany had lost World War I because craven politicians in Berlin had betrayed the generals. The newest plotters, he now said, had planned to "thrust a dagger into our back as they did in 1918. But this time they have made a very grave mistake." His voice rose to a shriek: "Every German, whoever he may be, has a duty to fight these elements at once with ruthless determination. . . . Wipe them out at once!"

Fearing for his life, Hitler never again spoke in public. By his orders, hundreds of suspected conspirators were arrested, tortured and executed. Another five thousand of their relatives and suspected anti-Nazi sympathizers were taken to concentration camps. A decree went out for Stauffenberg's family to be "wiped out to its last member."

Hitler ordered some of the chief plotters "strung up like butchered cattle." A motion picture of their execution was rushed to the Wolf's Lair for the Führer's enjoyment. By one account, Hitler and his chief propagandist, Joseph Goebbels, watched in the Führer's private theater as the shirtless men on the screen swung from piano-wire nooses, writhing and dying while their carefully unbelted trousers fell off to reveal them naked.

Goebbels had demanded for years that Hitler's enemies be stalked with "ice-cold determination." But when the top Nazis watched the ghoulish flickering images of the lifeless plotters, it was later said, even the cold-blooded Goebbels had to cover his eyes to keep from passing out.

AS HITLER FINISHED HIS SPEECH from the Wolf's Lair, Franklin Roosevelt gave his own radio address from California. Speaking from a private railroad car at the San Diego naval base, he accepted the 1944 Democratic nomination for President. For wartime security reasons, the public was told only that the base was on the "Pacific coast."

The President was taking a five-week, fourteen-thousand-mile military inspection trip of the Pacific Coast, Hawaii and Alaska. His special nine-car railroad caravan had moved slowly from Chicago to Kansas City, El Paso and Phoenix, to "kill time" before his arrival in San Diego and spare him from having to sleep at night in a moving train. Secret Service agents had tried to keep Roosevelt's exact whereabouts a secret. At each stop, the President and his party were asked to stay aboard the train. But Roosevelt's famous Scottie dog, Fala, had to be taken off to relieve himself. When Pullman porters and ticket takers saw Fala, they knew who was really aboard the train called "Main 985."

One might have expected Roosevelt to be delighted when he heard the news of a coup that might topple Adolf Hitler. If a new, post-Hitler government accepted the Allied demand for unconditional surrender, it would save millions of lives and let the Big Three—Roosevelt, Joseph Stalin and Winston Churchill—throw Allied forces fully into the war against Japan.

But Roosevelt knew that life was rarely that uncomplicated. For months, American intelligence had secretly warned him of plots against Hitler. In early July 1944, Allen Dulles of the Office of Strategic Services reported from Bern, Switzerland, that "the next few weeks will be our last chance to demonstrate the determination of the Germans themselves to rid Germany of Hitler and his gang and establish a decent regime." Eight days before Stauffenberg set off his bomb, Dulles warned that "a dramatic event" might soon take place "up north."[2]

Roosevelt would have certainly realized that a new, post-Hitler junta would probably demand a negotiated settlement. It might insist that certain members of the German military high command, government and other institutions stay in place. This would frustrate his declared intention to remake postwar Germany from the ground up so that it could never threaten the world again. Official Allied policy was unconditional surrender. But Roosevelt knew that if a rump post-Hitler government sued for peace, it would be difficult for Churchill and himself to persuade their war-exhausted peoples to keep fighting and lose hundreds of thousands more lives.

Dulles had reported that one group of anti-Hitler conspirators wanted "to prevent Central Europe from coming . . . under the control of Russia." As Roosevelt knew, Churchill might be sorely tempted by a deal with a new German government that could save British lives and block the Soviets in

2. With the time-honored self-protectiveness of intelligence chiefs, William Donovan of the OSS was worried that Roosevelt might be angry that Donovan had not sent him a more specific warning of the July 20 plot against Hitler. Covering his rear end, two days later he sent the President a transcript of a telephone conversation he had had with Dulles, saying that the attempt "did not come as a great surprise."

Europe, provoking an immediate confrontation with Stalin. Even worse was the possibility that a post-Hitler government might side with the Soviets against the Anglo-Americans.

Told of the attempted assassination, reporters in San Diego badgered Roosevelt's aides for the President's reaction to the news. The President offered no comment. Whatever he said would be playing with fire. If he publicly welcomed the plot, he might seem to be backing off from unconditional surrender. If he denounced it, he might appear indifferent to a development that might end the war quickly. If he opposed the plot and it proved ultimately to succeed, Stalin would have a better chance to make a deal with a new post-Hitler government that would let the Soviets dominate Europe.

Instead, Roosevelt wrote a carefully worded private message to Stalin suggesting that the plot was encouraging because it revealed a Nazi foe in disarray: "We have just received news of the difficulties in Germany and especially at Hitler's headquarters. It is all to the good." With the same cheerful presumption that the plot could be nothing but good news, Roosevelt wrote his wife, Eleanor, "Dearest Babs. . . . I might have to hurry back earlier if this German revolt gets worse! I fear though that it won't."

ON FRIDAY EVENING IN CHICAGO, with Roosevelt's consent, Democrats had chosen Senator Harry Truman of Missouri for Vice President. In San Diego, with Truman safely nominated, the President and Fala were driven in darkness to Broadway Pier and piped aboard the heavy cruiser *Baltimore,* bound for Honolulu. To protect Roosevelt from Japanese attack, the gleaming new ship was escorted by four destroyers. It followed an unpredictable route and was darkened from sunset to sunrise. During the voyage, sailors had to be stopped from cutting snippets of hair from Fala to send home.

The President slept soundly and sat on the vessel's flag bridge, enjoying the sun and cool breezes. During his Pacific idyll and later in the trip, Roosevelt received intelligence reports that after Hitler's near-murder, the "blood purge" of the Führer's internal enemies was "ruthless." So many Germans were being arrested that "schools and other large public buildings are being used as supplementary jails." Roosevelt was informed that after Hitler's clean sweep, Germans would now "probably have to wait for the complete military collapse of Germany to rid themselves of the Nazis."

When the *Baltimore* arrived in Honolulu, its presidential flag was hoisted. This upset the Secret Service, but by now, almost everyone in the Hawaiian capital knew that Roosevelt was coming. Staying in a mansion bequeathed to the United States by a hard-drinking millionaire who had committed suicide, the President had what he called a "splendid" talk with General Douglas MacArthur about the Pacific war.

Only a full week after Hitler's near-assassination did Roosevelt make his first public comment about the plot. As the President sat with reporters on the emerald lawn of the Hawaiian governor's palace, he was excruciatingly careful: "I don't think I know anything more about it than you do. . . . We can all have our own ideas about it."[3] He went on to reaffirm the Allied demand for unconditional surrender: "Practically every German denies the fact they surrendered in the last war. But this time, they are going to know it!"

From Moscow, Stalin's propagandists agreed: "Hitlerite Germany will be driven to her knees not by insurgent officers, but by ourselves and our Allies!"

CHURCHILL SCOFFED at the anti-Hitler plot. Before the House of Commons, he explained that high German officials were merely trying to elude their inevitable, absolute defeat by "murdering one another."[4]

The Prime Minister's icy dismissal concealed a secret that few in His Majesty's government knew. According to British intelligence documents released in 1998, Churchill's secret agents were themselves trying to have Hitler murdered. Under the code name Operation Foxley, they schemed to have Hitler's tea poisoned, his uniform doused with lethal bacteria, his train blown up, or for him to be shot during his daily walk.[5]

3. Roosevelt insisted that even this anodyne comment not be quoted.

4. After the war, Churchill made an *amende honorable,* insisting that he had been "misled" about the size of the anti-Hitler conspiracy: "These men fought without help from within or from abroad, driven forward only by the restlessness of their conscience."

5. Another related plan was to infiltrate a murderous British agent into the harem of Hitler's womanizing propagandist, Joseph Goebbels, whose wife had abandoned him: "Untrammelled in any way, Goebbels may pursue these affairs with an even greater zest than before." Still another would have Rudolf Hess, Hitler's onetime deputy, who was imprisoned in England, "hypnotized" to return to Germany and kill the SS chief Heinrich Himmler: "Hess is known to be an extremely nervous individual and should be very susceptible to hypnotic treatment."

One British colonel who knew about the operation could not understand why they were going after Hitler: He was doing such a good job of losing the war! Killing the Führer, he warned, might unite Germans against the Allied armies. Assassination would "canonize" Hitler and "give birth to the myth that Germany would have been saved had he lived." Another British officer said, "I think Hitler should be permitted to live until he dies of senile decay before the eyes of the people he has misled. . . . Make him a laughing stock."

A more sober British intelligence man insisted that they keep on trying. Hitler's "mystical hold" over the German people, he wrote, was "keeping the country together" as the Anglo-Americans struggled to free Europe.

ROOSEVELT AGREED WITH Stalin and Churchill that the paramount question left by the European war would be what happened to Germany. He believed that a lasting peace would depend on whether he and Churchill could maintain their friendship with the Soviet Union and whether Germany could be so transformed that it would never threaten the world again.

But how? Even with the European war rushing toward climax and Allied armies about to pierce the German border, the President refused to commit himself. He told exasperated aides that much would depend on "what we and the Allies find when we get into Germany—and we are not there yet."

With his extravagant confidence in his ability to master events, Franklin Roosevelt was keeping his options open until the final possible moment.

CHAPTER TWO

"Unconditional Surrender"

No other American President has had more early experience on German soil than Franklin Roosevelt. After his elderly father suffered a heart attack, his parents brought their only son to Germany eight times, where they took the cure at the famous health resort of Bad Nauheim.

During Franklin's first visit in 1891, at the age of nine, he was enrolled for six weeks in a local school—mainly to improve his German. "Rather amusing," recorded his mother, Sara, "but I doubt if he learns much." The Roosevelts stayed in a British-owned hotel called the Villa Britannia. Anglophile, partial to French culture, they considered most Germans crude and inferior. Sara complained about dining with "German swine."

The Germany that Franklin first encountered had been created twenty years earlier, after the Franco-Prussian War, by the "Iron Chancellor," Otto von Bismarck—twenty ancient kingdoms, free cities and provinces forged into a single Reich. In 1890, Bismarck was fired by Kaiser Wilhelm II, who spoke of Germany's "destiny" to rule.

By chance, in 1901, Roosevelt actually met the Kaiser. At nineteen, he and his mother were sailing the Norwegian fjords when they encountered Wilhelm II's gleaming white yacht *Hohernzollern* and were invited aboard for tea. As Roosevelt recalled, he filched a pencil bearing the bite marks of the Kaiser's teeth.

Years later, as President, Roosevelt liked to believe that his own early German experience gave him a special understanding of German politics and psychology. He recalled German schoolchildren chattering about "the inevitable war with France and the building of the Reich into the greatest world power." He insisted that on his first visit there, Germany was "not a military nation." Politics was local and there was "decent family life." But by the late 1890s, he recalled, boys and girls wore uniforms and were "taught to march."

Roosevelt shared his mother's social prejudices. In 1905, during his honeymoon with Eleanor, he wrote his mother from a German spa that "by a show of severity" he had arranged to sit as far as possible from where Germans dined—"four long pigsties, where the strange assortment of mortals (swine are mortal, n'est-ce pas?) consume victuals." He noted that when Germans spoke of his distant cousin, President Theodore Roosevelt, there was "a certain animosity and jealousy as usual." During the same trip, Eleanor and he were riding by train through the German countryside when a German passenger brusquely reached across him to shut the window without asking. Eleanor wrote her new mother-in-law that she "thought Franklin would burst and a duel would ensue."

During World War II, while waging war against Hitler, Roosevelt told friends and family colorful stories—possibly exaggerated or imaginary—about his youthful brushes with German authoritarianism. He claimed that while pedaling with his tutor through southern Germany, he had been arrested four times in a single day.[1]

In another tale, perhaps an embellishment of his honeymoon encounter with the rude German on the train, he claimed that while traveling with his mother and a friend of hers to Berlin, a "Prussian officer" had once closed the train window. Since his mother's friend had a "bad headache," Roosevelt reopened it. According to him, the Prussian twice again closed it. As Roosevelt claimed, he knocked the Prussian to the floor, for which he was thrown into a Berlin jail: "My mother called the American embassy, but it took them several hours to get me out of prison."

ROOSEVELT'S MORE SERIOUS EDUCATION on Germany came during World War I. When fighting broke out in Europe in 1914, he was a thirty-two-year-old Assistant Secretary of the Navy. President Woodrow Wilson

1. For swiping cherries, rolling over a goose, taking his bicycle into a train station and riding his bicycle into a German village after the sun had gone down.

decreed neutrality, but Roosevelt privately wrote, "I hope England will join in and with France and Russia force peace *at Berlin*!"

After American entry into the war in April 1917, Roosevelt gave speeches against "Kaiserism" and "Prussianism." He insisted that Germans were a "misguided" people "subjected to the rule of a military caste" and "led along a path they could not understand." In the summer of 1918, touring battlefields in France and Belgium, he wrote in his diary of "stolid, stupid" German prisoners and the "little pile of dead Boche" that offended "our sensitive noses."

President Wilson's decisions on Germany foreshadowed the decisions Roosevelt would have to make a generation later, during World War II. Committed by his Fourteen Points to self-determination and enforcement of the peace by a League of Nations, Wilson said he had "no desire to march triumphantly into Berlin."

Roosevelt insisted that if England, France and the United States did not plunge deep into Germany, the Germans would convince themselves that they had not really lost the war. Germany's aggressive militarism would survive. He wanted the Germans "cut down and purged." When he was asked for advice on peace terms for the German navy, Roosevelt argued for unconditional surrender. "The one lesson the German will learn is the lesson of defeat," he said.

In January 1919, after the armistice, he took his wife to the ancient fortress at Ehrenbreitstein, on the Rhine and Mosel Rivers. He had seen the bastion as a boy and wanted to see it flying an American flag. When he saw none, he was outraged to be told that the local American commander did not want to upset the Germans. Roosevelt took up the matter with General John J. Pershing, commander of the American Expeditionary Force, who ordered the Stars and Stripes hoisted "within the hour."

Under the Treaty of Versailles, Germany was ordered to slash its military; demilitarize the eastern bank of the Rhine; surrender its colonies; give land to Belgium, France, Denmark and Poland; accept absolute blame for World War I; and pay the Allies reparations for damage caused by the war—ultimately billions of dollars. The French Prime Minister, Georges Clemenceau, had insisted on much of this over Wilson's objections. The Allies also imposed a new political structure, based on proportional representation, to prevent another dictatorship.

Most of this ultimately fed German extremism. Adolf Hitler and others charged that their military had been "stabbed in the back" by "criminal" politicians and kept from winning the war. The new legislature was mired in deadlock and chaos, as none of the dozens of new political parties proved large enough to form a stable government.

Some Americans complained that the German peace had been too soft. The Allies had occupied only the western bank of the Rhine and allowed the German government to continue. Five years after the end of World War I, General Pershing complained that the Allies had never made sure the Germans "knew they were beaten," adding, "It will have to be done all over again."

Roosevelt agreed. In the 1920s, as a lawyer and private businessman recovering from infantile paralysis, which he contracted at the age of thirty-nine, he felt that Versailles had been both too hard, burdening Germany with financial and other obligations it would only resent and could never fulfill, and too soft, because it did not do enough to keep Germans from wishing for war and being able to wage it.[2] He watched gloomily as his worst fears unfolded. The Weimar democracy sagged under hyperinflation, war debt and reparations, resentment over the harshness of the Versailles treaty, and the conviction, fanned by Hitler, that betrayers of the German military had held back Germany from its historical destiny.

Roosevelt thought Wilson should have insisted that the victors occupy Germany and train the Germans to give up their old ambitions for dictatorship, a strong military and a world empire. When he saw Hitler come to power shortly before his inauguration in 1933, Roosevelt realized earlier than most Americans that during his term in office, the United States might be forced to pay for Wilson's mistakes.

In December 1941, during a radio speech to Americans after Pearl Harbor, Roosevelt insisted that the United States could "accept no result save victory, final and complete." Later in the war, the President said that when victory in Europe came, the Allies must heed the lesson of 1918. In Germany, they "must not allow the seeds of the evils we shall have crushed to germinate and reproduce themselves in the future."

IN JANUARY 1943, the President seized the opportunity to practice what he preached. After a bumpy forty-eight-hour flight in a requisitioned Pan American clipper, his first air journey as President, he landed in

2. Roosevelt did feel that the British economist John Maynard Keynes's well publicized argument that blamed Versailles for later German extremism was overdrawn.

the old Moroccan port city of Casablanca to meet with Winston Churchill.

Coping with the German thrust into the western Soviet Union, Joseph Stalin stayed home. Anglo-American forces had just halted Hitler's advance in North Africa, but the Nazis were in control in Europe from the Atlantic to Leningrad and Stalingrad. Before the Casablanca meeting, Roosevelt had warned Churchill that they should not "give Stalin the impression that we are settling everything between ourselves before we meet him."

Stalin was lambasting his allies in public for their refusal to open a promised second front against Hitler—the invasion of western Europe that would relieve German pressure on the Red Army. The British ambassador in Moscow, Clark Kerr, advised Churchill that the Soviets were threatening to break with Britain and America unless a second front was opened soon. Some Soviet officials were wondering aloud whether the Anglo-Americans were secretly plotting to let the Germans bleed the Soviet Union dry, after which they would make a separate peace with Berlin.

At Casablanca, Roosevelt and Churchill agreed to issue a public statement that the Allies were "resolved to pursue the war to the bitter end." From Roosevelt's point of view, this would prevent repeating Wilson's mistakes in handling Germany at the end of World War I, and calm Stalin's fears about Anglo-American determination. It would be a defiant statement at a moment when the Allies had been thrown back on their heels in Europe. It would also foreclose disagreements among the Big Three and within each of their governments about war aims. Over luncheon, Roosevelt suggested that they use the phrase "unconditional surrender."

Churchill had his private doubts but was so dependent on Roosevelt's support of England that he strained to show enthusiasm.[3] "Perfect!" he said. "I can just see how Goebbels and the rest of them will squeal."

"It's just the thing for the Russians. . . . Uncle Joe might have made it up himself!" Roosevelt said.

At a press conference marking the end of the Casablanca meeting, Roosevelt told reporters, "I think we have all had it in our hearts and heads before, but I don't think it has ever been out on paper . . . and that is . . . that

3. Churchill had cleared the demand against Germany with his War Cabinet before departure. He knew that it would reassure the United States that after victory in Europe, Britain would go to war against Japan.

peace can come to the world only by the total elimination of German and Japanese war power." This meant "unconditional surrender by Germany, Italy and Japan." The Allies would fight to destroy "the philosophies in those countries which are based on conquest and the subjugation of other people." He declared that Casablanca should be called the "unconditional surrender" meeting. Churchill chimed in, "Hear, hear!"

AFTER RETURNING TO LONDON, Churchill defended the policy of unconditional surrender before the House of Commons: "Twice within our lifetime" the Germans had "plunged the world into their wars of expansion and aggression. . . . Nazi tyranny and Prussian militarism are the two main elements in German life which must be absolutely destroyed . . . if Europe and the world are to be spared a third and still more frightful conflict."

The Prime Minister's eloquence concealed the fact that he did not quite believe what he was saying. He had been loathe to quarrel with Roosevelt at Casablanca, but he was pessimistic that unconditional surrender would placate Stalin. He told his War Cabinet afterward, "Nothing in the world will be accepted by Stalin as an alternative to our placing fifty or sixty divisions in France by the spring of this year."

More than Roosevelt, Churchill worried that unconditional surrender would cause Germans to struggle harder against the Allies and prolong the war: If the Germans had nothing to hope for after an Allied victory, why not fight until the bitter end? After Casablanca, Joseph Goebbels's propagandists warned the German people that the unconditional surrender demand was hard proof that if the Allies won the war, they would enslave and exterminate them.

Nor did Churchill share Roosevelt's utopian aspirations to transform postwar German society. Suspicious of Stalin, he knew that the chief bulwark against Soviet domination of postwar Europe might have to be Germany. To keep that bulwark in place, the Anglo-Americans might have to ensure that the German infrastructure was operating as soon as possible after their victory.

Churchill decided that he would interpret unconditional surrender in his own way. Privately, he told associates that, for him, it simply meant that after victory, the Allies would have a "free hand" in Germany, unbound by previous commitments—not that the victors should feel licensed to "behave in a barbarous manner" or "blot out Germany from among the nations of Europe."

STALIN WAS INFORMED ABOUT Roosevelt and Churchill's unconditional surrender declaration just as the Red Army turned back the Germans at Stalingrad. As Churchill had foreseen, the Soviet leader was not happy about it. He was angry that his allies had not consulted him in advance. He immediately understood that they might use it as a poor substitute for the second front he was waiting for. He feared, even more than Churchill, that the unconditional surrender demand would unite and steel the German people against the Allies.

Stalin was also reluctant to say things in public that might jaundice postwar Germans against the Soviet Union. He knew the difficulty of converting Germans to the Soviet way. Communism fits Germany," he once said, "like a saddle fits a cow." Still, like Lenin, he had never stopped dreaming of a Communist Germany—or at least that Germany, with its industrial might and skilled manpower, might be made to help modernize Russia. He was determined that millions of Soviet soldiers should not have lost their lives in World War II only to be faced with a hostile German nation. He was still in a cold fury over Hitler's surprise invasion of the Soviet Union in June 1941.

Stalin's approach to a postwar Germany was to play a double game. Publicly he would avoid the inflammatory anti-German rhetoric heard from Roosevelt and Churchill, subtly telegraphing to Germans that the Soviets might be the most friendly of their potential conquerors. Privately he would demand that his allies commit themselves to draconian methods to shatter postwar German power—partition, mass trials and executions, forced labor, expulsions of millions of Germans from German territory, as well as more traditional demands for reparations and disarmament. Such measures could keep Germany from threatening the Soviet Union again for a generation or so. They might also create a power vacuum allowing the Soviet Union to push into postwar central Europe.

In February 1942 Stalin made it clear to the world that he would not endorse the view that there was no difference between the Nazis and the German people. He declared, "Hitlers come and go, but the German people and the German state remain." Denouncing the "prattle" in the "foreign press" that the Red Army wished to "destroy the German state," he claimed that his only aim was to "drive out the German occupiers from our country."

In the summer of 1943, Stalin formed what amounted to his own German government-in-exile, the National Committee for a Free Germany. Its members included old German Communists who had fled to Moscow and high-ranking German prisoners of war whom the Soviets had captured at Stalingrad. Designed to entice German "working people," its platform extolled the glories of Soviet-German cooperation. Some of the committee's members were quietly told that after the war, unlike some of Germany's enemies, the Soviet Union was determined to preserve a unified German state and a strong German army.

Stalin publicly claimed that the Free Germany Committee was intended to reduce German resistance. But many American and British planners feared, with good reason, that its actual purpose was to serve as the political spearhead of Soviet influence in postwar Germany. Under the best of circumstances, from Stalin's point of view, the new committee could be the embryo of a puppet postwar German government under Soviet control. Some of its radio broadcasts to Germany clearly suggested that Soviet occupation would be more lenient than one by the Anglo-Americans.

William Bullitt, who had served as Roosevelt's ambassador to the Soviet Union and France, warned the President that "Stalin's objective is to set up a Soviet Quisling government in Germany."[4] After an Allied victory, he wrote, the United States must stop "the flow of the Red amoeba" and "keep the Bolsheviks from replacing the Nazis as masters of Europe."

While publicly using the Free Germany committee and other means to persuade the Germans of Soviet friendliness, Stalin was privately hustling his allies to make sure that postwar Germany was dismembered. As early as December 1941, in Moscow, meeting with British Foreign Secretary Anthony Eden, he had privately demanded that East Prussia, the Rhineland, Bavaria and Austria all be made into separate nation-states, and that France seize German territory all the way up to the Rhine. When Eden reported to Churchill, the Prime Minister replied that publicly raising the idea of dismemberment now would "rally all Germans around Hitler."

4. Meaning a Soviet puppet government. Vidkun Quisling was a Norwegian collaborator with the Nazis.

At the White House in March 1943, Eden warned Roosevelt that at the end of the war, Stalin, with his "deep-seated mistrust of the Germans," would "insist" on dismemberment. Unless Roosevelt and Churchill reached an "understanding" with Stalin about postwar Germany, "either Germany will go Communist or an out-and-out anarchic state will set in."

Roosevelt was still haunted by the failure of Woodrow Wilson. He told Eden that he hoped "we would not use the methods discussed at Versailles" to impose a division of Germany. Better instead to "encourage the differences and ambitions that will spring up within Germany" for separate states after the war. He recalled that before Bismarck, there had been many German states and peoples. Even if there should be no such spontaneous movement, Prussia, with its militaristic tradition, must certainly be removed: "The Prussians cannot be permitted to dominate all Germany."

The frustrated Eden left the White House appalled by what he privately called Roosevelt's "cheerful fecklessness." He sarcastically wondered whether the President had learned European history and geography through his passion for stamp collecting. He felt that Roosevelt "seemed to see himself disposing of the fate of many lands" like "a conjuror, skillfully juggling with balls of dynamite, whose nature he failed to understand."

Eden did not realize that Roosevelt's manner was to think aloud. He would soon discover that his advice about toughness toward Germany had made more of an impression on the President than he thought.

CHAPTER THREE

"Fifty Thousand Germans Must Be Shot!"

By the fall of 1943, Stalin was growing all the more impatient for the Anglo-Americans to open the second front they had pledged. That September, he was again outraged when Churchill and Roosevelt froze the Soviets out of the unconditional surrender by the new Italian government of General Pietro Badoglio, who had deposed Mussolini.

Roosevelt asked his Secretary of State, Cordell Hull, to fly to Moscow for a meeting with the Soviet Foreign Minister, Vyacheslav Molotov, along with Anthony Eden. Physically exhausted, Hull suffered from diabetes and tuberculosis, which he concealed. He was claustrophobic and had never flown on an airplane before. But he was so thrilled to be invited to make the journey that, without asking his internist or his wife, he quickly told the President yes.

For years, the old ex-congressman from Tennessee had operated less as Roosevelt's Secretary of State than as his aggrieved chaperone. With grace and loyalty, Hull had tried to provide structure to a President prone to chatting about unconventional ideas, and who made Hull's life miserable by flagrantly circumventing him with a ceaseless parade of personal envoys. He complained, "I just don't know what's going on and the President won't let me help him."

The President privately joked about Hull's lisp and loved to impersonate him, crying, "Jesus Chwist!" For a decade he had done much of his important business through Under Secretary of State Sumner Welles, an old Roosevelt family friend whom Hull hatefully denounced as an "all-American thun of a bitch."

Roosevelt had asked Welles to attend the Moscow conference instead of Hull. But by the fall of 1943, the President had concluded that widespread rumors about Welles's secret homosexual liaisons—eagerly spread by Hull with theatrical indignation—made him a security risk, forcing Roosevelt to sadly banish his old friend from public life.

Roosevelt had left Hull in Washington when he went to see Churchill at Casablanca. When Hull learned of Roosevelt's demand for unconditional surrender, he was upset. He feared that the demand would prolong the war against Germany and require the Allies to "take over every phase" of German life after victory in Europe. As Hull later recalled, he asked the President to show him the "political part" of his secret correspondence with Churchill. Roosevelt said "he would give it to me, and three hours later, I get a message that the President had decided he would not do it."

After Pearl Harbor, Roosevelt had assigned postwar planning for Germany and the rest of the world to Hull's State Department. From the President's point of view, somebody had to do it while he attended to the more urgent problems of winning the war. Although he conscientiously met with postwar planning committees, he believed that by the time World War II was over, any plans would have been revised a hundred times anyway and that, as always, he would keep the ultimate power of decision in his own hands.

While Roosevelt ran the war, Hull's planners envisioned a strong, self-supporting postwar German economy that would help restore sanity to its society and empower the rebuilding of Europe. Free trade would buttress German democracy and stability.

In September 1943, Roosevelt sent Hull a copy of a letter published in the *New York Times* by his friend Gerard Swope, president of General Electric. Swope had recommended that after the war, the Allies break up Germany, slap strict controls on German heavy industry and disperse the "Prussian military clique."

Roosevelt liked the letter. Hull was aghast. At the White House on Wednesday, October 5, he told the President that postwar Germany should remain unified, although stripped of East Prussia, with other minor border changes: "Imposed partition would be little short of a disaster both for Germany and for us."

Roosevelt disagreed. He reminded Hull that he had traveled and studied in Germany. He could speak German and he knew the country better than Hull did. Maybe his memories were "too old" to be "valid," he said, but to his mind, the only way to prevent another war was to partition Germany.

The immediate postwar period would be "trial and error," he told Hull. But first they should slice Germany into three or more states, bound only by a system of common services, and strip those new states of "all military activities" and "armament industries." East Prussia should be separated from Germany, "and all dangerous elements of the population forcibly removed." And postwar Germans should provide reparations to those countries that were Hitler's victims—"not money," as after World War I, "but equipment and manpower."

Roosevelt was drawing as usual from his half-remembered experiences in Germany, with little careful thought or reading about the country or its future. He showed little understanding, for instance, of the difference between the autocracies of the last Kaiser and Hitler—or of Prussia, which he incorrectly viewed as the militaristic nucleus of Nazi evil. It was not Prussia but Bavaria that was the seedbed for Naziism. The vulgar flamboyance of Hitler's circle flouted old Prussian instincts of self-restraint and respect for tradition.

Hull did not know it, since Roosevelt did not allow him to read the pertinent secret cables and documents, but Roosevelt's first priority at the moment was to mollify Stalin, whom he presumed to be interested in German reparations and dismemberment. He wanted Hull to let Stalin know that, even though opening the second front might take a little longer, on postwar Germany his American ally was sympathetic.

AFTER COUGHING UP a considerable amount of blood during his air journey, Hull arrived in Moscow on Tuesday, October 18, 1943. At Roosevelt's instance, he told Stalin's Foreign Minister, Molotov, that after the war, Prussia, the "taproot of all evil," should be severed from Germany. Many of his experts were "extremely skeptical" about further dismemberment, he said, but the idea had support "in high quarters" in Washington, and the United

States would keep an "open mind." Certainly German power should be "decentralized."

Molotov replied that the Soviets would endorse any measure to "render Germany harmless in the future."

Hull made offers stemming from what he and Roosevelt thought to be Stalin's demand for a hard peace with postwar Germany. Sounding tougher than his own planners, he proposed that the Allies dismantle the German military and stop the production of arms, including the materials that were "essential" to make them.[1] Postwar Germany must offer reparations in goods and services for its "physical damage" to the Soviet Union and other countries. This was no small enticement to the Soviets, who were eager to rebuild.

Hull proposed that after Germany's defeat, the country be jointly occupied by all three Allied armies and run by an Allied Control Council. Under a bill of rights, the council would help create a democratic German government that would provide Germans a "tolerable standard of living."

Molotov said that Hull's ideas sounded promising as long as they were "a minimum and not a maximum proposal." Molotov was much tougher on Germany than Hull, but the Secretary of State felt that the Soviet aggressiveness toward the Germans might keep Stalin from trying to make a separate peace with Berlin that might lead to a Communist postwar Germany.

When the discussion turned to German war criminals, Hull spoke up with untypical vehemence: "If I had my way, I would take Hitler and Mussolini and Tojo and their arch-accomplices and bring them before a drumhead court-martial.[2] And at sunrise on the following day there would occur an historic incident!" Molotov and his aides applauded and cheered.

At the end of the conference, Hull, Eden and Molotov issued what soon became known as the "Moscow Declaration" on war crimes. Using language drafted beforehand by Churchill, they decreed that Germans accused of atrocities would be "sent back to the countries in which their abominable deeds were done." The three victors would jointly try major war criminals whose offenses were not restricted to one country.

1. Misinterpreting what the State Department intended, Molotov may have presumed that this meant large categories of materials such as steel, chemicals, synthetic oil and rubber.

2. A summary trial for an offense committed during military operations. Such courts-martial had once often occurred around drumheads.

One purpose of the Moscow Declaration was to discourage Germans from committing new atrocities as Hitler's armies retreated. It warned that the Allies would pursue them "to the uttermost ends of the earth."

When Hull returned to Washington, Eleanor Roosevelt found him "enthusiastic about all the Russians," whom he had found "like your country cousins come to town." Hull was "convinced they will make no separate peace" with Germany.

THE MOSCOW CONFERENCE had been planned as a prelude to the first meeting between Roosevelt, Stalin and Churchill in Soviet-occupied Tehran. When Hull returned to Washington, he found the President "looking forward to his meeting with Stalin with the enthusiasm of a boy."

Stalin had demanded that the meeting be held at a place of his own convenience. With a not-too-subtle reminder that the Soviet Union was carrying the lion's share of the war against Germany, he had told Roosevelt that he could not leave his military post and threatened to defer the promised conference until after Roosevelt and Churchill opened their second front. The President agreed to Stalin's suggestion of Tehran, adding in his cable that he hoped the conclave would bring the "further disturbance of Nazi morale."

On Saturday morning, November 13, 1943, Roosevelt boarded the U.S.S. *Iowa* on Chesapeake Bay. Although Hull had not embarrassed him in Moscow, the President once again left him home.

"It's a lovely day but cold," the President wrote in a diary he briefly kept. "I am being showered with every security and every comfort—and I am optimistic about results." Referring to the secrecy of the trip, he added, "I much wonder when the cat will get out of the bag!" During the Atlantic voyage, he wrote, "I revel in an old pair of trousers and a fishing shirt."

Conferring aboard ship with his Chiefs of Staff, Roosevelt drew three lines across a *National Geographic* map of Germany. "Practically speaking," he said, "there should be three German states after the war." These would evolve out of the three zones occupied by the Americans, British and Soviets. That would be "okay" with Stalin. A southern German state would be Catholic, he said. The northwestern would be Protestant. He joked that the religion of the northeastern one would be "Prussianism."

Roosevelt predicted that Churchill would try to fob off the landlocked southern German state, adjacent to France, on the United States. He would refuse. He didn't want to get entangled in postwar French problems: "France is a British baby." Instead, Roosevelt wanted the northwestern state, which would include port cities such as Bremen and Hamburg. He also told the Chiefs, "The United States should have Berlin."

The President predicted that at the end of the European war there would "definitely be a race for Berlin." The United States must be ready to put its "divisions into Berlin as soon as possible" so that no Russians could seize Berlin before the Anglo-Americans could get there. Roosevelt's close aide Harry Hopkins chimed in that the United States should "be ready to put an airborne division into Berlin two hours after the collapse of Germany."

Roosevelt told the Chiefs that after victory in Europe, he expected to field an occupation force of about a million American troops. The Army's Chief of Staff, General George Marshall, asked him how long American soldiers would remain in Europe.

"For at least one year," replied Roosevelt. "Maybe two."

After stopping in Cairo for a meeting with Churchill and the Chinese leader Chiang Kai-shek, the President arrived in Tehran on Saturday, November 27, 1943. Although the scheduled meeting had been kept secret, there were death threats against the Big Three. Hitler's police chief, Heinrich Himmler, had gone to the extreme of asking German magicians and mystics when and where the Allied leaders would meet. Soviet intelligence warned Roosevelt's Secret Service that Nazi operatives had dropped by parachute into Tehran.

To avoid the threat, the President rode from the airport into the city in a plain Army staff car. Riding in the presidential limousine was a Roosevelt double, outfitted with the famous cape, fedora and cigarette holder, grinning at Persian troops lining the avenues. The President agreed to be lodged at a yellow-brick mansion within the Soviet embassy compound so as to avoid dangerous trips around the city.

At the Soviet embassy on Sunday afternoon, November 28, Stalin was clearly uneasy at his first encounter with Roosevelt. To set him at ease, the President offered him a cigarette. "The doctors don't allow it," said Stalin. Roosevelt replied, "Doctors should be obeyed."

Later, at the Big Three's first session, Churchill declared that the room held the "greatest concentration of power" the world had "ever seen." Roosevelt joked that as the "youngest of the three present," he wanted to welcome his "elders." He predicted that "our three great nations" would "work in close cooperation for the prosecution of the war" and "for generations to come."

To start the talks on the right footing, Roosevelt opened debate on an Anglo-American invasion of Europe for May 1944. He hoped the invasion would divert at least thirty or forty German divisions from the Soviet front. Stalin predicted that the Germans would "fight like devils" to prevent a landing in France.

That evening, over an American dinner of steak and baked potatoes, Stalin told Roosevelt and Churchill that they were "too lax" about postwar Germany. How could they ever reform a people so blindly obedient? He recalled that during a Leipzig visit in 1907, he had watched two hundred Germans miss an important mass meeting because there was no one on the train platform to punch their tickets.

To the President's surprise, Stalin badgered him about unconditional surrender. It was welding the Germans together and costing Allied lives. Holding out specific terms for surrender, "no matter how harsh," would hasten the day of German capitulation.

Anxious not to quarrel, Roosevelt changed the subject. Referring to the German word for empire, he said it was "very important not to leave in the German mind the concept of 'the Reich.' . . . The very word should be stricken from the language."

Stalin said it was "not enough to eliminate the word. The very Reich itself must be rendered impotent, so as never again to plunge the world into war." After victory in Europe, the Allies must retain "the strategic positions necessary to prevent a revival of German militarism."

Stalin insisted that German territory east of the Oder River be granted to Poland. Roosevelt and Churchill did not object. The President said that, in the same spirit, he wanted to make sure that access to the Baltic Sea was always open. Perhaps an international zone could be formed around the Kiel Canal, which connected the Baltic to the North Sea.[3]

Stalin flushed red. As Roosevelt's words were translated, he thought the

3. Roosevelt did not say so aloud, but American control of the northernmost zone in Germany would reassure the Soviets by maintaining their direct access to the Atlantic.

President was questioning the Soviet Union's seizure of Latvia, Lithuania and Estonia in 1940.

While the mistake was corrected, Roosevelt suddenly fell ill. With his face turning green and sweat pouring from his chin, he lifted a shivering hand to his forehead and was wheeled out of the room. "We've got to hurry," said the President's Secret Service agent Mike Reilly. "The Boss is sick!"

Roosevelt was suffering from his arduous trip, but some of the Americans in the room were terrified that their chief had been poisoned.

AFTER ROOSEVELT'S DEPARTURE, Stalin sat down on a sofa with Churchill and warned him that Germany had "every possibility of recovering from this war." The Germans were "talented people" and "could easily threaten the world again in fifteen or twenty years."

Churchill agreed. If that happened, "we would have betrayed our soldiers." Why not strip postwar Germany of all aviation and arms-related industries?

Not enough, said Stalin. "Furniture factories could be transformed into airplane factories. Watch factories could make fuses for shells." Churchill must remember that the Germans had used "toy rifles" to teach thousands of their people how to shoot in the 1930s. Stalin said he had ordered German prisoners of war called into his presence to explain why they had rampaged into Russian homes and raped Russian women. They replied that Hitler had told them to. Stalin said he had had them executed.

After Versailles, Stalin said, "peace seemed assured, but Germany recovered very quickly." Churchill said that the problem was that in 1919, the great powers were "inexperienced" about Germany—and Russia had not helped to devise the peace. After World War II, he said, there was no reason why Russia's army, Britain's navy and America's air force could not join to keep the peace in Europe for fifty years.

The Prime Minister allowed that he did not agree with Roosevelt's insistence that there was no difference between Hitler and the German people. During wartime, he said, you never distinguish between the enemy's leaders and its people. But he and Stalin must recognize, in truth, that this war was "largely the fault of the German leaders." The Allies could change the German people with a generation of "self-sacrificing, toil and education."

Listening to Churchill merely confirmed Stalin's view that, with a wary eye on Soviet power in the postwar world, Churchill was privately soft on Germany. He crisply told the Prime Minister that "nothing" he had suggested was enough to solve the "German problem."

ON MONDAY AFTERNOON, with Roosevelt feeling better, the meeting resumed. As at all of their wartime summits, the Big Three discussed a host of problems, but an abiding theme was Germany and its postwar future.

Stalin complained of what he saw as Churchill's strange diffidence about Germany. With the Franco-Prussian War of 1870 and two world wars in its history, why should Germany not be expected to start a third world war by 1959 or 1960?

Roosevelt described his hope for a postwar system of "four policemen"—the Soviet Union, Britain, America and China—and a United Nations organization that would protect the world against Germany and Japan.[4] They could "move swiftly" against the first hint that Germany was converting its factories to war.

Stalin disagreed. "The Germans have shown great ability to conceal such signs." He insisted that "something more serious" was needed.

That evening, with the Marshal hosting a dinner of borscht and fish, Churchill toasted "Stalin the Great." But Stalin responded, "You are pro-German!" He said that Churchill's attitude seemed to be "The Devil is a Communist and my friend God is a Conservative." Stalin added that his own attitude was that "if Germany moves a muscle, she will be rapidly stopped."

Stalin continued, "At least fifty thousand—and perhaps a hundred thousand—of the German command staff must be physically liquidated." Then he raised his glass. "I propose a salute to the swiftest possible justice for all Germany's war criminals—justice before a firing squad! I drink to our unity in killing them as quickly as we capture them. All of them! There must be at least fifty thousand."

4. On New Year's Day 1942, in Washington, D.C., twenty-six anti-Axis powers had signed a "Declaration by United Nations" pledging support for the principles of international cooperation listed by Roosevelt and Churchill in their August 1941 Atlantic Charter. In October 1943, in Moscow, the Soviet, British and American governments went further, pledging to found a world organization that would preserve security and peace.

What Churchill heard deeply disturbed him. He knew that Stalin's demand went far beyond October's three-power Moscow Declaration of War Crimes. He replied, "The British people will never stand for such mass murder. . . . I will not be a party to any butchery in cold blood." War criminals "must pay," but he would not agree to execute soldiers who had fought for their country: "I would rather be taken out in the garden, here and now, and be shot myself than sully my country's honor by such infamy."

Roosevelt said, "As usual, it seems to be my function to mediate this dispute." In jest, he asked them to compromise on a smaller number—"say, forty-nine thousand, five hundred."

One of the guests at the dinner was the President's son Elliott, a reconnaissance pilot based in England. He raised his glass and said, "Russian, American and British soldiers will settle the issue for most of those fifty thousand in battle, and I hope that those fifty thousand war criminals will be taken care of—but many hundreds of thousands more Nazis as well!"

Stalin rose to his feet, gave Elliott a bear hug and clinked glasses with him.

Outraged, Churchill addressed the President's son: "Much as I love you, Elliott, I cannot forgive you for making such a dastardly statement. How dare you say such a thing!" Churchill stalked away from the table, but Stalin chased after him, grabbed his shoulders and said he had only been kidding.

When the Prime Minister returned to his rooms after dinner, his doctor, Lord Moran, noted that he had fallen into one of his "black depressions." With his instinctive understanding of history and the vicissitudes of national power, Churchill predicted that there might one day be a war with the Russians "more bloody" than that with Germany: "I want to sleep for billions of years. . . . Stupendous issues are unfolding before our eyes, and we are only specks of dust that have settled in the night on the map of the world."

Elliott apologized to his father for offending Churchill, but the President simply laughed: "Forget it. Why, Winston will have forgotten all about it when he wakes up."

The President was wrong. Elliott later ruefully noted that before Tehran, Churchill had included him on country weekends at his official retreat, Chequers. But after hearing Elliott's toast to Stalin, the Prime Minister never invited him again.

• • •

ON WEDNESDAY EVENING, December 1, Roosevelt told Churchill and Stalin that the question before them was "whether or not to split up Germany." Determined to prove that he shared Stalin's ardor for shattering postwar German power, he upped the ante from three German states to five. He added that the port of Hamburg, the Kiel Canal and the rich industrial mining regions of the Ruhr and the Saar should go under international control.

Churchill said, "If I might use the American idiom, the President has said a mouthful!" He would consider some adjustments in the map of Germany but would commit His Majesty's government only to the separation of Prussia.

"If Germany is to be dismembered," said Stalin, "it should *really* be dismembered." Singling out Prussia wasn't enough. Prussian officers might provide the cement, but "all Germans fight like beasts," as the Anglo-Americans would discover when they started fighting in northern Europe.

Eager to keep Stalin friendly, Roosevelt quickly retreated from his armchair theories about Prussia. He conceded that since World War I, there had really been "no difference" between Prussians and Germans. Southern Germany had simply lacked the tradition of an "officer caste."

Churchill warned that even if Roosevelt succeeded in dividing Germany into seven parts, "sooner or later they will reunite into one nation. . . . The main thing is to keep Germany divided, if only for fifty years."[5]

Stalin scoffed that whatever the Allies did, the Germans would always want to reunite. The World War II victors must maintain the strength to "beat the Germans" if they ever tried to forcibly reunite and start "down the path of a new war."

Churchill said that Stalin seemed to want "a Europe composed of little states" that were "separated and weak." He did not need to add that such a Europe would be subject to the domination of a powerful Soviet Union. "Not Europe," said Stalin, "but Germany."

Roosevelt sided with Stalin: "Germany was less dangerous to civilization when it was in 107 provinces." Churchill told his allies that he hoped they would not go to that extreme.

5. Churchill could not know how prescient he was. Ultimately Germany remained divided for forty-five years after World War II.

CHAPTER FOUR

"On the Back of an Envelope"

By Wednesday, January 12, 1944, Franklin Roosevelt was back at the White House, suffering from what the doctors called influenza, caught during his Tehran journey. In the presidential bedchamber, propped up in his old three-quarter mahogany bed, surrounded by dozens of naval prints and family pictures, Roosevelt thrust out his hand to greet General Dwight Eisenhower.

He had just named Ike to be Supreme Commander of Operation Overlord, the Anglo-American invasion of northern Europe. When Stalin had asked Roosevelt at Tehran who would lead the great invasion, the President had said he had not yet decided. Stalin replied that therefore the British and Americans must not be serious. Roosevelt got the message. Stopping in Tunis on the way back to Washington, he told Eisenhower that he would be the commander.

Eisenhower had always been amazed by Roosevelt's mastery of geography. "The most obscure places in faraway countries were always accurately placed on his mental map," he later wrote. But he was also unsettled by Roosevelt's insistence on keeping his own counsel. Years later he privately caviled that Roosevelt was "almost an egomaniac in his belief in his own wisdom."

So secretive was Roosevelt about Tehran that he did not confide to Ike his discussions with Stalin and Churchill about dismembering Germany. Eisenhower pleaded against dividing the conquered state into three occupation zones. Letting a single commander and an Allied military government run all of Germany, he said, would be simpler and more likely to ensure that the Red Army would behave.

Roosevelt assured him that he could handle the Russians. Soon after he returned to Washington, he encouraged his Secretary of War, Henry Stimson, to scotch the earlier notion of an Anglo-American-Soviet joint occupation force. Instead, each country should appoint a military governor to run its own occupation zone.

AT TEHRAN, the Big Three had asked the newly established three-power European Advisory Commission to suggest zones for Germany. Roosevelt had conceived of the EAC as something that would buy time and get the Soviets into the habit of consulting the West on postwar questions.

The American commissioner, ambassador to London John Winant, considered himself not Hull's but the President's man.[1] Winant complained to Roosevelt that Hull gave him his orders, but the Secretary of State did not know what the President had said at Tehran about the permanent division of Germany or anything else. Winant did, since he had been at Tehran, but he didn't know how much he was supposed to tell Hull.

Winant later frankly told Roosevelt by cable that in all "recorded history," he did not think that any "commission created by governments for a serious purpose has had less support from the governments creating it than the European Advisory Commission." This was just what Roosevelt had in mind.

At the EAC, Winant was not inclined to submit State Department and other proposals that he knew had been drafted in ignorance of Roosevelt's tough private talk about Germany. Such papers envisaged Germany's return to its pre-Hitler borders, preservation of its centralized administrative machinery and rebuilding of its industry—with limits on warmaking potential—in order to ease the country's "integration" into the world economy.

In London, on the commission's opening day, Friday, January 14, 1944, the British member, Sir William Strang, proposed dividing Germany into a northeastern Soviet zone, a northwestern British zone and a southwestern

1. At the moment, Winant was having a discreet romance with Churchill's daughter Sarah.

· GERMANY in 1937 ·

American zone.[2] One hundred ten miles inside the Soviet zone, Berlin would be jointly occupied by all three powers and, unlike the zones, administered by a combined Allied Control Council.

Given the military facts of the moment, Britain's proposal was lavish to the West. Operation Overlord was still merely a promise. Who could know whether the Anglo-American invasion would succeed? Still, Britain was granting itself and America almost two-thirds of 1937 Germany.

Unbeknownst to the Anglo-Americans, Stalin had actually been considering a proposal that would have been even more generous to the West. Soviet archives opened in the 1990s include a draft document that would have had the Soviet zone extend no farther west than the Elbe River.[3]

Stalin's advisers wanted to endorse the British plan. According to the newly opened Soviet archives, they privately suggested that not only Berlin but Hamburg and the Kiel Canal should be jointly occupied, just as Roosevelt had suggested at Tehran. But Stalin refused. Nor did he revive his suggestion at Tehran that the Soviets deserved a stake in an internationalized Ruhr. Perhaps he hoped that the Anglo-Americans would reciprocate by renouncing their desire to jointly occupy Berlin. They did not.

When Roosevelt was informed of the zones agreed upon by the British and Soviets, he was irritated. He told the State Department that the zones must "conform with what I decided on months ago." But Hull and his new Under Secretary, Edward Stettinius, had no idea what the President meant. They suggested to Roosevelt that it might be helpful for them to see the secret records of the Tehran conversations. But the President refused.

The Joint Chiefs, of course, knew all about Tehran. They had dug up the *National Geographic* map that Roosevelt had scribbled on while sailing for the Big Three conference and translated it into a formal proposal. When Winant saw the map, he was astonished. The proposed zones would cut crudely across German geography and existing administrative boundaries. The American zone would include forty-six percent of German territory. For their years of blood and sacrifice, the Soviets would get a measly twenty percent.

2. The proposed western boundary of the Soviet zone was the same as the one that ultimately prevailed after VE-Day.

3. The draft proposal was dated January 11, 1944. If there was any chance that the Russians might have offered it at the EAC, they scrapped it when the British produced the more generous plan three days later.

When Winant presented the proposal to the EAC in London, the Soviet commissioner, Feodor Gusev, was furious. He complained that the United States was awfully grabby for a country whose only troops on the European continent were now stalled in Italy.

IN THE OVAL OFFICE ON MONDAY, April 3, 1944, the matter was brought to Roosevelt by Winant's counselor, George Kennan, the American diplomat who would later become famous for his strategic thinking after World War II. The President told Kennan that he would not accept Churchill's plan to saddle him with the southern zone and the problems of postwar France.

Kennan explained that he had come to discuss the boundary of the Soviet zone. He showed Roosevelt the plan drafted from his scratchings on the *National Geographic* map. The President laughed: "Why, that's just something I once drew on the back of an envelope." He ordered Winant to approve the British plan, with the exception of America's consignment to southern Germany.

Winant had another worry. The EAC had agreed on a three-power occupation of Berlin, which would be divided into three sectors, but no one had asked the Soviets to guarantee access rights across their zone to the city. Wary of depending on Soviet goodwill, Eisenhower suggested locating the Allied military government of postwar Germany not in Berlin but a "cantonment capital," to be built at the junction of the three occupation zones.

Winant was instructed by his State Department superiors that Berlin should be no problem. Not only would there be cooperation between the Soviets and the West, but if the Soviets accepted Western rights to be present in postwar Berlin, they must naturally also acknowledge the right to travel to and from the city. With this the British agreed.

In one of the great mistakes of modern diplomacy, Winant was ordered not to raise the matter of access with the Russians because it would make them too suspicious. Nor did Roosevelt or Churchill ever consider the issue serious enough to take up with Stalin.

AFTER TEHRAN, Stalin pressed Roosevelt to soften his demand for unconditional surrender by Germany. As Molotov told the American ambassador in Moscow, Averell Harriman, Stalin felt that unless the Germans were told exactly what to expect after defeat, Hitler and Goebbels would exploit their "fear of the unknown" and "stiffen the German will to fight."

As he planned his invasion of France, Eisenhower strongly felt the same way. His psychology experts had told him that if a "proper mood" were created in the German General Staff, there "might even be a German Badoglio."[4] Eisenhower asked both Roosevelt and Churchill to give some hope to the Germans that would weaken resistance when Anglo-American forces hit the beaches. The Prime Minister wrote Roosevelt to ask whether he would like to join him in exploring the matter with "Uncle Joe" Stalin.[5]

Roosevelt replied that they didn't know enough about whether unconditional surrender was really stiffening German resistance to go on any such "fishing expedition." He reminded Churchill that he had assured his fellow Americans on Christmas Eve by radio that the Allies had "no intention to enslave the German people," merely to "rid them once and for all of Naziism and Prussian militarism and the fantastic and disastrous notion that they constitute the 'Master Race.' "

Churchill told Eden that he could not disagree: "I must say I think it is all wrong for the generals to start shivering before the battle."

The Prime Minister told Eisenhower that, at Tehran, he and Roosevelt had agreed to let Russia seize a huge amount of German machinery after the war—and that Stalin wanted to take millions of Germans to help rebuild Russia. Therefore a "frank statement of what is going to happen to Germany would not necessarily have a reassuring effect upon the German people." They "might prefer the vaguer terrors of unconditional surrender."

Roosevelt complained to Hull about Churchill's and Stalin's efforts to whittle away at his policy. He said that in April 1865, before surrendering to General Ulysses S. Grant, General Robert E. Lee had talked of conditions and Grant had told him he must trust his innate fairness. When Lee mentioned the Confederate officers' horses, Grant replied that they should take them home, as

4. Referring to the new Prime Minister, Marshal Pietro Badoglio, who, after Mussolini's arrest in July 1943, negotiated with the Allies on terms for Italy's unconditional surrender.

5. Roosevelt and Churchill both jocularly referred to Stalin by this nickname, sometimes shortened in their correspondence to "U.J."

6. Despite Roosevelt's comparisons of his unconditional surrender policy to Appomattox, Grant's demand for unconditional surrender came not at Appomattox but Fort Donelson, when he accepted the surrender of General Simon Bolivar Buckner.

they would be needed for spring plowing.[6] "A few incidents like this," Roosevelt said, would have more effect on Germans than "lots of conversations."

In March 1944, Admiral William Leahy, who presided over the Chiefs of Staff, reported to Roosevelt that the Nazi "gangsters" in Berlin were telling Germans that their enemies intended their "extermination." Couldn't the Allies issue a pledge that only German "military aggression" would be destroyed?

Roosevelt replied that he was "not willing" to say "that we do not intend to destroy the German nation" as long as the Germans kept using the term Reich. His "somewhat long study and personal experience in and out of Germany" made him believe that "German philosophy cannot be changed by decree, law or military order." It must be "evolutionary" and might take "two generations."

Still, the President did not want to slam the door on Churchill or his Chiefs. With the cross-Channel invasion now planned for June, he asked Churchill, "What would you think of a statement by me alone along these lines, to be issued after D-Day?" He could declare that the Anglo-Americans sought the "total destruction" not of the German people but of "the philosophy of those Germans who have announced that they could subjugate the world."

Churchill replied, "If there were nothing between us except that the Germans have an evil philosophy, there would be little ground for the war going on."

Then, on June 6, 1944, the mighty Anglo-American armies landed on Hitler's Fortress Europe.

FROM BERN, Allen Dulles of the OSS insisted that Roosevelt's unconditional surrender policy was an "ideal gift" to the Nazis that would lengthen the war and cost Allied lives. For more than a year, Dulles had been anxious about signs that the Soviet Union might try to make a peace deal with Berlin. He considered the Free Germany Committee, Stalin's dream German government-in-exile, a menace to the "maintenance of Western democracy in central Europe." He warned Washington that with Churchill and Roosevelt so adamant about unconditional surrender, "Moscow has been the only source of hope for the Germans."

Dulles had developed fruitful sources among those Germans who were plotting against Hitler. When some raised the possibility of a separate peace with the Anglo-Americans, Dulles longed for the liberty to explore it. "I do not understand what our policy is," he carped to Washington, "and what offers, if any, we could give to the resistance movement."

In April 1944, one group of conspirators had asked Dulles for guarantees that if they toppled Hitler and his regime, Britain and America would negotiate a peace with the new post-Nazi government, after which the German army would turn full throttle against the Soviets. Dulles reported to Washington that the conspirators were eager to "prevent Central Europe from coming ideologically and factually under the control of Russia." He jocularly observed that the plotters seemed to be trapped in "the old predicament of capitulating to the East or to the West: the Germans can never perceive the third alternative of capitulating to both at the same moment."

On the afternoon of July 20, 1944, at the American embassy in Bern, Dulles learned that Stauffenberg had made his move. He later informed Roosevelt and OSS Chief William Donovan that according to one of his two primary contacts with the plotters, Hans Gisevius,[7] who had by then escaped from Berlin and fled to Switzerland, Stauffenberg might have tried to broker a separate German-Soviet peace and a "workers and peasants" government in Berlin. Gisevius claimed that the "old-line Generals" within the conspiracy had favored a separate peace with the Anglo-Americans but did not oppose Stauffenberg "since he was the only one willing to risk his life" and "the only person in a position to place the bomb."

After the failed assassination, and Hitler's blood purge of potential internal enemies, the war was likely to go on until the Allies marched into Berlin. Dulles found a fresh way to whittle away at unconditional surrender. He warned Roosevelt and Donovan that when Anglo-American soldiers stepped onto German soil, there might be "stubborn resistance" unless they chose the "right kind of Germans" as collaborators. He urged that Britain and America try to get local German military officers to smooth the way for Anglo-American occupation of towns and villages. If the German officers played ball, "assuming they are not marked as war criminals," they would be "treated with consideration."

7. Dulles did not name Gisevius in his dispatch.

Dulles insisted that his plan could "drive a wedge in the German army before the effects of the Soviet successes in the East create chaos in Germany." Without it, he warned, many Germans would accept a "Bolshevized Germany" in order to shorten the war.

ROOSEVELT WORRIED ABOUT fierce German resistance to the Anglo-American soldiers who were landing on Fortress Europe. He asked his speechwriter Robert Sherwood to try his hand at a statement that could be issued to German soldiers once the Allies were in France. Sherwood, who had written the popular dramas *Idiot's Delight* and *Abe Lincoln in Illinois,* produced a draft saying, "Your Nazi leaders, who led you into war from no better motive than the lust for power and conquest, have failed." The "one remaining hope" of those leaders was that "if you can be made to resist long enough, they can get a compromise peace.

"How utterly senseless!" the proclamation would say. "Victorious armies never compromise." Instead, Germany must "atone" for its "wanton destruction of lives and property," with Naziism "totally destroyed." The more quickly fighting and slaughter ended, "the more quickly can that better civilization come to the whole world." In that world, "Germany, in due time and as she . . . proves herself worthy, will have her due place."

In mid-July, a month after D-Day, Roosevelt told Hull that "Allied progress on all the fronts" of the war was not "sufficiently impressive" to issue such a statement.

DURING THE FIRST TWO YEARS that Americans fought the Germans, there was, at the center of Franklin Roosevelt's many private conversations about postwar Germany, a strange void. Throughout his fulminations against "Junkers" and "Prussian militarism" and the German love of marching in uniforms, he did not mention the biggest reason why any civilized human being of the 1940s should be uniquely anxious about the German national character.

CHAPTER FIVE

The Terrible Silence

Franklin Roosevelt began receiving information as early as 1942 that Adolf Hitler, under a veil of secrecy, was carrying out his threats to "annihilate the Jewish race." One might expect the President to have gone on radio and told Americans in stirring language exactly what his government was learning about the Nazi death camps, adding that this unimaginable crime was exactly what the Allies were fighting to banish from the world.

But Roosevelt made no such speech. Nor did he command American propaganda organs to publicize everything the government knew about the extermination of the Jews. Instead, through at least the early months of 1944, the President's references to the subject were vague and seldom. He did not mention the subject at the Big Three meeting at Tehran, in his private correspondence with Churchill or, except in the most oblique fashion, in his public statements.

In July 1942, the president of the American Jewish Congress, Rabbi Stephen Wise, asked the President for a statement that could be read to a Madison Square Garden rally against Hitler's oppression of Jews. Wise suggested that Roosevelt say that the Axis powers "will not succeed in exterminating Jews, as they have repeatedly threatened to do, any more than they will succeed in enslaving mankind." He should say that "every American" lamented "the savagery of the Nazis against their Jewish victims."

But the President did not mention extermination or "Jewish victims."

Instead, his statement said that Americans "sympathize with all victims of Nazi crime" and would hold the perpetrators to "strict accountability in a day of reckoning which will surely come."[1]

In December 1942, when Rabbi Wise and other Jewish leaders wished to give Roosevelt details on "the most overwhelming disaster of Jewish history," the President tried to fob them off on the State Department, but they demanded and won a personal meeting. At the White House, Wise handed Roosevelt a twenty-page memorandum on the Nazi "blueprint for extermination" and asked him to tell the world about the tragedy and try to "stop it."

Using one of his trademark maneuvers to control the conversation, the President chattered away for most of the half-hour session, scarcely letting anyone get a word in edgewise. Did they know that he had just appointed Herbert Lehman—his successor as New York Governor and a Jew—to head his new Office of Foreign Relief and Rehabilitation? It gave him "sadistic satisfaction," he said. After the Allied victory, German "Junkers" would have to crawl to Lehman on their knees and ask for bread!

When Wise finally managed to ask Roosevelt to tell the world about Hitler's war against the Jews and try to stop it, the President replied that while his government knew many of the facts, it was hard to know what to do. Hitler and his gang were "an extreme example of a national psychopathic case," but the Allies must not contend that the whole German people were murderers or endorsed Hitler's actions. He suggested that punishment would probably have to wait until after the war: "The mills of the gods grind slowly, but they grind exceedingly fine." Pressed for a statement, he advised the leaders to reissue the Madison Square Garden statement he gave them in July. He insisted that the statement be quoted precisely.

Wise and his colleagues ignored Roosevelt's stricture and issued a press release claiming that the President had been "shocked" to learn that, thanks to Nazi rule and Nazi crimes, two million Jews had already perished in Europe. On December 17, 1942, at the initiative of the British, the Allies issued a declaration against "exposure and starvation" and "mass executions" imposed by the Nazis on "many hundreds of thousands of innocent men, women and children."

1. Disinclined at the moment to take on another controversial issue, Roosevelt jettisoned altogether Wise's suggested statement of support for "the heroic Jewish population of Palestine."

In July 1943, at the White House, Lieutenant Jan Karski of the Polish underground army told Roosevelt about the mass murder of Jews he had witnessed taking place in a Polish concentration camp: "Our underground authorities are absolutely sure that the Germans are out to exterminate the entire Jewish population of Europe." The President listened intently, but when Karski implored Roosevelt to get the Allies to intervene, the President replied, "Tell your nation we shall win the war."

Neither, in 1942 or 1943, was Roosevelt willing to fight his own bureaucracy and hostile members of Congress to relax immigration restrictions in order to rescue European Jews. As the historian Richard Breitman has written, Roosevelt's government "did not match Adolf Hitler's single-minded frenzy to wipe out the Jewish 'race' with corresponding determination to save those Jews who could be saved."

WHY DID THE PRESIDENT RESPOND to the staggering news from Europe with near-silence? During World War I, no member of Woodrow Wilson's government had been more outspoken than Roosevelt about how the Kaiser's officers had relapsed "into the unlimited and horrible conditions of warfare in the Dark Ages." As Assistant Secretary of the Navy, Roosevelt had demanded that a German book on the subject be translated into English so Americans could know what kind of people the Germans were.

Although Roosevelt had seen concrete evidence of what the scholar Walter Laqueur has called Hitler's "terrible secret," like many other Americans, including some Jewish leaders, he could not comprehend that this was a crime unlike any other in world history—the systematic effort to murder an entire people, which later generations would think of as the Holocaust. As Laqueur has observed, information is not the same thing as knowledge. In the absence of that larger historical understanding of what Hitler's Germans were doing, Roosevelt remained riveted to the single goal of Germany's unconditional surrender. By this standard, any other war aim, even saving an entire people, was a distraction. That was why he told Karski in essence that his answer to the problem was to "win the war."

Roosevelt felt he had a limited amount of influence with Stalin and Churchill and with Congress and the American people, and of all those things he wished to use it for, as the historian Robert Dallek has said, "refugee matters ranked way down the list." The President was doubtless sensitive to old complaints that his government—the "Jew Deal"—was too abundant with Jews and that he had plotted to drag the nation into a "Jewish war" in Europe. He had never underestimated the anti-Semitism in American society. Before World War II, he had warned his ambassador to London, Joseph Kennedy, "If there was a demagogue around here of the type of Huey Long to take up anti-Semitism, there could be more blood running in the streets of New York than in Berlin."

Roosevelt might have feared that public complaint by the American President might spur Hitler to murder Jews all the more quickly. He may have felt that to dramatize Hitler's Final Solution and tell Americans that this was what the Allies were fighting against might weaken his unconditional surrender policy. The President would probably have argued that this might inflame Jewish leaders to demand that military aims be widened from fighting Hitler in general to include specifically going after those Germans and the machinery they were using to annihilate the Jews. Roosevelt might have feared that this would lengthen the war and divide the American people over what the war in Europe was really about—especially at a moment when it was not yet certain that the Allies would win the war in Europe.

Roosevelt was the architect of modern interest group politics in America, and from his point of view, in 1942 and 1943, Jewish voters were in his hip pocket. In each of his three presidential victories they had voted for him by majorities of from eighty-three to ninety percent. Furthermore, with some conspicuous exceptions, the pressure from many Jewish leaders to alleviate Jewish suffering in Europe was gentle. Many American Jews, even those who understood the magnitude of what was unfolding, were reluctant to look like special pleaders during wartime.

Roosevelt would also have argued in his own defense that he had to deal with his Allies. Widening Allied war aims to include the rescue of Europe's Jews would not have bothered Churchill. The Prime Minister was sporadically eager to take risks to help the Jews. He had never liked the unconditional surrender policy anyway.

But what about Stalin? In Roosevelt's probable calculation, the murderer of millions of Kulaks was not likely to feel much genuine outrage over genocide—and Stalin was anything but partial to the Jews. During a time when Roosevelt was using unconditional surrender as a means of keeping Stalin from growing too angry about his and Churchill's postponement of the D-Day invasion until mid-1944, the President might have felt that to depart from his promised single war aim could cause the Soviet leader to distrust his intentions—especially if he suspected that the sanction might be extended to all perpetrators of mass murder and genocide.[2]

BY THE FALL OF 1943, Winston Churchill was searching for some way to halt the German atrocities. He hoped that as the Red Army started rolling back Nazi occupation, Europeans could be intimidated from joining in Hitler's "atrocities, massacres and executions."

Churchill was the secret author of the Moscow Declaration by the Allied foreign ministers, Cordell Hull, Anthony Eden and Vyacheslav Molotov. Although it did not mention the Jews, it warned that those responsible for "abominable deeds" would be pursued "to the uttermost ends of the earth." Churchill told Eden that the Moscow Declaration would at least make "some of these villains shy of being mixed up in butcheries now that they know they are going to be beat."

But at around the same time, Churchill's War Cabinet resolved that the Allies should take final responsibility for punishing atrocities committed on enemy territory. Nevertheless, by November 1943, more than three million of Europe's Jews had perished.

As Hitler's war against European Jewry raged on, Franklin Roosevelt maintained his silence. Before 1944, he avoided discussing the matter. He did not publicize it. He did not spend his political coin on rescue and refugees. All of this undermined his lofty wartime premise that in planning for postwar Germany, he was plainly confronting the most fundamental issues of German morality and national character.

Unable or unwilling to comprehend the awful historical magnitude of what was happening in Europe, Roosevelt would have argued in his defense that throwing all resources behind the single goal of an early Allied victory was the best way to save the Jews. Nevertheless, the more Hitler felt in danger of losing the war, the more the Nazi extermination mills were speeded up. As some darkly observed at the time, by the moment the Allies won World War II in Europe, there might be no Jews left to save.

2. It was in April 1943 that the Germans revealed the Katyn massacre—the mass murder or more than four thousand Polish officers by the feared Soviet security organ, the NKVD.

• • •

By the end of 1943, Henry Morgenthau, Jr., Roosevelt's Secretary of the Treasury, Dutchess County neighbor and closest friend in the Cabinet, was deeply unsettled by the silence from the Oval Office.

So secular a Jew was Morgenthau that, although he was fifty-two, he had never attended a Passover seder. As Roosevelt knew, Morgenthau and his wealthy father, an early FDR supporter, were not Zionists. When an anti-Semitic journal castigated the Treasury Secretary as a "Leader in Zion," the President joshed to Justice Felix Frankfurter that he and Eleanor would cable Morgenthau that "we will not receive him unless he arrives with a large black beard," after which he would be "disavowed by his old man."

During his decade at the Treasury, Roosevelt's friend had avoided Jewish matters. But the evidence from the death camps radicalized him. When Rabbi Wise, who had celebrated Morgenthau's marriage to his wife Elinor, brought him a cable from Switzerland and other information about how Hitler's Germans were murdering millions of Jews, Morgenthau had told him, "Please, Stephen, don't give me the gory details." Wise pressed on, explaining how the inmates' remains were being made into soap. The Nazis, he said, were "making lampshades out of the skins of the Jews."

As the Treasury Secretary's confidential aide Henrietta Klotz recalled, her boss "grew paler and paler, and I thought he was going to keel over." Morgenthau cried out, "I cannot take any more!"

CHAPTER SIX

The "One Hundred Percent American"

Morgenthau's relationship with Franklin Roosevelt had been the lodestar not only of his public career but, to a great extent, his identity. He once told an aide that his friendship with the President was the "most important thing" in his life. It was Roosevelt who, as Governor of New York in 1929, had lifted him from the obscurity of being the shy only son of a self-made New York real estate mogul. And it was the friendship with Roosevelt that gave Morgenthau a sense of personal acceptance and security as a Jew who wished to be thought of, as his elder son later put it, as a "one hundred percent American."

Born in 1891, Henry Morgenthau, Jr., was descended from German Jews who were rabbis, cantors, Hebrew teachers, ritual slaughterers and financiers. His paternal grandfather, Lazarus Morgenthau, came to post–Civil War America after suffering financial problems in Germany.

The future Treasury Secretary spent much of his life differentiating himself from his vainglorious father. Henry Jr.'s namesake son much later recalled that Henry Sr. was "very ambitious for himself" and "my father was really a direct extension of his ego and his ambitions." Financier for Woodrow Wilson's first presidential campaign, ambassador to Turkey during World War I, Henry Sr. was eager to live among the American upper class and for his son to do things in life that were beyond his own social and professional reach. His daughter Ruth said that Henry Sr.'s life was "centered around his business, his ambition and his son."

Henry Jr. recalled how his father had had to "fight every inch of the way" in New York construction and real estate: "His theory for me was you can start at the top and save all that. . . . He was crazy to have me in business with him."

As a young man, Henry Jr. had suffered from a learning disability that made speaking and writing difficult. Miserable as an Exeter student, he dropped out after his second year. His father had him tutored and sent to Cornell for an architecture degree that would help him when he joined his business. But the son dropped out of Cornell. At his father's behest, he worked for a while as a timekeeper at a construction site, but soon he came down with typhoid fever.

Sent to recuperate at a Texas ranch, the young Morgenthau discovered that what he really loved was farming. He returned to Cornell to study agriculture and in 1913, at the age of twenty-two, used family money to buy a run-down thousand-acre farm in East Fishkill, Dutchess County, New York. As Morgenthau later said, it was a "desperate move to get out from under" his ambitious father. Farming was the "one thing" his father "knew nothing" about.

The father had hoped that his early support ($20,000—almost $200,000 in 2002 dollars) for the dark horse New Jersey Governor might lead the new President Wilson to appoint him to the Cabinet, perhaps the Treasury. But Wilson offered only the ambassadorship to Turkey. Morgenthau Sr. was furious. For years, that embassy had been a ghetto for Jewish contributors. With his more expansive view of himself, he complained to Wilson that American Jews were "very sensitive" to the notion that Turkey was "the only diplomatic post to which a Jew can aspire." Why not China?

Irritably Wilson replied that much of America's business in China was missionary work, which required a Christian envoy. And didn't Morgenthau understand that it was the Turks who oversaw the Jews of Palestine? When Morgenthau's friend Rabbi Wise endorsed Wilson's argument, Morgenthau took the job. As ambassador, he made a deep impression on his son by waging a lonely battle to get the United States to intervene when the Turks committed mass murder against the Armenians in 1915.

In 1916, Henry Jr. married Elinor Fatman, granddaughter of a Lehman Brothers founder, who made up for what he lacked in ambition and sociability. While keeping an apartment in New York, they bought another thousand acres in Dutchess County to create Fishkill Farms, where they raised potatoes, cabbage, squash, rye, corn, beef cattle, apples and, in time, three children—Henry III, Robert and Joan. Life as a country squire gave Morgenthau distance from a father who, as Elinor recalled, "tried to regulate his life and to dominate his thoughts."

HENRY MORGENTHAU III WROTE, "Early in life, I sensed my parents' malaise in their Jewishness, which they mocked good-humoredly, while remaining fiercely alert to attack from outsiders." To them, he said, being Jewish was "a kind of birth defect that could not be eradicated, but with proper treatment, could be overcome, if not in this generation, then probably in the next."

Asked at age five what his religion was, Henry III had gone to his mother for guidance. Even more "firmly assimilationist" than her husband, Elinor said, "Just tell them you're an American." As the son recalled, his parents did not attend a synagogue as he was growing up and "tended to avoid" the city and country clubs, the Americanized Temple Emanu-El, and the country places in Westchester County that gave wellborn New York German Jews a "comforting sense of community." [1]

As Henry III recalled, his grandfather was "afraid of anything that might threaten his Americanism" and thus "didn't want my father to be involved in Jewish things." The patriarch was put off by Zionism. Although once president of Rabbi Wise's Free Synagogue in New York, Henry Sr. had fallen out with Wise over the Rabbi's ardent wish for a Jewish homeland in Palestine. "We Jews of America have found America to be our Zion," scoffed the elder Morgenthau. "I am an American."

FRANKLIN ROOSEVELT WASTED NO TIME in welcoming the new arrival to his home county. The two men both loved the land and styled themselves as farmers. Their wives became close friends. When the Morgenthaus came

1. "Almost all of my parents' friends were Jewish," Henry III recalled, but "they never talked about anything Jewish" and "there were no Jewish artifacts or anything around." He recalled that when his mother took him for the winter to Augusta, Georgia, to recuperate from a riding accident, she "really resented" it when "the Jewish community there [reached] out to her," and she kept her distance.

for tea at the great house at Hyde Park, Roosevelt's mother Sara wrote in her diary, "Young Morgenthau was easy and yet modest and serious and intelligent. The wife is very Jewish, but appeared very well."

As an aspiring politician eager to be Governor of New York and then President, Roosevelt knew that there would be political benefits in friendship with the young Morgenthau. He knew that Morgenthau's father, whom he called "Uncle Henry," was a reliable donor to reform Democratic candidates. And in a state with so many Jewish voters, who were prone to wonder whether some Christian candidate was privately anti-Semitic, it would be helpful for Roosevelt to have at least one close Jewish friend.[2]

Roosevelt came to call his friend "Henry the Morgue," a playful jest at Morgenthau's doleful countenance, and asked for his help in politics. He prodded Morgenthau to run for sheriff of Dutchess County, probably knowing that, while a Democrat and a Jew was unlikely to win, the suggestion would boost Morgenthau's fragile ego. Above all, he was certain that Morgenthau was loyal, discreet and devoid of ambitions that would ever conflict with his.

For Morgenthau, his friendship with Roosevelt became something far more precious. Roosevelt was the older brother Morgenthau never had, who abounded with the qualities he lacked—loquaciousness, extroversion, exuberance, self-confidence. Being embraced by a Hudson Valley patroon went a long way to quash any social inferiority the younger man felt, especially in a county not partial to New York City Jews. And with his career hitched to Roosevelt's, the sky must have seemed the limit.

Morgenthau tended the friendship as if it were one of his orchards. In this he was guided by his shrewd and perceptive wife, whose friendship with Eleanor Roosevelt buttressed the tie between their husbands.[3] Elinor Morgenthau made herself politically useful by joining the women's division of the New York Democratic party.

Having shed the genteel anti-Semitism of her class, Mrs. Roosevelt took care to shield her Jewish friend from social slights. She once wrote to another friend, who was Protestant, "You are worse than Elinor Morgenthau and haven't her reason!" When Mrs. Morgenthau was blackballed from member-

2. Through the rest of Roosevelt's life, Morgenthau remained the only real Jewish friend he ever had.

3. Morgenthau's authorized biographer John Morton Blum privately felt that the "bond of affection" between the two women was "much greater" than that between their husbands.

ship in the elite Colony Club of New York, Mrs. Roosevelt resigned in protest.

In 1938, Elinor Morgenthau told the First Lady that she planned to give her daughter Joan a debutante party. Mrs. Roosevelt offered to have the affair at the White House. When the President was wheeled into the East Room, he kissed the young woman and said, "I am sorry I cannot have the first dance with you." Guests who heard him say this were in tears.

Still, Mrs. Roosevelt was exasperated that Elinor felt social discrimination that the First Lady considered to be only in her head. "I have always felt you were hurt often by imaginary things and have wanted to protect you," she once wrote her. "But if one is to have a healthy relationship . . . it must be on some kind of equal basis. You simply cannot be so easily hurt. Life is too short to cope with it!"

AFTER 1921, when Roosevelt's infantile paralysis sidelined him from politics, he spent more time in Hyde Park and thus with his Dutchess County neighbor. Advancing his ambition to be Roosevelt's farm expert, Morgenthau bought the money-losing journal *American Agriculturalist* and allowed people to believe that the money-losing Fishkill Farms was a successful enterprise. Henry III later felt that even his father came to believe in the "fabled success" of his farm—"although he was always very thin-skinned when anyone dared to question him too closely on this score."

Morgenthau's shyness remained. At a meeting of Dutchess County farmers, he was so ill at ease that Elinor, a onetime Vassar drama student, delivered the speech he was scheduled to give. When Roosevelt ran for Governor of New York in 1928, Morgenthau planned campaign stops, hired bands and drove the candidate seventy-five hundred miles in an old Buick. Once elected, Roosevelt named him chairman of his farm advisory board and then conservation commissioner. Elinor Morgenthau wrote the Governor of her pleasure that "while you are moving on in your work," he was giving "Henry a chance to grow." Knowing how it would delight Morgenthau, Roosevelt once inscribed a photograph of them in an open car "from one of two of a kind."

When Roosevelt was elected President in 1932, Morgenthau was hoping to be named Secretary of Agriculture, which would have made him the second Jew in history to join a President's Cabinet. But farm leaders in the Midwest and South scorned the idea of giving the job to a Jew and a New Yorker (despite New York State's considerable agriculture). Instead, Roosevelt made Morgenthau chairman of the Farm Credit Administration.

Then, in the fall of 1933, Roosevelt's first Secretary of the Treasury, William Woodin, fell mortally ill. Morgenthau told his confidential aide Henrietta Klotz, who had worked for him since 1922, that he wanted to buttonhole Roosevelt's devoted secretary Missy LeHand and his aide Harry Hopkins about getting the job. Klotz warned him that Missy and Hopkins "hated" him and would sink the notion if they knew that was what he wanted. Morgenthau took her advice to go straight to Roosevelt and "put it on the line." Withstanding pressure to appoint the conservative tycoon Jesse Jones of Houston, the President gave Treasury to his Hudson Valley friend. As Morgenthau recalled, when he heard the news, he "broke out in a cold sweat."

Fortune dismissed the new Treasury Secretary as the "son of a Jewish philanthropist" who had "spent most of his life farming." Others charged Roosevelt with cronyism. The New York Republican donor Gladys Straus, herself Jewish, wisecracked that Roosevelt had managed to find "the only Jew in the world who doesn't know a thing about money." Mrs. Klotz later recalled that when the senior Morgenthau learned that his son would get the job he had once yearned for, he said, "I don't know how [Roosevelt] could appoint my son Secretary of the Treasury. He's not up to it. . . . *I* could do the job."

At that moment Roosevelt's first demand of a Treasury Secretary was not expertise but steadfastness. The President's longtime political adviser and éminence grise Louis Howe told Morgenthau he had "earned" his new job with his "loyalty" while others had let Roosevelt down.

That fall, the President had come close to breaking the law when he devalued the dollar by purchasing large quantities of gold. Indignant, Under Secretary of the Treasury Dean Acheson had quit. By appointing Morgenthau, Roosevelt presumed that he would never have to worry about his Treasury Secretary going off the reservation.

EAGER TO ESTABLISH HIS PLACE IN HISTORY, Morgenthau installed in his Treasury office a recording system, activated by a button in his desk, that captured his most important conversations and telephone calls.[4] He was the only Cabinet member who had an old family relationship with the President, including a standing Monday lunch at the White House. Those who crossed the Treasury Secretary could never know what Morgenthau or his wife might say about them to the Roosevelts over family dinner at the White House or in Dutchess County.

During Cabinet meetings, Roosevelt and his friend passed silly notes to each other like schoolboys. Referring to the Secretary of Labor, Frances Perkins, Morgenthau once scribbled, "How do you like Madam Perkins' new hat?" Roosevelt replied, "CHIC(K)," to which Morgenthau countered, "CLUCK!

Morgenthau knew, nevertheless, that while he was Roosevelt's closest friend in the Cabinet, he was also its least independent member. Unlike most of his colleagues, he had no faithful outside constituency to defend him if he got into trouble—not even organized Jews, some of whom disdained him as indifferent to his heritage. Postmaster General James Farley, who knew patronage better than most in Washington, complained that Morgenthau's appointment was the worst of both worlds: The President got "no credit from the Jews" and was criticized by the anti-Semites.

Morgenthau knew the hazards of depending on the mercurial President. Years later he painfully recalled how Roosevelt played off "one person against another" and "never let anybody around him have complete assurance that he would have the job tomorrow. That gave you a sense of uneasiness, of insecurity." During his twelve years in the Roosevelt government, aware that his friend might throw him overboard at any time, Morgenthau never

4. The conversations were evidently recorded on discs. The discs have vanished, but the transcripts made from them survive. These transcripts provide much of the dialogue between Morgenthau and others in this book. Many Roosevelt officials knew and resented that Morgenthau was so precisely preserving their conversations. Many incorrectly presumed that the verbal exchanges were being transcribed in shorthand by Morgenthau's assistant Henrietta Klotz. Klotz later claimed that her boss told interlocutors "beforehand" that "your voice is being recorded." She recalled, "Some of them didn't care. Some did." Certain that his words were being transcribed by Klotz and unhappy about it, Joseph Kennedy, chairman of the Securities and Exchange Commission in 1934 and 1935, once started a telephone chat with Morgenthau with a burst of profanity. Covering the telephone mouthpiece with his hand, he told a friend, "A couple of more sentences, and Mrs. Klotz will hang up!" Morgenthau felt that it was wrong to record the President but he inadvertently captured some of their telephone conversations, for which transcripts remain. Mrs. Klotz recalled that after White House meetings with Roosevelt, her boss "would come back and dictate word for word what the President said to him." Morgenthau's authorized biographer John Morton Blum later recalled that Morgenthau captured his conversations because "all the New Dealers were scared to death that if they didn't keep a record, someone would knife them in the back."

bought a house in Washington. Instead, he moved his family from one furnished residence to another.

When Roosevelt smiled at him, Morgenthau was exuberant. When he ignored him, he was despondent. In 1939 he complained to Eleanor Roosevelt that the President had been "bullying me, browbeating me and being thoroughly unpleasant," adding that he wondered whether he was "trying to get rid of me." She consoled him by noting that her husband was particularly hard on "people close to him."

At the start of World War II, Roosevelt had flippantly raised Morgenthau's hopes by telling him, "You and I will run this war together." Then, like a jilted lover, Morgenthau watched mournfully as the President came to lean instead on his rival Harry Hopkins, whom Roosevelt had brought to the White House as a confidential wartime adviser.

JUST AFTER PEARL HARBOR, Roosevelt lunched with Morgenthau and Leo Crowley, a Catholic who was Custodian of Alien Property.[5] As Morgenthau later recorded, the President told them, "You know this is a Protestant country, and the Catholics and Jews are here under sufferance." Roosevelt went on to say that it was therefore "up to you" to "go along with anything I want."

Knowing Roosevelt so well, Morgenthau could not have been surprised by what he heard, but he had rarely, if ever, heard him state it so baldly. Being told they were in America on "sufferance" would not have encouraged Morgenthau or the few other Jews in the presidential circle, such as Samuel Rosenman, Roosevelt's special counsel, and David Niles, his administrative assistant, to press him on Jewish matters.

In 1938, after Hitler unleashed his pogrom against the Jews of Germany, Morgenthau had proposed that the United States acquire British and French Guiana as a haven for Jewish refugees in exchange for canceling the British and French World War I debt. But Roosevelt responded, "It's no good. It would take the Jews five to fifty years to overcome the fever." The President did sound out the President of Paraguay about harboring Jewish refugees for money and asked Morgenthau for a list of the thousand richest Jews in the

5. The Custodian of Alien Property oversaw assets in the United States belonging to citizens of countries with whom the country was at war.

United States. But Morgenthau replied, "Before you talk about money, you have to have a plan."

In November 1939, Rabbi Wise asked Morgenthau to intervene when the French were stopping Jewish refugees in French ports. Morgenthau replied that while his "personal feelings would lead me to take an interest in the matter," he would "stick to his rule" that as Treasury Secretary, he would not do this "kind of thing."

BEFORE WORLD WAR II, whatever guilt Morgenthau might have felt about his reticence in helping save Jewish refugees from Hitler was sublimated in his zeal for defense preparedness and aid to Britain. More than most members of Roosevelt's Cabinet, he was convinced that the United States would probably have to intervene in Europe. "If we don't stop Hitler now, he is going right on to the Black Sea," he told Roosevelt. "Then what? The fate of Europe for the next hundred years is settled." As Roosevelt's wartime Treasury Secretary, Morgenthau helped to finance the costliest struggle in world history. But soon Cordell Hull was complaining that Morgenthau was trying to be a "second Secretary of State."

In 1942 the Allies made Admiral Jean Darlan of the Vichy French regime, which was collaborating with the Nazis, high commissioner of North Africa in a wildly controversial deal to keep French troops from opposing their invasion. When Darlan enforced Nazi decrees, Morgenthau heatedly complained to the Secretary of War, Henry Stimson, that Darlan had "sold many thousands of people into slavery."

Unlike other American officials, Morgenthau refused to separate the German people from their evil government. He was an original believer in collective guilt for German war crimes. In April 1943, scheduled to speak about the war at Carnegie Hall in New York City, he planned to pledge that the Allies would "rock Germany to its rotten, bloodstained foundation." But an Office of War Information censor told him that "most Germans" were "fine people," and it was "a shame to talk about them this way." Under duress, Morgenthau was persuaded to change his statement to "Nazi Germany."

THROUGHOUT HIS LIFE, Morgenthau had suffered splitting migraine headaches and spasms of nausea, forcing him to stretch out for hours and days in a dark room. What he learned in 1942 and 1943 from Rabbi Wise and others about the death camps of Europe disturbed his sleep more than ever.

Henrietta Klotz, who worshiped Morgenthau while serving him for more than twenty years, hectored her boss about the Jews of Europe. With ash-blond hair and blazing blue eyes, Mrs. Klotz had grown up poor in an Orthodox Jewish household. As Henry Morgenthau III recalled, she was the "key to getting him interested in Jewish things." With her "sheer, raw emotion," she penetrated the "reserve" of his father, who was "so emotional underneath."

As Klotz's husband, Herman, recalled, she told Morgenthau with "much prodding, pressure and unpleasantness" that he must "go over to the White House and get the President to take some action that would minimize the killing of the Jews." Thus "every morning when she arrived in the office," Morgenthau "looked hesitantly at her, because she had the expression 'When?' "

Three Treasury Department lawyers—John Pehle, Randolph Paul and Josiah DuBois, all Christians—informed Morgenthau that Assistant Secretary of State Breckinridge Long, hostile to foreigners, especially Jews, had been deliberately obstructing the flow of money, information and passports that might save Jews from Hitler. State had also blocked efforts to find refuge for Jews in the United States, Turkey, Switzerland and Palestine.

In December 1943 the furious Morgenthau arranged a showdown with Long and told him, "Breck, we might be a little frank. The impression is all around that you particularly are anti-Semitic." When Long denied it, Morgenthau went on, "Breck, the United States of America was created as a refuge for people who were persecuted the world over, starting with Plymouth. And as Secretary of the Treasury for 135 million people, I am carrying this out as Secretary of the Treasury, and not as a Jew." This was not something Morgenthau might have said a year earlier.

Long's boss, Cordell Hull, was little more willing to expend himself in order to rescue Jews. One reason was that he was inclined to back career State Department men like Long. Another was that the department's most sympathetic advocate for helping Jewish refugees, before his ouster, had been Hull's archenemy, Sumner Welles.

Still another reason was more personal. Hull's wife, the former Frances Witz of Staunton, Virginia, was half Jewish. As the historian Irwin Gellman has written, for years Hull "hid his wife's Jewish heritage for fear that it would cause controversy and keep him from the Presidential nomination he so passionately desired." The August 1936 *American Bulletin* insisted that

Hull was a "slave" of the Jews, "betraying" his office "to satisfy the greed of the moneychangers." Other tracts charged that Frances had pressed Jewish banking interests to back Hull in politics so that he would be subservient to Zionists. As Gellman writes, Hull "consciously turned away from the refugee question," worried that anti-Semites "would argue that his wife had forced him to support Jewish causes."

Most of Hull's friends tiptoed around the subject of his wife's Jewish heritage. But by now, Morgenthau had no patience for niceties. He bluntly told Hull that if he "were a member of the Cabinet in Germany today, you would be, most likely, in a prison camp, and your wife would be God knows where."

Morgenthau found the Secretary of State "simply bewildered." Depressed, the Treasury Secretary complained to aides, "Roosevelt wouldn't move on Hull. He never has. And Hull wouldn't move on Long." Morgenthau wished the President would fire Hull, but knew that Roosevelt lacked the stomach: "I once told the President what does he want Social Security for—or old age pension? He never fires anybody!"

Morgenthau was pained to find General Eisenhower's attitude toward refugees "no different" from that of the British—namely that "this thing is a damned nuisance." Morgenthau's close aide Harry Dexter White replied that the American government's attitude toward the refugees was "worse than that of the British because it is covered by hypocrisy. We don't shoot 'em. We let other people do that. We let them starve!"

The Treasury Secretary knew that there was only one court of last resort. Pehle later said that Morgenthau "valued above everything else his relationship with the President," and "he didn't want to stand out as a Jew."[6] DuBois recalled having the "feeling" from "a few things" Morgenthau told him that "Roosevelt was not the greatest—let's put it this way—on this Jewish problem."

Since the start of the war, Morgenthau had quietly and cautiously tried to help Jewish refugees. But after he learned the full truth about the Nazi death factories and how Long and other American officials had slammed the door on the possibility that the doomed Jews of Europe might be somehow rescued, something in him snapped.

6. John Pehle recalled that Morgenthau was so protective of his relationship with Roosevelt that once when Pehle spoke to the President on his own and Morgenthau heard about it, the Treasury Secretary gave him "unshirted hell."

As Henry III recalled, Morgenthau's father and his wife "did not want to see him get involved in Jewish affairs." But by 1944, the senior Morgenthau was eighty-eight years old and Elinor Morgenthau was flagging from cardiovascular disease. Henry III noted that by then Elinor "had less influence on him, and Mrs. Klotz had more influence on him."[7] He speculated that the Treasury Secretary's new intensity on Jewish matters may also have been "a delayed rebellion against his father."

Whatever the reason for Morgenthau's transformation, it was the supreme moment of his career. If going to Roosevelt made the President think of him as a special petitioner for his fellow Jews, so it would have to be. If his boldness jeopardized his treasured presidential friendship, so be that too. As Randolph Paul recalled, his boss was "taking his political life in his hands."[8] Having made his choice, from that moment on, Morgenthau was a different person.[9]

Many years later, Morgenthau met Gerhart Riegner of the World Jewish Congress, whose telegram from Geneva had alerted him about the death camps and the plight of the refugees. Morgenthau greeted Riegner, "So this is the fellow who changed my life!"

Morgenthau made an appointment with the President for a Sunday in mid-January. He would take along a slightly toned-down version of a document given him by his aides, called "Report to the Secretary on the Acquiescence of This Government in the Murder of the Jews." The report began somberly, "One of the greatest crimes in history, the slaughter of the Jewish people, is continuing unabated."

Before Morgenthau left for the White House, his aide Josiah DuBois told him, "If it means anything, and if you want to, you can tell the President that if he doesn't take any action on this report, I'm going to resign and release the report to the press."

7. Henry Morgenthau III recalled that as his father's public career wore on, he "felt he didn't need" Elinor "as much, which must have hurt her a great deal."

8. Paul added that this was especially true because Cordell Hull, although often ignored by Roosevelt, was "known as a killer" who might try to avenge criticism of his State Department.

9. As his biographer noted in an interview in 1984, Morgenthau "regained some consciousness of his Jewishness, which he had perhaps not suppressed but ignored for many years" and "began, on occasion, to return to synagogue, which he hadn't done for years."

CHAPTER SEVEN

"Oppressor of the Jews"

On Sunday, January 16, 1944, just after noon, Roosevelt received Morgenthau and his aides in the upstairs Oval Room in the White House family quarters. The President was still suffering from the "grippe" he had caught during his trip to Tehran. Randolph Paul marveled that, despite his indisposition, Roosevelt was so "well-dressed."

As Morgenthau later recalled, he felt "very anxious" about this meeting. He gave the President his indictment of Breckinridge Long and the State Department for "gross procrastination" and "willful attempts to prevent action from being taken to rescue Jews from Hitler."

Roosevelt skimmed the report and listened closely as Morgenthau and John Pehle summarized it. The report warned that a "growing number of Americans" saw "plain anti-Semitism" behind the State Department's actions, which could "explode into a nasty scandal. . . . Rescuing the Jews from extermination is a trust too great to remain in the hands of men who are indifferent, callous and perhaps even hostile."

Roosevelt defended his State Department. Long, he said, had "somewhat soured" on the refugees after Rabbi Wise persuaded him to admit a long list of them, "many of whom turned out to be bad people."

Morgenthau retorted that Attorney General Francis Biddle had assured the Cabinet that only three Jewish refugees admitted during World War II had been found "undesirable." He demanded that Long be stripped of responsibility for refugees. Morgenthau gave Roosevelt a draft executive order "to forestall the plan of the Nazis to exterminate all Jews and other minorities." It would create a new War Refugee Board, including the Secretaries of State and Treasury, under the President's direct supervision. Morgenthau warned that members of the Senate and House were complaining about the State Department's foot-dragging. If Roosevelt did not act, Congress might, lambasting presidential "indifference" toward the doomed—and during an election year.

Roosevelt refused to commit himself. After forty minutes, his wife entered the room and ended the meeting: "Now, come on, Franklin. Remember, you've not been well."

Morgenthau was worried that his intensity had alienated the President. He told his diary, "I was very serious . . . and he didn't seem to like it too much." That evening, he took Roosevelt's temperature by telephoning him on the pretext of asking his opinion on a speech in which he would castigate German "ringleaders of hate."

"Fine," said Roosevelt. "Are you sure?" asked Morgenthau. "Yes," replied the President. "But you might add the word 'proven' before ringleaders."

Morgenthau told his diary, "He joked and kidded with me and seemed to be in a grand humor." The Treasury Secretary was hugely relieved that Roosevelt seemed to have "no unfavorable reaction in his mind about myself, which is encouraging. . . . I hope he will see the thing through that I went to see him about."

Six days later, Roosevelt created the War Refugee Board. But he took the precaution of installing his Secretary of War as a member. He knew that the presence of the sober Henry Stimson, who was skeptical of using military resources to help refugees, would keep the new panel from being too audacious.

Why had the President acted? He understood that as the Allies rolled back Nazi tyranny in Europe in 1944, and with greater confidence in victory, there might be new opportunities for rescue. He did not want Congressional hearings on his inaction. Roosevelt also may have worried that if so normally uninvolved a Jew as Morgenthau was so upset about the issue, he might be in imminent danger of alienating Jewish voters in big, crucial states.

In his first three presidential victories, Roosevelt had depended on a huge Jewish vote. He knew that if the election were close in 1944, reduced Jewish support could mean defeat. And there was a good chance that his November opponent would be New York Governor Thomas Dewey, who had excellent relations with Jewish leaders and might try to outbid the President for Jewish voters on the refugee issue and a Jewish homeland in Palestine.

Delighted by what their boss had done, Morgenthau's aides wrote him a letter applauding the "courage and statesmanship" with which "you and you alone" had helped to change "this Government's attitude toward saving the Jews and other persecuted peoples" from "extermination." Morgenthau had earlier told them, "But the tragic thing is that—damn it!—this thing could have been done last February." Remembering Mrs. Klotz's prodding, he later wrote her by hand that "whatever credit I deserve" for helping to save Jewish refugees, "I want to share it equally with you."

Roosevelt wanted a "big name" as director of the board. Morgenthau suggested the President's 1940 opponent Wendell Willkie, but Roosevelt's secretary Grace Tully told the Treasury Secretary that the President did not want to give Willkie any "buildup," since he was seeking the 1944 Republican nomination. Morgenthau then pushed for Pehle, knowing that having his own man as director would help him control the enterprise. Roosevelt consented. By the end of the war, the War Refugee Board would help to save perhaps two hundred thousand Jews in eastern Europe, France, Italy, North Africa and elsewhere.

In London, the British Foreign Secretary, Anthony Eden, who did not share Churchill's enthusiasm to help refugees, privately complained that Roosevelt had created the board to placate the "large Jewish vote" in America before the November election. Nor was Henry Stimson happy about the board. He feared that it would divert attention from winning the war and swell public pressure to send Jewish refugees to Palestine, antagonizing the Arabs and jeopardizing oil supplies. He handed the duty of dealing with the board to his assistant secretary, John McCloy.

Morgenthau asked McCloy by letter to send American military commanders a copy of Roosevelt's new directive that the board should do all it could to help those Nazi victims who were "in imminent danger of death," so long as it was "consistent with the successful prosecution of the war." McCloy did, but warned the General Staff that he was "very chary of getting the Army involved in this while the war is on."

• • •

As he took personal responsibility for Jewish refugees, Roosevelt ended his public quietude about what Hitler was doing to the Jews of Europe. In March 1944, Hitler gave the new government of Hungary instructions to act against the more than 750,000 Jews there. American Jewish leaders pleaded with Roosevelt and others to remind the new regime in Budapest that for those who harmed the Jews, there would be serious punishment once the Allies were victorious.

That month, prodded again by Morgenthau, Roosevelt did not temporize or issue a tightly worded written statement that scarcely mentioned the Jews. Instead, on Friday, March 24, 1944, during an Oval Office session with reporters, he made the most direct proclamation of his life about the Final Solution. For the first time he spoke to Americans in plain language about what would become known much later as the Holocaust. To ensure that his allies understood that he was not widening war aims, he cleared the statement with Stalin and Churchill in advance.

From a script, Roosevelt read out, "In one of the blackest crimes of all history—begun by the Nazis in the day of peace and multiplied by them a hundred times in time of war—the wholesale, systematic murder of the Jews of Europe goes on unabated every hour. . . . None who participate in these acts of savagery shall go unpunished. . . . All who knowingly take part in the deportation of Jews to their death in Poland or Norwegians and French to their death in Germany are equally guilty with the executioner himself.

"Hitler is committing these crimes against humanity in the name of the German people. I am asking every German and every person . . . everywhere under Nazi domination to show the world by his action that in his heart he does not share these insane criminal desires. Let him hide these pursued victims, help them to get over their borders and do what he can to save them from the Nazi hangman."

As "military operations permit," Roosevelt said, the United States would find "havens of refuge" for "all intended victims of the Nazi and Jap executioner."[1]

1. The original draft of this statement, submitted by the War Refugee Board, had been weakened by Samuel Rosenman, Roosevelt's counsel, who argued that mentioning the Jews too prominently might stir public opinion against Jews and against Roosevelt. The President had also vetoed a suggestion that the statement include a promise to temporarily admit to the United States large numbers of refugees. The British Foreign Office endorsed Roosevelt's proclamation. The Soviets ignored American attempts to win their consent to it.

Reporters had only one question about the proclamation: Did the President plan to bring any refugees to the United States? "No, not yet," he said, "because there aren't enough to come."

AS MORGENTHAU FOUGHT TO HELP REFUGEES, he butted heads with John McCloy, who agreed with Stimson that U.S. armed forces should not be used to rescue the victims of the Nazis unless doing so was the "direct result" of military operations intended to win the war. Years later, McCloy recalled that Morgenthau was so "irate" over Hitler's treatment of the Jews that "he was going to do everything in his power" to fight it. He thought Morgenthau was being "vindictive."

McCloy had started life in a modest framework. Born in Philadelphia in 1895, he lost his father, an insurance clerk, at four, causing his mother to "do heads" as a society hairdresser. After Amherst and Harvard Law, he fought in France in World War I and served briefly with the U.S. Army in Germany. In 1930 he married Ellen Zinsser, the rich American-born daughter of a German who had come to America at the start of the century.

As a Republican Wall Street lawyer in the 1920s, McCloy spent much time "picking up loans" in Germany. "We were all very European in our outlook," he recalled, "and our goal was to see it rebuilt." He believed that instead of the punitive peace imposed on Germany at Versailles, the victors should have pulled the defeated nation into the European economy and bolstered it as a bulwark against Soviet Bolshevism.

In 1939, after almost a decade of work, McCloy won considerable damages from the Germans for American plaintiffs in compensation for a 1916 explosion caused by alleged German saboteurs at a New Jersey munitions depot called "Black Tom." His victory gave him a reputation as an expert on German spies.

The next year, the new Secretary of War, Henry Stimson, who knew McCloy as a "top-notch" tennis player at the elite Ausable Club in upstate New York, asked him to advise Army intelligence on preventing German sabotage. Before long, Stimson was using his congenial consultant as broker, legman, expediter and troubleshooter. McCloy left Wall Street to become the Secretary's full-time assistant. Before Roosevelt's Lend-Lease plan of 1941, McCloy and Morgenthau worked together to funnel U.S. aid to embattled

Britain. As McCloy recalled, "I got to know him very closely, because he was after me all the time—'Tell me, where are these munitions going?' . . . 'Can't you ship them abroad any faster than you're doing now?' "

Like Stimson, McCloy insisted that the best way to help the Jews and other victims of Hitler was simply to win the war as quickly as possible. In February 1944 they approved a directive saying, "We must constantly bear in mind the most effective relief which can be given victims of enemy persecution is to insure the speedy defeat of the Axis."

McCloy's biographer Kai Bird believed that McCloy was not an anti-Semite but that he "shared some of the same prejudices" held by "many men of his generation and social standing." Recalling World War I atrocity stories that had proven untrue, McCloy was not certain how much of the information about the Nazi death camps he should believe. He felt that part of his job was to protect Stimson against special pleading. He told the British historian Martin Gilbert in the early 1980s about how much he had been "bothered generally by Jewish requests throughout the war."

In the late spring of 1944, Morgenthau was pressing the War Refugee Board to find an unused Army base or some other haven in the United States where a small group of mostly Jewish refugees from Italy could be temporarily housed. On Tuesday, June 1, when Josiah DuBois raised the matter with McCloy by telephone, McCloy told him it wasn't the Army's business to take care of refugees.

Morgenthau was outraged by McCloy's reaction and that afternoon took a record of the conversation to a Cabinet meeting, where he gave it to Roosevelt, Hull and Stimson to read. Stimson was irritated that McCloy had not briefed him about the refugees: "The trouble with McCloy is he always runs with the ball." But he frankly told the President that he agreed with McCloy that refugees were "no business of the War Department."

Roosevelt replied that "under no circumstances must these people be turned back."

After the meeting, Stimson dictated a memorandum saying that "someone" at Cabinet, referring to Morgenthau, had criticized McCloy as an "oppressor of the Jews." When McCloy read the document, he was furious. Learning of McCloy's anger, Morgenthau asked him to come early the next morning to his rented stone house on Belmont Road in the wealthy Kalorama neighborhood of Washington to clear the air.

Arriving ten minutes early, McCloy immediately told Morgenthau, "I understand that I was criticized at Cabinet." Several times he said, "Somebody in Cabinet said that I was the oppressor of the Jews. That is a terrible thing."

Morgenthau did not directly confess that he had made the comment, but said, "That is why I wanted to send for you and want to get you straight." He explained that he had complained to Roosevelt and Stimson about McCloy's foot-dragging on the refugees from Italy. Stimson had been "annoyed" that "we were discussing something that he didn't know about. . . . You know, you have to tell Stimson these things two and three times over before he gets it."[2]

Morgenthau was happy to exploit McCloy's discomfiture to get him to turn up a dormant Army base for the refugees: "This is a token to the rest of the world that we, the United States government, aren't high and mighty in asking the rest of the world to do something which we aren't willing to do ourselves. That is what the Germans keep saying."[3]

Abashed, McCloy told him that Fort Ontario, in Oswego, New York, could take eighteen hundred refugees. Eager to demonstrate that he was not an oppressor of the Jews, he said that the Army was "willing to be the 'overground railway' to bring these people out," but someone else should feed and care for the refugees after they arrived.[4] He promised to "clear it with Stimmie."

Exhilarated with his victory but exhausted by the confrontation with McCloy, Morgenthau told his aides at 9:15 A.M., "I am glad I acted promptly, and I am now ready to go to bed!" He said that McCloy was "a human fellow" and "frankly, the fellow was bothered."

IN BUDAPEST, in defiance of Roosevelt's spring warning, the new regime was starting to wage war against the Jews of Hungary. The President was informed that Adolf Eichmann of the Reich Security Main Office, who was

2. Morgenthau later told his aides that the elderly Stimson was in some ways "a very small fellow": "You are working with a mind which at one time was a very, very fine mind, but now is a very worn-out mind."

3. German propaganda was braying in 1944 that the United States hypocritically talked about helping Jewish refugees but would not take them on American soil.

4. Here, of course, McCloy referred to the "underground railroad" that helped nineteenth-century black refugees from slavery.

ardently helping to carry out the Final Solution, had presented an offer to trade a million Jews for trucks and other assets.[5]

Despite their revulsion at bargaining with Hitler, Morgenthau and Pehle asked Roosevelt to pursue the feeler, hoping that it might lead to the suspension of Jewish deportation. Roosevelt said he was willing to consider secret, indirect negotiations with the Germans if there were a "remote possibility of saving lives," as long as the United States could deny the talks if they were publicly exposed.

British Foreign Secretary Anthony Eden suspected that the only purpose of Eichmann's "goods for blood" proposal was to entice the Anglo-Americans into secret dealings with Hitler. Trying to divide the Allies, the Nazis would then reveal the talks to Stalin in order to pit him against Roosevelt and Churchill.

To keep Stalin from being provoked, the Anglo-Americans took the precaution of ensuring that Moscow was informed of Eichmann's offer. But the Soviets objected to "any conversations whatsoever" with Hitler's government. Churchill was eager to help the Jews, but he concluded, "Surely we cannot negotiate with the Germans on this matter."

BY EARLY JUNE 1944 the Nazis had deported over a third of Hungary's Jews in only three weeks. Jewish leaders were suggesting a more direct means of frustrating the murderers. Jacob Rosenheim, a leader of the world's Orthodox Jews, and others wrote to Morgenthau, the War Department, the War Refugee Board and other American and British officials, imploring them to bomb the railway lines from Hungary to the death camp at Auschwitz in Poland. Rosenheim warned, "Every day counts."

Operating under Churchill's instructions, Eden wondered whether the murder factory itself should not be bombed. Churchill ordered, "Get everything out of the Air Force you can, and invoke me, if necessary." He told Eden, "There is no doubt that this is probably the greatest and most horrible crime ever committed in the whole history of the world, and it has been done by scientific machinery by nominally civilized men in the name of a great state and one of the leading races in Europe." Churchill's Secretary of

5. Eichmann had spat out the offer to a Hungarian Zionist leader named Joel Brand, at SS headquarters in Budapest.

State for Air, Sir Alexander Sinclair, advised that American bomber pilots were in the best position to do the job, but that it would be "costly and hazardous."

On June 24, as executive director of the War Refugee Board, John Pehle cautiously asked McCloy to explore the matter. Almost certainly reflecting Morgenthau's position, Pehle wrote McCloy that he had "several doubts" about bombing Auschwitz.[6] Was it appropriate for the U.S. military to do the job, and would the rail lines be destroyed for long enough to save the Hungarian Jews?

The War Refugee Board concluded that, if bombed, the transport lines could be swiftly repaired. Nevertheless Pehle sent McCloy a copy of a War Refugee Board cablegram from Switzerland listing the five main deportation routes from Hungary and asking for them to be bombed. On receipt of the message, McCloy's assistant, Colonel Harrison Gerhardt, reminded McCloy that he had told him to "kill" the Rosenheim request, "but since those instructions, we have received the attached letter from Mr. Pehle."

McCloy saw the proposal as a clear violation of his and Stimson's dictum that military resources be used only for winning the war. He wrote Pehle on July 4, 1944, that bombing the rail lines would be "of doubtful efficacy" and "could be executed only by the diversion of considerable air support essential to the success of our forces now engaged in decisive operations" in Europe.[7] Later McCloy used almost the same language to veto requests to bomb Auschwitz itself.

AS THE HISTORIAN ARTHUR SCHLESINGER, JR., has rightly argued, Franklin Roosevelt, "more than any person, deserves the credit for mobilizing the forces that destroyed Nazi barbarism." Still, a half-century later, one of the most controversial aspects of Roosevelt's World War II leadership is the American failure to bomb Auschwitz.

6. Although he worked for the War Refugee Board, as Pehle later recalled, "the Board was in the Treasury, the staff was in the Treasury and we pretty well ran it without going back to the Board itself." Henry Morgenthau III later felt that Pehle would never have made such a request without his father's acquiescence. If Pehle echoed Morgenthau's views, he demonstrated the ambivalence of most world Jewish leaders in the summer of 1944 about bombing Auschwitz, which meant that there was no passionate, forceful effort to press the President to act.

7. Less than a month after D-Day, Allied forces were struggling to break out of the Normandy beachheads.

Roosevelt's most stalwart defenders insist that the best way to save Jews was to win the European war as quickly as possible. They concur with McCloy's view that diverting bombers and crews from the bombing of German industry and other strategic targets might have postponed VE-Day, costing more Jewish lives than might have been saved by bombing Auschwitz and/or the rail lines to the camp. Some scholars note that bombing might have only briefly stopped the slaughter, before the Nazis rebuilt the death chambers, crematoria and rail lines or used other swift and brutal means of killing Jews—and that bombing might have merely provoked the Nazis into speeding up the killing, perhaps by other means.

In contrast, Elie Wiesel, that most eloquent survivor of the death camp known as Auschwitz III, wishes that the Americans had bombed. Wiesel has written that even had the bombing killed the Jewish inmates, "we were no longer afraid of death—at any rate, not of that death."[8]

Others have insisted that bombing Auschwitz might have raised the spirits of the victims, who were being told that the Allies did not care about them—and that it might have deterred some of the perpetrators by warning them how seriously the British and Americans took their crimes and how severely they would be punished when the war was over.

With more than a half-century of hindsight, it is clearer now than in 1944 that the sound of bombs exploding at Auschwitz would have constituted a moral statement for all time that the British and Americans understood the historical gravity of the Holocaust. In the face of so monumental a crime, it is hard to accept that the War Department's doctrine on using military resources should have so rigidly prevailed. As the historian Gerhard Weinberg has written, the bombing of Auschwitz might not have saved many Jews, but nevertheless "the record of the Allies would have been brighter, and each person saved could have lived out a decent life."[9]

Much of the later indignation at the American failure to bomb Auschwitz has centered on John McCloy. The Assistant Secretary of War has been excoriated, at best, for bullheaded concentration on traditional military targets, and at worst, for callous indifference to the murder of the Jews.

Did McCloy take the matter to the President? For decades after World War II, when interviewed about the subject, McCloy let stand the notion that

8. Allied leaders, of course, could not know that this was how the prisoners felt.

9. Weinberg also notes the important fact that in the end, "the Allies saved about two thirds of the world's Jews from the fate the Germans intended for them."

he did not. He told the *Washington Post* reporter Morton Mintz in 1983 that he "never talked" with Roosevelt about the subject. He said that Harry Hopkins had told him that Jewish spokesmen had appealed to the President and "the Boss was not disposed to" such an effort.[10] Drawing on the available evidence, David Wyman, in his 1984 book *The Abandonment of the Jews,* wrote that the bombing requests "almost certainly" did not reach Roosevelt. In a chapter he contributed to the 2000 volume, *The Bombing of Auschwitz,* Richard Levy wrote, "If McCloy is to be faulted, his fault must lie in having failed to go to the President himself."

Thanks to new information, however, we may conclude that the man who ultimately refused to bomb Auschwitz may not have been John McCloy but Franklin Roosevelt.

For decades, McCloy had implied that he had blocked the proposal without consulting the President. But in New York in 1986, three years before his death, McCloy had an exchange, unpublished before now, with Henry Morgenthau's son Henry III, who was researching a family history and taped their conversation.[11]

McCloy recalled that when Jewish leaders "wanted me to order the bombing of Auschwitz," he took the matter to Roosevelt, who was "irate" at the suggestion. The President "made it very clear" to him that bombing Auschwitz "wouldn't have done any good" and that "we would have been accused of destroying Auschwitz [by] bombing these innocent people." As McCloy recalled, Roosevelt "took it out of my hands" and exclaimed, "Why, the idea! They'll say we bombed these people, and they'll only move it down the road a little way and [we'll] bomb them all the more. If it's successful, it'll be more provocative, and I won't have anything to do [with it]. . . . We'll be accused of participating in this horrible business."[12]

10. Hopkins may have told McCloy that Roosevelt was "not disposed" to bomb on the basis of his own self-confidence that he knew Roosevelt's mind on such matters, not necessarily after having consulted the President specifically about bombing Auschwitz. Hopkins was well known for issuing commands in Roosevelt's name that may or may not have actually come from the President. McCloy also told Mintz that Hopkins had asked him to "inquire of the Air Force what the logistics were" for bombing Auschwitz.

11. Straining to say kind things to Morgenthau about his father, McCloy used language that sounded stereotypical about Jews: "He was a man of culture, he was a man of sensitivity, and he was a deeply passionate member of the Jewish race. He felt his racial position was affronted by the activities of the Hitler regime."

12. An August 8, 1944, McCloy letter, turning down the World Jewish Congress's request to bomb Auschwitz, uses the same argument: "There has been considerable opinion that such an effort, even if practicable, might provoke even more vindictive action by the Germans."

McCloy told Morgenthau's son, "I didn't want to bomb Auschwitz. . . . It seemed to be a bunch of fanatic Jews who seemed to think that if you didn't bomb, it was an indication of lack of venom against Hitler. Whereas the President had the idea that that would be more provocative and ineffective. And he took a very strong stand."

If one assumes that the old man's memory was accurate and that he was telling the truth, McCloy had concealed Roosevelt's personal refusal to bomb Auschwitz for forty-two years. Perhaps he was motivated by his old-fashioned notion of public service, which commanded protecting the secrecy of presidential conversations and deflecting criticism from the boss. If McCloy's confession to Henry Morgenthau III can be believed, it might not be wholly coincidental that the one interlocutor to whom McCloy finally revealed he was not the one who ultimately vetoed bombing Auschwitz was the son of the man who in 1944 had considered him an "oppressor of the Jews."

ON THURSDAY, July 6, two days after McCloy wrote Pehle refusing to bomb Auschwitz, Morgenthau went to the White House for a meeting with the President on civil administration in occupied France. It was exactly a month after D-Day. The Treasury Secretary stayed behind for a private talk with Roosevelt. He asked whether it would be "all right for me to go to France" to see how U.S. occupation currency was "getting along."[13]

"That would be fine," said the President. For Roosevelt, who usually suffered from rhetorical inflation, such a reply did not suggest enthusiasm. Surprised that his dependable old friend had pressed him so hard about Jewish refugees, he may have been nervous about what Morgenthau, left to his own devices, might do next.

Knowing that it would strengthen his hand in Europe, Morgenthau asked Roosevelt if he could "take McCloy with me" and asked for letters endorsing his trip to the "various generals in charge." The President agreed and, in Morgenthau's presence, scrawled out a note for General George Marshall:

13. After American troops landed on D-Day, General Charles de Gaulle, chief of the provisional French government, had given the United States an "arrogant and belligerent" warning that only he had the right to issue French currency in liberated areas. But four days after the landing, General Eisenhower issued the proclamation validating the currency himself, gambling that de Gaulle would "come along."

"I think it would be a good idea for Sec. Morgenthau + Jack McCloy to go over about July 21 to 23 to see how the new currency is working in France. Will you transport? F.D.R."

Morgenthau insisted years later that his only purpose in asking to go to France was to study currency problems. But he doubtless had other motives. There was not much to discover from a quick tour that he could not have learned in Washington. And with the British and Americans still establishing themselves in France, Morgenthau knew how much high-level staff time and logistical support such a trip would require.

Morgenthau was exhilarated by the prospect of visiting the Allied battlefront, as he had earlier done in North Africa. Henry III recalled, "He got a great kick out of getting into the war zone and getting the . . . sounds and smells of war." He may also have hoped to use the trip to help win himself a major role, beyond merely planning the postwar financial system, in shaping the European peace—especially the fate of Germany, about which his emotions were now running at high fever.[14] Morgenthau wanted to stop in London, where he intended to see if more could not be done to rescue Jews. By the first week of July, almost a half million Jews had already been deported from Hungary to the Nazi death camps.

Brandishing Roosevelt's note to Marshall, Morgenthau invited McCloy to accompany him to Europe. Suspicious of Morgenthau's potential encroachment on his terrain, perhaps still smarting from Morgenthau's barb that he was an "oppressor" of the Jews, the overworked McCloy declined. He wrote in his diary, "Naturally I do not want to go to France to look at currency problems and have in mind going somewhere else anyway."

Undeterred, Morgenthau began expanding his mission. He envisaged a week in occupied France, a visit to American troops, including his son Henry III, and meetings in England with Eisenhower and British officials.

Marshall dutifully sent a radiogram to Eisenhower, who was outraged at the notion of devoting scarce resources to a tour by Morgenthau just six weeks after the British and Americans had landed in France. He cabled Marshall, "Should the President desire that Secretary Morgenthau visit France, we will, of course, make a virtue out of a necessity. However, you will under-

14. Early in 1944, when Roosevelt had to name a U.S. representative to the European Advisory Commission on postwar Europe, Morgenthau had proposed his old Treasury aide Lauchlin Currie, which might have given Morgenthau an opening wedge to help shape the postwar era. Roosevelt refused.

stand that there is nothing to be learned about currency problems in the little strip of France which we now possess." Eisenhower added that "at my personal request," Churchill had barred members of his own War Cabinet from France, and that "accommodations for dignitaries visiting in the lodgment areas do not now exist."

Apologetically, Marshall's aide Colonel Frank McCarthy told Morgenthau of Eisenhower's telegram and asked whether, as a compromise, the Treasury Secretary might be satisfied with a one-day tour of France. He was "certain" that during that day, Eisenhower would bring "the mountain to Mohammed." He added that even Marshall and the Chiefs had limited their visits to the bridgehead to one day. But Morgenthau persisted. He won a two-day overnight tour of France and lengthened his visit to England.

He knew that the trip would be emotionally and physically grueling. Before his departure, he asked his secretary for "some more half-grain Nembutal and also some more half-grain Codeine" for his trip.

At LaGuardia Field, New York, on Saturday afternoon, August 5, Morgenthau and his aides Josiah DuBois, Fred Smith and Harry Dexter White boarded a military plane for the long flight to Europe. A telegram went to Roosevelt, who was on his West Coast military inspection trip: "Leaving today for England and France. Best regards, Henry."

CHAPTER EIGHT

"We Will Have to Get Awfully Busy"

WITH A FIGHTER ESCORT, Henry Morgenthau's C-54 Skymaster, the same type of plane as the President's *Sacred Cow*, roared into the night over the Atlantic. During the twenty-two-hour flight, Harry Dexter White pulled out a memorandum by the State Department on "property rights" in postwar Germany that he knew would provoke his boss.

White, the Treasury's chief international economist, was eager to ensure a weak postwar Germany. To make sure the memorandum struck Morgenthau with the maximum emotional punch, he may have planned to give it to his boss when he was tired and trapped aboard a noisy, droning airplane.

Morgenthau read the document with rising anger. It noted that Germans would need to support themselves. Germany must promote the revival of Europe and provide manufactured goods to its victims. Therefore the Allied victors must shore up most of the country's industrial apparatus.[1]

To Morgenthau the paper ignored the most "basic question of all": how to keep Germany from ever again menacing the world. As his aide Josiah

1. In this and a later document, State Department planners suggested that, if necessary to "hold the economy together," the first occupying Allied forces should even keep well-known leading Nazis in place. The planners acknowledged that Nazi party influence must be eliminated "as soon as possible" and proposed other economic controls such as destruction of German monopolies and bans on discriminatory trade practices. But they argued that the best safeguard against future German warmaking was to knit the country into a "peaceful and expanding world economy."

DuBois recalled, "by the time we arrived in England," Morgenthau was "convinced" that something had to be done. Another aide on the trip, Fred Smith, recalled that "Morgenthau was sure that the Germans were a war-loving race, and possibly incurable."

MORGENTHAU AND HIS PARTY landed at Prestwick, Scotland, just after midnight on Monday, August 7, 1944. They were met by Colonel Bernard Bernstein of General Eisenhower's staff, who ushered them aboard the Supreme Commander's luxurious special train, bound for his headquarters in Portsmouth.

Bernstein was the financial adviser to Eisenhower's command but he had earlier been a lawyer in Morgenthau's Treasury. He revered his old boss and still thought of himself as a Treasury man. Over breakfast, as the sun rose and the English countryside rushed past the train's windows, Bernstein warned Morgenthau that his colleagues in the War Department's Civil Affairs Division[2] did not appear very motivated to restrict postwar Germany. They seemed more concerned that as U.S. troops conquered Germany, they would be mired in a "morass of economic wreckage."

Bernstein showed his old chief a draft *Handbook for Military Government in Germany,* for use once U.S. troops crossed the German border. Written by the German Country Unit of Eisenhower's Supreme Headquarters, Allied Expeditionary Force (SHAEF) but not yet approved, its purpose was to minimize the chaos as Anglo-American forces advanced through Germany.[3]

Conquering soldiers would be told that their "main and immediate task" was to ensure that the "machine" in Germany "works efficiently." They should "restore as quickly as possible" the "official functioning of the German civilian government in the area for which you are responsible." German industry must be buttressed to support the Germans and keep Europe on an

2. During World War II, the War Department created the Civil Affairs Division (G-5) to oversee relationships with civilians in occupied countries.

3. The *Handbook* had been written under an April 1944 directive by the Anglo-American Combined Chiefs of Staff (CCS-551), saying that while Naziism should be banished, normal German life should be restored "as soon as possible, insofar as conditions will not interfere with military operations." Although intended for the immediate period after Allied forces pierced the German border, the *Handbook* was likely to influence those planning the postsurrender occupation of Germany.

"even keel." Every German must be promised two thousand calories of food per day.

Bernstein complained to Morgenthau that no one at SHAEF seemed to care "that it is Germans that they are controlling." Still unsettled by the paper he had read on the airplane, Morgenthau acidly noted that SHAEF's plans for Germany resembled "a nice WPA job."[4]

IN PORTSMOUTH, Morgenthau, along with his aides Fred Smith and Harry Dexter White, lunched with Eisenhower in the General's mess tent. Flush with the success of the Normandy landings, Eisenhower jovially derided American critics who were complaining that after D-Day, he was too slow to plunge deep into France: "After you make a thrust, you have to wait until you can 'coil the tail' again before you move ahead."

At Morgenthau's cue White raised the subject of postwar Germany. Under existing plans, he said, German "life would be reestablished on as high a plane as possible." Certainly while advancing through Europe, Allied troops must "bolster" an enemy's economy to keep from "bogging down in a morass." But Germany was no "thoroughfare." It was "the end of the road."

Grimly Eisenhower replied, "I am not interested in the German economy, and personally would not like to bolster it, if that will make it easier for the Germans." As far as he was concerned, the German General Staff should be "utterly eliminated" and Nazi ringleaders given "the death penalty." Ike said that the German people, by supporting Hitler, had been accomplices to everything done in their name. They "must not be allowed to escape a sense of guilt, of complicity in the tragedy that has engulfed the world." The Germans had been "taught to be paranoid in their actions and thoughts, and they have to be snapped out of it. The only way to do that is to be good and hard on them."

Morgenthau told Eisenhower that after occupation, he wanted to "see the mark pegged low enough so that it could go only one way." That way, "if the mark rose, there could be no accusation that through stupidity we wrecked the German economic system."

4. In 1935, Roosevelt created the Works Progress Administration to put unemployed Americans to work on federal projects. It was said that War Department officials later struck back at Bernstein for provoking Morgenthau about the *Handbook* by blocking his ambition to become a general.

Descended from eighteenth-century Rhineland Germans, Eisenhower later wrote in his memoirs that "as the months of conflict wore on, I grew constantly more bitter against the Germans." To his wife, Mamie, he wrote, "The German is a beast" and "God, I hate the Germans!" Since D-Day, the Germans had killed sixteen thousand and wounded seventy-eight thousand of his American boys. The very morning of Morgenthau's arrival, Eisenhower had heard a ghastly account of the Nazi death camps.

But the General had another reason to sound tough on Germany in Morgenthau's presence. He knew that in November 1942, Morgenthau had been his "severest critic in the Cabinet" when he made his pragmatic deal with the Vichy French Admiral Jean Darlan. In exchange for Darlan's pledge to blunt French opposition to the Allied invasion of North Africa, Eisenhower and the Allies had agreed to tolerate local Vichy decrees, including sanctions against the Jews.

As party to that deal, Eisenhower had taken some of the most searing criticism of his life. Plaintively he wrote his son John, "I have been called a Fascist and almost a Hitlerite." When Morgenthau called on Eisenhower in Algiers in October 1943, the Secretary had made his views known.

This time the Supreme Commander was not going to give Morgenthau a second chance to imply that he was soft on the Nazis. In reply to the Secretary's questions, Eisenhower noted that his duties as Supreme Commander would end after victory. But if an inter-Allied commission were established to keep Germany "in line," he would probably be military governor, in which case he would have "something to say about Germany's economy."

He felt that a "hard peace" with postwar Germany would inspire the Soviets to redouble their efforts to win the European war. More than most of his British and American colleagues, Eisenhower was optimistic about postwar cooperation with Moscow, and thus less motivated than they to strengthen Germany as a barricade to Soviet power in postwar Europe. He told Morgenthau that Russia "has problems of her own which will keep her busy long after we are dead."

Morgenthau was exhilarated that the much admired military leader seemed to share his views on postwar Germany. He later told his aides that on the Germans, Eisenhower was "very positive that he was going to treat them rough" and let them "stew in their own juice." Before leaving, Harry Dexter White told the General, "We may want to quote you on the problem of handling the German people." Eisenhower said, "I will tell the President myself, if necessary."[5]

ON TUESDAY, August 8, 1944, with another fighter escort, Morgenthau flew to Cherbourg, the once-great French port that had been mined by the Germans, then shelled by the Allies. Morgenthau observed, "It is to hell and gone."

Eisenhower's chief of staff, General Walter Bedell Smith, had told Morgenthau that he could not travel beyond SHAEF forward headquarters, but Morgenthau pulled rank and told Smith he would let the local commander, General Omar Bradley, "decide how far I can go." He filmed the battlefront with a sixteen-millimeter camera and toured evacuation hospitals, which depressed him. He later said that the "odor of the wounded" was so strong "that I had all I could do not to vomit."

After a night at Carentan, where he received a briefing on French occupation currency, he was driven to Bradley's Normandy front headquarters, where the General speculated that the Nazis might be defeated by the end of September 1944.[6] Bradley boasted that he had "an opportunity that comes to a commander not more than once in a century. We're about to destroy an entire hostile army."

Morgenthau also had an emotional reunion with his oldest son, Henry III, who was serving in General George Patton's Third Army. While touring Omaha and Utah Beaches, the Secretary accepted the gift of a captured German helmet. Later, he sent Generals Bradley and Bedell Smith thank-you cases of bourbon, writing, "Here's hoping that you will be having a drink on me in Berlin in the not-too-distant future." Bradley replied that "a bottle has already been put aside for your visit with us in Germany."

5. In November 1947, Morgenthau drew on his diaries to publish an article in *Collier's* magazine about his wartime talk with Eisenhower. He also authorized an article by his Treasury aide Fred Smith saying that with their Portsmouth conversation, it was Eisenhower who had "launched" Morgenthau's effort to tame Germany. By then, the Cold War had begun and many Americans had come to think that the only Americans who had wanted a tough peace with postwar Germany had been pro-Soviet. Eager to protect himself from such accusations, Eisenhower asked his aides to find in his files his own contemporaneous record of his talk with Morgenthau that would support or refute the article. They could not. In his 1948 World War II memoir *Crusade in Europe*, Eisenhower offered his own version of his talk with Morgenthau, based on what he called his "rough" recollection of it four years later. Eisenhower's retrospective account of what he said to Morgenthau was considerably softer on Germany than what Morgenthau recorded him saying at the time.

6. McCloy felt the same way. Both men soon changed their minds.

During Morgenthau's visit to occupied France, Goebbels's propagandists were at work. Berlin radio let the German people know that while touring France, the "Jew Morgenthau" had stolen a priceless French tapestry.

Flown back to England, Morgenthau was grandly lodged at an eight-thousand-acre estate in Wiltshire called Red Rice, which was leased by the U.S. Army. Worried that the frugal Treasury Secretary might tell Roosevelt that Eisenhower was a spendthrift, Bedell Smith assured him that SHAEF did not "go to this extent in billeting the majority of our visitors."

On Thursday, August 10, over lunch, Morgenthau asked his British counterpart, Sir John Anderson, if permitting Germany "to continue as an industrial nation" would not mean that soon it would be "arming for another war." Anderson replied merely that the making of "war-related products" should be stopped.

Morgenthau was taken aback by Anderson's timidity. Drawing on his romantic Dutchess County notion of yeoman farmers, Morgenthau offered, as "purely my own" idea, that "we could divide Germany up into a number of small provinces, stop all industrial production and convert them into small agricultural landholders." Anderson merely responded with silence.

That afternoon, Morgenthau called on Churchill, who seemed "very glad to see me," he noted in his diary. The Prime Minister had good reason to try to make Morgenthau happy. He was eager to continue receiving U.S. Lend-Lease aid during the period from the German surrender through Japan's defeat, and Morgenthau was trying to keep the sum modest.

With Morgenthau, Churchill used the same combination of scare tactics and charm that he usually deployed on Franklin Roosevelt. Melodramatically he told his American visitor that England's prospects were "very, very dark." The country was "completely bankrupt" and there was "no future" for the returning British soldier. England could produce only half the food it needed and would need big postwar exports to survive. While troops were still fighting in Europe, Churchill said, he could not tell his people the awful truth, but after victory, he would have to "lay the whole thing before Parliament." Then he would become "the most unpopular man in England."

Morgenthau recorded in his diary, "The man was terribly depressed, and this talk to me was most shocking."

The Prime Minister told him, "Morgenthau, you have been reported to me in the last year as having turned against us and becoming rather hard in your attitude toward us." The Treasury Secretary pledged to "make an honest effort" to help, "guided by my emotions, rather than my pocket."

The previous month, Churchill and his War Cabinet had debated the Zionist leader Chaim Weizmann's old request that a Jewish brigade be formed to fight the Nazis. Churchill had been sympathetic, but others had warned that a Jewish brigade might evolve into a Jewish army, which, after the war, might go to Palestine and agitate for a Jewish state.

Now, playing to his audience, Churchill told Morgenthau that he thought a Jewish brigade, hoisting Star of David flags, should be sent into Germany: "To hell with the Arabs! They haven't helped to win the war anyway."

Morgenthau said he approved of such a brigade, but not with Jewish flags, which he feared would suggest that Jews were not loyal to their own countries: "It would just demonstrate to Hitler that what he said about the Jews was true." He added that he considered himself, first of all, an American.[7]

Just before Morgenthau's departure for Europe, the Nazi puppet regime in Budapest had offered to release "certain categories of Jews," if the British and Americans would take them. As DuBois recalled, British diplomats feared that more than a hundred thousand Jews might demand entry into Britain: "They actually said in so many words that 'we can't accept this proposition because what do we do with these Jews if they are released?'" DuBois recalled that when Morgenthau had heard about this attitude, he "got very worked up."

Morgenthau now asked Churchill whether Britain would join the United States in finding "havens of refuge" for the Jews of Hungary. Churchill said yes, but that Palestine could not be one of them. He had promised the Arabs that as long as the war was on, he would not exceed the agreed-upon quota for Jews residing there. Churchill added that his capacity to "accommodate refugees" on British soil was "limited."

Later, Morgenthau complained that when suggesting a Jewish brigade, Churchill could say "to hell with the Arabs," but "when it comes to this quota, he doesn't want to let the Jews come into Palestine."

7. Later that month, Churchill indeed approved establishment of a Jewish brigade in Siena, Italy, to fight alongside General Sir Harold Alexander's army.

At the end of their visit, Churchill took the American into his fabled War Room, which Morgenthau found "quite a thrill." The Prime Minister also showed him a model of the British landing beach at Normandy. Morgenthau later told his aides, "Of course, I have no way of knowing which was better—the English or ours—but certainly the two beaches I saw looked damned good."[8]

On Saturday, August 12, 1944, Morgenthau sat on the wide green lawn at Red Rice with Harry Dexter White, other aides and Roosevelt's ambassador to London, John Winant. He reported that Eisenhower had told him that "we must take a tough line with Germany." He said he himself felt that the conquered state could be reduced to a "land of small farms," like Denmark, where farmers close to the land were unaggressive and "peaceloving." Morgenthau felt that the Jefferson agrarian philosophy that he considered himself to share with Roosevelt could purge the German spirit.

Winant did not buy it. He said, "Farmers make good fighters."

"Not farmers without modern industrial equipment!" said White.

Winant remarked that as the American representative on the European Advisory Commission in London, he had tried for months to get instructions from Washington. But he had no idea what Roosevelt wanted to do about postwar Germany.

White complained that the British were saying that Britain needed a "strong, healthy Germany" for its export market. If the victors put postwar Germany back on its feet and freed it of the need to produce armaments, then a few years after its defeat, the aggressor nation might be "better off" than its European victims. "To return Germany as a respectable member of the family of nations is to put Germany in a position where she will again endeavor to become master of the world," he said. "Twice in our generation she has tried, and the third time, she may well be successful."

8. At Morgenthau's insistence, DuBois stayed on in London to press the British for a public declaration that both countries would find havens for Jews who fled Hungary. The British consented, but only after making a secret side deal that the United States would actually take any refugees released. "How much good it did psychologically is anybody's guess," said DuBois long afterward. "I don't know how many Hungarians were actually released as a result of it." Pehle advised Morgenthau on August 17, 1944, that the Germans were "now taking this position" that "nobody can leave Hungary unless they get ransom." Nevertheless, the courageous Raoul Wallenberg of Sweden, financed by the U.S. War Refugee Board, managed to save more than twenty thousand Jews or converted Christians of Jewish descent in Budapest.

• • •

ON SUNDAY AFTERNOON, August 13, Morgenthau took Winant and White to Anthony Eden's house, where they had tea on the lawn. He told the Foreign Secretary he had gathered from Churchill that, at least for the early months after victory, Germany would be forced to fend for itself.

Eden responded that at the Tehran conference, Roosevelt, Churchill and Stalin had agreed to dismember the country: "Uncle Joe Stalin was determined to smash Germany so that it would never again be able to make war."

Eden did not know that Roosevelt had refused to confide the substance of the Big Three's private conversations at Tehran to Morgenthau or other high American officials. But now the cat was out of the bag. Morgenthau quickly asked Eden to show him the British records of the secret Tehran talks on postwar Germany before he left London. Desperate for Morgenthau's help on Lend-Lease, Eden was hardly in a position to say no.

Provocatively, Harry Dexter White told Eden he understood that the British wanted to restore the German economy in order to regain their "most important customer." Startled, Eden replied that any such soft-on-Germany talk would cause the Soviets to worry that the Anglo-Americans were going to go their own way. Nothing must impede the "closest possible postwar cooperation" among the three powers. A strong postwar Germany, he said, would be more dangerous than a strong postwar Russia.

Hearing more than the Foreign Secretary had said, Morgenthau later marveled to his aides that Eden "wants to take Germany apart—completely apart," and "he doesn't pull his punches either."

ON TUESDAY, Morgenthau and White went to Eden's office at Whitehall. As the American visitors listened with fascination, the Foreign Secretary read aloud from the records of the Tehran talks in which the Big Three had spoken of dividing Germany and Roosevelt had insisted that the vanquished country be split into three or more parts.

Morgenthau said that if the Allied intention was to divide postwar Germany, State Department and Pentagon officials talking about reviving the German system were violating official policy.

Eden was clearly embarrassed by the entire scene. He may have worried that Roosevelt might penalize him and Churchill for showing Morgenthau the Tehran records that the President had clearly intended him not to see. He asked Morgenthau to please explain to Roosevelt that he had not even meant to raise the subject of Germany with him.

Morgenthau insisted that he had not "come to England to discuss the matter" either, but said that when he returned to Washington two days hence, he would talk to Roosevelt and Hull about postwar Germany.

MORGENTHAU HAD ASKED to tour the London air-raid shelters. Churchill had thought of accompanying him himself but by the summer of 1944 he was sometimes booed on the streets by Britons impatient with the long war. Rather than risk embarrassment in front of the visiting Treasury Secretary, Churchill had his wife, Clementine, escort Morgenthau.

As a respite from British food rationing, Morgenthau gave Mrs. Churchill newly laid eggs and hams from Fishkill Farms. She wrote her husband that Morgenthau was a "funny vague old thing" and that it was "difficult to imagine him managing a whelk stall[9]—but perhaps the Treasury is easier, with no competition!"

After midnight in London, Morgenthau gave an address on CBS Radio to the American people, which Roosevelt's speechwriter Robert Sherwood and the CBS London correspondent Edward R. Murrow helped to write. He told his audience that while touring the fallout shelters, the "principal thought that filled my mind and heart" had been "we must never forget!"[10] It was not enough to hope that postwar Germans and Japanese would "behave themselves as decent people": "Hoping is not good enough. . . . Germany and Japan must be kept disarmed."

Afterward, Clementine Churchill wired Morgenthau, "Your voice was warm and true and all you said showed such understanding of our people." Morgenthau's wife cabled from Fishkill Farms, "Your speech was excellent. All well."

BEFORE FLYING HOME FROM LONDON, Morgenthau asked his Under Secretary, Daniel Bell, to arrange an appointment for him with the President.

9. Churchill had once criticized his opposition by saying that they "were not fit to run a whelk stall," meaning a sidewalk vendor's stall.

10. Coincidentally, Morgenthau was using a phrase that would be uttered by postwar Jews and others about the Holocaust.

To keep the Axis from learning Roosevelt's whereabouts, Bell replied with an obliquely worded radiogram that on Saturday evening, three days hence, the "gentleman with whom you wish appointment" would be leaving Washington for Hyde Park.

Morgenthau got Bell to arrange a White House appointment for Saturday morning. Exploiting his advantage over other Cabinet members who were not family friends, Morgenthau also arranged for himself and his wife to hop a ride with Roosevelt on the presidential train to Hyde Park, which would give him more time to bend the President's ear. Roosevelt's aide William Hassett, a hard-drinking Vermont ex-newspaperman who did not like the Morgenthaus or Jews, wrote in his log that "the Morgenthaus muscled in for the ride to Dutchess County."

ON THURSDAY, August 17, in Washington, Morgenthau had lunch with his staff, which, in contrast to the top echelons at the State and War Departments, was heavy with liberal, reformist New Dealers who were indignant at the notion of German economic revival.[11] Morgenthau told his aides that during his European trip, "I spent most of my time on . . . how they are going to treat Germany. We will have to get awfully busy."

Morgenthau warned that their old bureaucratic adversaries seemed to be thwarting Roosevelt's intentions. "It took me days and days and days, but I got the story." He was glad that he got his "nose under the tent": "Thank heavens the President did let me go to England and find the stuff!" Hull's "boys" at State were "the worst," saying, "Keep a central Germany. Keep a strong Germany." Morgenthau concluded, "I don't know how much Mr. Hull knows, but he is certainly going to get an earful."

ON FRIDAY MORNING, Morgenthau went to Cordell Hull's large office in the gray French Renaissance edifice next to the White House that housed the State Department.[12] He told the Secretary of State that "from all appearances," the Germans were to be "built up" after World War II so that in ten years, they

11. That summer, Harry Dexter White had been struggling against State Department officials who insisted that the postwar International Monetary Fund avoid New Deal–type social reforms in Europe.

12. Now called the Eisenhower Executive Office Building.

would be ready "to wage a third world war." He reported that Eden had read aloud to him from the minutes of the Tehran meeting, which showed that the Big Three had decided to divide Germany "into three or fifteen parts."

Hull gasped: "Henry, this is the first time I have ever heard this! I have never been permitted to see the minutes of the Tehran conference. I have asked [the President] and I have not been allowed."

Morgenthau pledged to "keep it absolutely amongst ourselves." He said that no one was working along the lines agreed upon at Tehran: "I appreciate the fact that this isn't my responsibility, but I am doing this as an American citizen . . . and I am going to stick my nose into it until I know it is all right."

Ruefully, the Secretary of State said that Roosevelt never let him do "anything" important in foreign policy: "I am not told what is going on. That's on a higher level. . . . When they talk about the state of Germany, I am not consulted." Hull said he was "exhausted fighting the different people around town": "The President could stop it in a minute—if he wanted to do it."

Morgenthau was amazed. He knew that Roosevelt had circumvented his Secretary of State, but he had not realized it was that bad. He asked Hull where he stood on postwar Germany. The frail old Tennessean wistfully recalled the single excursion into urgent Allied diplomacy that Roosevelt had allowed him—the Moscow meeting with Eden and Molotov. "The reason I got along so well with the Russians was because . . . I [said] I would hold a secret trial [of] Hitler and his gang . . . and . . . shoot them all. . . . Then I would let the world know about it a couple of days later. That's my position!"

Morgenthau told Hull that if he read what his own planners were writing on Germany, he would find that he and they were "about as far apart as the North and South Pole."

Back at the Treasury, Morgenthau told his aides of the scene in Hull's office: "If Eden hadn't actually read from the minutes of the Tehran conference and Hull hadn't told me, face to face, that he hadn't seen them, I wouldn't believe it. . . . I am sure if Hull got a directive on the dismemberment of Germany, he would go to town. My trip to Europe was many, many times worthwhile—just for what I learned and what I told Hull. And we will see what happens when I see the President."

CHAPTER NINE

"Not Nearly as Bad as Sending Them to Gas Chambers"

On Friday, August 18, 1944, after his tour of military installations in California, Hawaii, Alaska and the Pacific Northwest, Franklin Roosevelt spent his first day at the White House in more than a month. Under Andrew Jackson's magnolia tree on the South Grounds, wearing a polka-dotted bow tie and shirtsleeves, he lunched with his new Democratic running mate, Senator Harry Truman of Missouri. Truman thanked him for "putting the finger on me" for Vice President.

Joseph Baldwin, a Republican Congressman from New York, later said that Roosevelt and Truman both told him that during their tree-shaded lunch, the President said to his new running mate, "When you have made as much progress as we have . . . in the last few years, you have to digest it. . . . I want someone to succeed me who is . . . a little right of center." Truman presumed that the President was referring to him.[1] Roosevelt told him to stay off airplanes because one of them had to stay alive.

Truman had not seen Roosevelt for a year and was shocked by how much he had aged. After the lunch, he told his aide Harry Vaughan, "I had no idea he was in such a feeble condition. . . . It doesn't seem to be a mental lapse . . . but physically he's just going to pieces. I'm very much concerned about him."

A few weeks later, while coming out of the White House, an old Army

1. If Roosevelt thought of Truman as "right of center," that may have reflected his awareness of Truman's border state origins more than Truman's actual sympathies and voting record.

friend told the Missouri Senator to "turn around and take a look," because he would be living there before long. "I'm afraid I am," said Truman, "and it scares the hell out of me."

By the summer of 1944, a New York cardiologist named Howard Bruenn had been quietly added to the President's entourage, examining him three or four mornings a week. During his first encounter with Roosevelt in March at Bethesda Naval Hospital, he found the President "very tired" and "very gray." Though in "good humor," Roosevelt moved with "considerable breathlessness."

The doctor found that, after what was diagnosed as influenza dating from after the Tehran conference, Roosevelt had "failed to regain his usual vigor," complaining of "undue fatigue." Bruenn concluded that he was "in cardiac failure," with a "grossly enlarged" heart and "tortuous" aorta. "Appalled at what I had found," Bruenn said in 1992 that if he had ever been asked, he would have advised that a fourth term for Roosevelt was "impossible medically."

Modern antihypertensive drugs could have relieved the burden on Roosevelt's arteries, but those did not exist in 1944. As Bruenn recalled, there was little he could do but "protect him from stress, keep down his excitement, insist on him having rest after lunch," cutting back his smoking to six cigarettes a day and reducing his weight. After "obstinately" obeying a rigid diet, Roosevelt lost more than twenty pounds, which left him looking gaunt and hollow-cheeked.

"His mind was unaffected," wrote the historian Robert Ferrell. "His problem was an inability to concentrate for long periods." Sometimes he dozed off during conversations. By 1944, Roosevelt was engaged in intense public business no more than two to four hours a day.

About the severity of Roosevelt's condition the public was told nothing, although the forty-two-year-old Republican candidate Thomas Dewey scored points by attacking the "tired old men" in the White House. Roosevelt's aides, Cabinet members and family seldom permitted themselves the thought that the President was suffering from anything graver than the pressures of a global war.

Roosevelt himself asked his doctors as few questions as possible. Bruenn noted that "at no time" did the President ever ask why he was seeing him so frequently and insisting on electrocardiograms, other tests and medications like digitalis. Almost certainly Roosevelt knew that if he asked, the doctor would tell him something he would not want to hear.

Roosevelt's declining condition eroded his ability to operate more than it might have done to other Presidents. His approach to leadership was to play Cabinet members off against one another, hold a dozen conflicting ideas in his head at any one time, and to keep the mechanics of control firmly in his grasp. But with his energy and concentration ebbing, he no longer had the patience and command of detail that had once let him keep important policies from going off the rails and Cabinet members from exceeding the roles he envisaged for them. Cordell Hull's new deputy, Edward Stettinius, found Roosevelt "increasingly difficult to deal with because he changed his mind so often."

Roosevelt's physical decline therefore was more and more a problem as World War II approached its climax and he tried to plan for the postwar world. In August 1944, Eleanor Roosevelt wrote her young friend Joseph Lash, serving in the Army in New Zealand, that the President "complains of getting tired too quickly and he looks older. Whatever he had last spring took a toll, but I guess he still feels his experience and equipment will help him do a better job than Mr. Dewey."

ON SATURDAY MORNING, August 19, Henry Morgenthau arrived at the White House. He was told that the President was running late and could only give him five minutes, but that they could talk on the train to Hyde Park that evening. As Morgenthau later recalled, when he was admitted to Roosevelt's presence, "I stayed for a half hour, but I couldn't do justice to my subject because I felt I was under pressure, and I talked terribly fast." Reporting on his trip, he said that Churchill had confided to him that England was broke.

"What does he mean by that?" snapped the President.

"England really is broke," said Morgenthau, adding that Churchill presumed that when he told the bad news to the British people and Parliament, he would be "through."

Roosevelt scoffed at that, saying that Churchill was only trying to sweeten his chances to get more American Lend-Lease aid. The Prime Minister was "taking those tactics now" but "more recently his attitude was that he wanted to see England through the peace." He joked that if what Churchill was saying was really true, "I will go over there and make a couple of talks and take over the British Empire!"

Morgenthau told about his trip to Europe and how "little by little, I put pieces together" to find that planning for postwar Germany was in disarray. Eisenhower was "perfectly prepared to be tough with the Germans when he first goes in" but at lower levels, SHAEF was planning to "treat them like a WPA project." He told Roosevelt that he had gotten Anthony Eden to read to him from the secret records of the Big Three's conversations about Germany at the Tehran conference. He added that "Hull told me that he had never been told what was in the minutes of the Tehran meeting." Thus State Department planners were writing memos while knowing nothing about what Roosevelt, Stalin and Churchill had agreed on at Tehran.

As Morgenthau recorded in his diary, "The President didn't like it, but he didn't say anything. He looked very embarrassed, and I repeated it so that he would be sure to get it."

Roosevelt was probably angry at Eden for divulging the information to Morgenthau when it was clear to Eden that this contravened the President's wish. But he was doubtless especially piqued at his Hudson Valley friend for sticking his fingers where they did not belong, giving the irascible Hull new ammunition for his eternal complaints about the President bypassing him—and most of all, for pressing the President to commit himself on postwar Germany before he wanted to.

Morgenthau reminded Roosevelt that State Department officials planning for postwar Germany "couldn't get any instructions from Hull because Hull didn't know what had been agreed upon" at Tehran. "The sum and substance is that from the Tehran conference down to now, nobody has been studying how to treat Germany roughly—along the lines you wanted."

Because he had not intended his private talk at Tehran to be ironclad policy on Germany, Roosevelt tried to keep Morgenthau from what he presumably considered further meddling. He tried to signal Morgenthau that since they agreed completely, he should now butt out and let the President handle it.

"Give me thirty minutes with Churchill and I can correct this," Roosevelt said. "We have got to be tough" with "the German people—not just the Nazis. You either have to castrate the German people or you have got to treat them in such a manner so that they can't just go on reproducing people who want to continue the way they have in the past." Why not be tough with Germany? "They have been tough with us!"

Morgenthau recorded in his diary that Roosevelt had "left no doubt whatsoever in my mind that he personally wants to be tough with the Germans. . . . He and I are looking at this thing in the same way." He told Harry Dexter White, "I think he is going to act on it now. I think it is going to turn the whole thing upside down."

THAT EVENING, MORGENTHAU and his wife rode with Roosevelt on the presidential train to Dutchess County, but there is no record that during the trip the President gave his friend any further chance to lobby him on postwar Germany.

In fact, without Morgenthau knowing it, Roosevelt took action to stop his friend's freelancing. With the balance-of-power approach that he employed to keep his own people in line, he asked his aide Harry Hopkins to ask Henry Stimson to have a "talk" with Morgenthau. He knew that Hopkins disliked the Treasury Secretary and coveted the family intimacy that the Morgenthaus enjoyed with the Roosevelts. Stimson invited Morgenthau for lunch at the Pentagon on Wednesday, August 23.

Before the lunch, Stimson saw Roosevelt for the first time since his return from the Pacific Northwest. He later recorded in his diary that it was "a great day in the war news. Paris has been freed." The war's end "seems to be approaching on a galloping horse."

During what Stimson called a "rapid fire talk," he told Roosevelt that he needed "a decision on what we are going to do to Germany." It was "of primary importance in the peace settlement." The Allies were "drifting into a chaotic situation." American troops were about to march into Germany and Eisenhower had not yet been instructed about "vital points" of policy.

Roosevelt noted that he was scheduled to see Churchill in Quebec in mid-September.[2] There he planned to "settle all these questions" about Germany.

• • •

2. Roosevelt and Churchill had met once before in Quebec, in May 1943.

Born in 1867, Henry Lewis Stimson was descended from what he called "sturdy, middle-class people—religious, thrifty, energetic and long-lived." With his thin gray-white mustache, his stiff public demeanor and ancient suits, the seventy-six-year-old Secretary of War seemed like a nineteenth-century outlander in Roosevelt's entourage.

Stimson's father had hated being a New York stockbroker. He quit and took his family to live in a modest hotel in Berlin. As Stimson recalled, the father grew "disgusted by the martial swagger of the youthful German empire" and moved them to Paris. Then, when Stimson's mother died, the eight-year-old Henry and his sister were sent to live with their grandparents in a New York brownstone. Stimson went to Andover, Yale and Harvard Law School, married Mabel White of New Haven and joined a white-shoe Manhattan firm. He found the law too "devoted to the making of money." Appointed U.S. Attorney by his hero President Theodore Roosevelt, he was, improbably, the Republican candidate for Governor of New York in 1910.

Defeat suggested that he was better suited to appointive office, and President Taft named him Secretary of War. At age fifty, Stimson fought as an artillery officer in the trenches of France, writing his sister, "I have seen and felt real war now." For the rest of his life, people were encouraged to address him as "Colonel Stimson."

Appointed in 1929 as Herbert Hoover's Secretary of State, Stimson dealt with the subject of German reparations. The First World War's victors had demanded that Germany repay its victims in cash. At the same time, Germany was stripped of its overseas colonies, the steel and mining region of Alsace-Lorraine and the coalfields of Silesia and the Saar, which reduced the defeated nation's ability to pay the debt. Stimson saw how the deadweight of reparations swelled German hyperinflation, unemployment and depression. Still, his biographer Godfrey Hodgson wrote, Stimson's "probity and rationality"—his conventional mind—kept him from grasping the "enormity of the disaster impending in Germany" with the rise of Adolf Hitler.

As a charter member of the Northeastern Republican Establishment, Stimson abhorred much of the New Deal but admired Roosevelt's efforts to prepare an isolationist nation against fascism. In June 1940, after the fall of France, with Britain in jeopardy and a perilous third-term campaign ahead, the President put aside "strictly old-fashioned party government" by installing the 1936 Republican vice presidential nominee Frank Knox as Secretary of the Navy and persuading Stimson to return to his old job at the War Department.

Fifteen years Roosevelt's senior, Stimson was instantly the commanding figure in the Cabinet. He was an emblem of bipartisanship, with a deep experience in foreign and military affairs to which the President could not pretend.

Stimson was the only figure in Roosevelt's circle, save General Marshall, with whom the President did not dare play too many games. With Stimson, Roosevelt kept his own counsel, as he did with everyone, but he felt lucky to have him and knew the public price he would pay if Stimson ever resigned over principle. This gave the Secretary of War an imposing advantage in bureaucratic conflicts with others, such as Hull and Morgenthau, whom the President took less seriously.

Stimson was appalled by Roosevelt's harum-scarum delight in pitting people against one another. He wrote in his diary that Roosevelt was "the poorest administrator I have ever worked under. . . . He is not a good chooser of men and he does not know how to use them in coordination."

An insomniac who suffered from poor digestion, chronic fits of weakness and a surprising temper, Stimson was a Victorian. At Woodley, his Washington estate, and Highhold, his home on Long Island, Stimson and his wife refused to have in their home people who had been divorced. He had once moved to prevent a donation from going to Columbia University because of what he considered the "tremendous Jewish influence" there. As Secretary of State, he had championed the National Origins Act of 1929, which discriminated against immigrants from lands outside of northwestern Europe.

Confident that he knew what constituted patriotism and selflessness, Stimson's definition of the national interest compelled him to view such appeals as those of Morgenthau and others to bomb Auschwitz and be harsh on postwar Germany as the special pleading of an influential American ethnic group that did not necessarily harmonize with the supreme goal of winning the war.

Henry Morgenthau III recalled how, before his father's eminence as Secretary of the Treasury, his parents had recognized Stimson as a fellow guest at the Ausable Club in upstate New York: "Awestruck, they kept their distance."

When Stimson joined the Cabinet, he and Morgenthau were natural allies in military preparedness. But by August 1944, Morgenthau had come to view Stimson as an obstacle on Jewish refugees and perhaps as one of the men who were flatly refusing to consider bombing Auschwitz.

STIMSON AND MORGENTHAU took their lunch in the Secretary of War's huge new office in the just-built Pentagon. Stimson had hated the faceless building in the Foggy Bottom section of the capital that had originally been planned for the War Department. He thought the place looked like a provincial opera house and refused to move in.[3]

Instead, across the Potomac, the largest building in the world was erected in eighteen months. Roosevelt hoped that the postwar world would be so placid that the War Department would not need so large a headquarters. He thought the Pentagon would prove a white elephant, useful for little beyond storing military records. But Stimson's men, more pessimistic about Soviet-American friendship, expected that they might need more space, not less. They imagined augmenting the new building with a twenty-four-story office tower, crowned by an eternal flame. As David Brinkley later wrote, the flame would symbolize "the new American imperium over which Washington would preside."

Morgenthau noticed that Stimson "tires very easily." The War Secretary told him that surgery on his back was giving him a lot of trouble. Soon he must "get away again for a rest."

Turning to business, Morgenthau told Stimson how he had discovered from Eden that the Big Three had agreed to dismember Germany. Stimson replied that the conversations on dismemberment had been "a most tremendous surprise to all of us," but he was "not sure" that the Chiefs of Staff saw it as a "fait accompli." The conversation at Tehran may have been "more informal" than Morgenthau realized. Stimson said that Germany must indeed be "policed" for at least twenty years after World War II, until there was a new generation of Germans.

Morgenthau was angered by what he took to be Stimson's equanimity: "If you let the young children of today be brought up by SS troopers who are indoctrinated with Hitlerism, aren't you simply going to raise another generation of Germans who will want to wage war? Don't you think the thing to

3. The scorned building was adopted by the postwar State Department and, with later additions, remains its headquarters to this day.

do is to take a lead from Hitler's book and completely remove these children from their parents?"

He proposed that "ex–U.S. Army officers, English Army officers and Russian Army officers" run German schools "and have these children learn the true spirit of democracy." (He did not specify how Red Army officers might teach German children democracy.) Stimson conceded that something like this might have to be done.

Morgenthau mocked Roosevelt's insistence that he and Churchill could settle the problem in thirty minutes: "I don't think Churchill is going to worry about it, and the President hasn't time to think about it." He proposed that he, Hull and Stimson draw up a common proposal for Roosevelt on postwar Germany "before he meets Churchill again."

Stimson consented, saying that one solution might be to internationalize the industrial Ruhr and Saar, throwing the region under joint multipower control. Morgenthau was intrigued, but he said he favored "removing all industry" from the Germans and "reducing them to an agricultural population of small landholders."

"Germany was that kind of a nation back in 1860," said the Secretary of War, "but then she had only forty million people. . . . You might have to take a lot of people out of Germany."

Morgenthau replied, "Well, that is not nearly as bad as sending them to gas chambers!"

CHAPTER TEN

"Somebody's Got to Take the Lead"

BACK IN HIS TREASURY OFFICE, Henry Morgenthau reported bitterly to his staff that Stimson had told him that the Army spent "five years at peace for one at war" and was "accustomed to doing relief work—floods and general things like that." That was what Stimson was "proposing" for postwar Germany.

He asked his aides to "draft the Treasury's analysis of the German problem." He told Harry Dexter White, "It may be a question of taking out this whole SS group—because you can't keep the concentration camps forever—and deporting them somewhere. . . . I wouldn't be afraid to make the suggestion just as ruthless as is necessary to accomplish the act. . . . Let somebody else water it down!"

By now Morgenthau was on a mission. He told White, "This is the most important thing that I'll ever handle while I'm in government service." His elder son felt that by now his father was a man "obsessed."

TWO DAYS LATER, on Friday morning, August 25, Morgenthau telephoned John McCloy at the Pentagon: "Henry talking. Now, look, I just feel somebody's got to take the lead about 'let's be tough to the Germans.'" He told McCloy that when American soldiers went into Germany, there should be a military rate of twenty German marks to the dollar. From Morgenthau's point of view, this would allow the soldiers to dominate the postwar Germans like miniature Goliaths, striking "a keynote of toughness."

McCloy reminded Morgenthau that "the British take a different view."[1] But Morgenthau said, "They can do any damn thing they want. . . . Jack, from the experience I've had the last month or two, if we tell them this is what we want, and we stick to it, they've got to go along." Issues like this were "straws in the wind as to how we're going to treat Germany."

Fifteen minutes later, Morgenthau called on Roosevelt in the Oval Office. He wrote in his diary that although he had seen his old friend a week earlier, today "I was shocked for the first time, because he is a very sick man and seems to have wasted away."

Morgenthau told Roosevelt that in the British government, he had found two schools of thought on postwar Germany. Eden felt "we must trust Russia for the peace of the world." But Churchill was asking, "What are we going to have between the white snows of Russia and the white cliffs of Dover?"

"That's very well put," said Roosevelt. "I belong to the same school as Eden."

"Look, Mr. President, you can't be expected to give these directives on how to treat Germany unless somebody does the work for you. Everything that has been done so far is worthless." Morgenthau suggested a committee composed of State, War and Treasury, not unlike the War Refugee Board, to write memos on "how to proceed against Germany."

"No, that's no good," said Roosevelt. "Hull doesn't like it—these kinds of committees." Morgenthau knew that this was an excuse. Roosevelt had never cared much what Hull thought.[2]

"Well, I have dug this thing up and it is a little hard not to go along with it," Morgenthau said, "but at least I have the satisfaction of having gotten everyone around town excited." He did not seem to understand that the last thing Roosevelt wanted to hear was that he was stirring up the whole of Washington about a decision Roosevelt wished to defer until the last possible moment.

1. Worried that pegging the mark so low would topple the German economy, the British government was proposing five marks to the dollar. The State Department was suggesting eight.

2. Morgenthau once told aides that if Roosevelt wished to kill an idea, he would say, "You go see Cordell."

Morgenthau tried to smoke out his boss on why Stimson had invited him to lunch and disdained his plans to be tough on Germany. Was this the work of Morgenthau's old rival Harry Hopkins?

"No, I told Stimson to see you," said Roosevelt.

Unwilling to accept that it was Roosevelt himself trying to blunt his interventions on Germany, Morgenthau wrote in his diary that Roosevelt's comment "may or may not be true."

Morgenthau told the President he wanted the occupying U.S. soldiers to get twenty German marks for a dollar. "Nothing doing!" said Roosevelt. "I want to give them dollars, and let each soldier make his own rate."[3]

Morgenthau handed the President a copy of the SHAEF *Handbook for Military Government* that he had been shown on the way to England, and a collection of provocative excerpts from it compiled by the Treasury staff. Roosevelt pooh-poohed the manual, insisting that it could be read as "both hard or soft" on Germany.

Morgenthau suspected that, on Germany, Roosevelt was now under the thrall of Stimson and McCloy. Like a jealous sibling to a father, he told the President that he was apparently getting his advice on Germany from Stimson—"and I don't want to annoy him, so I think maybe you better give me back the memorandum and the *Handbook.*"

Roosevelt responded to Morgenthau's petulance by saying, "No, if you don't mind, I would like to keep it and read it tonight, and then I will return it to you."

Changing gears, Morgenthau pronounced himself "the only person in town" worried about postwar unemployment. If Germany surrendered before the November election, there might be several hundred thousand jobless men "walking the streets of Detroit. . . . The whole CIO[4] could very easily turn against you."

Roosevelt shrugged. Morgenthau later complained to his diary that "here is another vitally important matter," but the President "doesn't seem bothered or surprised that no preparations have been made at all to cope with this thing."

Widening his compass, Morgenthau told the President, "Sometime when

3. In the end, the President agreed with the British government to set a rate of ten military marks to the dollar.

4. Congress of Industrial Organizations.

you have time, I would like to talk to you about myself. Because, looking forward to the next four years, I am kind of getting bored over at the Treasury and I don't think you are making use of all of my talents. . . . I would like to do a little daydreaming with you as to the next four years."

What Morgenthau meant he did not explain in his diary. But if he was fishing for another government job, there were only two he would have wanted—Secretary of State or War—and he knew that for both there were likely to be openings soon, because Hull and Stimson were old men in bad health. Morgenthau would also be far more able to ensure that America was tough on postwar Germany in one of those two posts than from the Treasury.

Roosevelt quickly scotched any ambitions Morgenthau had to be Secretary of State or War: "Now look, Henry, you and I will gradually ease out of our present jobs and become country gentlemen. . . . There is going to be an organization of the United Nations, with which I expect to be associated, and you should go with me."

Roosevelt was serious. From time to time, among those in his close circle like Morgenthau, he talked about resigning the presidency when the war was over and perhaps even becoming Secretary-General of the new postwar United Nations. Sometimes he spoke of locating the U.N. near Hyde Park, with a little airstrip on which visiting foreign leaders could land. Roosevelt may have been musing on some variation of this idea when he hinted to Truman over lunch at the White House that he had chosen him with the presidential succession in mind.

Disappointed by Roosevelt's reply, Morgenthau told his diary, "I couldn't help but flash through my mind to how, a couple of years ago, the President said, 'You and I will run this war together,' and then it was . . . Hopkins and himself, and me out on my ear. But I certainly planted the seed with him, and he keeps associating myself with himself, which is very pleasant. . . . I am certainly going to remind him from time to time."

As for postwar Germany, he wrote, "I am going to continue to feed the President suggestions, but it is quite obvious that he wants to keep me very much in the background, and wants to do it in his own way—as usual."

THAT DAY, OVER LUNCH, Stimson warned Roosevelt that American troops were about to enter Germany with "no instructions" on "vital points." His own view, he said, was that Germany should not be dismembered.[5] Nor should German industry be destroyed. That could cause thirty million people to starve. Stimson told the President that if American officers were to shoot high-ranking Nazis, "it must be immediate," and they should have "definite instructions" on exactly who should be executed.

At a Cabinet meeting that afternoon, Roosevelt used Morgenthau's memo to complain about the SHAEF *Handbook for Military Government.* After reading out some of the *Handbook*'s more egregious recommendations,[6] he said that Germans could "live happily and peacefully on soup from soup kitchens if she couldn't make money for herself." Roosevelt also said he had accepted Morgenthau's recommendation to appoint a "Cabinet Committee on Germany," composed of Hull, Stimson and Morgenthau, with Harry Hopkins as coordinator.

Euphoric that Roosevelt now seemed to share his revulsion against the SHAEF *Handbook,* Morgenthau took the President's decision as a triumph for himself. After the Cabinet meeting, he told his aides that he had "definitely convinced the President" and "that was very hard." Stimson and McCloy "could not wash their hands of the fact that if we hadn't gone to Europe and dug this stuff up, the *Handbook* would have gone into effect. . . . Now the President is hungry for this stuff, because every time I tell him something . . . he immediately uses it."

That same afternoon, Roosevelt wrote what McCloy called a "spanking letter" to Stimson, saying, "This so-called *Handbook* is pretty bad. . . . It gives me the impression that Germany is to be restored just as much as the Netherlands or Belgium, and the people of Germany brought back as quickly as possible to their prewar estate. . . . I do not want them to starve to death, but . . . if they need food to keep body and soul together . . . they should be

5. Stimson was willing to consider trimming Germany of the outlands of East Prussia, Alsace-Lorraine and possibly Silesia, but nothing more.

6. Roosevelt was especially repelled by the *Handbook*'s insistence that after the German surrender, the Allies "restore as quickly as possible" the "regular German civil service" and the "highly centralized German administrative system" and "import needed commodities" to feed the Germans.

fed three times a day from Army soup kitchens. . . . They will remember that experience all their lives."

The President wrote that he would not accept the view of those who said that "the German people as a whole are not responsible for what has taken place, that only a few Nazi leaders are." The Germans must have it "driven home" that they were a "defeated nation" so that they would "hesitate to start any new war." The Allies must make the Germans understand that their "whole nation" had been waging "a lawless conspiracy against the decencies of modern civilization."

McCloy did not think the *Handbook* was "as bad as the President did." He noted that its purpose was merely to cover battle conditions "before defeat or surrender." But as a good soldier, Stimson replied to the "spanking letter" by conceding to Roosevelt that the *Handbook* was indeed "unduly solicitous of the future welfare of Germany."[7]

LATER THAT DAY, Stimson rode with McCloy to National Airport, where a military aircraft was waiting to fly him to Saranac, New York, for his August holiday at the Ausable Club.[8] Morgenthau was to spend his vacation at a nearby fishing camp, so Stimson had offered him a ride on his plane.

Greeting McCloy at the airfield, Morgenthau boasted of getting Roosevelt to agree to a military occupation rate for the German mark that would punish the Germans: "Jack, I told you this morning I was fishing for much bigger fish, and I caught the fish!" During their flight, Stimson and Morgenthau took turns lampooning the hapless Cordell Hull. Stimson carped that Hull "keeps referring to these things" that he probably hadn't "ever read himself."

As Morgenthau later told his staff, Stimson told him "that we should take all the members of the SS troops and put them in the same concentration camps where the Germans have had these poor Jewish people . . . and make an exhibit of them to the whole world. . . . Beyond that, he hadn't thought."

Morgenthau did not perceive that under Stimson's old-school facade the Secretary of War was smoldering at him. Stimson was annoyed that Morgen-

7. In its defense, Stimson explained that the *Handbook* was based on "the usual short-term policy" of keeping the area behind military operations "in order" and thus "further the advance and welfare of the Armies." Morgenthau and McCloy later agreed that a revised *Handbook* would prevail only until surrender.

8. In Stimson's absence, McCloy would be Acting Secretary of War.

thau had provoked the President into reprimanding him. He was determined to block Morgenthau's freelancing on postwar Germany.

At the Ausable Club, Stimson and his wife, Mabel, were joined by McCloy's wife, Ellen, and two McCloy children. He rode horseback and fished in the shadow of the Adirondacks. As usual, Stimson told his diary, the club was "very pleasant, particularly on account of the character of the people who assembled there."

From his cottage, Stimson regularly spoke to McCloy at the Pentagon, using an Army-installed telephone line equipped with a scrambler. He warned McCloy that Morgenthau was trying to foment "a very bitter atmosphere of personal resentment against the entire German people," leading to "clumsy economic action" as a weapon of "mass vengeance."

CHAPTER ELEVEN

"Christianity and Kindness"

FROM HIS FISHING CAMP AT MALONE, New York, south of the Canadian border, Henry Morgenthau kept in touch by telephone with Harry Dexter White and other aides, who were drafting a Treasury proposal for the President on postwar Germany. He told White to make sure that the industrial Ruhr was put "out of business." Perhaps that would induce Churchill to be tough on Germany: Before World War II, competition from the Ruhr had been "partly responsible for the great unemployment in England."

Morgenthau considered dropping in at Fort Ontario, the newly established emergency refugee camp in Oswego, New York, that President Roosevelt and John McCloy had promised him. His aide Josiah DuBois recalled long afterward that the State Department had complained that the refugees would try to stay in the United States, and that "they'll be staying here without a proper immigration visa and all that bullshit." In DuBois's sarcastic memory, the President "magnanimously" let in only a thousand refugees. Oswego proved to be the only place during World War II where the United States tried to establish a refugee haven on its territory.[1]

Morgenthau decided not to visit Fort Ontario. Perhaps he feared that,

1. Seven months after VE-Day, President Harry Truman resisted considerable congressional objection to give visas to the Oswego refugees, who were 90 percent Jewish, and let them remain in the United States. In July 1945, one Paul Sheehan of Buffalo wrote Truman that Roosevelt had "contrived" to admit the thousand Jews "in open and flagrant defiance of law": "Every one of those Jews illegally in this country should be deported at once. . . . There is no reason why Jews should be a privileged class any longer in America."

with the fall presidential campaign about to begin, it would inflame the refugee issue and provoke anti-immigration members of Congress.[2]

On Saturday, September 2, 1944, the President and First Lady motored from Hyde Park to have tea with the Morgenthaus at Fishkill Farms, where the Treasury Secretary had returned from his retreat.

Near the unpretentious farmhouse, which the family called "the Homestead," loomed a spreading elm that state troopers used as a lookout during the President's frequent visits. Under its branches the Morgenthaus gave an annual clambake for the White House press corps. Inside the house, Morgenthau's red-pine study was furnished with early American reproductions and Rooseveltiana—a chair from Eleanor's Hyde Park workshop, a desk ornament made from wood removed from the old White House roof that the President had given to his Cabinet members.

Unlike other Dutchess County farmers, Morgenthau was not known for donning overalls, but he loved his red roses and his apples. When he arrived exhausted from Washington, he would tell the gardeners that he didn't want to talk "for a day or two." Today, as Morgenthau told his diary, he was glad to have the President "quietly and uninterrupted" for a talk about Germany.

He dreaded the way Roosevelt jocularly deflected earnest conversations that bothered or bored him. While talking with the President in May, for example, Morgenthau had described a new War Bond drive being planned by the Treasury. By radio, the actor Orson Welles would explain what Naziism could mean to every American home, including the President's. To the taciturn Morgenthau, Roosevelt had wisecracked, "We don't have any Naziism in *our* home!" The President had gone on to say he wished Welles would repeat "The War of the Worlds," his 1938 radio simulation of a Martian attack, adding that Welles's drama had "scared the pants off a lot of people."[3]

2. Instead, Elinor Morgenthau and Eleanor Roosevelt went to the camp a few weeks later. The First Lady observed, "The people were so evidently happy to be free from fear, but pathetic beyond words because they were such good people. . . . The attempt to make the partitioned-off barracks like homes is heartbreaking."

3. Roosevelt liked to mask his seriousness by joking about grave subjects. In November 1943, while flying to Tehran at a time when American Jews were pressing him for a Palestinian homeland, FDR looked down at the barren Palestine wasteland and observed, "I don't want Palestine as *my* homeland!" Years after his death, Eleanor Roosevelt sentimentally observed of her husband, "The nicest men in the world always keep something of the boy in them."

This afternoon, Roosevelt and Morgenthau spent an entire hour talking about Germany. The President reported that he had written to Stimson and McCloy about the SHAEF *Handbook*, quoting "directly from your memorandum," and "certainly put them in their place."

Morgenthau handed the President a draft he had just received of the Treasury's current suggestions on Germany, including a map. He said that it didn't go "nearly far enough."

Mischievously Roosevelt said, "I wonder if you have the three things that I am interested in. . . . We will see as we go along." He read the document and then revealed his three demands. "Germany should be allowed no aircraft of any kind, not even a glider."[4] Germans should not be allowed to wear military uniforms. Nor should they be permitted to march: "If you don't allow them to wear a uniform and there was no marching, that would do more to teach the Germans than anything else that they had been defeated."

Morgenthau would have been right to wonder whether Roosevelt was pulling his leg. Politely he said, "That's very interesting, Mr. President, but . . . the heart of the German war machine is the Ruhr." If the Ruhr merely became an international zone, "it is just time before Germany will attempt an *Anschluss.*"[5] Instead, dismantle the Ruhr's factories and give the machinery to countries that need it—even if that put "eighteen or twenty million" Germans "out of work."

Roosevelt said he did not care how many Germans were put out of work: "Just feed them out of American Army soup kitchens!"

Morgenthau said that the "other big problem" was the "mentality" of Germans between twenty and forty who had been "inculcated with Naziism": "You may have to transplant them out of Germany to some place in Central Africa, where you can do some big TVA project."[6]

Roosevelt said, "You will have to create entirely new textbooks for the Germans."

4. Roosevelt had pledged this at Tehran.

5. At Tehran, Roosevelt had privately discussed internationalizing the Ruhr. On September 7, 1944, during a lunch with their French friend Jean Monnet, Stimson and McCloy suggested a potential board of trustees for an internationalized Ruhr. Stimson felt that "Russia must certainly be included. . . . Leaving her out would bring disaster to the confidence which must exist between the three great Allies in Europe." To Stimson's surprise, as he wrote in his diary, McCloy "was alarmed at giving this addition to Russia's power." Morgenthau used the term *Anschluss* to suggest annexation of land, as Germany had with Austria in 1938.

6. Roosevelt's Tennessee Valley Authority was a Depression-era public works project to bring electric power to the region.

When Morgenthau mentioned McCloy, Roosevelt played to his audience: "Oh, the trouble with him is he is just an appeaser."

Morgenthau later wrote in his diary that this comment was "very, very unfair." He worried that his rival Harry Hopkins had poisoned Roosevelt against McCloy in order to eliminate a competitor who might block Hopkins's ambition to become American military governor of Germany. Despite their disagreements over Auschwitz and postwar Germany, Morgenthau felt that McCloy was "amongst a half dozen civilians" who had done the most to prosecute the war.

Morgenthau warned the President against Robert Murphy. Just appointed as General Eisenhower's political adviser on the Germans, Murphy had also been mentioned as a possible U.S. military governor. Morgenthau complained that as American liaison in North Africa, Murphy had been "living in the pocket" of Admiral Jean Darlan.[7] As Morgenthau recorded, Roosevelt "got quite excited" about Darlan. Dealing with the Vichyite had been his own decision. Murphy had been merely his "agent." Distasteful as the Darlan deal may have been, it had "saved ten thousand lives of American soldiers."

Eleanor Roosevelt interjected that asking a Catholic like Murphy to be military governor, with so many Catholics in Germany, was a bad idea. She added that Pope Pius XII had been too lenient on the Nazis.

The President reminded his wife that the Pope had always stood up "for private property" and "against Communism." Morgenthau felt that Roosevelt's reply was not "very reassuring or convincing."

To nail Murphy's coffin shut, Morgenthau informed the President that Murphy's closest aide was Carmel Offie, who had spread the rumors about Sumner Welles's homosexuality that forced Roosevelt to fire his old family friend. As Morgenthau recorded, Roosevelt promised "quick as a flash" to "get rid" of Murphy "tomorrow."[8]

Morgenthau then suggested his own candidate for military governor—Alexander Kirk, then serving as ambassador in Cairo: "He hates the Nazis." Roosevelt said that Kirk was "namby-pamby" and "doesn't know America" because "he has been out of the country too long."

Morgenthau said that to augment Kirk, his own Treasury aide John Pehle could serve as deputy military governor. He did not need to add that if Pehle

7. In November 1942, when Morgenthau complained to Stimson about the Darlan deal, he had found the Secretary of War "flabbergasted by my vehemence."

8. Roosevelt did not keep his pledge.

were appointed to oversee the postwar Germans, he would serve as a cat's paw for Morgenthau.

Before the conversation ended, Roosevelt said he would raise Morgenthau's prescription for a harsh German peace at Quebec: "I don't know how far I will get with Churchill on this."

"I think Eden will go along with you," said Morgenthau.

Roosevelt replied, "It will be tough sledding with Churchill."

LATER THAT AFTERNOON, the Morgenthaus drove to Mrs. Roosevelt's cottage, Val-Kill, in Hyde Park. Morgenthau asked the First Lady if he had been "too aggressive with the President." She said, "No."

Morgenthau seized the opportunity to plunge a knife into Harry Hopkins. Did she know that Hopkins wished to be military governor of Germany?[9] "Does the President know that Hopkins receives secret cables from Churchill?" Eleanor said she didn't know about the cables, but would find out.

Morgenthau told her he was "convinced that the President wants to do the right thing" about the Germans: "But he hasn't got the time to look into it thoroughly, and everything that has been done so far is useless, so some of us have to do it for him."

In his diary, Morgenthau recalled that Mrs. Roosevelt had been "slightly pacifist before the war." He feared that she might be "too sentimental" about the problem. "That was one of the main reasons why I went up to see her. I thought she might think we should go a little easy on the Germans, but she doesn't."[10]

Mrs. Roosevelt said she agreed with what Morgenthau had told the President about Germany. But she had been told that there were German prisoners of war "with whom we can deal" after surrender.[11]

9. Morgenthau was right. Hopkins had told Stimson that he was "deeply interested in postwar problems" and would like to go to Germany as governor, but Roosevelt scotched the idea, citing Hopkins's bad health.

10. Morgenthau was not entirely correct. During the summer of 1944, Trude Pratt, a German émigré engaged to Eleanor's friend Joseph Lash, sent the First Lady a copy of the manifesto of the Council on German Democracy, headed by the theologian Paul Tillich. It called for the denazification of Germany, but not dismemberment or destruction of German industry. Eleanor told Mrs. Pratt, "Everything in it seems reasonable to me."

11. Morgenthau did not say so, but he thought she "has this thing a little twisted." Alarmed, he later consulted the First Lady's source, a colonel in the War Department, who told him that actually the German POWs were "very difficult" and "you could do nothing with them."

The First Lady had recently been reading a widely publicized book by a New York psychiatrist named Richard Brickner, called *Is Germany Incurable?*[12] Boasting a jacket blurb from the anthropologist Margaret Mead, the volume concluded that German society was "paranoid" and "megalomaniac." Mrs. Roosevelt was unconvinced. She concluded that "one cannot treat a whole people that way."

After Morgenthau's visit to Val-Kill, she wrote Joseph Lash that while Morgenthau seemed to think he knew the President's thinking on Germany, Franklin probably had not yet made up his mind. She observed that he usually kept his thoughts to himself, "even from people like Henry," while "he lets them all talk."

Like a nervous schoolboy, Morgenthau later asked his wife how he had "handled" himself with the Roosevelts. "Extremely well," she said.

TWO DAYS LATER, on Monday, September 4, Morgenthau was back at his Treasury office in Washington. He told the aides who were drafting his blueprint that the President was "willing to go as far as I am" or "farther" on Germany. "Now the man is hungry, crazy to get some stuff to work with," Morgenthau said. "When he saw what we were talking about, he said, 'I don't know how far I will get with Churchill on this.' . . . But he is very, very anxious to get something down in black and white on this thing."

Alluding to Roosevelt's mid-September meeting with Churchill, scheduled for Quebec, Morgenthau warned his staff that they now had only a week "to reach the President, if you get what I mean, before he has another important meeting, see?"

Morgenthau reported that Roosevelt was "entirely agreeable" to closing down the Ruhr: "Just strip it. I don't care what happens to the population. I would take every mine, every mill and factory and wreck it. . . . Steel, coal, everything. Just close it down. . . . Make the Ruhr look like some of the silver mines in Nevada."

"Sherman's march to the sea!" said Daniel Bell.

"No, some of those ghost towns," said Morgenthau. "Make this a ghost area." If the region were "stripped of its machinery" and its mines "flooded,

12. Philadelphia: Lippincott, 1943.

dynamited, wrecked," he said, Germany would be "impotent to wage more wars."

Harry Dexter White proposed putting the Ruhr under international control. Other countries could "strip it of any machinery they want."

Morgenthau said no. He warned that if the Ruhr were internationalized, the Germans would stage a "revolution" and seize it, and the region would revert to "the German war people": "All the war has sprung from that area. They cannot make war if that area is shut down." As for the Saar, "shut that down or give it to France."

White warned that shutting down the Ruhr would exile millions of Germans and harm the rest of Europe.

"May I just stop a minute?" said an irritated Morgenthau. "I have brought back a message to you as to where the President stands and where I stand. Why don't you go to work on it, see?"

Morgenthau went on, "I am for destroying it first and we will worry about the population second. . . . I am not going to budge an inch. . . . The President is adamant on this thing. Sure, it is a terrific problem. Let the *Germans* solve it! Why the hell should *I* worry about what happens to their people?"

Morgenthau recalled his father's World War I experience as Wilson's ambassador to Turkey: "One morning, the Turks woke up and said, 'We don't want a Greek in Turkey.' . . . They moved one million people out. They said to the Greeks, 'You take care of them.' . . . The people lived. They got rehabilitated in no time. . . . It seems inhuman. It seems cruel." But "we didn't ask for this war. We didn't put millions of people through gas chambers." The Germans had "asked for it. . . . For the future of my children and my grandchildren, I don't want these beasts to wage war. . . . I am not going to be budged."

Morgenthau reminded his aides to recommend harsh punishment for German war criminals. John Pehle replied, "It's got to be limited in scope."

Morgenthau, recalling the records of what was said at Tehran but unaware that the Soviet leader was perhaps joking, said, "Stalin has a list with fifty thousand."

Taking it that Stalin had been speaking literally, Pehle replied, "But we wouldn't get that, I don't think."

• • •

STIMSON WROTE IN HIS DIARY that by late afternoon, "I felt I had had a full day but I had an engagement to dine with Morgenthau. So I went home and rested for an hour and then went to dinner at his house." Morgenthau had also invited McCloy and Harry Dexter White.

Of the evening Stimson recorded, "Morgenthau is, not unnaturally, very bitter, and as he is not thoroughly trained in history or even economics . . . he would plunge out for a treatment of Germany which I feel sure would be unwise." Morgenthau's intentions for Germany reminded the War Secretary of the vindictive peace that Rome had imposed on Carthage. During dinner, Stimson infuriated his host by saying, "I think we can't solve the German problem except through Christianity and kindness."

THE NEXT MORNING, Tuesday, September 5, in the office of the Secretary of State, Hull, Stimson, Morgenthau and Hopkins had their first formal session on Germany. Hopkins had told Morgenthau, "We will have to meet with Roosevelt quick, before somebody else changes his mind." As Stimson wrote in his diary, "Hull has been rather crotchety about the whole thing and showed it in this meeting. I fear that he regards it as a reflection upon the prerogatives of the State Department."

To Stimson's "tremendous surprise," during the meeting, Hull sounded "as bitter as Morgenthau against the Germans." He suspected that Morgenthau had been "rooting around the scene and greased the way for his own views by conference with the President and others." He was shocked that Hull was suddenly so ready to jettison all the free trade principles that for twelve years he had been "laboring for."

Although a Southerner, Hull, knowing that Roosevelt was in a tough mood, suggested the American Reconstruction as a model for treating Germany. After the Civil War's devastation, he said, it took Southerners "seventy-five years to get back again. Germany's living standard should be "held down to subsistence levels," its economic power crushed. The Ruhr might have to be closed. "We may even have to sacrifice a little of our trade to make the Germans suffer. . . . This Naziism is down in the German people a thousand miles deep, and you have just got to uproot it. And you can't do it by just shooting a few people." Once again Hull recalled what a hit he felt he had made with the Russians in Moscow by saying he would have a "drumhead court-martial and shoot all the people."

Stimson crisply insisted, as he had the night before, that Germany be treated with "Christianity and kindness." They must follow some kind of "legal procedure" before people were shot. Stimson said it was "very singular" that he, the man in charge of the department that had done "the killing in the war," was the "only one" who seemed to have "any mercy for the other side."

The exchange grew so testy that Hull and Stimson began addressing each other not by their first names, as usual, but as "Mr. Secretary of State" and "Colonel Stimson."

Stimson warned his colleagues that "thirty million people will starve if the Ruhr is closed down. . . . This is just fighting brutality with brutality."

"Do you mean to say that if we stop all production of steel in Germany that would be a brutal thing to do?" asked Hopkins.

Stimson felt that such a prohibition would "pretty well sabotage everything else." But he found himself "a minority of one." He told Hull that he was ignoring what his own planners had proposed.

"Let's forget the papers," cried Hopkins. "There are too damn many papers. We can't read them all. We have got to start fresh."

Stimson objected to Morgenthau's demand that Germans be stripped of military uniforms. Why should German war veterans be "deprived"? It would be "impossible to administer" anyway. He warned against forcing American troops to occupy Germany in a "chaotic situation."

When the meeting broke up, as Stimson observed, they were "irreconcilably divided." Hull said it was obvious that they would not be able to agree on a proposal on Germany to send to the President: "If anybody has a plan, let him send it separately."

WHEN STIMSON RETURNED to the Pentagon, McCloy had never seen him so depressed. Stimson wrote in his diary, "In all the four years that I have been here, I have not had such a difficult and unpleasant meeting, although there were no personalities. We all knew each other too well for that. But we were irreconcilably divided."

Stimson complained that everyone had "ganged up" on him—especially Hull, who had battled on a "pretty low level." He could not understand the "wave of hysteria" that was "sweeping" over his colleagues, making them "shallow and vindictive" against Germany. He dictated a record of his own views "for history," to show future generations that not every high official under Roosevelt had run "amuck at this vital period."

JUBILANT, MORGENTHAU TOLD HIS STAFF that Stimson had been outnumbered. Stimson and Hull had argued like schoolboys: "They are both going back to their second childhoods." He reported that Stimson "seems to be afraid to talk about Christianity in front of me—I don't know why." He himself had told Hull, "Cordell, you go back to the teachings of Jesus. . . . I would love to be able to live up to them all myself."

Morgenthau told his aides that even his rival Hopkins was "so keen" about his ideas on Germany that Hopkins had told him, "We will have to meet with Roosevelt quick before somebody else changes his mind." Now he called Hopkins and said, "That was a most encouraging meeting."

"God, wasn't it?" said Hopkins. "I nearly fell through the floor."

Morgenthau said, "I wanted to get up and kiss Cordell for the first time."

Hopkins criticized Stimson's comment about "Christianity and kindness": "Ridiculous! . . . My God, he was terrible. . . . It hurts him so much to think of the non-use of property. He's grown up in that school so long that property, God, becomes so sacred. . . . It's terrible, and I tell you, Henry . . . it's fruitless to talk with him anymore."

Hopkins said he felt "confident" about where Roosevelt would "land on this. Now if Hull will keep going to bat, we're going to be all right here pretty soon."

Morgenthau said they should let Stimson hang himself by giving him an opportunity to "blow off like that in front of the President."

"If I get a chance, I'm going to tip off the Boss, because I think he might blow up right into Stimson's face," said Hopkins. "That would settle it, you know."

"Of course . . . he didn't come quite clean," said Morgenthau. "What he wants is a strong Germany as a buffer state [against the Soviet Union], and he didn't have the guts to say that."

At 5:45 P.M., McCloy called Hopkins to tell him that the morning meeting had made the Secretary of War depressed and angry. If Roosevelt did not do something fast, McCloy said, the President would be confronted with a majority recommendation for turning Germany into farmland that might be very hard for him to veto. If Roosevelt wanted to keep his options open, he had better give his Secretary of War some encouragement—now. Hopkins quietly passed McCloy's warning to the President.

ON WEDNESDAY MORNING, September 6, alarmed by the warning from Hopkins and McCloy, Roosevelt called his committee on Germany to the Cabinet Room at the White House. "After what had happened yesterday," wrote Stimson in his diary, "I was much alarmed about this meeting and expected to be steamrollered by the whole bunch."

Gazing at Stimson, Roosevelt repeated his insistence that Germans could live from "soup kitchens." He said that "our ancestors" lived "successfully and happily" without "many luxuries." In Dutchess County in 1810, people had worn homespun wools. As a boy, he had used a "Chic Sale" outhouse: "People could get along without bathrooms and still be perfectly happy."[13]

Impatient with Roosevelt's chatter, of which he had heard more than he wished during four years as Secretary of War, Stimson reminded him that the issue was Morgenthau's plan to make an "ashheap" out of the Ruhr. He was "utterly opposed" to destroying "such a gift of nature." It should be "used for the reconstruction of the world," which "sorely" needed it now. Unless the German economy were quickly revived, there would be a "dangerous convulsion in Europe." They must not burn down the house of the world just to get "a meal of roast pig."

To Morgenthau's shock, Roosevelt now agreed with Stimson. He said there was "no particular hurry" to decide "right away" on the Ruhr. They could leave the steel mills intact and then act in six months or a year. He reminded Hull that they both had long worked for free trade, and "we have got to do just that in Germany." Britain was "going to be in sore straits after the war." Perhaps the Ruhr could furnish raw material for British steel companies.

Hopkins said it was possible to revive the Ruhr while "all German steel-making and war factories" were "immediately shut down."

13. Chic Sale was a vaudevillian who in 1929 wrote a short bestselling book called *The Specialist,* on the building of outhouses, which sold two million copies and made his name synonymous with the word. After the Cabinet Room meeting, when Morgenthau related this exchange to his aides, his press secretary Herbert Gaston joked, "We are going to destroy the plumbing in the Ruhr—is that the idea?" Harry Dexter White shot back, "That would dispose of many millions of people!"

Morgenthau could not believe what he was hearing. Roosevelt told him, "The Germans are very wonderful in agriculture, aren't they, Henry? With their methods, they could take care of another million people, couldn't they?"

The President's appointment's secretary Edwin "Pa" Watson stepped into the room and began pacing up and down, a blunt signal that the meeting was over. When that did not work, Watson brought in the Governor of Texas, Coke Stevenson.

Morgenthau realized that Roosevelt had arranged with Watson to stop the conversation before it could be hijacked by Morgenthau. Upset, Morgenthau marched to Hopkins's office, but Hopkins was not there. He left a message for Hopkins to telephone him, but Hopkins did not call. Finally Morgenthau made the call himself. Hopkins conceded that the meeting with Roosevelt had been "a little disappointing."

"Terrible!" cried Morgenthau. Later he told his Treasury aides and others that he was "just heartbroken." It "couldn't have gone worse." How could the President have lent "aid and comfort" to Stimson? He realized that the battle was not "lost, by any means." The "sad part" was that Roosevelt "just won't give you time enough to talk the thing out." He declared, "I'm discouraged, but not licked."

THAT AFTERNOON, McCloy sent the President's son-in-law, John Boettiger, who worked in the War Department's Civil Affairs Division, to see Morgenthau.

A former *Chicago Tribune* reporter, Boettiger lived at the White House with his wife, Anna, the President's only daughter. Secretary of the Interior Harold Ickes noted how Roosevelt was "leaning" on Boettiger "more and more." Ickes found him "slow and unimaginative and stubborn, a truly Germanic character." When McCloy told him that Boettiger was a "distinct embarrassment," Ickes asked why Stimson didn't fire him. "White House pressure!" replied McCloy.

Perhaps projecting his own problems onto Morgenthau, Boettiger privately felt that the Treasury Secretary had exploited his relationship with Roosevelt. Morgenthau thought that Boettiger was out of his depth.

Boettiger now told Morgenthau that the Combined Chiefs of Staff in

London had revised what Morgenthau considered the "God-awful" *Handbook,* although it still "has bad spots in it." The problem was that the original version had already been printed, and the Army was "desperate" for guidance. McCloy wanted Morgenthau's endorsement of a cable to Eisenhower that the book should be released to the soldiers, but with a corrective flyleaf pasted to the cover.

Outraged, Morgenthau reminded Boettiger that Roosevelt had "killed" the *Handbook:* "Am I making myself clear?" He asked to see the new version of the manual, but Boettiger told him that there were only two copies in Washington—in the Oval Office and at the War Department.

"Before I become a party to that cable, I would like to see the *Handbook,*" said Morgenthau. "If the thing is so precious . . . bring it over with an armored escort. . . . I am serious." He called McCloy and said, "If it can't be brought here, I'd come to Mr. Stimson's office with my gang." [14]

"What we're trying to do is to meet Eisenhower's needs," said McCloy. "He let out a great cry of pain. . . . We always try to lean over backwards to do what is convenient to him." McCloy suggested that they satisfy Eisenhower by issuing the *Handbook* with the flyleaf as a "little device" to cover them through Germany's surrender. Then, "in our leisure," they could do a "complete rewrite," to be issued after victory.

Morgenthau consented. He said he could study the new draft of the *Handbook* and flyleaf at "any hour tonight or tomorrow," except for a five o'clock appointment with his osteopath.

"Your bones aren't breaking up, are they?" asked McCloy.

Still reeling from Roosevelt's surprise turnabout that morning, Morgenthau exclaimed, "The head is!"

THE NEXT MORNING, Thursday, September 7, the Great White Father called Morgenthau to the Oval Office for some stroking. He greeted his friend more warmly than usual and said, "Don't be discouraged about yesterday's meeting. I had Cordell trembling."

Morgenthau told his diary, "I don't know what he meant by that, because

14. The revisions indeed reflected Morgenthau's thinking. Among other changes, the new *Handbook* prohibited the "economic rehabilitation" of Germany, except to support the occupation, and banned importation of relief supplies, except to prevent epidemic.

Cordell certainly was not trembling. . . . But the amazing thing was that he should have greeted me the way he did, because he must have realized the way I felt, and this was most encouraging."

Trying to smooth over their differences, Roosevelt told him that the "whole question" seemed to be about "closing down the plants" in the Ruhr, "and we have got to do the thing gradually."

Morgenthau knew that if the Ruhr were not closed down immediately after the German surrender, it almost certainly never would be. He left the White House dejected and tense.

At 12:45 P.M., Morgenthau blew up while haggling with Robert Brand of the British Exchequer over an occupation rate for the German mark that would punish the Germans. When Brand asked him if his view had the President's backing, Morgenthau cried, "Now, look, do you suppose I would not tell the President of the United States? . . . Of course, I told him!"[15]

After Brand left, Morgenthau told aides he had nearly "hoisted" Brand out of the window: "I am not going to take much more of his . . . God-damned lip!" Years later, Morgenthau's son observed that when his father got angry, it often meant that he was afraid.

AT THE PENTAGON, Stimson complained to General George Marshall about Morgenthau's eagerness to shoot Nazi war criminals without trial. He was "not a bit surprised" by what he had heard, but "I was appalled—a different thing." Marshall felt it was "the same sort of thing that happens after every war," and the "bitterness after this one" was "sure to be extreme."

Stimson later observed, "It was very interesting to find that Army officers have a better respect for the law in those matters than civilians who talk about them and who are anxious to go ahead and chop everybody's head off without trial or hearing."

At Morgenthau's request, Roosevelt called a new meeting of the Cabinet Committee on Germany for Saturday at noon. To make sure that the President did not once again foreclose a serious debate, Morgenthau asked Pa Watson to give them two hours.

"Christ!" replied Watson. "He isn't going to give you any two hours. God!

15. The next day, the British agreed to a rate of ten cents to the German mark.

. . . When I talk about two hours, [he'll say], 'Oh, Henry can go chase himself!' "

After McCloy heard about the Saturday meeting, he warned Stimson that Morgenthau still "sticks to his guns" and was using the "entire forces of the Treasury" to "demolish" Stimson's position on Germany. Stimson wrote in his diary, "So we are in for some fireworks."

CHAPTER TWELVE

"It Is Very, Very Necessary"

TO COLLECT HIS "resources for the coming battle," as he recorded in his diary, Henry Stimson invited his friend Justice Felix Frankfurter to dine with him at Woodley, his eighteen-acre rolling green estate in northwest Washington, crowned by a tall eighteenth-century Federal house.[1]

Woodley helped the Secretary of War keep the rigors of global conflict at bay. When Stimson heard the "sweet" song of the wood thrush, he wondered whether the bird was perched in the copper beech tree or the maple. In the cool late afternoon, before his dinner with Frankfurter, he enjoyed a "very refreshing" ride on a Tennessee walking horse in Rock Creek Park.

When Stimson sought advice from Frankfurter, as he often did, he joked that he was visiting the "cave of Adullum."[2] Tonight, when he brought up postwar Germany, he was relieved to find that, "although a Jew like Morgenthau," Frankfurter approached the subject "with perfect detachment and great helpfulness."

Frankfurter dismissed Morgenthau as a "stupid bootlick" who did not deserve his high post. As Stimson described Morgenthau's designs on the Ruhr and punishing the Nazis, the Justice "snorted with astonishment and disdain." Frankfurter emphatically agreed with Stimson that "we must give these men the substance of a fair trial" and that "they cannot be railroaded to

1. Woodley is now the site of the Maret School.

2. In the Bible, under threat, David took refuge in the cave of Adullum.

their death." The Justice added that "most of these Nazi crimes have not been directed at the American government or at the American Army but at the people and armies of our allies."

Frankfurter left eager to help Stimson do battle with Morgenthau. As Stimson recorded, he later discovered that the Justice was "flying around trying to help on the sidelines so actively that he rather alarmed us for fear he would commit some indiscretion."

ON FRIDAY, September 8, the day before the new meeting of the Cabinet Committee on Germany, Morgenthau called on Hull and told him that on Germany the President now "seemed to be influenced by Stimson."

Hull insisted that Roosevelt would not let Stimson stampede him: "Forget about him."

But Morgenthau sensed a change in Hull's demeanor toward him. Morgenthau wrote in his diary, "I felt Hull was holding back on me, and . . . that he wasn't telling me anything. . . . Of course, underneath it all . . . Cordell resents my being in on this."

Morgenthau thought Hull looked "very tired and very badly." For the millionth time, Hull complained about his circumvention by the President. The previous June, he said, Roosevelt had sent Vice President Henry Wallace to China without bothering to consult him. Hull said that to his surprise, Roosevelt had invited him to next week's meeting with Churchill at Quebec, but he had declined on grounds of exhaustion. He told Morgenthau that he hoped Roosevelt would not talk seriously about Germany at Quebec. Stalin might be angry if important decisions were made in his absence. And Churchill would be listening "to some squeaky-voiced man from the Foreign Office."

"The trouble is, Cordell, the President has never given a directive on how he feels Germany should be treated," said Morgenthau. "The first thing we know, we will be in Germany and we will have no policy."

ON SATURDAY MORNING, September 9, before the Cabinet Committee meeting on Germany, Roosevelt saw Robert Murphy, who was leaving for England to join Eisenhower's staff. Morgenthau had warned the President a week previously about Murphy's ambition and unfitness to go to occupied Germany as military governor.

Roosevelt launched into one of his rhapsodies about the Germans he had discovered as a nine-year-old in 1891—"their music and their love of liberty"—and how four years later, boys were "wearing uniforms and marching in formation." After the German surrender, "all of this must be eradicated." The transformation "might well take forty years."

He told Murphy that the United States did not want postwar reparations from Germany, but the Soviets, British and other countries should get "German labor and equipment." The Allies should deal with "local commanders and authorities" in Germany, not "a central authority and the German high command." This would "protect us from the charge of having made a deal" with any person or group who, "while pretending to be anti-Nazi, might be a cover for unwelcome elements."

Roosevelt said that German war criminals should be "dealt with summarily." No "long, drawn-out legal procedure." After proper identification, they should simply be executed. Above all, he wanted to arrange the occupation in a way that would convince the Russians that America "really" wanted to work with them. His primary postwar aim was Soviet-American cooperation. Germany, he said, would be the "proving ground."

THAT MORNING AT THE TREASURY, Morgenthau's aides gave him black, loose-leaf-bound copies of the final version of his plan for postwar Germany. Larded with charts, maps and graphs, the report's formal title was "Program to Prevent Germany from Starting a World War III." But from this moment on, it would always be known as the "Morgenthau Plan."

At Morgenthau's instance, copies of the plan had been prepared not only for the Cabinet Committee on Germany but also for Roosevelt's use with Churchill the following week in Quebec. The document was studded with talking points, such as "How British Industry Would Benefit by Proposed Program."

Under the Morgenthau Plan, all German heavy industry would be destroyed. The Ruhr and adjacent areas[3] would be internationalized and "not

3. Including the Rhineland and German territory from the Kiel Canal northward.

again be allowed to become an industrial area." All Germans in the Ruhr with industrial training or skills would be "encouraged" to leave the country forever. German plants and equipment, German labor and other assets would be given to the Soviet Union and other nations that were Germany's victims. There would be no reparations in the form of recurrent payments or goods, which would require the German economy to be rebuilt and ultimately give it a larger share of foreign markets than in the 1930s. The Allied armies' only involvement in the German economy should be to aid their own military operations. Feeding, housing and clothing the Germans should be the burden of the German people.

Ignorant of Roosevelt's private instructions on precisely how Germany should be divided into Allied occupation zones, Morgenthau had ordered his staff to propose how Germany should be permanently dismembered. Under the Morgenthau Plan, East Prussia would be divided between the Soviet Union and Poland. France would get the Saar and nearby lands. A northern German state would be organized around the old Prussia, Saxony and Thuringia. A southern state would include Bavaria, Württemberg and Baden.

All German schools, universities, radio stations and periodicals would be shut down until the Allies restructured them. In deference to Roosevelt's wish, spoken to Morgenthau at Fishkill Farms, all German aircraft, military uniforms, bands and parades would be banned.

The Allies would draw up a list of "arch-criminals of the war." These villains would be "apprehended as soon as possible" and "put to death forthwith by firing squads."

Sharing Roosevelt's dark views on German national character, the Morgenthau Plan said, "The Nazi regime is essentially the culmination of the unchanging German drive toward aggression." German society had been "dominated for at least three generations by powerful forces fashioning the German state and nation into a machine for military conquest and self-aggrandizement."

German industrial growth had "immeasurably strengthened the economic base of German militarism without weakening the Prussian feudal ideology or its hold on German society. . . . What the Nazi regime has done has been to systematically debauch the passive German nation on an unprecedented scale and shape it into an organized and dehumanized military machine." Therefore "German militarism cannot be destroyed by destroying Naziism alone."

Before leaving for the White House, Morgenthau thanked his staff: "I am very glad we are doing what we are. I should think it would be very useful to the President at Quebec. Please don't stop. Please keep right on. It is very, very necessary."

AT NOON, looking gray and exhausted, Roosevelt met in the Cabinet Room with his committee on Germany. For days, he had been feeling "low" and "logy."

The Secretary of the Treasury passed out copies of his program to his colleagues. "None of us had seen this until we got into the room," Stimson recorded, "and therefore it was impossible to discuss it intelligently."

From Morgenthau's document Roosevelt read one of the talking points aloud: "It is a Fallacy that Europe Needs a Strong Industrial Germany." Roosevelt said this was the "first time" he had seen it stated: "All the economists disagree, but I agree with that. . . . Furthermore, I believe in an agricultural Germany."

Stimson retorted, "It would breed war, not peace. It would arouse sympathy for Germany all over the world."

Hull and Stimson continued their schoolyard bickering. Hull said he had sent the Secretary of War a report on the German economy and was still "waiting for an answer from you, Colonel Stimson." Coldly Stimson replied, "Mr. Secretary of State, I have not received it."

Morgenthau was disappointed that "Hull just wouldn't get into the discussion," he later wrote in his diary. "Just what his game is, I don't know." When Roosevelt once again invited Hull to the forthcoming meeting with Churchill in Quebec, Hull said he was "too tired."

Stimson declared he was "unalterably opposed" to Morgenthau's desire that German industry be "substantially obliterated." He also derided the eagerness to put "so-called arch-criminals" to death without trial. Better to try the "chief Nazi officials" with an "international tribunal."

Roosevelt said he backed some sort of international trusteeship for the Ruhr, the Saar and the Kiel Canal, and division of Germany into three parts. As Morgenthau recorded, the President was "in favor of doing it now and not waiting." Stimson objected to any "permanent" partition of the country.

"I think there will be two things brought up at Quebec," said Roosevelt. "One is military and the other is monetary, because Churchill keeps saying he is broke." He added, "If they bring up the financial question, I will want Henry to come to Quebec."

MORGENTHAU FELT THAT AFTER MOVING "inch by inch all week," the President seemed to be taking his side, after all. He wrote in his diary, "I evidently made a real impression on the President the time he came to my house."

Having watched Roosevelt's twists and turns on Germany, Harry Dexter White was more skeptical. When Morgenthau reported that Roosevelt had endorsed the briefing book's section title that said it was a "fallacy" that Europe needed an industrial Germany, White sardonically observed, "Having read the title, he was convinced of it."

Stimson wrote in his diary that the Cabinet Committee meeting had been "very discouraging," and "I came away rather low in my mind." He felt "much troubled by the President's physical condition." At the meeting, Roosevelt was "distinctly not himself."

That afternoon, Stimson took a military plane to Mitchel Field on Long Island for a weekend rest at his country estate, Highhold. As the plane soared up the Eastern Seaboard, Stimson studied his black-bound copy of the Morgenthau Plan, which he found "a new diatribe" against the Nazis, "full of the bitter spirit of his old paper" but "buttressed by alleged facts drawn by the Treasury." Angrily he scrawled in the report's margins, "Childish folly! . . . A beautiful Nazi program! . . . This is to laugh!" Next to the section on how the Morgenthau Plan would benefit British trade, he wrote, "Bribe to U.K."

From Highhold, Stimson spoke by telephone with Justice Frankfurter, who advised him to let the black book "fall to the wayside by its own weight": The President would "catch the errors" and see that its "spirit" was "all wrong."

"I wish I was as sure as he was," Stimson wrote in his diary. He feared that Morgenthau's plan would "make an impression" on Roosevelt. At Stimson's behest, McCloy flew to New York City to rally opposition to Morgenthau among bankers, corporation chiefs and economists. Stimson asked him to gather expert views on Germany to be used against the "curbstone opinion" of the Treasury Secretary.

Stimson was worried about Roosevelt's meeting with Churchill at Quebec. He was especially worried about the Commander in Chief's health. As Stimson told his diary, the President "had a cold and seemed tired out." He feared that Roosevelt would be pummeled by a "hard conference" with Churchill. The President was "going up there" with "absolutely no study or training" in the "very difficult problem" of Germany. And now he would "have to decide."

THAT EVENING, Morgenthau caught a ride with Roosevelt aboard the presidential train ("Main 36205"), which pulled out of its secret depot under the Bureau of Engraving and Printing Annex at 10:27 P.M. On Sunday morning, when the train arrived at Highland, New York, the President was driven to Hyde Park and Morgenthau to East Fishkill.

Roosevelt spent the morning working in his new Dutch colonial fieldstone presidential library, built on the grounds of his family estate with $350,000 in public contributions. Here he planned, after his presidency, to write his memoirs while scholars examined his papers and tourists gaped at his collection of naval prints, ship models and presidential geegaws.

With his ambition to benefit from his old boss's mistakes at the end of World War I, Roosevelt increasingly had Woodrow Wilson on his mind. As the late summer sun streamed through the windows of his library office, he sat behind a desk that Wilson had used while sailing to Paris aboard the *George Washington* after World War I to write the peace at Versailles that had ultimately failed.

Roosevelt told his adoring Hudson Valley friend Margaret Suckley, who was serving as his archivist, that the past four days had been "awful" and he felt "really tired." The previous weekend he had told her that he wouldn't be at all surprised if Dewey defeated him in November: Democrats seemed "so confident" that Roosevelt would win that they were "just not bothering to register for victory."

He drove Suckley in his blue Ford sedan, equipped with hand controls, to his new little house, Top Cottage, which he had designed, for a picnic lunch of fried chicken and stuffed eggs. But he had no appetite.

Word came that Churchill and his party, who had crossed the Atlantic on the *Queen Mary,* would arrive in Quebec the next morning. Roosevelt sent Eleanor a message that they must board their special railroad car, the *Ferdinand Magellan,* "at four sharp." Long after darkness fell, the President's train crossed the Canadian border.

Eleanor had written Joseph Lash that "this Canadian meeting will not be all smooth sailing, since many things put aside in the past must now be settled."

CHAPTER THIRTEEN

"Do You Want Me to Beg Like Fala?"

At nine o'clock on Monday morning, September 11, 1944, under glowing sun and azure sky, with the tart fragrance of early autumn in the air, the President's train arrived at Wolfe's Cove station in Quebec. Roosevelt was carried to an open black Phaeton, where he sat waiting for Churchill.

When the Prime Minister's train arrived, Churchill emerged, wearing a blue uniform, naval cap, vest and gold watch chain, swinging a cane and smoking a large cigar. He walked to Roosevelt's car and shook hands with the grinning President. The crowd cheered.

The motorcade snaked up a steep hill and across the Plains of Abraham, where in 1759 the British had defeated the French in the Battle of Quebec. Roosevelt and Churchill lunched at the towering old Citadel, built to defend the city after the failed American attempt at conquest in the War of 1812. The two leaders did not dwell on past wars. They wondered to each other what might have happened had Adolf Hitler "got into Britain."

On Tuesday morning, after Roosevelt woke up in his large bedchamber at the Citadel, he was given a "My dear Friend" message from Churchill. The Prime Minister said it was "painfully apparent" that "one of the most important things I have to discuss with you" was future American Lend-Lease aid to England: "Would Thursday, 14th, do for that?—in which case I hope you could have Morgenthau present."

On Tuesday evening, at East Fishkill, a Secret Service agent handed the Treasury Secretary a telegram from the President: "PLEASE BE IN QUEBEC BY THURSDAY, 14 SEPTEMBER, NOON. ROOSEVELT." Delighted, Morgenthau boarded a military plane for Quebec.

At the Citadel on Wednesday morning, September 13, as a rainstorm drenched the beautiful city, Roosevelt and Churchill met with their Combined Chiefs of Staff. Churchill said that historians would give a "great account" of the ten months since the Tehran meeting. Since D-Day, "everything we have touched has turned to gold." He was proud that the British Empire could claim "equal partnership" with the United States, "the greatest military power in the world."

Roosevelt reminded Churchill that Stalin deserved "no little of the credit." Especially in Stalin's absence, he wanted the conference record to show nothing that might look like an Anglo-American conspiracy against the Soviets. He was anxious that Stalin keep his commitment to fight the Japanese after Germany was defeated. He had once hoped that this conference, code-named OCTAGON, would be another Big Three conclave, perhaps aboard battleships off Scotland. But Stalin had sent word that he could not leave his command post in Moscow.

Roosevelt now told Churchill it was still "not quite possible to forecast the date of the end of the war with Germany." Hitler's armies were retreating from the Balkans and Italy, but the Germans had always been "good at staging withdrawals." If they gathered behind a "west wall" on the right bank of the Rhine, they couldn't yet be "counted out." The Anglo-Americans might have to fight "one more big battle."

Raising the subject of postwar Germany, Roosevelt noted that there were "certain groups" in both of their countries who have "a kindly attitude toward the Germans." Such people presumed that evil could be "eradicated from the German makeup" and that Germany could be "rejuvenated by kindness."[1]

"Such sentiments would hardly be tolerated in Great Britain," Churchill replied. "The British people would demand a strong policy against the Germans. The German working man should be allowed sufficient food for his bare needs, and work, but no more. The more virulent elements, such as the

1. Stimson's exhortations for "Christianity and kindness" toward Germany must have registered on Roosevelt.

Gestapo and the young fanatics, should be deported to work in rehabilitating the devastated areas of Europe."

CHURCHILL HAD SPENT his adulthood dealing with the tides of German power. In 1911, with the Germans expanding their navy and deepening the Kiel Canal to let German battleships rush to the North Sea, Churchill was First Lord of the Admiralty, preparing Britain for war.

No Englishman was more eager for victory, but when World War I was over, as Minister of Munitions, Churchill warned Lloyd George's War Cabinet that they "might have to build up the German army" and "get Germany on her legs again" to stop Bolshevism. In April 1919 he pronounced Lenin's atrocities "incomparably more hideous" than the Kaiser's. He wished to build a "strong but peaceful Germany" as a "moral bulwark" against Soviet power. "Kill the Bolshie," he told his friend Violet Asquith. "Kiss the Hun."

In the 1920s, Churchill had vainly pressed to relax the Versailles treaty's harsh sanctions against Germany. He reasoned that Germany could not be kept "in permanent subjugation." Better to show mercy toward a weakened Germany now than later have to fight the nation when it was emboldened by desire for revenge.

In 1936, when Hitler broke the treaties of Versailles and Locarno and seized the Rhineland, Churchill felt sadly vindicated. "British policy for four hundred years has been to oppose the strongest power in Europe," he wrote his cousin Lord Londonderry. "Sometimes it is Spain, sometimes the French monarchy, sometimes the French Empire, sometimes Germany. I have no doubt who it is now." After Prime Minister Neville Chamberlain made his appeasement pact with Hitler at Munich, Churchill warned Parliament that England was now "dependent" upon the "goodwill or pleasure" of Nazi Germany for its "existence."[2]

Although a deeply emotional man, Churchill was able, even more than Roosevelt, to keep his personal feelings out of his balance-of-power calculations. He told Harry Hopkins in early 1941 that he had no enemies "except the Huns"—and "that was professional!"

After the Soviets joined Great Britain against Hitler in 1941, as Churchill

2. In almost identical language Churchill would warn the Anglo-Americans against Soviet power after World War II.

himself said, the Prime Minister "wooed Joe Stalin as a man might woo a maid." By radio, he assured the British people that "the cause of any Russian fighting for his hearth and home is the cause of free men and free peoples in every quarter of the globe." But among intimates, he worried about a postwar Europe dominated by Stalin: "I do not want to be left alone in Europe with the bear."

Throughout the war, Churchill expected that postwar Germany might have to be buttressed to stop the Soviets in Europe. In October 1943, he told Foreign Secretary Eden, "We mustn't weaken Germany too much—we may need her against Russia." By the summer of 1944, he was unsettled by the speed of the Red Army's march through Eastern Europe and the Balkans.

Churchill's doctor Lord Moran observed in his diary that "Winston never talks of Hitler these days. He is always harping on the dangers of Communism." The month Churchill went to Quebec, Moran wrote, "The advance of the Red Army has taken possession of his mind."

ON WEDNESDAY AFTERNOON at four o'clock, Henry Morgenthau arrived at the President's grand suite at the Citadel for tea with the Roosevelts.

Roosevelt turned to his dog Fala: "Say hello to your Uncle Henry!" He told Morgenthau that the Prime Minister had brought along his close adviser Lord Cherwell, whom Churchill called by his nickname "the Prof": "I have asked you to come up here so that you could talk to the Prof." Roosevelt said that he and Churchill were "doing shipping" that evening,"[3] but "you might as well come too."

Morgenthau asked how freely he might talk with the Prof. "You can talk about anything you want," said Roosevelt. Thinking of his plan for Germany, Morgenthau asked, *"Anything?"*

"I wouldn't discuss with him the question of the zones to be occupied by our armies," Roosevelt advised. "That's a military question. Nor would I discuss the question of partitioning, as that's a political question. But you can talk about the fact that we are thinking of internationalizing the Ruhr and the Saar, including the Kiel Canal."

Knowing that Hull would not be in Quebec, Churchill had not planned to bring his foreign secretary. But Roosevelt grandly reported, "I have sent

3. Roosevelt had also summoned his war shipping administrator, Emory Land, to Quebec.

for Eden," adding, "Churchill, Eden, yourself and I will sit down to discuss the matter."[4]

As Morgenthau later wrote in his diary, he supposed that Roosevelt wanted Eden in Quebec because he had told the President that Eden would be tough on Germany. "Don't worry about Churchill," Roosevelt now said. "He is going to be tough too."

As the Treasury Secretary departed, Roosevelt handed his copy of the Morgenthau Plan to his secretary Grace Tully: "Put that book right next to my bed. I want to read it tonight."

CHURCHILL TOOK MORGENTHAU'S presence at dinner as a sign that Germany must be foremost on Roosevelt's mind. Earlier that day, Roosevelt had tried out on Churchill one of Morgenthau's arguments for a tough German peace: "How would you like to have the steel business of Europe for twenty or thirty years?" He presumed that Churchill could not turn down his nose at such a glittering prospect.

As they dined, Churchill asked Roosevelt, "Why don't we discuss Germany now?" At the President's invitation, Morgenthau described his plan, showing how closing down the Ruhr would bolster the British steel industry and help stave off postwar British bankruptcy.

Indignantly, Churchill asked Roosevelt, "Is *this* what you asked me to come all the way here to discuss?" He replied to Morgenthau's proposals with anger. Churchill declared that he would not chain himself to "a dead German": "I'm all for disarming Germany. But we ought not prevent her living decently." Germans must not be allowed to starve. "You cannot indict a whole nation."

The British people would never "stand" for such measures, he said. They were "unnatural, un-Christian and unnecessary." Seizing Germany's old steel business would bring England little economic relief. Churchill did not add that his Foreign Office had warned him that if postwar Germany could not produce, British exports would sag along with world trade, and that "a starving and bankrupt Germany would not be in our interest."

Morgenthau later recorded, "I have never had such a verbal lashing in my life." He wondered whether Roosevelt had deliberately let Churchill "wear himself out attacking me."

4. Actually Churchill had asked Eden, on Roosevelt's recommendation, to fly in from London.

Churchill and most of his people disliked Morgenthau. They considered him anti-British and hell-bent on shifting postwar political and economic influence from London to Washington. The Prime Minister was still irritated at Morgenthau for going around his back to Eden and lesser British officials in August to press for harsh measures toward Germany.

Morgenthau reminded Churchill of his lamentation during their conversation in London that Britain would be destitute after the war. How could the Prime Minister keep his people from starving without expanding his export business? Churchill replied that he knew his people: In five years, after passions had cooled, they would not stand for repression of Germany.

Roosevelt reminded Churchill that it was Stalin, at Tehran, who had demanded that German industry be destroyed. Admiral William Leahy interjected that the only way to ensure the peace would be for a Big Three police force to "crack down" on Germany if it tried to expand again.

Churchill replied that the three Allies had better do the job in rotation, adding that his military people "get dirty when they associate with the Russians."

The Prime Minister was clearly worried that Roosevelt would use the Morgenthau Plan as an excuse to reduce future Lend-Lease aid to Britain: If crushing German industry gave new export opportunities to Britain, why should Churchill need so much American cash? He insisted to Roosevelt that Morgenthau's plan could not substitute for postwar aid: "If you do not do something for Britain, then the British will simply have to . . . do business largely within the Empire." Churchill was threatening to close British markets to American exports.

Roosevelt replied that "the Prof" should "go into our plans with Morgenthau" in the morning.

As they left the room, Morgenthau warned Roosevelt that the Russians seemed to be "holding back" from full cooperation out of fear that "we and the British" would "make a soft peace with Germany and build her up as a future counterweight against Russia."

"You are right," said Roosevelt. "And I want you to read a telegram I just received from Harriman."

Averell Harriman, the American ambassador in Moscow, had cabled that the Soviets had lately started trying to "force us and the British to accept all Soviet policies, backed by the strength and prestige of the Red Army." Unless this were stopped, "the Soviet Union will become a world bully wherever their interests are involved."

IN WASHINGTON, Stimson learned the "outrageous" news that Morgenthau had "got himself invited" to Quebec. He recorded that when he informed McCloy, he had "never seen him so depressed as this made him." He complained to his diary, "Here the President appoints a committee . . . and when he goes off to Quebec, he takes the man who really represents the minority and is so biased by his Semitic grievances that he really is a very dangerous adviser to the President at this time.

"I cannot believe that he will follow Morgenthau's views. If he does, it will certainly be a disaster." Morgenthau would try to "beguile the British" with his "poison poured into the President's ears." Stimson called Cordell Hull to suggest that they stage an emergency meeting of the Cabinet Committee on Germany to stop whatever damage Morgenthau was doing in Quebec.

Hull refused. Perhaps he was worried that it might look like a palace coup in the President's absence.

AFTER HIS LACERATION BY CHURCHILL, Morgenthau did not sleep that night. At ten o'clock on Thursday morning, September 14, Lord Cherwell came to his rooms at the turreted Hotel Chateau Frontenac. To support himself, Morgenthau had Harry Dexter White close at hand.

Churchill's biographer Martin Gilbert called Cherwell the Prime Minister's "closest friend and confidant." Arch, unmarried, partial to Rolls-Royces and country weekends, the Prof was known as Churchill's "one-man brain trust." He was born Frederick Lindemann[5] in 1886 to an affluent Alsatian father and American mother. During World War I, he was refused a British Army commission because of his German name and birth certificate. One colleague felt that after the episode, "to avoid exposing himself to slights and insults," Cherwell formed a lifelong secretiveness that was "easily mistaken for arrogance."

His Oxford friend Roy Harrod thought that "because he was by birth a foreigner," he was "anxious to assimilate himself completely to England."

5. When offered a title, Cherwell named himself after the river that runs through Oxford.

This may have manifested itself in Cherwell's outspoken antipathy to Germany. Churchill's assistant private secretary, Jock Colville, recalled that Cherwell "detested Germans." Perhaps his hostility came from growing up in a region newly under German domination. In 1871, France had surrendered Alsace to the just-unified Germany.

Cherwell had long been Churchill's traveling companion and man-of-all-work. During World War II, the Prof counseled him on almost everything, including the secret race by Americans and Germans to produce an atomic bomb.[6]

Some, including McCloy, wondered whether Cherwell was Jewish. In a 1959 book-length biography of Cherwell, *The Prof,* Harrod wrote that "the question of whether the Prof was a Jew was a subject of frequent discussion" and that "it will always remain something of a mystery."[7] Cherwell's brother Charles insisted to a later biographer, the Earl of Birkenhead, that there was "not a shred of foundation" for the belief that his brother "had Jewish blood," noting that "had there been any suspicion of Jewish blood," he himself would "never have been allowed" to marry his French wife.

After dinner on Wednesday night in Quebec, Cherwell reminded Churchill that Morgenthau's plan "would save Britain from bankruptcy by eliminating a dangerous competitor." Cherwell insisted that "somebody must suffer for the war," and it shouldn't be Britain. He later recalled, "Winston had not thought of it that way, and he said no more about the cruel threat to the German people."

WHEN MORGENTHAU HAD LEARNED that he would be dealing with Cherwell at Quebec, he consulted an Oxford cousin, Arthur Goodhart, who told him that Cherwell was "not popular at Oxford because he is more interested in politics than scientific work."

6. In 1939, to keep Prime Minister Neville Chamberlain from making new concessions to Hitler out of worry that the Germans were developing a new "secret weapon," Cherwell had gleaned information that allowed Churchill to assure Chamberlain that the Germans would not have "new explosives of devastating power" for at least "several years."

7. During his three-page discussion of the subject, Harrod wrote, "There were many touches in his deportment, in his manner of conversation, in his modes of thought, and notably in his social attitudes, that suggested the Jew to the Gentile mind. . . . It seems curious that he never cleared the matter up. . . . It is possible that the reader who knows the Prof only through these pages will find, if he perseveres to the end of the book, that he has formed his own opinion on whether the Prof had Jewish blood."

Starting the bargaining on Thursday morning, Cherwell told Morgenthau that Churchill wanted to know how much Lend-Lease aid the United States had in mind before making any commitments on Germany. Morgenthau said he imagined granting Britain six billion dollars in postwar credits.

Leafing through a copy of the Morgenthau Plan, Cherwell said he couldn't understand why Churchill had been so "contrary" last evening. Perhaps he hadn't fully comprehended what Morgenthau had in mind.

Morgenthau replied that the real problem might be that Churchill wanted a strong Germany between Russia and the "white cliffs of Dover." Did they want "a strong Germany and a weak England, or a weak Germany and a strong England?"

Cherwell said he thought the Plan could be "dressed up" in a way Churchill might find more attractive.

At 11:30 A.M., the two men joined Roosevelt and Churchill at the Citadel. The President told Churchill that they should have their people work out terms for future Lend-Lease aid to Britain. Not surprisingly, Churchill suggested Harry Hopkins, whom he considered a great friend of Britain, as chairman of the negotiating committee, but Roosevelt appointed the more tough-minded Morgenthau.

Cherwell declared that he hadn't had the time to study the Morgenthau Plan in detail but was "definitely attracted by the possibilities." Framing the plan in more modest language than Morgenthau's, he said that his understanding was that machinery would be seized from the Ruhr and granted to those countries most devastated by Germany. An international authority controlling the Ruhr "and perhaps other areas" would decide "whether, when and how" German industry should be rebuilt. German "exports would be reduced," but Germans would not "starve." Germany's postwar living standard would be higher than that of the Hitler era, "when so much national effort was put into preparations for war." And if German markets should be "available" for Britain and the United States, that seemed no "disadvantage."

To Morgenthau's astonishment, Churchill reversed himself from the previous evening. The Prime Minister said there was "a good deal to be said for this approach." The Allies were "entitled to make sure Germany could not commit wanton acts of aggression."

Roosevelt said he did not think it "an undue hardship" to turn Germany back into the agricultural nation she had been before the late nineteenth century.

Churchill abruptly pronounced himself "converted." He later told his doctor, Lord Moran, "Why shouldn't it work? I've no patience with people who are always raising difficulties."

That afternoon, when Roosevelt and Churchill were about to initial a memorandum authorizing Lend-Lease negotiations, the President changed the subject and began telling stories. Churchill, who knew Roosevelt so well, feared that he was scheming to postpone or avoid signing the document he was so desperate for. Finally he burst out, "What do you want me to do? Get on my hind legs and beg like Fala?"

ON FRIDAY, September 15, at noon, Roosevelt signed a document pledging the United States in principle to more Lend-Lease aid. With tears in his eyes, Churchill said they were doing this for "both countries."

They were joined by Anthony Eden, just arrived from London. To preserve the fiction that Quebec was a military, not a political conference, Churchill insisted that Eden was present not as Foreign Secretary but as "unofficial Deputy Defense Minister." Back in Washington, when Hull heard that his British counterpart was in Quebec, he was furious. He complained to Stettinius that "if the conference went into political matters," the President had promised to send for him.

The Prime Minister turned to Cherwell: "Where are the minutes on this matter of the Ruhr?" Cherwell said they weren't ready yet. Roosevelt joked that the reason was that "Henry" had been telling "too many dirty stories."

At Churchill's behest, Cherwell and Morgenthau drafted an Anglo-American statement on Germany. But Churchill said, "This isn't what I want." With his secretary called in, he dictated his own memorandum. When Churchill spoke of crushing industry, Roosevelt insisted that he insert the phrase "in Germany," not just the Ruhr.

As Lord Moran recorded, Eden "flew into a rage." Within earshot of the Americans, he told Churchill, "You can't do this! After all, you and I publicly have said quite the opposite."

Annoyed by Eden's defiance, Churchill told him that under the plan, Britain "would get the export trade of Germany."

"How do you know what it is?" retorted Eden. "Or where it is?"

Churchill snapped, "We'll get it wherever it is. . . . The future of my people is at stake, and when I have to choose between my people and the German people, I am going to choose my people."

Eden later recalled that this was the only time Churchill ever upbraided him in front of Roosevelt. Of Morgenthau, Eden wrote in his diary that he himself felt "irritated by this German Jew's bitter hatred of his own land."

The President and Prime Minister now solemnly read the endorsement, drafted by Churchill, of Germany's conversion "into a country primarily agricultural and pastoral in its character." On the 226-word memorandum Roosevelt scrawled, "O.K. F.D.R." Churchill wrote his initials and the date: "W.S.C. 15 9."

Churchill's language did not include the destruction of all German mines and factories, but as Morgenthau wrote in his diary, he was "terrifically happy" that he had achieved "just what we started out to get," and that "Churchill has dictated this himself."

WHY HAD ROOSEVELT PRESSED Churchill to agree to the memorandum?

At that moment, with various German anti-Hitler plotters having pressed both Stalin and the West to make a separate peace, the President wished to ensure that the Soviets stayed in the war to unconditional surrender. Nervous about Stalin's conspicuous absence from Quebec, Roosevelt doubtless hoped that the document would be a dramatic statement to the Marshal that he and Churchill still stoutly endorsed Stalin's demands at Tehran for toughness on Germany and that they had no intention of making a separate deal with Hitler. The memorandum pointedly said that "it must also be remembered" that the Germans had "devastated a large portion of the industries of Russia."

Roosevelt was also worried that his own officials would combine with Churchill and his Foreign Office to undercut his determination to avoid the mistakes of the First World War and build a new, democratic Germany from the ground up. The President, of course, knew that the Quebec document was not binding. The real decisions on Germany would be made by the Big Three. But even if the memorandum were later weakened, it would be a bulwark against the soft-on-Germany crowd in Washington and London.

The Quebec memorandum also indulged Roosevelt's habit of using his sentimental predispositions in his diplomacy. Like Morgenthau, he believed that Jeffersonian democracy was best nurtured on the farms and countryside. Roosevelt fantasized that Germany could actually be turned into a nation primarily of yeoman farmers close to their own land. When he reminisced about his German boyhood, he always insisted that the trouble came when the arcadian Germany he once knew was transformed by the industrial revolution.

Roosevelt also wished to get U.S. troops out of Europe as soon as possible after victory. A weakened Germany might make that more possible.

Throughout the wartime alliance, Churchill was always the weakest member of the Big Three, and he knew it. At crucial moments in his diplomacy, he performed surprising flip-flops, trying to maximize British influence, even if it cost him consistency. The Prime Minister's overnight reversal on the Morgenthau Plan was the latest such example. It was rooted in cold calculation.

Churchill realized that the memorandum might be needed to mollify Stalin. He may have also supposed that Roosevelt's offer to open longtime German markets to Britain was a welcome signal that the Americans would not grab for them first. He certainly felt that signing such a document was Roosevelt's price for more Lend-Lease aid, especially since the American broker was going to be Morgenthau. In his war memoirs, Churchill claimed that he did it because Morgenthau, "from whom we had so much to ask," was "so insistent."[8]

Like Roosevelt, Churchill knew that unless and until it was endorsed at a Big Three meeting, the document would have no force. But he could console himself that he and Cherwell had gotten Roosevelt to sign a memorandum, dictated by Churchill, that was less brutal than Morgenthau's actual plan.[9]

ON FRIDAY AFTERNOON, Roosevelt and Churchill discussed occupation zones in Germany. The President told Morgenthau he had postponed this question until he could get "everything else settled" and Churchill would be "in a good humor."

8. Churchill was never above rewriting history. Although he was the one who asked Roosevelt to bring Morgenthau to the Big Three meeting, he claimed in the same memoirs that he was "surprised to find" Morgenthau at Quebec.

9. For instance, it did not mention dismemberment of Germany and did not demand the complete shutdown of the Ruhr.

He had used three colored pencils to sketch out German zones on a map of Europe. As long planned, the Soviets would be granted the northeastern zone. But as he had told Churchill in February, he was "absolutely unwilling" to be saddled with the landlocked southwestern zone, whose owner would have to "police" adjacent France and deal with a possible postwar French revolution. "France is your baby," he had told Churchill. Instead, the United States should have the northwestern zone, with access to the North and Baltic Seas.

Roosevelt had told Hull that when victory came, he would have to ask war-weary Americans to keep troops in Europe. A landlocked zone would make that more difficult. Since "all supplies have to come 3,500 miles by sea," the United States must use "the ports of northern Germany—Hamburg and Bremen."

Stimson wrote in his diary that for Roosevelt to be so "hell-bent" on the northeastern zone was "ridiculous": "We all think that is a mistake, that it will only get us into a head-on collision with the British." In late August, Stimson had told the President that they were having "such great success with our invasion in France" that it was "a good time to be generous" toward the British. He told him not to worry about France. There "couldn't be any revolution" until the war was over." By then "our troops would be out of France." If the United States took the southwestern zone, it would be "further away from the dirty work that the Russians might be doing with the Prussians in eastern Germany."

Reassured by his Secretary of War, Roosevelt did not argue too fiercely with Churchill. The Prime Minister promised to ensure him sea access if Britain were granted the northwestern zone. Roosevelt gave in.

When Morgenthau dropped by the President's Citadel suite before dinner on Friday, he found Roosevelt "completely relaxed." The President said he was toying with the notion of an opening meeting of the postwar United Nations organization ten days before the November 1944 election. He noted that one reason why Wilson's League of Nations failed was that it took "much too long" to convene after World War I.

Morgenthau remarked that a late October meeting would also make "good window dressing" for Roosevelt's presidential campaign. Candidly Roosevelt replied, "Yes!"

"Look, Mr. President, now that we have this Ruhr and Saar stuff straightened out, the thing should be presented to Stalin. And I think if Stalin knew how we felt, you would find he would act much better."

Roosevelt said he would have Ambassador Harriman "sell it to Stalin."

"Listen, Harriman can't do this," said Morgenthau. "You ought to send me. I get along very well with the Russians—and you can check with Stalin as to whether I do or whether I don't."

Already nervous about Morgenthau's aspirations for more influence over the postwar world, Roosevelt replied, "Oh, I have far too important things for you to do around Washington."

After dinner, while Churchill met with his aides, Roosevelt and Clementine Churchill screened the just-released Twentieth Century–Fox picture *Wilson,* starring Alexander Knox. As Roosevelt watched the scenes of the twenty-eighth President collapsing from a stroke while fighting for his postwar League of Nations, he cried, "By God, that's not going to happen to me!"

WITH THE QUEBEC MEETING OVER, the Churchills were to be houseguests at the Big House at Hyde Park. Eleanor had some trepidation. She once complained that Churchill "knew Franklin rose early and did not take two-hour naps in the afternoon, as he did." Yet Churchill kept him "up till all hours of the night" and "wore Franklin out."

Eleanor abhorred Churchill's conservatism and colonialism and did not mind telling him so. "Poor Winston!" she once said. "Whenever he is here for dinner, he has to sit by me."[10] She complained to Joseph Lash that although she and Churchill differed on fascist Spain, "he insists on bringing it up at every meal." She thought Churchill spoke "picturesquely" but sometimes "stupidly."

On Monday, September 18, the Roosevelts and Churchills lunched at the Big House with the Duke of Windsor, the former King Edward VIII, who had abdicated in 1936 after eleven months on the British throne. Roosevelt's aide William Hassett recorded that the Duchess was "having something done to her innards" at a New York hospital.

For Roosevelt to have Windsor in his home had its ironies. According to

10. When FDR met Churchill in Quebec, he cried out, "Eleanor's here!" Some aides, knowing the friction between Churchill and the First Lady, suspected that their boss was twitting the Prime Minister.

FBI documents released in 2002, after the war began in Europe, the President had ordered the FBI to keep both the Duke and Duchess under surveillance because of their "Nazi sympathies" and suspicions that the Duchess had given secret information to Joachim von Ribbentrop, Hitler's prewar ambassador to London and later Foreign Minister, with whom she had allegedly had an affair. One FBI report had it that if Hitler defeated England, he would restore the Duke to the British throne as King, with his twice-divorced wife as Queen.

That afternoon, the President and Prime Minister motored to Fishkill Farms for tea. Smiling, Roosevelt sat in the sun on the open portico while Morgenthau proudly showed Churchill the ripe apples hanging from his trees. Morgenthau's son Robert, on leave from the Navy, mixed mint juleps for Roosevelt and Churchill. Knowing of Churchill's intemperance, he was surprised when the Prime Minister had just one.

The next day, Roosevelt and Churchill initialed one more Churchill-drafted memo, on the secret atomic bomb program, which they referred to by the code name "Tube Alloys." When the bomb was ready, "it might perhaps, after mature consideration, be used against the Japanese."

By the time the Churchills left Hyde Park, Roosevelt was exhausted. Hassett recorded that the President had been "under a heavy strain ever since he went to Quebec—continuous talking." Roosevelt told Margaret Suckley that he had had a "good conference" with Churchill, but now he wanted "to *sleep* all the time."

CHAPTER FOURTEEN

"A Hell of a Hubbub"

BACK IN HIS TREASURY OFFICE, Morgenthau told his aides that Quebec was "the high spot of my whole career in the government. I got more personal satisfaction out of those forty-eight hours than with anything I have ever been connected with." Roosevelt had told him that he "had been groping for something" and "we came along and gave him just what he wanted. But I don't know how they are going to announce it, or what they are going to do about it."

DURING THE WEEKEND, McCloy had called Stimson at his Long Island estate, where an Atlantic hurricane had felled trees and wires, forcing him to use an old heavy-duty telephone line installed when Stimson was Hoover's Secretary of State. McCloy told Stimson that in Quebec, Roosevelt had ruled "flatly against us."

Into his diary Stimson angrily wrote, "Apparently he has gone over completely to the Morgenthau proposition and has gotten Churchill and Lord Cherwell with him." Cherwell was "an old fool" who had "loudly proclaimed that we could never cross the Channel"—a "pseudoscientist" for whom "nobody has much respect. . . . The cloud of it has hung over me pretty heavily over the weekend." It was a "terrible thing" for such a "critical matter" to be decided by Roosevelt and Churchill, "both of whom are similar in their impulsiveness and their lack of systematic study," with nobody to advise them at Quebec except "yes-men."

Everyone Stimson had spoken to was "horrified" by Morgenthau's "Carthaginian" attitude: "It is Semitism gone wild for vengeance and, if it is ultimately carried out (I cannot believe that it will be), it as sure as fate will lay the seeds for another war in the next generation."

Stimson resolved to send a written protest to Roosevelt: "It will undoubtedly irritate him, for he dislikes opposition when he has made up his mind. But I have thought the thing over and decided to do it. I should not keep my self-respect if I did not."

Stimson addressed his appeal to the "farsighted and greatly humanitarian President." He reminded Roosevelt that the Atlantic Charter he and Churchill had signed in 1941 promised that "victors and vanquished alike are entitled to freedom from economic want." They must not reduce seventy million Germans "to a peasant level."

IN WASHINGTON, McCloy was busy recruiting allies to fight Morgenthau, saying that Morgenthau's linkage of postwar Germany to Lend-Lease aid "couldn't be more sordid." McCloy warned James Forrestal, Secretary of the Navy, that over Stimson's "violent disagreement," Morgenthau was battling for the "conscious destruction" of Germany's economy and "a state of impoverishment and disorder."

Lunching with Harold Ickes, McCloy carped that Morgenthau had returned from Europe talking "very glibly about the conduct of the war and about who were good generals and who were not." The cantankerous Interior Secretary said that he himself was "too prejudiced" against the Germans to give a "fair judgment." Emotionally he felt "they all ought to be sterilized." With his abiding passion to increase his political domain, he wanted Roosevelt to install him on the Cabinet Committee on Germany.

Ickes agreed with McCloy that "Morgenthau ought not to have anything to do with this matter for the simple reason that he is a Jew, and the charge will be made that through him, the Jews are dictating peace terms that no one in the end will be willing to accept." He told his diary, "Such a plan as Morgenthau proposes is the worst possible. . . . Much as I hate the Germans and mistrust them, I do not believe that a vindictive peace would mean anything but another war, even if the Germans had to fight with their hands." He noted that Stimson and McCloy realized that they were "up against a stiff game, with Morgenthau running into the White House through the side door all the time."

ON WEDNESDAY, September 20, at 9:30 A.M., at the State Department, Morgenthau reported on the conference to Hull, Stimson and McCloy. The news from Quebec had left Hull sleepless and depressed. Suffering from a bad cold, he had not been able to fathom how Roosevelt could behave "with such irresponsibility and deviousness." He privately thought Morgenthau's plan was "mad."

In Hull's office, Morgenthau waved a copy of the Roosevelt-Churchill memo in the air. He said he did not know why the President had summoned him to Quebec, but he had gone "fully prepared" and planned to keep "active" on postwar Germany.

As Stimson wrote in his diary, Morgenthau spoke "modestly and without rubbing it in, but it was the narration of a pretty heavy defeat for everything that we had fought for."

When Morgenthau asked the War Secretary whether he knew Cherwell, Stimson replied, "Very well." But, he said, he did not know whether "the Prof" meant "the Professor" or "the Prophet." All he remembered about Cherwell was his false prophecies that the cross-Channel invasion would fail and that Hitler's robot bombs "would never do any harm" to London.

Hull said bitterly that since he was being excluded from such vital matters as postwar Germany, he was "rapidly losing interest" in his job.

Morgenthau left the meeting outraged by Stimson's opposition. He warned the President by letter that Stimson's approach to postwar Germany was "appeasement." Within fifteen to twenty-five years, it would allow Germany "to become so strong" that she could bring "even greater death, horror and destruction than she has caused in this war."

Stimson dined at Woodley with Frankfurter, who assured him that the Roosevelt-Churchill agreement on Germany would evaporate because the British people "wouldn't stand for it." Stimson found the Justice "so cheerful and optimistic" that he "cheered up the evening of a gloomy day."

The next morning, Thursday, September 21, was Stimson's seventy-seventh birthday. Knowing that Stimson was disgruntled about Quebec,

Roosevelt sent him a bouquet of roses. The birthday was shadowed, however, by a Drew Pearson column in that morning's *Washington Post,* almost certainly leaked by one of Morgenthau's men—perhaps Harry Dexter White, who was close to Pearson.[1]

Quebec was not mentioned, but Pearson reported that people at the State and War Departments had been "quaking in their boots" after Roosevelt "blew up" over their failures on occupation plans for Germany. Morgenthau, "in disgust," had "tossed" the *Handbook* on Germany on the desk of the President. In a letter to Stimson, an angry Roosevelt had denounced passages in the *Handbook* that were "especially weak or stupid" and ordered that the Germans be fed nothing more than "three bowls of soup a day."

Furious, McCloy told Stimson that Pearson had "practically quoted word for word the spanking letter the President sent you." There was "every indication" that the column "emanated from the Treasury." He said that they could leak their own story, but that would only reveal more embarrassing details about the controversy "in front of our enemies."

Nevertheless, at 12:40 P.M., by telephone, McCloy gave the *New York Times* columnist Arthur Krock discreetly chosen details about the Cabinet Committee on Germany and Morgenthau's presence at Quebec. Krock had already been tipped off by Hull and James Byrnes, director of the Office of War Mobilization, that Morgenthau had gone to Quebec and that Hull and Stimson were "very much disturbed" about it.[2]

Krock's column that next morning was titled "WHY SECRETARY MORGENTHAU WENT TO QUEBEC." Krock did not reveal the Morgenthau Plan or the Roosevelt-Churchill memorandum, but he reported that Morgenthau had become Roosevelt's "central" adviser on postwar Germany.

ON FRIDAY, September 22, Ickes lunched with Roosevelt and his daughter, Anna, under the Andrew Jackson magnolia. He felt the President was "decidedly showing the wear and tear of the past eleven and a half years."

1. Leaking to the press was one of the services White performed for Morgenthau. He told Morgenthau the following week that he had been trying to plant favorable stories on the Morgenthau Plan with columnists Clifton Fadiman, Raymond Gram Swing and Max Lerner and a correspondent for the Associated Press.

2. During the Quebec meeting, Byrnes had told Krock over drinks that asking Hull about Morgenthau "might be rewarding." He had detested Morgenthau since 1942, when they had broken over tax policy. When Morgenthau had tried to win an agreement, Byrnes replied, "I wouldn't agree with you on anything!"

The Interior Secretary mentioned a rumor that Morgenthau intended to give campaign speeches for Roosevelt "across the country." He noted "how intense the feeling of anti-Semitism is" and "how disliked Morgenthau is." Roosevelt said he understood, but that Morgenthau was simply planning his next War Bond drive. Ickes asked whether Morgenthau had "slipped up to Quebec to get the jump on Hull and Stimson" and force the President's hand on postwar Germany. Roosevelt replied that he had summoned Morgenthau because he had "the only definite information" on Germany "that anyone seemed to have."

Ickes warned that "the Pearson story about soup for the Germans" would be "very bad politically."

Roosevelt disagreed: "There might be a situation where the Army would have to set up soup kitchens." The soup would be "ample and nourishing." The President wondered aloud how Pearson got so much information.

Ickes later wrote in his diary, "Morgenthau is taking advantage of his personal relationship with the President, and the situation is not a good one."

Like Ickes, Roosevelt's daughter also resented Morgenthau's backdoor influence. She strongly felt that, as a Jew, Morgenthau should have nothing to do with postwar Germany. It would damage her father politically, and German propagandists could exploit Morgenthau's role to stiffen resistance by claiming that the Jews would run Germany after an Allied victory.

After listening to Ickes inveigh against Morgenthau, Anna told him, "It was almost as if you had taken the words out of my mouth." Roosevelt, who knew his daughter's feelings well, later joked that she must have told Ickes what to say.

THE NEXT MORNING, Saturday, September 23, the *Wall Street Journal,* on page one, revealed the Morgenthau Plan to the world for the first time: "Treasury Plan Calls for Dismemberment, Ban on Most Heavy Industry." The story, by Alfred Flynn, called the plan "Carthaginian," the same term Stimson and McCloy were using in private, which suggests that it was leaked by the War Department.

On Sunday morning, September 24, John Hightower of the Associated Press added another piece to the puzzle. On the front pages of the *Washington Post,* the *Washington Star* and the *Chicago Tribune,* he revealed that Morgenthau had presented his plan at Quebec and left with the "impression" that

Churchill found it "acceptable." The Morgenthau Plan had "split" the Cabinet Committee "wide open," with Hull unhappy about it and Stimson "violently opposed."

Morgenthau usually read the major newspapers before breakfast. This morning, he knew he was in big trouble. Just six weeks before a close presidential election, despite Roosevelt's will to present a united front during wartime, Americans had now been told that his Cabinet was at war over the Morgenthau Plan. His only comfort was that no one yet had discovered the signed agreement between Roosevelt and Churchill at Quebec.

Desperately anxious that Roosevelt would be furious about the stories, Morgenthau called the President at Hyde Park at 9:45 A.M., but the President did not take his call. Ingratiatingly, Morgenthau asked Roosevelt's secretary Grace Tully to tell the President that he had heard last night's speech to the Teamsters on radio, with its droll response to attacks on "my little dog Fala."[3] Please convey his compliments to the Boss: the "old master" was "back again."

To stem the damage of the news, Morgenthau suggested that Roosevelt's press secretary, Stephen Early, prepare a statement that he, Hull and Stimson would sign, conceding that they had given certain private advice on Germany and that they "naturally would abide by any decision the President made."

Six agonizing hours later, Morgenthau heard back from Tully. She told him that the President "didn't want to do anything about it." It was "simply a newspaper story." Nonetheless, Roosevelt was "curious to know" how the article had been hatched. Morgenthau replied, "Well, you can never find out where those things come from."

ON MONDAY MORNING, September 25, Morgenthau turned on his radio to hear his plan for Germany being debated. At 8:30 A.M., he called Hull and asked if there was "something we can do to stop the talk" about the Cabinet split.

Hull promised to tell reporters that the stories were "pure fiction" but complained that "somebody down the line in the Treasury has been talking

3. Roosevelt's address, at the Statler Hotel in Washington, became one of the best-remembered speeches of his career. As the President replied to Republican charges, including that he had sent a ship to the Aleutian Islands at public expense to retrieve his Scottie, his vigorous delivery helped to quash rumors that he was seriously ill.

to the press." Morgenthau had better speak to Stimson, who was "very much worried over the newspaper leaks."

(Morgenthau later complained, "Hull is always very quick to suggest that I do the job.")

Hull told him, "The President ought to get a dozen people together around the table and thrash this thing out."

"He won't do it," replied Morgenthau. "That isn't the way he works. The unfortunate thing is that . . . it all could be stopped if the President would insist on it."

Afterward, Morgenthau told his aides, "Everyone is saying what I have said and what I haven't said." Drew Pearson was writing "that Hull and his cookie-pushers are all against us." Morgenthau said he would tell the press, "I never tell what I recommend to the President."

"I don't think they would let you get away with that kind of answer," said Harry Dexter White.

"Take it from me," said Morgenthau. "Somebody in the Republican party is going to pick this up as an illustration that Mr. Roosevelt is a bad administrator. . . . Somebody is going to get dirty about me, and I am going to get sore and answer them, and the whole fat is in the fire."

Morgenthau kept trying to reach Roosevelt at Hyde Park by telephone, but the President refused his calls. Exasperated, he asked Grace Tully to ask the President for permission to show his plan to the press. It would be "a sort of red herring" to get the press to discuss the plan, not "the split in the Cabinet."

Roosevelt did not respond. Morgenthau told Tully, "I would like to give a copy of it to the Russian ambassador." Tully said she would have to let him know.

On Tuesday morning, September 26, in his Treasury office, Morgenthau told Harry Hopkins he was worried that "some unfriendly soul" who knew about the initialed document at Quebec might "let that get out in the paper" and "make a liar out of Roosevelt."

Unable to get the President to return his calls, Morgenthau was reduced to asking Hopkins to place a call to Hyde Park. When Roosevelt came on the line, Morgenthau suggested that the White House try to calm the fracas with a statement that the President was mulling over advice on Germany from Hull, Stimson and Morgenthau and that a directive endorsed by all three men was "on its way" to Eisenhower at Supreme Allied Headquarters in Europe. The President refused.

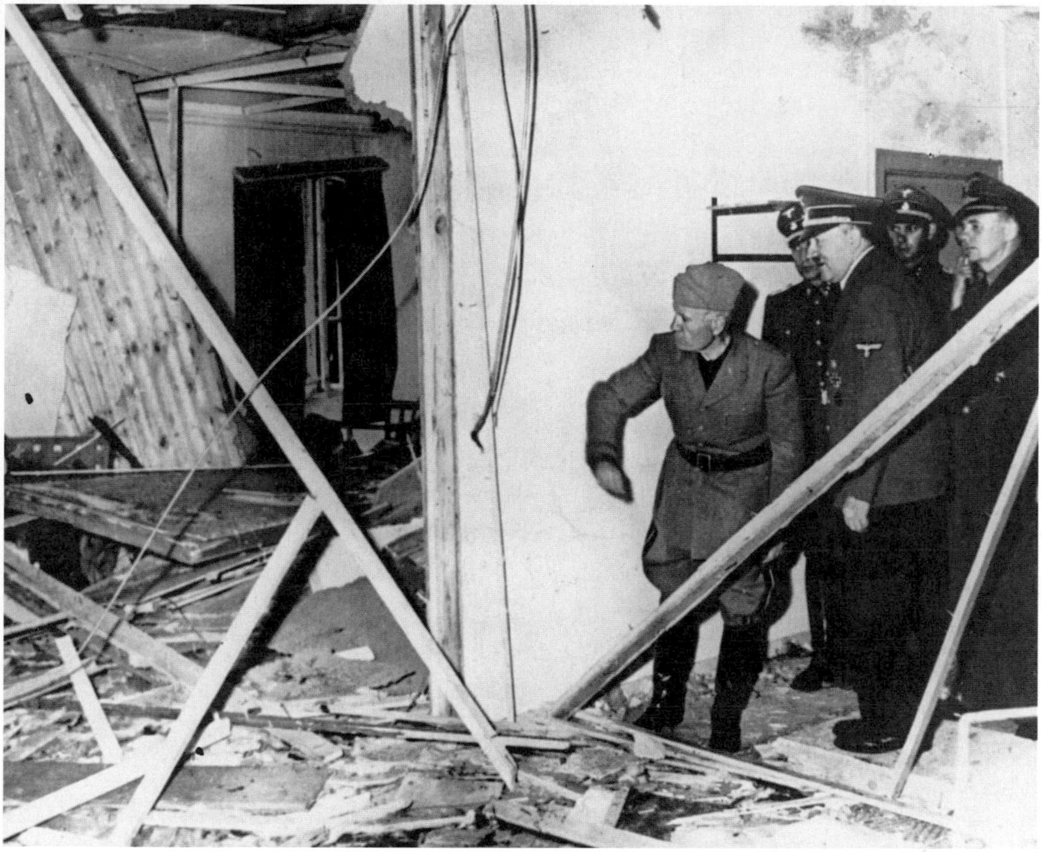

July 20, 1944. Adolf Hitler narrowly escapes assassination by anti-Nazi Germans. 1
Hours later, pretending bravado, the Führer shows the bomb damage to the ousted Italian dictator Benito Mussolini, crying, "Look at my uniform! Look at my burns!" Had the plot succeeded, Franklin Roosevelt and Winston Churchill might have had to bargain with a new German junta over stopping the war in Europe before their armies invaded Germany.

Colonel Claus von Stauffenberg, who detonated the bomb and was executed that night by a Nazi firing squad. A vengeful Hitler ordered all members of Stauffenberg's family murdered, and a "blood purge" of thousands of other potential plotters within Germany. The Führer never dared to speak in public again. Newly released British documents show that British agents were trying to murder Hitler under a secret plan called Operation Foxley. 2

3 At the Casablanca conference, January 1943, FDR demanded that World War II be fought until the Germans accepted unconditional surrender. Churchill worried that the policy would stiffen German resistance, but he acceded to his more powerful ally.

At Casablanca, FDR tells reporters that the Allies will accept nothing less than unconditional surrender. Despite his private doubts, Churchill says, "Hear, hear!"

4

Tehran, November 1943: Behind closed doors, FDR seconded Stalin's demand 5
that the Allies shoot fifty thousand Germans to death. Disgusted, Churchill stormed out of the room. Stalin grabbed his shoulders and pulled him back, claiming that he and Roosevelt had only been kidding.

6 Eleanor Roosevelt with Hudson Valley neighbors Secretary of the Treasury Henry Morgenthau, Jr., and his wife Elinor. Morgenthau was FDR's closest friend in the Cabinet and only the second Jew in American history to hold a Cabinet post. Eager to be considered a "one hundred percent American," for years Morgenthau refused to raise Jewish issues with the President.

Rabbi Stephen Wise, whose private alarms that the Nazis were "making lampshades out of the skins of the Jews" moved Morgenthau to confront FDR in January 1944 about his "acquiescence" in the Holocaust and risk his cherished friendship with the President.

7

Secretary of State Cordell Hull, Morgenthau and Secretary of War Henry Stimson—members of the War Refugee Board hastily established by Roosevelt in 1944 to save Jews from Hitler. Stimson argued that his job was to win the war, not to rescue Jews. Hull was deeply worried that if he tried to help Jews, anti-Semites would publicize his wife's little-known Jewish heritage and charge that he was a tool of Jewish interests. 8

Secretary of the Interior Harold Ickes privately told FDR that as far as he was concerned, the Germans "all ought to be sterilized."

9

Assistant Secretary of War John McCloy refused to let American military resources be earmarked for rescuing Jews. He also refused pleas to bomb Auschwitz. Angry about McCloy's footdragging on Jewish refugees, Morgenthau attacked him as being an "oppressor of the Jews." New information reveals that McCloy secretly submitted the Auschwitz bombing requests to FDR, who turned them down flat.

10

11 Fort Ontario, Oswego, New York, 1944. At an unused Army base, the United States took in about a thousand mostly Jewish refugees from Nazi-dominated Europe—the only such American haven of the war. Even this tiny number of Jews caused some Americans, including vocal anti-Semites, to demand their deportation.

August 1944: Henry Morgenthau tours liberated France, taking home movies with his sixteen-millimeter camera. During this trip, he conceived his secret plan to keep postwar Germany on its knees. Told privately by Henry Stimson and other officials that the Morgenthau Plan was too harsh, he replied that it was "not nearly as bad" as sending people "to gas chambers." 12

Below left: FDR's aide Harry Hopkins failed to persuade the President to let him be U.S. governor of postwar Germany.

Below right: Harry Dexter White, Morgenthau's close adviser. Newly released Soviet documents show that White met secretly with Soviet intelligence agents, raising the suspicion that the Soviets may have been trying to manipulate FDR and Morgenthau to crush postwar Germany.

13

14

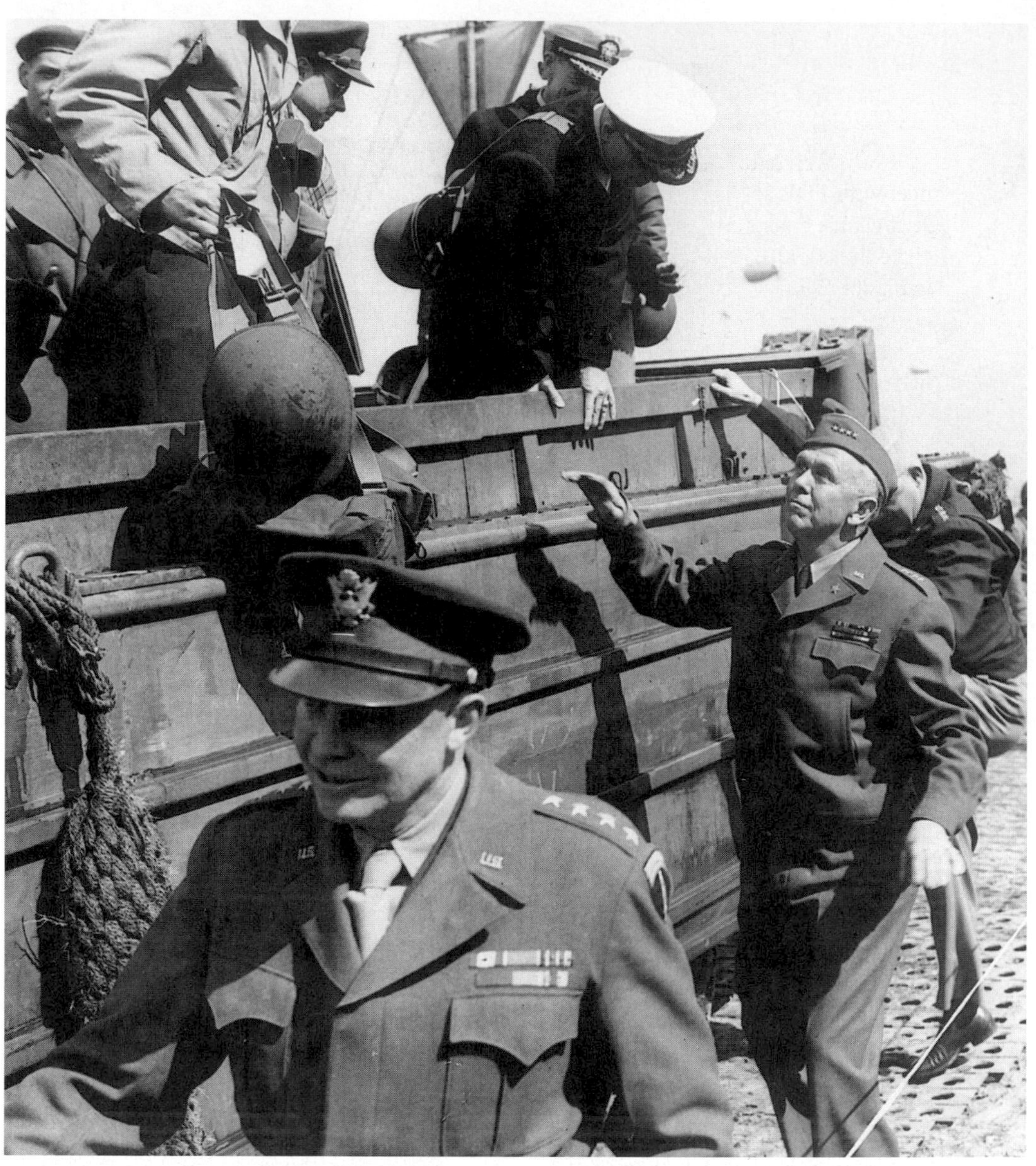

15 Supreme Allied Commander General Dwight Eisenhower and U.S. Army Chief of Staff General George Marshall *(behind)*, inspecting the battlefront in France after D-Day 1944. Within two months after D-Day, sixteen thousand American soldiers had been killed. Ike wrote his wife Mamie, "God, I hate the Germans." He told Morgenthau that Germans "must not be allowed to escape a sense of guilt, of complicity in the tragedy that has engulfed the world. . . .The only way to do that is to be good and hard on them."

Marshall, in contrast, told Morgenthau that "the American soldier" did not want the Germans treated harshly. He recalled that after World War I, despite anti-fraternization orders, U.S. troops "would go in the back door and sit down with German families and enjoy themselves."

16

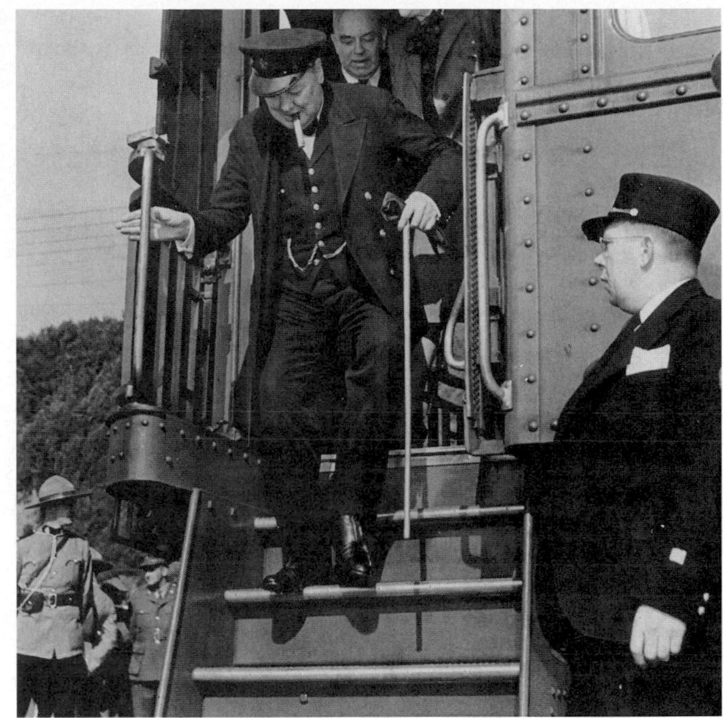

September 1944: Churchill arrives to meet with FDR at Quebec. He boasts to the President that since D-Day "everything we have touched has turned to gold."

Churchill and FDR meet reporters in Quebec. (Canadian Prime Minister Mackenzie King is at right.) In private, FDR lobbied Churchill to endorse the key points of Morgenthau's plan to punish Germany. Churchill refused, insisting that he would not chain himself to "a dead German." But when Roosevelt threatened to cut postwar financial aid that Britain desperately needed, Churchill quickly pronounced himself "converted." 17

In October 1944, Joseph Goebbels, Hitler's propaganda chief, denounced Morgenthau's blueprint as a "Jewish murder plan" to "exterminate forty-three million Germans." Goebbels told Germans that to prevent the Allies from imposing the Morgenthau Plan, "every house" in Germany "should resemble a fortress."

18

November 1944: Republican Presidential candidate Thomas Dewey charges that the Morgenthau Plan has aided Hitler as much as "ten fresh German divisions." Dewey complains that the "blood of our fighting men" is being shed for "Roosevelt's improvised meddling."

19

November 1944: Just before FDR wins a fourth term, he and Morgenthau make their traditional pre-election motorcade tour of the Hudson Valley. Shunned by Roosevelt during the furor over the Morgenthau Plan, the Treasury Secretary was anxious about his place in the presidential circle.

Armistice Day, November 1944: FDR at the Tomb of the Unknown Soldier. With the European war almost won, the President was eager to avoid the mistakes made by President Woodrow Wilson at Versailles in 1919, which, he believed, led to Adolf Hitler and World War II. Roosevelt is accompanied by *(left to right)* Secretary of the Navy James Forrestal, Secretary of War Henry Stimson, appointments secretary General Edwin "Pa" Watson and Admiral Wilson Brown.

22 Yalta, January–February 1945: Visibly failing from cardiovascular disease, FDR told Stalin that seeing the destruction in the Soviet Union has made him even "more bloodthirsty" against the Germans. In private, Roosevelt and Stalin agree to dismember postwar Germany. "But you don't want to tell them!" exclaimed Churchill. "That will make the Germans fight all the harder."

23

Edward Stettinius, Roosevelt's hapless final Secretary of State. In March 1945, after Yalta, Stettinius's insubordinate aides tricked him into getting the President to sign a document overturning FDR's own plans to be tough on postwar Germany. When Roosevelt discovered what had happened, he complained that he had been "sold" a "bill of goods." FDR's daughter Anna told intimates that her father's "increasing incapacity" frightened her.

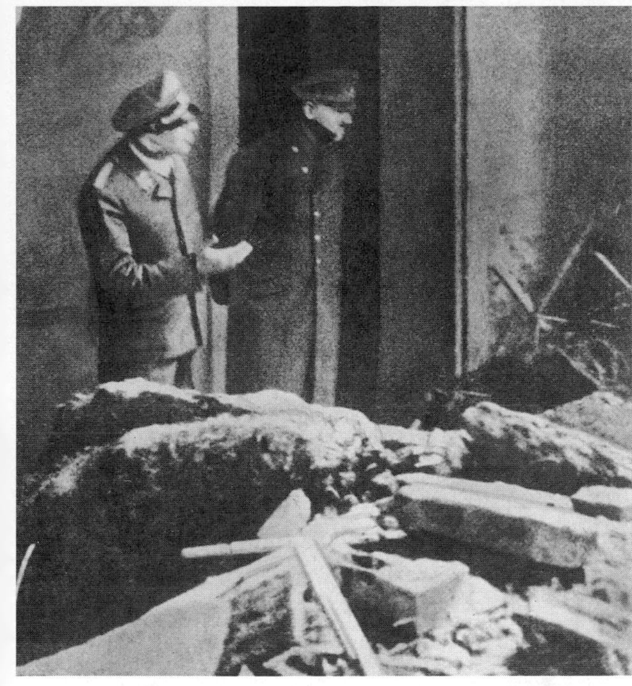

24

A broken Hitler in his ruined chancellery under Allied bombing, April 1945. Later, when President Truman learned that Hitler had killed himself, he was surprised. Truman had expected “many high German officers” to commit suicide, but Hitler, “in his fanaticism,” to “resist to the very end.”

British soldiers cheer Hitler’s demise. According to newly opened Soviet documents,
after Hitler shot himself, the Soviets secretly had the Führer’s jawbones and teeth
flown to Moscow for identification. Nevertheless Stalin speculated to his allies that
Hitler had escaped from Berlin. He may have felt that the specter of a live Hitler
25 might keep the Anglo-Americans from going soft on Germany.

26

Liberation of the Buchenwald death camp, April 1945: "You are free! You are free!" Secretary of the Interior Harold Ickes wanted the "simply horrifying" pictures of the camps to be widely publicized so that American public opinion would "really assert itself" against the Germans. Secretary of War Henry Stimson icily continued to refer to the German "so-called atrocities."

27

28

July 1945: President Harry Truman and Secretary of State James Byrnes aboard the *Augusta,* sailing to Europe to meet Stalin and Churchill at Potsdam, in vanquished Germany. By now Truman had scrapped the Morgenthau Plan and fired Morgenthau. Truman had assured Henry Stimson that neither Morgenthau nor "any of the Jew boys" would be going to Potsdam.

At Potsdam, Stalin, Truman and Churchill divided Germany into occupation zones that foreshadowed the postwar division of Europe and forty-five years of Cold War. While visiting Hitler's bombed-out chancellery, Truman said that he wasn't sure the Germans had "learned anything" from the Nazis' miserable end. Yet the sight of defeated Germans marching along a highway reminded him of his homeless Confederate grandmother and her family after the Civil War. 29

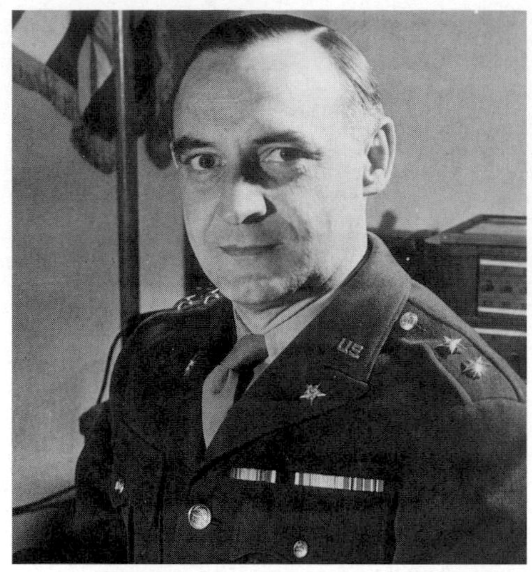

General Lucius Clay, Harry Truman's viceroy in postwar Germany. His difficult task was to punish the Nazis while attracting the Germans to American-style democracy. In July 1945, Clay warned Washington that the conquered Germans were showing no "feeling of war guilt or repugnance for Nazi doctrine." He found that the Germans "blame [the] Nazis for losing the war, protest ignorance of the regime's crimes and shrug off their own support or silence as incidental and unavoidable."

30

July 1945: In Berlin, Truman watches the American flag being raised over Hitler's old capital. Flanking him *(left to right)* are Generals Dwight Eisenhower and George Patton, Secretary of War Henry Stimson and General Omar Bradley. The President tells the crowd of U.S. soldiers, "We are not fighting for conquest. There is not one piece of territory or one thing of a monetary nature that we want out of this war." The President wrote his wife, "This is a hell of a place—ruined, dirty, smelly, forlorn people, bedraggled hangdog look about them. You
31 never saw as completely ruined a city."

• • •

Back at the White House on Wednesday morning, September 27, Roosevelt called Stimson to ask who was responsible for making the Morgenthau Plan public.

Stimson blamed the Treasury Secretary, noting that Drew Pearson's column had "violently criticized both Hull and me" and "played up Morgenthau."

Having read Stimson's protest letter, Roosevelt distanced himself from what he had done in Quebec. He didn't "really intend to make Germany a purely agricultural country," he told Stimson. His "underlying motive" was "very confidential"—England was broke: "Something must be done to give her more business to pull out of the depression after the war."

Relieved, Stimson felt that Roosevelt now realized "he had made a false step and was trying to work out of it."

Indignant at Stimson's opposition, Morgenthau fought back. On Wednesday afternoon, he told Harry Dexter White, "I want you to put some of your boys to work to study Stimson's record on German reparations when Stimson was Secretary of State."[4] He noted that in 1931, while serving President Herbert Hoover, Stimson had called on Mussolini, who gave him a speedboat ride.

Morgenthau clearly hoped to jaundice Roosevelt against Stimson by reminding him of Stimson's service to Hoover, who, as he well knew, was one of Roosevelt's pet hates. He said, "This is where Mr. Stimson stood with Herbert Hoover in 1932 or 1933 . . . and the man hasn't changed since. . . . Sure, this is why Stimson is against this."

On Thursday, September 28, over lunch at the Treasury, General George Marshall warned Morgenthau that publicity about his plan was increasing German resistance: "We have got loudspeakers on the German lines telling them to surrender and this doesn't help one bit."

4. In 1930, in a vain effort to improve the deepening world financial crisis, Stimson had persuaded Hoover to propose a moratorium on both German reparations and repayment of the European debt held by the United States. Morgenthau presumably thought that this record could be exploited to depict Stimson as soft on Germany.

"Well, General, you don't think this has come out of the Treasury? It must come either from War or State." Marshall drew himself up and defended his boss: "You're not talking about my Secretary of War, are you?"

Morgenthau told Marshall that "the Germans were almost successful in the First World War . . . even more successful in the Second, and might win in the third. You, as a soldier, know that as soon as this is over, the German General Staff will immediately plan another war."

Marshall replied, "You will find that the American soldier doesn't want the German treated harshly." He recalled that after World War I, despite the strict orders of General Pershing, commander of American forces in Europe, "American soldiers would go in the back door and sit down with German families and enjoy themselves." One of his own worst headaches since entering Germany had been photographs of American troops "fraternizing with the Germans."[5]

Later, McCloy complained to Morgenthau about the fracas over his plan: "There has been a hell of a hubbub and a very deplorable one."

"And I have had to take it on the chin!" Morgenthau replied. He said he wished America would adopt the British penalty of two years in prison for revealing classified information in the newspapers.

JOSEPH GOEBBELS WAS WORKING overtime to exploit the frenzy. The *Völkischer Beobachter* brayed, "ROOSEVELT AND CHURCHILL AGREE TO JEWISH MURDER PLAN!"

German radio announced that Roosevelt's "bosom" friend Henry Morgenthau, "spokesman of world Judaism," was singing "the same tune as the Jews in the Kremlin"—dismember Germany, destroy its industry and "exterminate forty-three million Germans." At that moment, Americans were fighting against surprisingly fierce German resistance to seize their first major German city—Aachen, near the Belgian-Dutch border, once the home of Charlemagne. Goebbels warned Aachen's citizens that to avoid the fate of the Morgenthau Plan, "every house in Aachen should resemble a fortress."

The *Washington Post* complained that the "senseless" Morgenthau Plan

5. That week, Harriman's embassy in Moscow warned Hull that the Soviet press was seizing such evidence of fraternization to claim that the Anglo-Americans "do not intend to adopt a severe policy against Germany."

would implant a "festering sore" at the "heart of Europe," leaving "a chaos which would assuredly end in war." If Germans suspected that "nothing but complete destruction lies ahead, then they will fight on. Let's stop helping Dr. Goebbels."

A naval officer replied by letter that "twice in my lifetime," he had had to "halt the bestial blood-letting of the Huns. In the name of God and decency, of little children brutally starved and slain, helpless women burned in Gestapo furnaces, isn't it time we stopped it once and for all?"

Leaders of the anti-Semitic American Right proclaimed that the Morgenthau Plan confirmed their direst alarms. One was Father Charles Coughlin, the once-popular Roman Catholic radio priest, who had railed against the Jews through the 1930s, before his church had ordered him silenced. Coughlin privately grumbled that Morgenthau wanted to "emasculate the German men."[6] He later insisted that Morgenthau's sterilization plans "didn't get out in public" but "got to me." Coughlin claimed that a disgusted Roosevelt had upbraided Morgenthau, saying, "You S.O.B., how inhuman can you become?"

Coughlin would have been startled to discover that the private jokes in Washington about "castrating" the Germans had been made not by Morgenthau but by the President and Ickes.

On Friday morning, September 29, Arthur Krock reported in the *New York Times* that Roosevelt was about to perform an "about-face" on the Morgenthau Plan. He wrote that "high administration sources" were "passing out word" that Roosevelt "does not favor" the Plan and "never really" did. Goebbels was making "obvious use" of the Morgenthau Plan, asking "why Germans should not die to the last man" to "resist" such an Allied conquest.

Morgenthau was certain that Hull or one of his people at State had leaked the story to Krock. It was only 8:15 A.M., but he called Roosevelt's appointments secretary, Pa Watson, and asked for a "very urgent" meeting with

6. Coughlin had a special hatred for Morgenthau. In 1934, after Coughlin had shrieked to his large radio audience against Jewish traffickers in silver, the Treasury Secretary humiliated him by issuing a list of the largest silver owners in the United States. To Coughlin's horror, it included the name of his personal secretary, who, by investing the ample cash that Coughlin took in from his listeners, had become the largest silver investor in Michigan. Coughlin publicly declared that Morgenthau's "investigation smells to high heaven."

Roosevelt: "Please give the President my message. I want to see him." Roosevelt refused to receive him.

With two sons on active duty, Morgenthau was tortured by Krock's charge that his plan was increasing German resistance. An hour after calling Watson, he told his aides, "Am I going to sit in the Cabinet, knowing that the American people and the soldiers are being sold down the river on the entrance to Germany?" Emotionally Morgenthau insisted that he had "a right" to give the President, at his "request," written advice on Germany: "It doesn't aid and comfort the enemy until the time it is made public. It is the person who made it public who is responsible!"

"I think you have to take whatever rap is coming during the next month," replied Harry Dexter White. "The President will do whatever he thinks is of interest to him politically. After the election, it will be a different story."

Morgenthau said that if he could prepare "a nice one-page memorandum showing him how nice a job has been done on him," Roosevelt might get "very angry" at Hull and Stimson, and "not do what Krock prophesies." He said a more "severe" option was for the President to convene the Cabinet Committee and use Morgenthau as a "whipping boy" to "stop this thing from leaking any further. . . . Maybe the President thinks it came from the Treasury. . . . This isn't the first time that I have been the whipping boy for the President. . . . I can take it."

Morgenthau's press aide, Herbert Gaston, speculated that Hull and Stimson had changed Roosevelt's mind about the Plan: "Even an agreement at Quebec isn't finally binding. They are working here and abroad to upset it."

Morgenthau replied that Roosevelt had shown him no sign that he had reversed himself "one iota."

UNBEKNOWNST TO MORGENTHAU, Hull spoke that morning "in profound confidence" to Krock about Morgenthau's "mad German plan." He claimed that he hadn't realized Morgenthau would be in Quebec until he read it in the newspapers. He could not understand why Roosevelt had allowed Morgenthau to do such "damage."

Hull said he often talked the President out of "some folly," but Roosevelt always kept "someone" between them. Hull was sick and tired. He confided to Krock that after the November election, he would quit his job.

• • •

THE PUBLIC FUROR was giving Morgenthau fierce new migraine headaches. Seizing a humiliating last resort, he walked to the White House, took the elevator upstairs and camped out beside the closed door of the President's office in the family quarters. He had no appointment. He was intent on seeing his friend.

Anna Roosevelt Boettiger was acting as her father's guard. Years later Eleanor Roosevelt recalled that increasingly during the war even she had had to go through Anna to see her husband. Her friend Edna Gurewitsch wrote that Eleanor "said no more about it, but one knew it had hurt her."

Morgenthau gave Anna a sheaf of positive clippings on his plan for Germany and asked her to make sure the President saw Krock's column. "Oh, the President knows all about that," Anna gruffly replied.

"Please take it in and show it to him," said Morgenthau. "I think he ought to get Hull, Stimson and me together in the same room and read the law to all of us and tell us to stop talking." He was worried that the press would find out about the Roosevelt-Churchill memorandum at Quebec. He told her that the public uproar was "bad politically" and "bad by the inference on the Jewish angle": "I will stay here outside the President's door in case he should want to see me."

Anna disappeared into the office. A few minutes later, she returned, took Morgenthau's arm like a pincer and pulled him away from her father's door. Despite Morgenthau's efforts to resist, she put him on the elevator, saying, "All I know is the President said he definitely doesn't want to see you."

Asked that day by the White House press corps about the "reported split" in the Cabinet, Roosevelt replied that "every story" had been "essentially untrue": "I might emphasize the word *essentially.*"

The President said he would ask Leo Crowley, now at the Foreign Economic Administration, to advise him on German postwar exports and trade—a clear suggestion that he was tabling the Morgenthau Plan. If German industry were to be destroyed, why would he be thinking about postwar German trade?

Roosevelt abolished his month-old Cabinet Committee on Germany and mollified Hull by privately asking him to "study and report" to him:

"No one wants to make Germany a wholly agricultural nation again, and yet somebody down the line has handed this out to the press. I wish we could catch and chastise him."

The President told Hull that he opposed "complete eradication" of German industry in the Ruhr and Saar, yet "I just cannot go along with the idea of seeing the British Empire collapse financially" while Germany rearmed "to make another war possible in twenty years." As for the Soviets, "we have no idea as yet what they have in mind, but we have to remember that in their occupied territory, they will do more or less what they wish."

ON TUESDAY, October 3, Stimson came to the White House family quarters for a long, conciliatory lunch with the President and his daughter, Anna. As he later told his diary, he was struck "for the first time" by Roosevelt's "fatigue and illness." Their table was set in the mansion because "the mere lunch with me was a violation of his doctor's orders that he should not waste strength at lunches in his office."

After the roller-coaster ordeal of the past month, Stimson found the President "very friendly." Stimson still felt "a very real friendship for him." So eager was Roosevelt to cement their relationship that he did not talk business until the end of the meal.

In preparation, Stimson had scribbled notes to himself on Germany: "Objective of punishment is *prevention* but not vengeance. . . . Reason why Jew is disqualified." Plunging a dagger into Morgenthau, Stimson icily told Roosevelt that if the Treasury Secretary had "seen fit" to discuss the *Handbook* directly with him and McCloy, "corrections could easily have been made" and "there would have been no hubbub."

As Stimson noted, Roosevelt "grinned and looked naughty." Shirking all responsibility, the President cried, "Henry Morgenthau pulled a boner!"

Stimson declared that throughout the war, Roosevelt's leadership had been on a "high moral plane." He must not poison it with "hatred or vengeance." He had "shuddered" when Morgenthau launched his "campaign against Germany, knowing how a man of his race would be misrepresented for so doing." Roosevelt and Anna emphatically agreed with him.

Lamenting the "unfortunate publicity," the President insisted that he had no desire to turn Germany into an agrarian state. He had merely wished to save some of the Ruhr's proceeds for Britain, which was "broke."

Wagging his finger, Stimson reminded the President of the memo he had initialed at Quebec.

"About this pastoral, agricultural Germany, that is just nonsense," said Roosevelt. "I have not approved of anything like that. I am sure I have not."

"Mr. President, please don't say that abroad until you have refreshed your memory with this paper, which I have here in my pocket." Stimson pulled out a copy of the Roosevelt-Churchill memorandum with the initials "O.K. F.D.R."

As Stimson later recalled, the President was "not a man to get flustered," but the Quebec document left him "perfectly staggered."

Roosevelt replied that he had no idea how he could have endorsed such language. Whether affected by his deepening illness or sheer deceitfulness, he told Stimson, "Henry, I have not the faintest recollection of this at all!"

CHAPTER FIFTEEN

"As Useful as Ten Fresh German Divisions"

On Thursday, October 5, 1944, Harry Dexter White went to the unproletarian marble beaux arts Soviet embassy on Sixteenth Street in Washington, once the mansion of Mrs. George Pullman, widow of the sleeping-car magnate. Over vodkas, the Soviet ambassador, Andrei Gromyko, asked White where he stood on Germany. White replied sardonically that all Gromyko had to do was read the *Washington Post.* "Where does Russia stand?"

Gromyko said, "I don't know anything official, but I would think that they stand very close or closer to what is spoken of as the Morgenthau Plan."

White asked Gromyko how his efforts to get American Lend-Lease aid were going. The ambassador said, "Fairly satisfactory." But he complained, "It is like pulling teeth to get what we need."

Back at the Treasury, White recounted the conversation for Morgenthau, who lightheartedly asked him "how many vodkas" he had drunk with Gromyko. "Just one!" said White. "He tried to push more on me, but I thought I had better take just one."

Morgenthau could not have imagined, but Gromyko certainly knew, that Harry Dexter White had a close secret relationship with Soviet intelligence.

White was born in 1892 in Boston to Russian Jewish immigrants, who later Anglicized the family name from "Weit." He added the English-sounding "Dexter" while in high school. When the United States declared war against Germany in 1917, he immediately enlisted in the Army and fought in France. At the age of thirty, by then married to Anne Terry, another child of immigrant Russian Jews, he enrolled in college, studying economics at Columbia and Stanford, and taught for five years at Harvard. Unable to win tenure, he took a job in 1932 at Lawrence College in Wisconsin.

"I think Harry was exposed to all sorts of prejudice as a Jew," recalled White's Treasury associate Edward Bernstein. "It was very hard to get a professorship in Harry's day if you were a Jew."

White told friends he was learning Russian in order to study the Soviet method of central planning. His ambition was to win a yearlong fellowship to study in the Soviet Union. But in 1934 he jumped at the chance to return east and work at the Treasury on monetary and banking legislation. By 1938 he had made his way into the "9:30 Group" of Morgenthau's senior aides. After Pearl Harbor, Morgenthau told them that White would be "in charge of foreign affairs for me. . . . I want it all in one brain, and I want it in Harry White's brain."

Blunt, sardonic, hardworking, rapaciously ambitious, White strode with blue eyes darting from side to side down the Treasury halls. The stocky, mustached White became Morgenthau's Director of Monetary Research and chief source of intellectual capital. Despite an increasing number of allies, he had few friends. McCloy considered him a "gadfly." Morgenthau's biographer John Morton Blum thought him a "son-of-a-bitch."

White said he had learned to flatter superiors from boyhood, selling crockery and hardware for the family business. White's constant praise appealed to a Treasury Secretary insecure about his own abilities.

In Dale Carnegie fashion, White concentrated his charm on the boss's chief assistant and doorkeeper, Henrietta Klotz. "Harry was very, very nice to me," she recalled. With her shrewd intelligence and lack of schooling, she was "hungry for an education." White took the time to teach her about the economic issues she heard about all day long but did not understand. Anne White taught Klotz about psychiatry, knowing that she needed help with her daughter Elinor, who had been born without irises. Soon, as Klotz recalled, she was "in Harry's house at least two or three times a week."

By 1944, White was closer to Morgenthau than ever. Along with the

British economist John Maynard Keynes, he was an architect of the postwar world economic order that would be centered around an International Monetary Fund and World Bank.

According to recently opened evidence, White was also secretly meeting with Soviet intelligence agents. On Monday, July 31, 1944, four days before he accompanied Morgenthau on his plane journey to Europe, White met with a Soviet agent whose code name was Kolstov.[1] As Kolstov reported to Moscow, White (code-named "LAWYER") briefed him on Morgenthau's forthcoming mission. He said he was "ready for any self-sacrifice" but warned that "compromise" would bring "political scandal," so he must "be very cautious."

According to the Kolstov cable, White arranged for another meeting after his return with Morgenthau from Europe in mid-August. But the anxious White wanted to meet more privately. As Kolstov reported, White proposed "infrequent conversations lasting up to half an hour while driving in his automobile."

Four years later, in August 1948, after he was accused by the famous American Communist defectors Elizabeth Bentley and Whittaker Chambers, White told the House Un-American Activities Committee (HUAC), "I am not now and never have been a Communist." He died five days later of a heart attack.

In November 1953, President Dwight Eisenhower's Attorney General, Herbert Brownell, announced that his review of the evidence showed that White had been "a Russian spy" who "smuggled secret documents to Russian agents for transmission to Moscow." (Brownell's evidence turned out years later to have been little more than a classified FBI summary of the Chambers-Bentley charges.)

Morgenthau, by then retired from public life, was tortured by charges that his close aide had abused his trust and duped him into making decisions that benefited the Soviet Union—denying large amounts of cash to the Nationalist foes of the Chinese Communists, altering the postwar economic system to favor Moscow, endorsing a large American loan to the Russians,

1. According to FBI documents newly unearthed by the historian Bruce Craig, Kolstov was probably Nikolai Chechulin, a member of the Soviet delegation working with the Americans on the postwar economic system.

granting them a duplicate set of American printing plates to issue their own German occupation currency.[2]

In January 1952, Morgenthau went to the FBI and asked one of J. Edgar Hoover's top assistants, D. M. Ladd, "what definite information" he had of White's disloyalty. He knew what "the Bentley bitch" had said, but wanted "more concrete evidence." When Ladd showed him the files, according to FBI documents, Morgenthau said he was "very upset" because there seemed "no question but that White was working for the Russians."

With horror Morgenthau wondered whether White had somehow manipulated him to launch what became the Morgenthau Plan—handing him the offending document on the noisy plane to Europe, badgering Eisenhower, Winant and Eden about postwar Germany, compiling the thick "black book" that Morgenthau handed to Roosevelt in the Cabinet Room, steeling Morgenthau for battle in Quebec with Churchill.[3]

Had White maneuvered him, on behalf of the Soviets, to help keep Germany from blocking their domination of postwar Europe? As Henry Morgenthau III recalled, for the rest of his life his father "was never able to resolve the question of White's Communist affiliations in his own mind." Since White was the chief spur to one of Franklin Roosevelt's chief advisers on postwar Germany, whether or not White was secretly acting on behalf of the Soviet Union is no small matter.

According to Whittaker Chambers's public testimony, White in 1937 described for him a proposal he was writing on reform of the Soviet monetary system. Later a copy was passed to Chambers, who gave it to a Soviet intelligence agent, Boris Bykov. By Chambers's account, White passed him four pages of handwritten notes on confidential Treasury matters (later one of the crown jewels of Chambers's infamous "Pumpkin Papers," named for the three rolls of microfilm he had hidden in a pumpkin

2. This decision stimulated inflation in postwar occupied Germany, forcing Americans to pay a quarter of a billion dollars to redeem the Soviet-printed marks. Although it emerged from intense debate, the decision may have seemed more heinous in retrospect than at the time.

3. In fact, White had actually questioned some of the more draconian measures of Morgenthau's plan, such as closing down the Ruhr to force out millions of Germans. (See page 104.)

on his Maryland farm), as well as other original documents and information.[4]

Chambers told the FBI that White would usually pick him up at a movie theater on Connecticut Avenue and drive around, while White told him what he had seen and heard. Chambers recalled that White talked "endlessly" about Morgenthau: "If White's spirits were up, I knew that the Secretary was smiling. If he was depressed, I knew that the Secretary had had a bad day."

In 1939, after bolting the Communist party himself, Chambers gave Assistant Secretary of State Adolf Berle a list of Communists, spies and sympathizers. He later said he did not mention White because White had pledged to stop collaborating with the Russians.[5] Chambers told the FBI in March 1945 that White was a Party "member-at-large" who, though "rather timid," had brought other Communists to the Treasury.[6] That November, Elizabeth Bentley gave the FBI a list of officials passing sensitive documents to the Soviets, including White.

Bentley later testified that "on our instructions," White pressed Morgenthau "hard" to sponsor the plan on postwar Germany, adding that "every time Morgenthau got a little weak," White "pushed him."[7] She charged that White put new Soviet "contacts" into "sensitive positions" at the Treasury.

Starting in 1995, the U.S. government released thousands of messages between Moscow and Soviet agents in America during the 1940s that had been intercepted and decrypted by the Army Signal Intelligence Service[8] under the code name "VENONA." Sixteen declassified cables mentioning White (also code-named "JURIST" or "RICHARD") revealed that he personally met once with Kolstov and at least twice with Soviet intelligence officials in late 1944 and early 1945. A November 1944 message said that White would take an "offer of assistance favorably." White was reported to be

4. Still Chambers told a grand jury in 1949, "I don't think White ever personally gave me material." To the historian Bruce Craig, Chambers's comment demonstrates the "inherent difficulty" of reconciling his various testimonies. Craig notes that White's Treasury files reveal no evidence of such a document, arguing that the Soviets were unlikely in the 1930s to have solicited advice from an American official on reforming their economy.

5. Isaac Don Levine, who accompanied Chambers to the meeting, later insisted that Chambers did mention White.

6. Chambers could not prove that White knew they were Soviet agents.

7. As dramatic as Bentley's claim sounded at the time, we now know, as described in this book, that the Soviets were ambivalent about Morgenthau's plan and his approach to postwar Germany.

8. A forerunner of today's National Security Agency.

inclined to refuse "a regular payment" but "might accept gifts as a mark of our gratitude." Strapped on his nine-thousand-dollar-a-year government salary, he had to pay for his daughter's college education. There is no evidence that White asked the Soviets for money, or that he received any.

One cable reported that White's "data" showed Vice President Henry Wallace in support of giving the Soviets a five-billion-dollar loan.[9] Another showed White tipping off the Russians that if they held out, they could win a more generous loan than the Americans were currently offering. He chatted about the postwar German economy, the chances that Roosevelt (code-named "KAPITAN") would get a fourth term and other issues. The cables demonstrate that some of White's associates in Treasury were indeed Soviet agents, including Nathan Gregory Silvermaster, Ludwig Ullman, Harold Glasser and George Silverman, White's close friend since Stanford.[10]

In 1999 the American historian Allen Weinstein and an ex-Soviet intelligence agent named Alexander Vassiliev published *The Haunted Wood,* based on Soviet intelligence files shown to Vassiliev in exchange for a fee paid by the book's publisher, Random House. The Weinstein-Vassiliev research suggests that White was terrified of public exposure. In a 1942 cable cited by the two authors, one Soviet intelligence officer, Vassily Zarubin, described him as "very nervous and cowardly." In a 1945 message that probably shed important light on White's ambitions, Silvermaster complained that White would not "pass information or documents" because he more grandly envisioned his role as giving the Soviets "advice on major political and economic matters."

9. White's defender James Boughton of the International Monetary Fund dismisses this cable as apparently a "secondhand account" on the grounds that White "would not have been privy to a conversation between the Vice President and the Secretary of State." But in fact White knew Wallace well, collaborating with him to organize support for his controversial nomination as Commerce Secretary in 1945. Morgenthau wrote his sons that White had organized "a meeting at our house" to see "what could be done for Wallace." Wallace later said that, if elected President in 1948, he would appoint White his Treasury Secretary. Hull also knew White well, finding him a "very high class fellow."

10. Chambers testified that, in 1936, Bykov wanted to pay several Americans to spy for the Soviets, saying, "Who pays is boss, and who takes money must also give something." Chambers advised him that it would be counterproductive because they were Communists in principle. Instead, according to Chambers, Bykov gave him cash that he used to buy four costly Oriental rugs, two of which Chambers gave to Silverman, who had introduced him to White. (Chambers testified, "On the four rugs we marched straight into active espionage.") Silverman testified that he gave one of the rugs to White but as a thank-you gift for allowing him to live in his house without rent, and that White did not know it came from Chambers or Bykov. During the HUAC hearings, White was questioned about his frequent visits to Silvermaster's house, where Silvermaster's tenant Ullman maintained a basement darkroom allegedly used to photograph documents for the Soviets. White told the FBI in 1947 that Silvermaster, Ullman and Silverman were his "close" friends.

According to Weinstein and Vassiliev, Silvermaster more dubiously claimed that before Morgenthau (code-named "NABOB") was Treasury Secretary, he had an affair with Mrs. Klotz ("MORA"), who bore him a daughter. Silvermaster insisted that Klotz was eager to help him get promoted, but that White refused, shouting at him that an FBI check would jeopardize both himself and Morgenthau.

White's defenders have correctly noted that meeting with Soviet officials was an important part of White's wartime job. As James Boughton has written, Roosevelt had told his people "to treat the Soviets exactly like any other ally, and White did so with full conviction." White required no Soviet manipulation to believe that American-Soviet collaboration was the key to the postwar future. Still, while the United States and Soviet Union were wartime allies, their interests did not always converge.

In his instigation and support of the key elements of the Morgenthau Plan, we may never know whether White was chiefly moved by his own economic-political philosophy, Soviet bribes or other forms of pressure, a higher allegiance to the Soviet Union or an arrogant certainty that he knew best how to handle America's trusted Soviet ally. The hidden motivation of so opaque an operator as White is difficult to prove.[11]

But had KAPITAN and NABOB known in the fall of 1944 what we know now about White's covert relationship with Soviet intelligence, they certainly would have fired him. Had White's Soviet connections then been publicly revealed, an ensuing scandal could have undermined Roosevelt, Morgenthau and the effort to win both the war and the peace. It might have put Thomas Dewey in the White House. Thenceforth any American effort to be tough on Germany might have had a fatal pro-Soviet taint.

But in ignorance of White's secret life, Morgenthau asked Roosevelt that fall to elevate him to Assistant Secretary of the Treasury.[12] The President said he thought White had "earned it" and that the new title would help since "so much of his work is with the foreign governments."

Roosevelt asked Morgenthau to "please clear" the nomination with the

11. For example, if White endorsed internationalization of the Ruhr, did he do that in order to give the Soviets, who would almost certainly have been a trustee, a spearhead into Western Europe?

12. Morgenthau may have delayed White's promotion through the war in order to avoid giving too many visible Treasury positions to Jews. White's new title was a recognition of his de facto role at the Treasury, his work to found postwar international economic institutions and his need for a title that would help him persuade Congress to ratify them.

Democratic chairman, Robert Hannegan, who predictably wanted to give the job to a political "fat cat."[13] But Morgenthau prevailed after warning Roosevelt that if he didn't approve White's promotion, "about half of my best people would leave."

SINCE STALIN HAD NOT COME TO QUEBEC, Churchill flew to see him in Moscow in October 1944. Playing to his audience, he said that "for about a month or so" in public, he had been "shy about breathing fire and slaughter" in Germany "because it would make the Germans fight harder." But in private, he was "all for hard terms." The "best thing" would be to "beat the Germans into unconditional surrender, and then tell them what to do."

Stalin replied that if they did not use "hard measures," Germany would start a new world war every twenty-five or thirty years. Thus the "harshest measures" could prove "the most humane." Germany must be partitioned, its heavy industry destroyed.

Foreign Minister Molotov asked Churchill what he thought of the Morgenthau Plan. The Prime Minister reported that Roosevelt was "not very happy about its reception." He added that the British people would never allow the mass execution of Germans. But it was "necessary to kill as many as possible in the field." After the war, the Hitler Youth must be taught that it was "more difficult to build than to destroy."

Stalin warned that to do the job correctly, the Allies would have to occupy Germany for many years. Churchill said that the Americans were not likely to stay in Europe very long.

Some Soviet officials were privately imagining the possibility of a postwar Anglo-Soviet entente, including a more distant relationship with the United States. According to Soviet documents opened in the 1990s, Maxim Litvinov, former ambassador to Washington, advised Molotov that autumn that the contradictions of capitalism would cause the British and Americans to fall out over competition for markets and geographical influence. After the Americans departed Europe, the Soviets and the British should divide the continent: "Our maximum sphere of security should include

13. Morgenthau was told that Hannegan's objection was that White had not worked in the 1944 Roosevelt campaign. "How could he," asked Morgenthau, "being a civil service employee?" One wonders what both men might have said had they learned what party White may have been really supporting!

Finland, Sweden, Poland, Hungary, Czechoslovakia, Romania, the Slavic countries of the Balkans, as well as Turkey. The British sphere should undoubtedly include Holland, Belgium, France, Spain, Portugal and Greece." Germany should join Austria, Norway, Denmark and Italy in a "neutral zone."[14]

Before Churchill departed Moscow, he and Stalin returned to the subject of Germany. Churchill said he wished to "put the Ruhr and Saar permanently out of action." After the war, Russia and other victims of Hitler could take away as much German machinery as they needed. This was the policy of Morgenthau, whose "hatred of the Germans" was "indescribable." As for Britain, it was "only justice" for his country to inherit Germany's old markets.

Stalin pledged to support "any steps" Britain took to be compensated "for the losses it has suffered."

Churchill insisted that the German metals, chemical, electrical and other industries that made war be closed "for a generation at least." Prussia, the military "taproot" of the German "arch-evil," should be amputated from Germany. The industrial region along the Rhine should go "under international control."

Stalin agreed.[15] Churchill marveled that they had so few differences: It was a "pity" that when "God created the world," the two of them were not consulted. Stalin liked the joke. "It was God's first mistake!" he replied.

MORGENTHAU WAS SUFFERING under the whip of public criticism. During a telephone talk with Stettinius, he was so combative that he later called back to apologize: "This terrific drive on me has sort of got under my skin and I'm kind of snappish about it." Later he told Stettinius he was being "unfairly treated." He charged that the State and War Departments were waging a "coordinated attack" against him that was "unfair and anti-Semitic."

Roosevelt sent Morgenthau a report from the OSS chief William Donovan saying that a majority of prewar Europe's farm machinery had been pro-

14. In a later paper, in January 1945, Litvinov moved Norway to the Soviet orbit and gave Sweden, Denmark and Italy to Britain, adding that these countries and Turkey and Yugoslavia should be left to "bargaining and compromise."

15. He also insisted that the Kiel Canal be internationalized.

duced by Germany. The tacit message: Shutting down German industry might force all Europeans to starve. Morgenthau scrawled back, "I would like to say in the words of your son Johnny, 'So what?' "

As Morgenthau wrote in his diary, that same month Stimson handed him "an olive branch, which I accepted with pleasure." He approved the War Secretary's request to make a deposit "in a secret account, the purpose of which will not be known to anyone in the Treasury or elsewhere." The secret purpose was development of an atomic bomb.

As THE FALL OF 1944 WORE ON, predictions of a quick German surrender were evaporating. Only on October 22, after Germans fought with desperate brutality, did American troops raise the Stars and Stripes over Aachen, their first major conquest on German soil.

Morgenthau had tried his hand at the proclamation by General Eisenhower to be posted in English and German as his troops scrambled across the border. His version was to begin, "We come as militant victors to ensure that Germany shall never again drench the world with blood. The German people must never again become the carriers of death, horror and wanton destruction to civilization."

McCloy told Morgenthau, "I don't like the 'death and destruction and drenching with blood' business myself." The language was "a bit lurid" and "out of keeping" with Eisenhower's approach. Morgenthau said that his draft may be "theatrical" but in his speeches "I have talked about dripping of blood and bodies hanging on trees, and the people eat it up. My God, I don't know why we should be pussyfooted!"

McCloy prevailed. In the end, Eisenhower's Proclamation Number One "to the people of Germany" began, "The Allied forces serving under my command have now entered Germany. We come as conquerors, but not as oppressors. In the area of Germany occupied by the forces under my command, we shall obliterate Naziism and German militarism."

Roosevelt lamented to Hull that the Anglo-American advance into Germany was going more slowly than they had expected: "I dislike making detailed plans for a country we do not yet occupy." He wrote to him, "I cannot agree at this moment as to what kind of a Germany we want in every detail," and sent a copy of his memo to Stimson and McCloy, pointedly excluding Morgenthau. When the Treasury Secretary asked to see it, McCloy brusquely told him that he lacked "the right to show it to him."

McCloy privately chortled that Roosevelt was taking "a very much chastened approach" to Germany. The President told Ambassador Winant that he had "made a mistake" to bring Morgenthau to Quebec.

STIMSON NOTED IN HIS DIARY in October 1944 that Roosevelt's campaign against Thomas Dewey was "getting hot and uncertain." The British ambassador cabled Eden that Dewey might win "unless the President seizes the initiative."

On Wednesday, October 18, for the first time, Dewey exploited the Morgenthau Plan as a campaign weapon. In a speech at the Waldorf-Astoria in New York, broadcast on radio, Dewey recalled that when Roosevelt went to Quebec, he took not his Secretary of State or War but Morgenthau, "whose qualifications as an expert on military and international affairs are still a closely guarded military secret." The result? "A first-class Cabinet crisis." Dewey complained that Joseph Goebbels had used the Morgenthau Plan "to terrify the Germans into fanatical resistance": "Now they are fighting with the frenzy of despair."

Worried that Dewey's charges would inflict real damage, Roosevelt had Stephen Early, his press secretary, ask Stimson to issue a rebuttal.[16] But Stimson thought it would be "ridiculous and undignified" for him to respond to "a campaign attack." The White House should not make any comment, "simply stating correct facts, with no reference to the Dewey speech."[17]

Roosevelt could scarcely object. But Harold Ickes told his diary that he couldn't see why Stimson should "hesitate" to support the administration "of which he is such an important part." After all, "one can't expect an immaculate conception in politics."

16. The statement would say that "basic plans" for U.S. occupation of Germany had been "unanimously agreed upon" months ago. The Allies did not want the "destruction or enslavement of the German people," but to ensure that the Germans "will not have the will, power and capacity to make war again."

17. Finally the State Department issued a rebuttal.

Harry Hopkins told McCloy that while Roosevelt "would not think" of enmeshing Stimson in partisan politics, perhaps McCloy could make a speech. McCloy declined.[18]

Stimson wanted to do something for Roosevelt. He felt it would be "inconsiderate and unfair" not to "back him up." So he went as far as he could by sitting on the dais during a Roosevelt campaign speech to the Foreign Policy Association in New York, where the President lauded him as a "great Secretary of War" who had "rendered magnificent services."[19]

MORGENTHAU WAS TERRIFIED that publicity about the Morgenthau Plan might provoke the Germans to "capture" and be "extremely cruel" to his son Henry III. He asked his friend and private lawyer, Edward Greenbaum, whether Henry might be given a false identity and dog tags.

McCloy told Greenbaum that the Germans were "constantly" equipping their spies with false identification. If the Germans caught Henry III with counterfeit dog tags, the U.S. Army would have to "completely disown" him. Greenbaum advised Morgenthau instead to ask Eisenhower's aide Bedell Smith to have SHAEF "pull Henry out of his outfit and send him to a quiet sector."

"Henry would never forgive me," replied Morgenthau. "I do not want to have the boy touched."

ROOSEVELT WAS TAUNTED about the Morgenthau Plan by both foe and friend. In the Oval Office on Thursday morning, October 26, Joseph Kennedy demanded to know why the President had let Morgenthau go to Quebec. It was "sheer madness," the meddling of a "proved incompetent."

Roosevelt confessed that the Morgenthau Plan had caused him a great deal of worry.

Kennedy disliked Morgenthau in part because he had the one job in the

18. He told his diary, "One of the great strengths of the Administration is that it was willing to take on Mr. Stimson, a Republican, and to give him and the Generals the management of the war. . . . Any effort to bring the War Department into the political picture at this time would detract from that position."

19. Covering the speech, *Time* violated the informal agreement that kept the press from reporting on Roosevelt's infirmity by informing readers that the President had been "wheeled in" to his place at the head table.

Roosevelt administration that Kennedy had wanted. Instead, Kennedy had had a tumultuous run as Roosevelt's isolationist ambassador in London before the two men fell out and Kennedy resigned after the 1940 election.

Roosevelt's campaign handlers hoped that the President could attract Northeastern Catholics and prewar isolationists by wangling Kennedy's endorsement in 1944. But Kennedy was convinced that his old boss would entangle the nation in Europe's postwar problems. He was in agony over the death of his eldest and favored son, Joseph Jr., whose plane had exploded over the English Channel in August. When Truman stumped in Boston, Kennedy upbraided him: "Harry, what the hell are you doing campaigning for that crippled son of a bitch that killed my son Joe?"

With effrontery that the President seldom encountered, Kennedy now told Roosevelt that he could not abide "the crowd around you"—people like Sam Rosenman and Harry Hopkins: "They have surrounded you with Jews and Communists and alienated the Catholics. . . . They will write you down in history, if you don't get rid of them, as incompetent, and they will open the way for the Communist line."

Lunching afterward with Arthur Krock of the *New York Times,* Kennedy said that Roosevelt "looks sick" and should never have sought reelection. Now he understood how Morgenthau had pushed through his plan for postwar Germany: "That crowd can put anything over on him. He hasn't the mental energy to resist." He told Krock that he was voting for Dewey.

Of Morgenthau's plan, Kennedy later wrote his nineteen-year-old son Robert, "I don't think anybody really had an idea of what the plan was because it was never fully explained. Of course, it was never his plan—he wouldn't know enough to have a plan. It was conceived by a Jew named Bernstein, who is now Assistant Secretary of the Treasury." [20]

FOUR DAYS BEFORE THE ELECTION, on Friday, November 3, Arthur Krock reported in the *New York Times* that Roosevelt and Morgenthau had "bribed" Churchill to accept the Morgenthau Plan by promising generous Lend-Lease aid.

20. Kennedy was probably confusing the Treasury's Edward Bernstein, who had actually opposed the plan, with Colonel Bernard Bernstein of SHAEF, who had first brought the offending *Handbook* to Morgenthau's attention in England.

As he read the *Times* at Fishkill Farms, Morgenthau was apoplectic. Calling an aide, he noted that the Sulzbergers, who owned the paper, were old Morgenthau family friends: "How Arthur Sulzberger, who wants to see the President elected, could run a story like that!" he cried. "Today is Friday. Dewey can use it tonight or tomorrow."

Morgenthau doubted that the leak came from the Pentagon: McCloy would not "deliberately cut my throat." Pointing the finger at State, Morgenthau called Stettinius and said he was "mad." The Under Secretary of State replied, "Henry, I just can't believe that one of our boys has done any dirty work."

Morgenthau said he was "sick" of this kind of behavior. He said that the inference was "so dirty" and that it might damage the President.

A reporter friend warned Morgenthau the next day that Dewey was going to "skin" him "alive" that evening during his final campaign speech at Madison Square Garden in New York City. Dewey planned to speak on "the Morgenthau Plan and how it prolonged the war."

Deeply upset, Morgenthau tried to reach someone on the President's train but found that it had just pulled out. He left messages for Grace Tully and Sam Rosenman that after Dewey's speech, "either Stimson or General Marshall should deny it tonight." At 8:45 P.M., he called Stimson at Highhold on Long Island and pleaded with him to "do something."

But as Morgenthau recorded, Stimson "sounded overtired and resisted all suggestions I made." Stimson told him it was "ridiculous" for anyone to believe that publicity about his plan had lengthened the combat: "Our soldiers have not changed their fighting one bit. . . . They have been delayed due to lack of port facilities."

Morgenthau asked him, "Why can't you say something like this?" Stimson promised to think about it, but he wrote in his diary that this was "foolish." He was "entirely opposed to allowing the Army to enter last-day politics." He told McCloy that it wouldn't be "in either Morgenthau's or Roosevelt's interest" because "it would only accentuate the attack."

In that evening's oration, Dewey declared that the Morgenthau Plan was "so clumsy that Mr. Roosevelt himself finally dropped it. But the damage was done." The Republican candidate claimed that the plan had been as useful to Hitler "as ten fresh German divisions. It put fight back into the German army. It stiffened the will of the German nation to resist. Almost overnight the headlong retreat of the Germans stopped. They stood and fought fanatically." The "blood of our fighting men" was being shed for Roosevelt's "improvised meddling."

Listening on the radio, Stimson thought Dewey's charge so overheated that no reply was needed. He told his diary he felt "sorry for Morgenthau, for never has an indiscretion been so quickly and vigorously punished as his incursion into German and Army politics at Quebec."

The next morning McCloy told Morgenthau that if he or McCloy replied to Dewey, it would be a "last-minute bombshell" that would drag the War Department "into politics." The rebuttal must come from "somebody who has been campaigning."

Morgenthau asked who that might be. "Anybody," said McCloy. "But not Roosevelt or Truman."

Morgenthau said, "Well, I don't think that would carry much weight." He later told his press aide, Herbert Gaston, that the elderly Stimson had at least managed to "stay up and hear the broadcast last night, which is a phenomenon in itself."

ROOSEVELT HAD WOUND UP past campaigns with a "sentimental journey" up the Hudson, with Morgenthau riding beside him in an open car, just as they had driven around New York State together during the gubernatorial campaign of 1928. Despite the fracas over the Morgenthau Plan, on the day before the 1944 election, the Treasury Secretary was in his customary position in the left-hand backseat. But this year he and Roosevelt were surrounded by bulletproof glass. With the chill of late autumn, Morgenthau had arranged for a Poughkeepsie roadhouse to serve hot coffee and sandwiches to the motorcade riders.

On Election Night, Morgenthau and Elinor took their usual place among Roosevelt aides, relatives and neighbors to receive the election returns in the Big House. While guests waited in the long, dark-paneled library, Roosevelt sat with various aides in his mother's old dining room, computing returns.

At 3:16 A.M., as Hassett recorded, "the graceless Dewey" gave a concession speech but "sent no message to the victor." Retiring for the night, Roosevelt told his aide, "I still think he is a son-of-a-bitch." Hassett replied, "Back to his grandparents on both sides!"

Roosevelt had been reelected by 432 to 99 electoral votes, but his popular margin was the narrowest since Wilson's reelection in 1916. As Morgenthau's elder son recalled, his father "remained gloomily unsure of himself and uncertain as to where he stood with Roosevelt."

Back in Washington, Harold Ickes told Roosevelt's daughter, Anna, that thanks to Dewey's campaign charges, Morgenthau had become "a pretty heavy load to carry." Noting that "anti-Semitism is on the increase," he told her that "the less Henry has to do with the German settlement, the better."

But that was not what Morgenthau had in mind. He was planning to take his case to the American public by publishing a book on the Morgenthau Plan, "to be released on the day after Germany collapses."[21] Mrs. Klotz told him she would bet "two bucks" that Roosevelt would stop him: "If he says no, you put it out anyway."

Morgenthau agreed. He told his staff, "You people have to be prepared for a lot of things from me after the election."

21. Ickes had a similar idea. After learning that several Jewish groups were contemplating books on the German war against the Jews, he warned them that it might stir anti-Semitism. Instead, he thought of writing a book himself called *No Soft Peace,* detailing German crimes against Jews, Catholics, Protestants, Belgians, Hollanders and other peoples. In his diary, he wrote, "My idea would be to show as a matter of history that Germans always had a lust for conquest and that they probably always will have." But soon Ickes's fertile imagination turned elsewhere.

CHAPTER SIXTEEN

"Lord Give the President Strength"

WITH HIS FOURTH-TERM VICTORY IN PLACE, Roosevelt retrieved his old Hudson Valley companion from the outer darkness. On Wednesday, November 15, 1944, the President had Morgenthau to lunch upstairs at the White House.

Two days earlier, the old West Virginia liberal Harley Kilgore, chairman of the Senate Subcommittee on War Mobilization, had issued a report demanding that German industry be "so altered that it cannot again serve the purposes of war."[1] Morgenthau called Kilgore and said, "I thought you got out a swell report." Kilgore replied, "Your plan and mine fairly well coincide," adding, "You were badly misinterpreted."

Over luncheon with Morgenthau, the President called Kilgore's report "wonderful." Morgenthau felt that Roosevelt no longer cared "what the public thinks" and that the President's coolness toward his plan for Germany was "just lifting like a cloud." Roosevelt told Morgenthau that he had asked Hull and Stettinius for their recommendations on Germany. Morgenthau should read them and tell Roosevelt what he thought of them.

1. Like many liberals of the time, Kilgore, a former judge, was concerned about how international cartels "exploited" colonial peoples and bred "totalitarianism and war." He thought the Morgenthau Plan would help to solve the problem in Germany.

• • •

AT THAT MOMENT, although the public was told he was suffering from a "cold," Hull was being treated for advanced tuberculosis and diabetes in a VIP suite at Bethesda Naval Hospital. His wife, Frances, told a friend that the "Morgenthau episode" at Quebec had taken a toll on his health and morale. After years of Roosevelt's abuse, the "Morgenthau business was the final blow."[2] She had "made him promise to go to the hospital" and retire as Secretary of State. To avoid harming Roosevelt's reelection chances, Hull had deferred his resignation announcement until after the balloting.

Roosevelt announced in late November that Hull's successor would be Edward Stettinius. A former Morgan partner and U.S. Steel president, with his snowy mane and theatrically groomed eyebrows, Stettinius could have been Hollywood's idea of a Secretary of State, just as Warren Harding might have been its image of a President. One of his subordinates acidly recalled that Stettinius was "about as much Secretary of State as I was King of Spain." Since Stettinius was mainly a show captain, Roosevelt could remain his own Secretary of State, which was exactly what he wanted. He hoped that Stettinius had the clout with Republicans and Big Business that would persuade them to support his cherished dream of a postwar United Nations organization.

Morgenthau was disappointed. He recorded that Stettinius was "a lifelong Republican," and Roosevelt had clearly wanted a "good clerk" at State. Stimson complained that his new colleague was "pretty ignorant of international history." McCloy wickedly lampooned Stettinius's efforts to "make everyone feel happy in good Rotary Club fashion."

Harold Ickes wrote in his diary that Stettinius's appointment had driven him to "depression." Roosevelt's choice was "a douche of cold water to most of the intelligent people in the Administration." The new Secretary of State was "a backslapper. He likes everyone and is liked by everyone." Ickes spread a rumor that his archenemy Harry Hopkins had arranged the appointment because Stettinius had given Hopkins "money on the side."

Stettinius warned Morgenthau that his new memo to the President on

2. For his part, Roosevelt told Ickes that Hull had "wife trouble," noting that Mrs. Hull "nags him and is overanxious about him."

Germany "might not go far enough to satisfy you. And if it doesn't, why, we ought to thrash it out."

Morgenthau agreed to "thrash it out with you" before appealing to Roosevelt: "Is that fair enough?"

McCloy warned Stimson that with the election over, Morgenthau was back in business on Germany. Astonished, Stimson exclaimed, "He can't keep his hands out of it! And he is going to get into trouble again, if he doesn't look out."

McCloy responded to the news by thinking up silly ways to pastoralize Germany and repeating them with guffaws to his friends. He knew that Morgenthau had transcripts made of his conversations. During one meeting with the Treasury Secretary, he pulled out a tiny spy camera and jocularly said, "Since you've been recording everything without our permission, I thought you wouldn't mind if I did too!"

When Morgenthau and John Pehle of the War Refugee Board made a public statement against new German atrocities, Stimson told the Treasury Secretary that he should have been consulted in advance. Morgenthau apologized, but Stimson wrote in his diary that it was "just an example of how he likes to push into that kind of matter. He, as a Jew, is the last man who ought to do it."

Morgenthau advised his aides that while Stimson and McCloy "dislike us heartily," they would treat him with "a wholesome respect": "They just don't want to start anything with me."

Roosevelt told Stettinius he was "determined to be tough" with the Germans. But until Allied troops marched into Germany, "we have no way of knowing what we shall find." He said he knew the country well from his student days, but "would not want to rely on that as a basis of reliable judgment."

Stettinius wrote the President, "We can't make Germany so weak that it will be impossible for her to recover." Give the Germans a "rock-bottom standard of living." But only within a "liberal world economy" would there be a "stable, non-aggressive Germany." If the victorious Allies were "prepared to use force," they could prevent Germany from starting another world war. If not, "once-and-for-all economic destruction won't make much lasting difference."

Roosevelt replied, "We should let Germany come back industrially to meet her own needs, but not to export for some time until we know better how things are going to turn out."

This was a long way indeed from the Morgenthau Plan. After reading the exchange, the Treasury Secretary told Stettinius it had "set me back on my heels": "If they're going to let them manufacture and come back industrially, hell, they can make anything under that!" Stettinius mollified him by insisting that the President's position on Germany had not yet "jelled."

Morgenthau confided to his aides that he would treat Stettinius "as frankly and openly as I can—up to the time that he does something to me."

Since Roosevelt's complaint about the SHAEF *Handbook* on Germany, Stimson and McCloy had been working on a directive for Eisenhower. JCS 1067 had much of the sound of the Morgenthau Plan. Eisenhower should exert "such control" over German industry, farms and other facilities as necessary to stop war production, starvation and sabotage, but not to rehabilitate the economy. Germans must be "made to understand that all necessary steps will be taken to guarantee against a third attempt by them to conquer the world."

JCS 1067 also ordered that Germany "will not be occupied for the purpose of liberation, but as a defeated nation." The "principal Allied objective" would be "to prevent Germany from ever again becoming a threat to the peace of the world." The commander should "take no steps looking towards" Germany's economic revival. Responsibility for housing, transportation, reconstruction and other economic problems "will remain with the German people and the German authorities."

But McCloy had quietly inserted important loopholes. The U.S. commander in Germany could "impose such economic controls as he may deem essential to the safety and health of the occupying forces." His actions "must be of short-term and military character, in order not to prejudice whatever ultimate policies may be later determined upon." This meant there would be no large-scale immediate destruction of mines and factories. It also gave wide authority to the American commander, who would be overseen by Stimson, McCloy and their War Department.

Under JCS 1067, the commander would arrest Germans suspected of war crimes or who might endanger the occupation. Categories for arrest would include high officials, Nazi leaders down to the local level and Nazi party members and sympathizers in key posts in industry, finance, education, publishing and the press. Morgenthau insisted on a sentence saying that "in the absence of evidence to the contrary," any German government official must be presumed to be a Nazi or Nazi sympathizer. On war crimes, JCS 1067 softened the American position. It included nothing about summary executions and gave the commander considerable latitude.

For months, Morgenthau had been arguing that the governor of the American zone in Germany should be a civilian. But Stimson and McCloy persuaded Roosevelt that the American should come from the War Department, preferably the Army. Unlike the State Department, which thought that postwar Germany would best be governed by a central Allied machinery in Berlin, McCloy envisaged a commander who would be a viceroy in his zone. As the historian Carolyn Woods Eisenberg has written, by agreeing to tether the new governor so closely to the Pentagon and give him so much autonomy, Roosevelt was taking a step toward the possible postwar division of Germany.

THE AMERICANS HOPED to get the British to agree on a joint directive to govern both of their zones. But as McCloy found, the British military was terrified that "chaos in Germany" would bring "chaos in Europe." They thought JCS 1067 "too vague." In London, Lord Cherwell told Eden that he agreed with Morgenthau's complaint that the British were putting "administrative convenience" above "principle." But Eden told Churchill that the "attack" was "unfair and ill-informed": Morgenthau might wish "to let the Germans stew in their own juice," but "we want to set the Germans to work for us."

McCloy warned colleagues that the British believed mistakenly that "they are going into a country where there will be a government, and they are going to have control of that government." In contrast, the Americans wanted "no government but the military government." McCloy said that his own approach was "I am a jealous God and there are no other gods but me."[3]

Thankful for JCS 1067's militant language, Morgenthau chose to ignore how McCloy had used the directive to weaken his plan with his loopholes and by granting the commander such wide authority. To Morgenthau, McCloy's willingness to do battle with the British suggested that he must really be on the Treasury's side after all.[4]

3. "For I the Lord thy God am a jealous God. . . ." and "Thou shalt have no other gods before me" appear in Exodus.

4. A better window on McCloy's intentions was the less-noticed decree that he and Stimson sent in late October 1944 to the Civil Affairs Division of SHAEF, saying that the development of the German economy would depend on "an orderly process of trade."

• • •

ROOSEVELT WAS PRIVATELY MEDITATING on the race against the Germans to build an atomic bomb. On Saturday, December 9, he confided to Margaret Suckley over dinner, as she recorded in her diary, that he had just gotten "a secret report from a German source" that the Germans had developed a "bomb which will kill by concussion everything within a mile. They are planning to use it on New York [to break American] morale . . . not seeming to realize that it will have the exact opposite effect. . . . He said that in the next war, the side which first uses these new explosives will undoubtedly win."

The President inaccurately told his friend that "the Germans are way ahead of us in that direction, though we are doing a lot of research trying to catch [up] to them." In a premonition of the postwar world, Suckley wrote in her diary that "the human race is out to destroy itself. Only the few who live in isolated places may survive."

ON MONDAY, December 11, William Donovan of the OSS sent Roosevelt a cable from Allen Dulles, his man in Bern, warning that the Morgenthau Plan, by showing "that the enemy planned the enslavement of Germany," had "welded" ordinary Germans to the Hitler regime. It said that the "Germans continue to fight" because they were convinced that defeat would bring only "oppression and exploitation."

Five days later, Hitler launched the counteroffensive soon known as the Battle of the Bulge. "A complete surprise to our people," wrote McCloy in his diary. General Marshall gravely warned Stimson that if the counterattack succeeded and the Russians refused Anglo-American pleas for help, the United States would have to "recast the whole war," retreat to the German border and let the American people "decide whether they wanted to go on with the war enough to raise the new armies which would be necessary to do it."

Three days after the Bulge began, McCloy sent John Boettiger to see Morgenthau. The President's son-in-law had just returned from Aachen, the first significant German city under American occupation. After American troops crossed the German border in mid-September, Hitler had hoped that Aachen would be his Stalingrad, the high watermark of the Anglo-American offensive against Germany. The Führer had ordered the SS and police to evacuate Aachen's citizens, at gunpoint if necessary, and defend the city to the death.

But on October 21, Colonel Gerhard Wilck defied Hitler and surrendered more than three thousand remaining citizens, most in hiding.[5] American aerial bombardment had destroyed seventy percent of the city. The next day, an American colonel from Montana, John Harrison, wrote in his diary, "If every German city that we pass through looks like this one, the Hun is going to be busy for centuries rebuilding his country."

As Aacheners climbed out of cellars and smoking ruins, blinking from their first rays of sunlight, the local U.S. military government, led by an ex–New York State policeman, Thomas Lancer, looked for a new mayor. On the recommendation of the city's Catholic bishop, Lancer appointed Franz Oppenhoff, a lawyer who had abjured the Nazis and whom the bishop had hidden from the SS.[6]

McCloy hoped that Boettiger's firsthand description of the hazards in Aachen might move Morgenthau to relax his strict demands of American occupying troops. "I can't overemphasize the secretiveness of what I am going to say," Boettiger told Morgenthau. He said that "our men are doing the best they can without quite understanding what is wanted of them."

Boettiger reported that U.S. troops had not discovered any Germans in Aachen who were "sympathetic" to the Allies. The bishop's recommendation for the new mayor had been based on the man's success in defending "fifty or sixty Nazis who were on trial." There was "no money in the city to pay anybody." If the military government got coal miners to work again, they would have to feed them and "transport the coal out." Unless the Allies got the economy moving, "all of Europe will have a revolution." They should treat the Germans "rough" but "not completely destroy them."

Boettiger asked Morgenthau if he could tell McCloy that the Treasury Secretary was willing to take a "fresh look" at the problem. Morgenthau refused: "My position hasn't changed one iota. But I don't want you to go away saying I want to destroy Germany. . . . I want them to take care of themselves as we leave it."

"Well, if you don't do something, there is going to be this complete

5. Aachen's normal population was 175,000.

6. Oppenhoff ensured that his appointment was not publicly announced out of fear that Hitler would retaliate by sending his relatives, elsewhere in Germany, to concentration camps.

chaos," said Boettiger. He reminded Morgenthau that U.S. troops in Aachen had had to fight for five weeks against heavy German resistance. He said they had complained to him that the Morgenthau Plan was "worth thirty divisions to the Germans."

Angry but chary of antagonizing the President's son-in-law, Morgenthau replied, "What do they think about Mr. Churchill when he says he is going to hand East Prussia over to the Poles? I suppose *that* doesn't bolster German morale."

Recalling Morgenthau's intervention against the SHAEF *Handbook,* Boettiger demanded, "Why didn't you take it up with the Army? Why did you give it to the President? That wasn't the way to do the thing. Why did you go to Quebec with a plan? . . . That wasn't the right way, to put Mr. Stimson in a bad position. And of course, there had to be leaks on a thing like this."

Morgenthau told Boettiger that he did not intend to butt out on postwar Germany: "Make a list of the things you don't think are going right in Aachen. Let's study it and get together." Boettiger was not interested. He warned Morgenthau not to start another "tough wrangle."

Anxiously Morgenthau wondered whether Boettiger was speaking on behalf of his father-in-law. "When you go up against a fellow like that," he told his aides, "you can't forget that he eats one or two meals a day with the President." He warned his staff, "It is getting lonesomer and lonesomer." He wrote his sons, "Nobody is starving in Aachen, and the responsibility for what they get to eat and how they live is entirely up to the Germans. And if it doesn't work, it is their fault and not ours."

THE NEXT MORNING, Wednesday, December 20, McCloy told Morgenthau that the German counterattack was growing more dangerous. It would be awhile "before we occupy all of Germany."

"It doesn't look too good, does it?" Morgenthau asked.

"It's bound to throw us off our schedule," said McCloy. "It's just a heavy punch in the nose." He said that he and Stimson had had no idea that the Germans had been "ganging up" with such force: "It was staggering that they could deliver such strength so rapidly and in such completely concealed form, especially when we had command of the air."

McCloy exclaimed, "Those fellows! . . . I've been competing with them, I think, probably more . . . consistently than any other fellow in the United States since young manhood.[7] They always bring you to the point of exhaustion before you prevail. . . . Just when you think they're down, they come back with these staggering blows that shake your back teeth."

Still fuming over his conversation with Boettiger, Morgenthau suggested that they needed someone else to report on occupied Germany. Why not send his former aide Colonel Bernard Bernstein, now on Eisenhower's staff?

By now, Colonel Bernstein had been marked as the man who in August had handed Morgenthau the SHAEF *Handbook,* offering him the opportunity to meddle on postwar Germany.[8] McCloy told Morgenthau that he was willing. But he effectively killed the idea by cabling Eisenhower that Bernstein's absence from London might harm the conduct of the war.

ROOSEVELT HAD HOPED that by the end of 1944, the war against Germany would be over. When victory came, he and Eleanor planned to make an immediate journey to see American troops on the battlefront, after which they would celebrate with the Churchills in London. But now, with the surprise German counteroffensive, that dream seemed distant.

Stimson wrote in his diary that the "pressure of the great battle" of the Bulge "lies on everyone, and I would not be human if I didn't feel it." They now faced a "somber future," with "heavy casualties and hard fighting through a long, cold winter."

At Sunday noon, December 31, 1944, in the President's White House bedroom, Stimson told Roosevelt that the Germans had massacred dozens of American prisoners at Malmedy, Belgium. The President replied, "Well, it will only serve to make our troops feel toward the Germans as they already have learned to feel about the Japs."

He told Stimson about the meeting with Stalin and Churchill planned for late January. The top-secret site would be Yalta, the old Russian spa on the Crimean coast.

Stimson said that Yalta seemed a "very long distance" from home. The

7. McCloy's earlier experience as a Wall Street lawyer involved much exposure to German businessmen and financiers.

8. Bernstein's role had been publicized during the autumn public furor over the Morgenthau Plan, when it probably cost him his aspiration to become a general.

clearly ailing Roosevelt replied, "Stalin gave as the reason that his own doctor had forbidden him to travel far."

FOUR DAYS AFTER NEW YEAR'S 1945, the isolationist Senator Burton Wheeler, Democrat of Montana, demanded that with the Battle of the Bulge raging, Roosevelt drop his "brutal and costly" insistence on unconditional surrender. Wheeler said that the "majority of Americans are unwilling to sanction a peace of vengeance" against Germany. Nor did they want America to police Europe, "a seething furnace of fratricide, civil war, murder, disease and starvation."

The British embassy in Washington recorded that Wheeler was "a cold-blooded demagogue in action" whose "isolationism made him anti-Soviet and anti-Semitic." Ickes wrote in his diary, "If we negotiate a peace, which would necessarily be a soft peace, we might as well prepare ourselves for the next war with Germany, which might well open with bombs launched from Germany itself, blasting away at Washington, New York, Philadelphia and other East Coast or even Middle West cities."

Democratic Senator Claude Pepper of Florida told Morgenthau he would try to put Wheeler "on the defensive." Morgenthau could help by explaining his plan on Germany to key Democrats. Unwilling to throw himself into the firing line, Morgenthau told his aides, "I just wasn't going to give anybody a chance to tie me—what do they call it?" Harry Dexter White said, "Hog-tied." Morgenthau joked, "But it wouldn't be Kosher!"

THE MORGENTHAUS HAD GIVEN Roosevelt three pairs of Brooks Brothers pajamas for Christmas. From France, his son Henry sent the President a case of champagne. The President wrote the father, "I am always amazed when these youngsters who are fighting the war have time to think about Christmas presents for their relatives and friends back home."

In the European war, the tide was turning. Morgenthau exulted by letter to his sons overseas that the U.S. Army was "beating back the Germans": "For a while, things certainly looked bad, and I hope that this time it is the real thing and 'it's on to Berlin!' "

Soon after New Year's, Stettinius had invited Morgenthau to a "very sumptuous luncheon" with him at Blair House. Morgenthau wrote his sons overseas, "I do think that from now on, we'll get better cooperation."[9]

Then Morgenthau discovered that Stettinius and McCloy were excluding him from meetings and correspondence on postwar Germany. He planned to complain to Roosevelt after Cabinet on Thursday, January 11, but changed his mind when he saw how "very tired" the President looked. Instead, he sent a memo to be included in Roosevelt's weekend reading at Hyde Park.

Morgenthau wrote that "the real motive of most who oppose a weak Germany is . . . fear of Russia and Communism. . . . This thing needs to be dragged out into the open. I feel so deeply that I speak strongly. If we don't face it, I am just as sure as I can be that we are going to let a lot of hollow and hypocritical propaganda lead us into recreating a strong Germany and making a foe of Russia. I shudder for the sake of our children to think of what will follow."

ON FRIDAY, January 19, Roosevelt joked to his Cabinet, "The first twelve years are the hardest!" He reported that his trip to see Stalin and Churchill would take four or five weeks. He did not tell them the site.

The President recalled that the stricken Woodrow Wilson had fired his Secretary of State for convening the Cabinet in his absence. Roosevelt said that since Stettinius would be traveling with him, he would not mind if Morgenthau, the next-ranking Cabinet member, had to call them together. Morgenthau wrote his sons that he hoped that did not happen, "because it does place considerable responsibility on my shoulders, but frankly it rather thrills me." After the meeting, he was "more tired than I had ever been in my life, because I had steeled myself to taking a rebuff and I didn't know how to take success."

Morgenthau was not immune to Stettinius's bonhomie. He wrote his sons, "I think that Stettinius and I see almost eye to eye on the future treatment of Germany." He claimed that support for "the so-called Morgenthau Plan" was "spreading and growing amongst the Administration." After the Cabinet meeting, he told his diary that the Cabinet meeting had shown his relationship with Roosevelt to be "just as good as it has ever been. I have every reason to believe it will continue to be, because I think Stettinius lacks courage. But time will tell!"

9. Morgenthau also wrote his sons, "Any time you have three minutes, do sit down and scribble off something, even if it's on a sheet of toilet paper."

• • •

THE NEXT DAY, at noon, Roosevelt was sworn in, without overcoat, for his fourth term on the White House South Portico, in deference to a nation at war. Standing in the crowd on the snow-dusted lawn, McCloy wrote in his diary, "The President looked distinguished, determined and solemn. He spoke briefly. It was not a great speech, but a good one."

The next day, Monday, January 21, Morgenthau wrote his sons, "Tonight we are going to the White House to celebrate the President's birthday." Hinting that Roosevelt was leaving for a Big Three meeting, he wrote, "You know his birthday isn't until the 30th, so you can put two and two together and I hope it doesn't make five." [10]

Late that night, after celebrating his sixty-third birthday, along with thirteen grandchildren and sundry daughters-in-law in town for the inauguration, Roosevelt, his daughter, Anna, and the rest of his party slipped out of the White House and boarded his train, bound for Norfolk, where the cruiser *Quincy* was waiting to take him across the Atlantic.

As Anna recalled, she had "wanted desperately" to go to Yalta, "but I also knew that if Mother went, I couldn't go. The other thing was that Averell Harriman and Churchill were bringing their daughters, and there would be no wives. So I just fell in with this, just blocked it out for my own purposes very selfishly."

Leaning out of the presidential train to wave good-bye to her husband, John, Anna "got deluged with soot," as she later wrote him. "Had to go in and brush it out of my hair, off my clothes and wash face, neck and hands. But at least I saw you as long as it was physically possible!"

At the White House, William Hassett recorded in his diary that few had been told where the President would meet "Joe and Winnie," and "I am not among that limited number." He wrote that "having achieved every political ambition a human being can aspire to," Roosevelt had now to think of his place in history. "So F.D.R. will win his niche or pass into the oblivion which in a quarter of a century has swallowed all of the statesmen of the First World War. . . . Who am I to ponder the imponderable? Lord give the President strength, courage and heavenly wisdom."

10. The Morgenthaus gave him a set of tumblers and Old-Fashioned glasses, which Roosevelt ordered sent to his house in Warm Springs.

CHAPTER SEVENTEEN

"The Only Bond Is Their Common Hate"

On Saturday morning, February 3, 1945, Roosevelt and his entourage were flown aboard the *Sacred Cow* from Malta to the Crimean town of Saki.

During the six-hour drive to Yalta in a chilly Packard on a twisting, bumpy, primitive road, Roosevelt catnapped in the backseat. When he awoke, he was appalled to see the detritus of German conquest—blackened tree stumps, burned-out houses, tanks and railroad cars. The President told Anna that the sights moved him "even more" to "want to get even with the Germans." She wrote that "wanton destruction makes even me bloodthirsty!"

Arriving after dusk, Roosevelt and his party were housed in the white granite Livadia Palace, once the summer home of the Czars. When the Germans fled, they had ransacked the place, stealing even the toilets and doorknobs.

"About two weeks ago," Anna wrote her husband, "some of our people went through it and discovered it to be occupied only by creepy-crawly creatures! It was thoroughly deloused but still there were complaints from a good many this A.M. of unwelcome bedfellows. I was lucky, but the delousing is still going on."

Anna reported that it was "a block to the bath I'm supposed to use." The mattress in her bedroom, down the hall from her father's, was "so thin I could feel the springs." To her disgust, a Soviet military intelligence chief had "tried to pet me." She wrote that her father had found the man "a most sinister appearing pest" who reminded him of some "big businessmen" he knew.

Anna was secretly worried about the President's health. Soon after the Yalta meetings began, Anna wrote her husband that "just between you and me," she was watching her father "very carefully. . . . He gets all wound up, seems to thoroughly enjoy it all, but wants too many people around and then won't go to bed early enough." She was trying to "keep the unnecessary people" away from his rooms and "steer the necessary ones in at the best times." She was irritated that most of the aides Roosevelt had brought to Yalta "just sit on their fannies and play gin rummy."

She wrote that her father's doctors, Howard Bruenn and Ross McIntire, "are both worried because of the old 'ticker' trouble—which, of course, no one knows about but those two and me. . . . I have found out from Bruenn (who won't let me tell Ross that I know) that this 'ticker' situation is far more serious than I ever knew. And the biggest difficulty in handling the situation here is that we can, of course, tell no one of the 'ticker' trouble. It's truly worrisome—and there's not a helluva lot anyone can do about it. (Better tear off and destroy this paragraph.)"

By the second day of the conference, Roosevelt had received no letter from his wife. Anna wrote her husband, "This is a very sad situation, Honey, because the only times he has mentioned her on this trip have been when he has griped about her attitudes towards things he's done and people he likes."

ON SUNDAY, February 4, at 4:15 P.M., Stalin arrived for a private meeting with Roosevelt in his Livadia Palace suite. The President told him that seeing the residue of German destruction had made him "more bloodthirsty" toward the Germans than when they had met at Tehran. Jocularly he expressed the hope that Marshal Stalin would once again toast the execution of fifty thousand German officers.

Stalin replied that the Crimean destruction was "nothing compared to that which occurred in the Ukraine."

Currying Stalin's favor by exaggerating his problems with Churchill, Roosevelt said he had had "a good deal of trouble with the British." Professing to be "indiscreet," he said that the British were a "peculiar people." He had not wanted the U.S. occupation zone next to France, but the British seemed to think that he should "restore order in France" and then "return political control to the British." They wished to "have their cake and eat it too." He did not mind giving France a zone, but "only out of kindness."

"That would be the *only* reason to give France a zone!" Stalin replied.

THE AMERICAN MINISTER-COUNSELOR in Moscow, George Kennan, who had served on the European Advisory Commission, was doubtful that the Soviets and the West could ever govern postwar Germany together. Almost alone in the American government, Kennan had heretically concluded that after surrender, Germany should be immediately divided along the western boundary of the Soviet zone, letting the American and British zones be combined in a democratic West German federation. He knew that this would mean the division of Europe, but he saw no alternative.

From his long diplomatic experience with the Russians, Kennan felt that even if they did not try to seize all of Europe, they were destroyers by nature and could not tolerate "balance" or "harmony" in the rest of the continent. He suspected that Stalin would find it hard to tolerate a democratic Germany, and that if the Germans, so accustomed to dictatorship, rejected democracy, Stalin would find it hard to keep his hands off.

ON MONDAY AFTERNOON, February 5, the Big Three sat down with their aides at the large round table in the Livadia's ballroom. The day before, Churchill had decreed that they would discuss "the future of Germany—if she has any." According to the Soviet record, Stalin replied, "Germany will have a future."[1]

By now, under pressure from Eden, Churchill had renounced his commitment with Roosevelt at Quebec to make Germany a "pastoral" state. In early January, he had told Eden that it was "much too soon for us to decide" such an "enormous" question. He said it was a "mistake" to set down in writing "what the vast emotions of an outraged and quivering world" might be "after the struggle is over."

1. Stalin's comment appears only in the Soviet official version of the talks. The Soviets may have fabricated the quote to suggest to the postwar Germans they were courting that, at Yalta, Stalin had defended their country against the Anglo-American Germanophobes.

Two years later, when McCloy mentioned the Morgenthau Plan during a visit with Churchill, the old man "hastily repudiated" it. In his diary, McCloy wrote, "Damned Morgenthau and the Prof. Said they were Shylocks."

Now, in the palace ballroom, Roosevelt brandished a map of Germany showing the three occupation zones already assigned. Stalin said, "We all favor dismemberment, but in what form?" Should they create an all-German government, or three separate ones? Roosevelt replied that such questions would "grow out of the zones of occupation."

"That we shall find out!" said Stalin. He recalled that at Tehran, Roosevelt had favored five Germanies and Churchill some sort of partition: "Hasn't the time now come for a decision?"

Churchill slammed on the brakes: "The actual tracing of lines is much too complicated a matter to settle here in five or six days." There must be "elaborate searchings" and "prolonged study." If Germany surrendered soon, "we have only to march in and occupy."

Stalin recalled the Stauffenberg plot of July 1944: "Suppose a group declares it has overthrown Hitler. Should we deal with them?"

"We must make up our mind whether the group is worth dealing with," said Churchill. "Present the terms of unconditional surrender." If they didn't sign, "continue the war and occupy the whole country."

Stalin pressed: Shouldn't they add a surrender demand "that Germany will be dismembered"? Churchill replied that he felt no need to consult "any German" about "their future." Dealing with eighty million people required "more than eighty minutes to consider."

"A decision should be made now," Stalin said.

Roosevelt said that what Stalin really meant was whether they should agree on dismemberment "in principle." Using a crucial change of word, Roosevelt said, "As at Tehran, I am very much in favor of decentralization." This ignored the fact that at Tehran the President had specifically called for five "self-governed" German states.

Trying to defuse the tension, Roosevelt prattled away about his boyhood in Germany, when there were small, semiautonomous states like Darmstadt and Rothenburg: "There was no word for the Reich. Affairs were managed at the local level." Eden averted his glance. Churchill played with his cigar.

In retrospect, Charles Bohlen, the President's interpreter-notetaker, who had often heard Roosevelt rhapsodize about his German boyhood, found this the one moment at Yalta when "his ill health might have affected his thinking." Bohlen felt that Roosevelt sounded so "rambling and inconclusive" that it might unsettle the British, who had feared for Roosevelt's life from the moment they saw his wasted face when he arrived.

Churchill considered German dismemberment an invitation for Soviet power in Europe. He said bluntly that during this conference, he would not consent to "any specific method." Roosevelt suggested that they simply tell the Germans "that we are going to dismember, and do it *our* way."

Stalin agreed to Roosevelt's compromise: The surrender terms would include a provision that Germany would be dismembered.

"But you don't want to tell them!" cried Churchill. "Eisenhower doesn't want that. That will make the Germans fight all the harder."

Roosevelt replied that "the German people have suffered so much that they are now beyond questions of psychological warfare."[2]

Stalin agreed that as long as dismemberment appeared in the instrument of surrender, they could conceal the demand from the Germans for now.[3]

Roosevelt and Churchill sympathized with Stalin's wish to compensate Poland for its loss of eastern lands, including Byelorussia and the western Ukraine, when Hitler and Stalin divided Polish territory in 1939, by granting the Poles all German territory east of the Oder and Neisse Rivers. Displacing six or seven million Germans, this would strip Germany of its richest farmland, dooming the Morgenthau notion that postwar Germans could sustain themselves as an agrarian state.

Churchill appealed for a French occupation zone, carved "out of the British and possibly the American zones." It would not "affect the Soviet zone." The Prime Minister hoped that the French would help resist Soviet power in postwar Europe, but he spoke only of restraining postwar German power. The occupation "might be a long time" and the British might grow tired. France could provide "real assistance."

Stalin suggested "another method." The British could solicit "the help of

2. During this colloquy, Stalin leaned toward Gromyko and asked whether Roosevelt actually disagreed with Churchill, "or is it just a ploy?" Gromyko assured him that they had genuine differences.

3. The falsified Soviet public version of this conversation claims that the Anglo-American "ruling circles" wanted dismemberment of Germany but the issue "was taken off the agenda at the initiative of the Soviet government."

France, Holland or Belgium in occupation, but not give them rights" in the control machinery for Germany.[4]

Churchill rejoined that the French had had "long experience in occupying Germany. They do it very well, and they would not be lenient. We want to see their might grow to help keep Germany down." He added, "I do not know how long the United States will remain with us in occupation."

Roosevelt said that American troops were not likely to stay in Europe "much more than two years." He could not persuade "our people and Congress" to "keep an army in Europe for a long time. Two years would be the limit."

The President was presuming that relations between the Soviets and the West would remain harmonious. But Stalin may have inferred from the remark that if the Soviets waited two years, they might enjoy a power vacuum in Europe.

Annoyed, Churchill wished that Roosevelt had not been so specific. When the President said "two years," he quickly said, "I hope that would be according to circumstances."

Stalin said, "I agree that the French should be great and strong." But the defeated land should be ruled only by those powers who stood "firmly against Germany" and "made the greatest sacrifice for victory."

"I admit they have not been much help," said Churchill. But the French were "the most important neighbor" of the Germans. "We will need her defense against Germany. . . . We have suffered badly from German robot guns and, should Germany again get near to the Channel coast, we would suffer again. After the Americans have gone home, I must think seriously of the future."

Eden asked, "If the French are to have a zone, how can they be excluded from the control machinery?" Stalin replied, "By the power who gave them the zone." Churchill said, "We cannot undertake to do that, and the French would never submit to it."

Stalin desperately wanted reparations from Germany. Much of his country was in ruins, the United States had yet to pledge him serious postwar aid and the zonal division of Germany would leave most German industry in Anglo-

4. The official Soviet version, published in the 1960s, omits Stalin's objections to a French zone. By then, the Kremlin was anxious not to alienate French President Charles de Gaulle. Eager for an independent France, resentful over U.S. leadership and the Anglo-American alliance, de Gaulle was forming his own relationship with Moscow.

American hands. "What does Russia want?" asked Roosevelt. The President noted that neither he nor Churchill wished for "reparations in manpower."

Stalin's Deputy Foreign Minister, Ivan Maisky, said that the Soviets wanted forced German labor, to be used to help rebuild their country. For two years after victory, the Soviets should also be able to seize German machinery, rolling stock and other assets. And over a decade, Germany should give them goods worth "not less than ten billion dollars." German heavy industry should be reduced by eighty percent, leaving only enough to cover the needs of the Germans.[5]

Churchill said that he sympathized with Soviet suffering, but could promise "nowhere near" ten billion dollars: "No victorious country will come out so burdened financially as Great Britain. If I could see any benefit in reparations, I would be glad to have them, but I am very doubtful." The Prime Minister said he was "haunted" by the "specter of a starving Germany." If eighty million Germans were hungry, who would pay to feed them? If you wanted a horse to pull a wagon, "you would at least have to give it fodder."

"But care must be taken to see that the horse doesn't turn around and kick you!" replied Stalin.

Roosevelt said that the Soviet Union should get "maximum reparations." The Germans shouldn't enjoy "a higher standard of living than the Soviet Union," but "we don't want to kill people." He recalled that after Versailles, Americans had lost a lot of money because "we lent Germany far more" than the United States "got back."

Roosevelt urged the Soviet Union to take "all it can in manpower and factories." The British should take "all they can in exports to former German markets." But they must "leave Germany enough industry and work to prevent her from starving" and becoming "a burden on the world."

Maisky retorted that by retaining its farming and light industry and being free of military spending, Germany would have a "modest but decent" living standard. As Gromyko later recalled, Stalin was piqued by the apparent

5. Before Yalta, Maisky had advised Stalin that the Soviets should demand seventy-five percent of all German reparations, "with a calculation of ultimately getting sixty-five": "We should make them understand that both the United States and England in the long run would only gain economically from the disappearance of such a dangerous competitor as Germany. But this should be done rather carefully because, due to their intrinsic hypocrisy, the Anglo-Americans would not want to openly admit the correctness of this conclusion."

Anglo-American indifference to his request: "Were our allies perhaps thinking that the Soviet economy should not be allowed to recover too quickly?"

The Big Three agreed to create a commission, meeting in Moscow, that would decide on reparations. Stalin said, "We three have the first claim on reparations, since we have borne the burden of the war."

Churchill replied that "exertion in the war" should not be considered. He added that if he agreed to the Soviet figure, he would be driven from office. Stalin retorted, "Victors are not driven out."[6]

Churchill teased his host by quoting Lenin: "To each according to his needs!" Stalin was not amused. Rising from the table, he said suspiciously, "It is possible that the U.S.A. and Britain have already agreed on this with each other."

ON FRIDAY AFTERNOON, February 9, the Big Three discussed what they should do with Nazi war criminals.

The previous November, Stimson had advised Roosevelt over lunch at the White House that after the war, an international tribunal should investigate the Nazi "conspiracy," to "give us a record" and persuade future generations of "the evil of the Nazi system."[7] Herbert Pell, the American delegate to the year-old United Nations War Crimes Commission in London, went further than Stimson.[8] Pell opposed an international tribunal and demanded a more sweeping definition of war crimes, including offenses committed because of race or religion and those before the war. During a visit before Yalta, Roosevelt smilingly told Pell, an old family friend, that he "absolutely" agreed with him.[9] That same day, he had Stettinius fire him.

Roosevelt assigned his aide Samuel Rosenman, a former New York Supreme Court justice, to be his new man on war crimes. He reminded Rosenman that after World War I, it took years to get trials going and the criminals had gotten away. This time, "make the punishment of the guilty swift." Like Stimson, he thought indictments should include "waging aggressive war."

6. That summer, the British electorate would prove Stalin wrong.

7. Stimson recorded that Roosevelt "was very nice about it."

8. The commission was established in October 1943 to pursue war criminals and bring them to justice. The Soviet Union was not a formal member but agreed to cooperate.

9. James Dunn told McCloy that Pell had been appointed for "sentimental" reasons: Roosevelt's and Pell's mothers had been "schoolgirls together."

At Morgenthau's behest, his aide Josiah DuBois went to Rosenman's apartment at the Wardman Park Hotel and warned him that a "mass conspiracy" trial might fall into a "legal shambles": Didn't the Moscow Declaration of 1943 order arch-criminals "dealt with on the political level"?

Rosenman explained that he was eager to have as many criminals as possible shot: "At a minimum, two hundred and fifty thousand people should be executed." U.S. authorities were "anxious to get the people who murdered our soldiers in Belgium," But you couldn't have individual trials for so many criminals. The conspiracy formula was a "very ingenious way" to "get large numbers of people."

Stimson persuaded the President to insist at Yalta on a "state trial" of the "highest-ranking German leaders." This would "show the full nature of the Nazi conspiracy" to "wage a war of terrorism on the European world." In a memo to Roosevelt, Stimson and Attorney General Francis Biddle argued that a world tribunal should try the highest-ranking leaders, beginning with Hitler, as well as top Nazi organizations like the SS and Gestapo. Charges would include waging "an illegal war of aggression" and prewar atrocities against German nationals. Later, presuming that one or more Nazi groups were found guilty, lesser defendants would go before "occupation courts," where the "only necessary proof of guilt" would be "membership."

As he sat with his allies, Churchill recalled that he had drafted the Moscow Declaration of 1943—"an egg that I myself laid." That document had dealt with the chief Nazi criminals whose crimes crossed national boundaries. Why not draw up a list of those outlaws, to be "shot once their identity is established"?

Stalin tossed out a firecracker: "What about Hess?" By this he meant Rudolf Hess, Hitler's old deputy, who in 1941 had parachuted into Scotland, ostensibly to contact "Aryan bloodbrothers" who might help him make peace with the British. Some Soviets suspected that Hess, now jailed in the Tower of London, knew enough potentially embarrassing secrets about treasonable doings within the British establishment to make Churchill eager to keep him locked up.[10]

10. One possibility was the story that Hess had been sent to Britain to make a deal that would let the Nazis turn full force against the Soviets—and that eminent British figures had been eager to play ball.

"Events will catch up with Hess," Churchill replied cryptically. He said that Hess and other lesser criminals should be granted "a judicial trial." He agreed with his colleagues to refer the matter of war crimes to their foreign ministers.

On Saturday afternoon, February 10, Roosevelt presented Stalin with a photograph book called *Target Germany,* showing the damage incurred by U.S. bombers, an unsubtle reminder of the American contribution to the war. He told Stalin that he had grown convinced it would be "impractical" for France to have a zone but no seat on the control commission. It would also make the touchy Charles de Gaulle harder to deal with.

With bigger fish to fry, Stalin laughingly raised his hands: "I surrender!"

Stalin's ready concession had been greased in advance by the American ambassador, Averell Harriman. Bohlen worried that it might reinforce Roosevelt's illusion that he had "great personal influence" on the dictator.

Stalin was still irritated that Roosevelt and Churchill had brushed off his demand for ten billion dollars in reparations. He said that if Britain felt the Soviets "should receive no reparations at all," they should "say so frankly."

Churchill refused to commit himself. He said that if the Germans could not pay their bills, "other countries" would wind up "paying for German reparations."

Stalin said, "We will bring our figures before the commission, and you bring yours."

The Allies finally resolved that Germany would pay its victims "in kind"—first to those nations "which have borne the main burden of the war, have suffered the heaviest losses and have organized victory over the enemy." For two years after surrender, those countries could help themselves to Germany's national wealth, "destroying" its war potential. Then, for an undecided period, they could claim annual deliveries of German goods and use of German labor. The Moscow reparations commission would work out the details.

The President jovially called out, "Judge Roosevelt approves!"

• • •

AT A DINNER HOSTED BY STALIN at the Yusupov Palace, the Marshal toasted Churchill for defying Hitler alone, "while the rest of Europe was falling on its face." He knew few such cases "when the courage of one man was so important to the future history of the world."

Churchill replied, "In peace, no less than in war, Marshal Stalin will continue to lead his people from success to success." Turning to Roosevelt, he toasted "the chief forger of the instruments that led to the mobilization of the world against Hitler." With his customary grandiloquence, Churchill declared that they were "standing on the crest of a hill, with the glories of future possibilities stretching before us. . . . It would be a tragedy for which history would never forgive us if we let this prize slip from our grasp through inertia or carelessness."

On Sunday afternoon, February 11, on his departure from Yalta, Roosevelt told Stalin with a broad grin, "We will meet again soon—in Berlin!"

But after Churchill said good-bye, he morbidly told Eden, "The only bond of the victors is their common hate."

CHAPTER EIGHTEEN

"Arguing About the Future of the World"

DURING HIS VOYAGE BACK to America aboard the *Quincy,* Roosevelt worked on a speech about the Yalta conference that he planned to deliver to a joint session of Congress. His daughter Anna was worried. She thought he "should really spend the entire crossing resting up." As she wrote her husband, her "fear" was that when her father got home, he would have a "terrific let down" and "possibly crack under it," the same as when he had returned home sick after meeting Churchill and Stalin in Tehran. "But all we can do is hold our fingers crossed."

On Wednesday morning, February 28, 1945, after five weeks away, Roosevelt was back at the White House. The next day Stimson wrote in his diary that Eisenhower's "big offensive" in Germany was succeeding: "The Germans are losing courage and are beginning to crumple up a little in some of their resistance. Not all—a good many of them are fighting vigorously. But there are more indications of a breakup than there have been at any time yet."

At Wednesday noon, exhausted from the fourteen-thousand-mile trip, Roosevelt addressed the House and Senate while seated. For the first time, he mentioned his infirmity in public, saying that it made it "a lot easier for me" not to carry "about ten pounds of steel around on the bottom of my legs."

The President told the Congress that Germany must never again be allowed to "wage aggressive war." This would "not harm the German people."

On the contrary, it would remove "a cancer from the German body which for generations has produced only misery and pain for the entire world." Echoing Stimson, he said, "I know there is not room enough on earth for both German militarism and Christian decency."

Vice President Truman sat on the podium behind Roosevelt. He privately observed in 1954 that "with all the ad libs and side-statements," it was "the most poorly delivered speech he ever made." Roosevelt's frailty made Truman feel "more than certain that the President wouldn't last" through his term.

The poet Archibald MacLeish, just appointed as an Assistant Secretary of State, wrote that he would "never forget" seeing the President after Yalta, "with the cold spring light on his face and death in his eyes."

After his speech to Congress, Roosevelt met with his Cabinet. Stimson felt "the expression on his face has changed somewhat, and he looks older." Henry Morgenthau noted that the President looked "very tired" and had "lost a great deal of weight."

Just as with Tehran, Roosevelt confided little of what had been said at Yalta. There had been a discussion of whether the "very bad Germans" should be tried for war crimes, but no decision. Wishfully he said that his days with Stalin had suggested that perhaps there was "something in him besides this revolutionist, Bolshevist thing." Perhaps during Stalin's training for the priesthood, "something entered into his nature of the way in which a Christian gentleman should behave."

ON SATURDAY, March 3, at 12:40 P.M., Roosevelt saw Stimson, who wrote in his diary, "Very generous of him, because it was cutting into his lunchtime."

Stimson was troubled by the "terrible and probably unnecessary" killing of perhaps fifty thousand people during the previous month's Allied bombing of Dresden. The German city had been bombed under a British plan to provoke chaos by disrupting the stampede of refugees from the latest Soviet offensive. In his diary, Stimson noted that the city, known for its china and architecture, was the capital of Saxony, "the least Prussianized part of Germany," which should be "the center" of a new, "less Prussianized" Germany that would be "dedicated to freedom."

Stimson reminded the President that Eisenhower had agreed to serve as military governor of Germany for a few months after surrender. But then he would step aside. With the Allies smashing into German territory, Eisenhower's successor had better be named "at once."

Roosevelt had sometimes fantasized that he himself would "like to try" being military governor. He reminded Stimson, who required no reminder, that he had studied in Germany "in the old days, before she was corrupted." He would love "to try to bring her back to the old Germany of Schiller and Goethe and the old Emperor."

During the summer of 1944, when Morgenthau had heard that McCloy was interested in the job, he indignantly asked Harry Hopkins how, with prewar clients like Westinghouse and General Electric, McCloy could "deal with such companies' big claims against postwar Germany." Eisenhower backed McCloy's candidacy, but Stimson told McCloy that he could not afford to lose him.

Hull had suggested James Byrnes of South Carolina, director of the Office of War Mobilization. Agreeing that Byrnes would be "sufficiently tough," Roosevelt had offered him the job. But Byrnes had wanted to be Secretary of State. He excused himself on grounds that he couldn't speak German.

Stimson suggested his Under Secretary, Robert Patterson, a former federal judge who still wore the belt he had snatched from a German soldier he had killed in World War I. Roosevelt had agreed that Patterson's "judicial poise, ability and character" would serve him well. Morgenthau thought the idea was "perfectly swell."

But now, in March 1945, Stimson told Roosevelt that after the Battle of the Bulge, the Pentagon must completely revise its production program. He needed Patterson to oversee it "without scandal or delay." He had decided that the right man for Germany was General Lucius Clay, Byrnes's deputy at War Mobilization. He told Roosevelt that the military governor should be a soldier, at least during the early occupation.

Clay was a military man, an engineer and "a most effective organizer," with deep experience in Washington politics and logistics, which reflected the Pentagon's aversion to letting Germany founder. In the fall of 1944 he had helped Eisenhower break a dangerous logjam at Cherbourg, allowing enough goods to flow through that vital port to hasten the Allied advance.

McCloy had established in advance that Clay was willing to make ample use, if necessary, of the loophole in JCS 1067, allowing the American commander to stop "disease and unrest and disorder" in Germany. Clay's background offered an important clue showing the kind of work Stimson and McCloy expected him to do in postwar Germany: He was an expert in reconstruction.

Roosevelt knew about Clay's excellent wartime performance, but could not recall having met him. With a laugh, he warned Stimson, "You will break Jimmy Byrnes's heart. He is so dependent on him."

ON FRIDAY MORNING, March 9, McCloy told Morgenthau he had heard that Roosevelt had asked Stettinius to write "a full statement of what was decided at Yalta," including "a good bit" that "nobody else has seen yet."

Morgenthau said, "I can't wait!" During the Big Three meeting, he had written his sons that he was "dying of curiosity to know what is going on."

After Stettinius returned to his office from Yalta, by way of Mexico City, he received his new number-three man, James Dunn. When Stettinius had asked the President to promote the old State Department veteran in December, Roosevelt was worried about Dunn's reputation for legerdemain and his conservatism, but he consented. Stettinius told his diary that Roosevelt did not realize that Dunn's new job would cover "all political matters" except Latin America, and that Stettinius had made no effort to tell him.

When Eleanor Roosevelt heard about Dunn's appointment to State, she was outraged. By letter she reminded her husband that Dunn had backed the Spanish fascist Francisco Franco and hankered to use "German industrialists to rehabilitate Germany." Dunn would be "clever enough to tell you he will do what you want" while pursuing his own agenda. How could he appoint someone "in whom you know you cannot put any trust?"

Stettinius had wanted to bring Dunn to Yalta. Roosevelt had refused, saying, "He'll sabotage everything."

Still piqued by the President's rebuff, Dunn handed Stettinius a "Draft Directive for the Treatment of Germany," dated Saturday, March 10. Dunn falsely assured the Secretary of State that he had merely put the Yalta decisions down on paper, with no change in policy involved. Four days later, Stettinius innocently took the Draft Directive to Roosevelt for his signature. Misinformed, he told the President that Stimson had seen and endorsed it. With that recommendation, Roosevelt initialed the document.

The hapless Stettinius did not know that Dunn had played him for a fool. Both JCS 1067 and the Yalta talks had stressed decentralizing German political power and limiting Allied responsibility for the German economy. In contrast, Dunn's paper stressed that economic controls would be dictated by the Allied Control Council, whose influence would be "paramount throughout Germany." Dunn had felt emboldened by Roosevelt's flagging health. As he later recalled, he had recently watched the President deal with a cable: Roosevelt was "seeing the paper, but not reading it . . . picking out something to show he was alert. He was in no shape to do anything."

Having sneaked the document past Roosevelt and Stettinius, Dunn exulted that he had cinched the victory for State Department planners on Germany that they had failed to win by other means. When he saw the "F.D.R." on his directive, he called up McCloy and told him he had better now revise JCS 1067 "at the earliest possible moment."

When McCloy read the Draft Directive, he was furious. On Thursday morning, March 15, he warned Stimson that the paper ordered "very close control" of German prices and wages, and pinched the authority of the American zonal commander. Quickly recruiting allies against the State Department, he called Morgenthau and urged him to "raise hell" with Stettinius. Disgusted by the Draft Directive but averse to a fight with another Secretary of State, Morgenthau said, "It's up to Stimson to take the lead on this thing."

Nevertheless, at 2:45 P.M., Morgenthau joined Stimson and McCloy in the Secretary of State's office. McCloy noted that the atmosphere was "very tense" and that Morgenthau was "very unhappy." The Treasury Secretary asked whether "any decision at Yalta" justified the Draft Directive's suggestion that the German Reich be "preserved." The paper appeared to say "that the power of the German empire would be continued and reconstructed." He was "very anxious to know" whether it was "definitely settled at Yalta that Germany should be treated as one nation."

McCloy said the Army presumed that Germany would be run from the zones, not by the Control Council in Berlin: "Any change in this principle would cause an extensive revamping of plans."

Stettinius reported that the Big Three had agreed to treat Germany "as a single country for the period of immediate military occupation." He pleaded that the directive was only an "interim document." He pledged to tell Morgenthau more about what was said at Yalta about dismemberment.

After the meeting, McCloy called Morgenthau: "That was quite a party!" Joking about the new Secretary of State's brainlessness, Morgenthau told McCloy that he had been "scared to look at you" while Stettinius spoke for fear of laughing out loud. McCloy replied, "I deliberately didn't look in your direction!"[1]

The next day, Stimson stayed behind after a Cabinet meeting and asked Roosevelt why he had approved Stettinius's terrible Draft Directive. The President replied that he had "not paid attention to it." He told Stimson, "I can't remember if I signed it. I have no idea what I signed."

There is no way to know whether Roosevelt was giving Stimson an excuse or whether he was growing so frail that he was signing vital documents without thinking. At about this time Harold Ickes anxiously confided to Anna Boettiger that the President did not "seem to understand at times what people are saying to him" and seemed "to forget quickly."

ON SATURDAY MORNING, March 17, Morgenthau told McCloy he had just had a "very frank talk" with Stettinius, "and I shook him terrifically." Under Morgenthau's interrogation, the apologetic Secretary of State had explained how Dunn had put one over on him. Morgenthau told McCloy, "He was tired and he really didn't know what was in it."

McCloy replied that the people at State clearly "went off on a frolic of their own" and "we've got a right to sulk on it."

Morgenthau agreed: "They just handed this thing to Stettinius. . . . He gave it to the President, and evidently the President didn't read it. And the whole future of Germany is at stake. It's damnable! An outrage!" McCloy agreed that it was "an incredibly fantastic way to treat such an important subject."

Morgenthau said, "I'm not going to take it lying down. Is that English? . . . And I hope that Mr. Stimson doesn't."

1. Stimson had been quiet through the meeting. Morgenthau asked McCloy "why you don't train your boss the way you train me." McCloy replied that before the meeting he hadn't had a chance to prime Stimson.

McCloy reported that Stimson's attitude was to do "something which is administratively possible" from a "military point of view."

Morgenthau pledged, "come hell or high water," to kill the Draft Directive. He found John Boettiger as shocked by Dunn's perfidy as his bosses Stimson and McCloy. Although he disliked Morgenthau, Boettiger promised to "help" him with his father-in-law: "This is terrible what Stettinius has done."

Morgenthau wrote in his diary, "If Anna and John go to work on this with the President, we will have a good chance to block it."

ON MONDAY, March 19, despite his pledge to inform Morgenthau about Yalta, Stettinius refused to show him the secret meeting records: "You go and ask the President. The thing is locked up in the safe."

Morgenthau's aide Josiah DuBois told him, "Stettinius isn't dealing with you aboveboard." Eager, after years of fighting Hull, to have a Secretary of State so pliable, Morgenthau replied, "Well, he is my white-haired hope, so I have to hang on." He planned to go over Stettinius's head to the President: "Ed is scared to death on this because he is absolutely wrong."

Harry Dexter White warned that Stettinius would be angry. "So what?" replied Morgenthau. "There is too much at stake to worry. . . . I want to put it to the President—'I'm simply upholding your hand, knowing there is going to be dismemberment, and everybody is going to try to doublecross you.' . . . It makes me so mad. I think the President should fire Jimmy Dunn and two or three other fellows."

McCloy called Morgenthau: "The more I think about this thing, the more outrageous it becomes in my mind." Morgenthau replied, "The position I'm taking sums up to one thing—leave 1067 as it is!"

ON TUESDAY, March 20, Morgenthau lunched with Roosevelt at the White House. Repeating what he had told Stimson, the President said he could not recall having read or initialed the Draft Directive. Morgenthau handed Roosevelt a memo opposing the document.[2] After reading the first and last

2. "I am confident that this Directive goes absolutely contrary to your views." It would "build up a strong central German government and maintain and even strengthen the German economy."

page, Roosevelt said that if Morgenthau and Stimson could "come to an agreement" with Stettinius, he would revoke the Draft Directive. He agreed with Morgenthau that after this episode, he should fire Dunn and several others at State.

The two men were joined by Anna and John Boettiger. Privately Anna felt that the President had "not been himself" since Yalta. She told Jonathan Daniels, an old family friend who had just become Roosevelt's press secretary, that her father's "increasing incapacity" frightened her.[3]

Anna was contemplating some kind of "regency," so Daniels recalled, with her and Boettiger in "dynastic positions," shielding the President from people who might annoy him and wear down his health. As he understood it, Anna aspired to be another Edith Bolling Wilson, who had acted as President-in-fact, protecting her invalid husband. "It scared the pants off of me."

The public controversy over the Morgenthau Plan had made Anna dislike her father's friend more than ever. She complained to Ickes that Morgenthau always went "weeping" to her mother, using her to "fight his battles," complaining that he wasn't "trusted anymore."

Roosevelt was absorbing a little of Anna's poison against Morgenthau. Before a White House dinner that month for the Canadian Prime Minister, Mackenzie King, Anna reported that her mother had told her that the Morgenthaus were King's "great friends."[4] Roosevelt shot back, "Who told her that? The Morgenthaus?"

To ensure that the Treasury Secretary did not cause the President any more trouble, Anna and her husband rode shotgun on his luncheon with her father.[5] Boettiger irked Morgenthau by carping within the President's hearing that "people down the line" in the Army didn't understand JCS 1067. It wasn't "workable." The Germans mustn't be forced to stew in their own juice.

"Let them have soup kitchens!" cried Roosevelt, repeating his old mantra. "Let their economy sink!" Boettiger prompted him: "You don't want them to starve." The President snapped, "Why not?"

3. Daniels's father, the North Carolina newspaper publisher Josephus Daniels, had been Roosevelt's boss in the Wilson Navy Department. His son recalled, "This is a vulgar way to put it, but I was more their kind of people than most of the other people around the shop."

4. Morgenthau had spent time with King during the Quebec meeting.

5. Roosevelt may have encouraged their presence as a foil to Morgenthau.

Morgenthau was startled to hear Boettiger undercutting his own Pentagon bosses by criticizing JCS 1067. As he later told his diary, Boettiger had "got the President so confused he didn't know what was going on, and I didn't know either."

Morgenthau told Roosevelt that while postwar Europe undoubtedly needed German coal, U.S. authorities shouldn't supervise the mining. "All right," the President replied, "I'll appoint a committee of three German businessmen to run the coal mines, and we'll supervise them in Washington. If they don't get the coal out . . . we'll shoot them!"[6]

After Morgenthau finished his lunch, Boettiger took him aside and sat him on a sofa: "I want to say something to you nobody else can hear." He upbraided Morgenthau once again for the fracas after Quebec. He said he would "implore you and beg you" to change his recommendations on Germany "because you are going to start the whole thing over again. And look at the mess you are going to get the President in."

"Listen, John," said Morgenthau. "If the President got in it," it was "because a Cabinet member talked" to the press after Quebec. He wasn't going to "change my principles" when the person to be "chastised" should be "the Cabinet member."

"It wasn't a Cabinet member," said Boettiger.

"A Cabinet member or his assistant," said Morgenthau. "If this town is too small to hold me and the other Cabinet member, I will go home. . . . Any time I am embarrassing the President, he knows what he can do."

Boettiger said, "Nobody is suggesting that."

Morgenthau exclaimed, "Well, I *am!*"

Back in his Treasury office, Morgenthau told his aides, "I had my day in court. . . . The President read all this stuff carefully . . . and said this was perfect, fine. Then, bingo, in comes Boettiger. . . . Well, you may read all about it in the columns. That is the way they will fight me."

Harry Dexter White said, "It may have been a tough time, but the result was good." Morgenthau said, "No, no, listen—I have been around the Roosevelt family personally, and I'm very low."

Morgenthau called McCloy: "This is sort of embarrassing, but everything

6. One wonders whether an outsider, hearing this entire exchange, might have had worries about the President's stability.

is embarrassing." The President was in "thorough agreement," but Boettiger was there "to keep me from making my case." Morgenthau telephoned Stettinius's new deputy, Under Secretary of State Joseph Grew. With slight embroidery, he reported that Roosevelt had changed his mind about the Draft Directive. Grew gasped: "He wants to *withdraw* it?"

"Yes, definitely," replied Morgenthau. "And he wants us to come to an agreement as to what we do from there on." Grew exclaimed, "Amazing!"

AT THURSDAY NOON, March 22, Roosevelt assembled McCloy, Grew, Boettiger and others to discuss the Draft Directive. To bolster himself, McCloy had tried to shoehorn Morgenthau into the meeting, but later learned that someone—probably one or both of the Boettigers—had told Roosevelt, "Don't have Morgenthau here. He only excites you."

Before the meeting, Roosevelt saw McCloy alone. With a stiff-armed Hitler salute, the President cried, *"Heil McCloy, Hochkommissar für Deutschland!"* He said, "I've made up my mind. McCloy, you're going to be the first high commissioner for Germany."

Staggered, McCloy replied, "Mr. President, we haven't won the war yet." He added that it would be better not to appoint a civilian governor. Whoever went to Germany would find something "like a Mississippi River disaster. Where are the rations going to come from? How are the people to be fed? Basic logistics."

"McCloy, I'm too tired to argue with you," said Roosevelt. "I think you're wrong, but you tell me—amongst the soldiers, who could do this job?" McCloy recommended Lucius Clay, knowing that Clay was inclined to enact JCS 1067 leniently.

At the larger meeting, Roosevelt complained that State had "sold" him a "bill of goods." The Draft Directive had been "slipped over" on him. If he didn't have a substitute by morning, he would take them out and "shoot" them.

Assistant Secretary of State William Clayton warned that without centralized power, there would be "chaos" in Germany. "Maybe so," replied the President. But they wouldn't know until they could "go in" to Germany and "take a look and see": "Why not let nature take its course?" Give the choice to "the man who is on the ground there."

Roosevelt confessed that he had "made a mistake" at Quebec. Astonishingly he tried to blame Churchill for the memorandum endorsing the Morgenthau Plan. Anyone "could tell by reading" it that Churchill was behind it. He himself "would never have thought" of using a word like "pastoral." The President said he wanted to "change the character" of German industry, but not to "eliminate" it. "I'm not for throwing salt into the mines." He wanted Germany's factories maintained to the "fullest extent necessary" so that Americans wouldn't "have the burden of taking care of them."

By telephone McCloy described the meeting to Morgenthau, including Roosevelt's insistence on preserving German industry. Disappointed, Morgenthau asked, "That's the *President*?" Improvising, McCloy tried to mollify him by saying that Roosevelt's instinct was to control the Germans "as little as you can. Let the Germans run the thing."

Relieved that at least the President did not wish to build up the German economy, Morgenthau said, "I'm a new man. . . . I'm very happy." He told McCloy that "it may sound silly to say thank you," but it was "so unusual" for him to be "treated squarely."

"Oh, for goodness's sake!" said McCloy. "We are right about the damn thing, and there is so much intrigue around here."

On Friday morning, March 23, Morgenthau took the elevator to the White House family quarters and asked Eleanor Roosevelt if he could see the President. He told her he wanted permission to publish a book on postwar Germany. After peeking into her husband's bedroom, she said that the President hadn't finished his breakfast.

At Morgenthau's behest, she relayed his message to her husband. "That's all right," Roosevelt replied. "Let him go ahead and make the study."

Knowing how often a Roosevelt yes really meant no, Morgenthau took the precaution of sending his boss a written request: "With your approval, I want to work on this at once."

THAT AFTERNOON, after the regular Friday Cabinet meeting, Morgenthau and Grew presented Roosevelt with a new document that would replace the Draft Directive. Written mainly by McCloy, it essentially reinstated JCS 1067. As McCloy had candidly told Morgenthau, the document reflected Roosevelt's current instinct to change, not destroy, German industry. Morgenthau took comfort from its decrees that reparations should not "foster" German economic revival, that no credit be extended to postwar Germany (except by Allied Control Council permission), and that Germans bear the burden of running their own economy.

Buoyantly Roosevelt asked McCloy and Grew how to spell the word *supersede.* Having been through this so many times, Morgenthau worried that while Roosevelt was stalling, he might change his mind and refuse to sign. But the President finally scrawled on the final page, "O.K. F.D.R., superseding memo of Mar 10, 45." He asked who the "drinks" should be on. Morgenthau cried, "On me!"

Roosevelt also appointed a sub-Cabinet Informal Policy Committee on Germany, soon branded IPCOG, that would deal with postsurrender planning.[7]

Into his diary Stimson fulminated about Roosevelt's "indecision" over Germany: "Never has anything which I have witnessed in the last four years shown such instance of the bad effect of our chaotic administration and its utter failure to treat matters in a well organized way." He lambasted Roosevelt's "looseness" in running his government and his eagerness to "sign any paper" that one adviser presented to him "without waiting for the criticism and counsel of the others."

MORGENTHAU CALLED MCCLOY from the Treasury: "Well, the President signed it. . . . It's in his own handwriting and his own pen and ink. . . . He's very happy. . . . I'm happier than I've been since March tenth. That was quite a setback!" McCloy said it was like the Battle of the Bulge.

At 4:45 P.M., Morgenthau called in his aides. Roosevelt had signed "a good, tough document," the "first step towards a kind of peace which, I think, will last. . . . And if we get Treasury policy accepted on reparations, why I think it was worth all the buffeting I have taken since Quebec."

Strangely, although it was the beginning of Roosevelt's term, Morgenthau spoke in a valedictory mood: "Let's get serious for a minute. . . . If I am ever short with you, well, you will just have to be a little charitable, because you can't be fighting a thing like this with all your soul and mind and body and,

7. Chaired by Assistant Secretary of State Will Clayton, it included Harry Dexter White, McCloy and representatives of the Navy and Foreign Economic Administration.

at the same time, always be one hundred percent pleasant." He had never felt "under such pressure in my life to give way on principle."

But the President had backed him up. The "State Department crowd" had "fought against us, with no rules," to get Roosevelt to change, "and they couldn't." People like Jimmy Dunn were "fascists at heart . . . just a vicious crowd, and sooner or later, they have to be rooted out."

But on postwar Germany, "this document sets the tone." The Treasury might not get invited to all meetings, but "by hook or crook, we get there uninvited. So I just want to say I am happy, and I like my official family."

On Saturday, March 24, at 2:30 P.M., Roosevelt's secretary Grace Tully asked Morgenthau, "You think it has worked out satisfactorily all the way around?"

"Entirely," he replied. "After all, what we are arguing about . . . is the future of the world." He asked her if she could "get an answer for me" to his letter about his book on Germany. Tully promised to "look in the box" and "see if I can get an O.K. on it."

Morgenthau asked her not to "rush" the President, who was going to Hyde Park. Let him consider the matter "in that good Dutchess County fresh air." He told Tully that he and Elinor were leaving that evening for Florida: "We'll let you take care of the world."

At 5:45 P.M., Morgenthau warned Boettiger about a speech on postwar Germany to be given on the radio that evening by his State Department foes Robert Murphy and James Dunn: "They have been beaten, and now we have smoked out the people who are really fighting the President. . . . I think they have hung themselves with their own rope."

With his nerves ragged from the battle over the Draft Directive, Morgenthau escorted his wife onto a sleeping car on the East Coast Champion, for a vacation in Daytona Beach. When they arrived, they checked in at the Sheridan Plaza Hotel.

A local woman, Gertrude Lerner, had written Morgenthau that he was "probably not aware" that the hotel was normally "restricted to Jews." She had asked him, "as an outstanding citizen of the United States," to "take a stand."

Morgenthau did not cancel his reservation, but he attended his first Passover seder, held at the Daytona city hall for men and women in uniform. "As you know, it is the celebration of the freedom of the Jews from bondage in Egypt," he wrote his sons. The "young rabbi" had asked him to speak, "but I felt that I didn't know enough about the service to get up and make a semi-religious speech, so I begged off."

ROOSEVELT WAS PLANNING his own railroad trip to his self-designed cottage, which the press called the "Little White House," at Warm Springs, Georgia.

Before he left on Thursday, March 29, he called in General Lucius Clay for a final audition to be Eisenhower's successor as governor of the American zone in Germany. While walking over to the White House, Jimmy Byrnes had warned his deputy, "He's going to ask you some trick question like, 'What would you do if, in Heidelberg during the night, Germans rose up and attacked and killed a few soldiers?' "

In the Oval Office, after his perennial reminiscence about his childhood in Germany, Roosevelt told Clay that the problem in Europe would be "energy." They should build "a giant TVA."[8] for the whole continent. Aides tried to break up the meeting, but Roosevelt was so obviously enjoying it that they failed.

Clay passed the test. Afterward, Byrnes told him, "You didn't say very much." Clay replied, "The President didn't ask me any questions. But I'm glad he didn't, because I was so shocked watching him that I don't think I could have made a sensible reply. We've been talking to a dying man."

8. Tennessee Valley Authority.

CHAPTER NINETEEN

"No Earthly Powers Can Keep Him Here"

On Good Friday, March 30, 1945, after lunch, Roosevelt's train arrived in Warm Springs. The President told his Hudson Valley friend Margaret Suckley that he wanted to "sleep and sleep and sleep."

"He is steadily losing weight," William Hassett wrote in his diary. "Told me he has lost 25 pounds—no strength—no appetite—tires so easily." There was "less and less talk about all manner of things—fewer Hyde Park stories—politics, books, pictures." Hassett told Dr. Bruenn, "He is slipping away from us, and no earthly powers can keep him here."

On Monday, April 2, a thunderstorm kept Roosevelt awake for much of the night. That day, General Marshall sent him an Army intelligence estimate on Adolf Hitler and the impending defeat of Germany. "Any cowardice, faltering or negotiating with the Allies in this last hour would destroy the great tragic myth he is seeking to create," it said. Hitler was likely to end his life "bravely and dramatically and thus remain a psychological force for his enemies to reckon with for decades."

Marshall's men did not know that in his underground bunker in Berlin, Hitler had secretly decreed his own version of the Morgenthau Plan. As Allied troops conquered Germany, mines should be flooded, power and telephone plants destroyed. No large installations usable for rebuilding Germany should be left. If the Führer did not rule the Germans, no one should.

• • •

IN WARM SPRINGS, Roosevelt received a cable from Churchill demanding that the Anglo-American armies compete with the Soviets to seize Berlin. Soviet brutality in Poland was making the Prime Minister even more pessimistic about postwar Soviet behavior. Churchill had argued for weeks that taking Hitler's capital would be a vital boost to British and American prestige in postwar Europe. The more territory to the East the Anglo-Americans held, the more influence they might wield against whatever dark plans Stalin had for Europe.

The Prime Minister noted that by late March 1945 the Red Army was just thirty-five miles from the city. Anglo-American forces were over two hundred miles away.

General Omar Bradley warned that seizing Berlin before the Russians would require a hundred thousand casualties—a "pretty stiff price" for "prestige," especially since the Anglo-Americans were committed to "fall back" and give the Soviets their zone in Germany.

Eisenhower felt that after the years fighting Germany, the Soviets deserved the honor of taking Berlin, and that few things would antagonize Stalin more than trying to deprive them of it. Backed by General Marshall, he ordered the Allied Expeditionary Force to march through central Germany and then link up with the Russians at the Elbe.

Still Churchill warned Roosevelt that if the Russians took Berlin, they would seem "the overwhelming contributor to our common victory," raising "grave and formidable difficulties in the future." Should Berlin "be in our grasp, we should certainly take it."

Roosevelt turned him down. Under "Eisenhower's present plans," the Anglo-Americans would ensure that German forces would be "completely broken up." Then they should "destroy in detail the separated parts of the Nazi Army."

Churchill consented. He wrote the President, "I regard the matter as closed, and to prove my sincerity, I will use one of my very few Latin quotations—'Amantium irae amoris integratio est.' "[1]

1. Roosevelt's aides in the White House Map Room translated the quotation for him as "Lovers' quarrels always go with true love."

• • •

On Tuesday, April 3, Roosevelt received the angriest letter Stalin ever sent him. The Marshal said he had reliable information that one of Hitler's commanders had agreed to open his theater to the Anglo-Americans "for a lenient truce." Why had the President concealed this development "from your allies, the Russians?"

Roosevelt knew the background. In early March, Allen Dulles of the OSS had met in Zurich with General Karl Wolff of the Waffen-SS, who wished to explore an unconditional surrender of German forces on the Italian front.[2] Wolff warned that he was acting alone and might not be able to sway the German high command. Roosevelt and Churchill had the Kremlin informed of the feeler, to avoid any hint of double-dealing.

Molotov wrote Ambassador Harriman that he did not object to talks with General Wolff but wanted two or three Soviet generals to join in. Stimson wrote in his diary, "It was a very quarrelsome letter and indicated a spirit in Russia which bodes evil in the coming difficulties of the postwar scene."

Roosevelt and Churchill balked at the notion that Soviet generals should be invited to pursue a peace feeler in an Anglo-American theater. Stalin would never offer such a courtesy. They told Moscow that Dulles's next meeting with Wolff was only for the purpose of "establishing contact." If there were actual surrender talks, the Soviets would be welcome.

Stalin did not buy it. Suspecting that Wolff was the linchpin of the separate peace between the Germans and the West that he had feared for so long, he had Molotov demand that contact with Wolff be broken off. Harriman felt that the Soviet complaint showed that Soviet leaders "believe that they can force their will on us on any issue."

In late March, Dulles met Wolff in a hillside villa in the Italian town of Ascona. He was accompanied by a British general, Terence Airey, and an American general, Lyman Lemnitzer, who declared that they would discuss nothing but the unconditional surrender of all German forces on the Southern front. They told Wolff that any German who had the authority to offer it should go to the Supreme Commander for the Mediterranean, Field Marshal Sir Harold Alexander, and sign the proper instruments. Nothing happened.

2. According to new information released by the CIA in 2000, Wolff had been much involved in the deportation of Italian Jews to Auschwitz.

Now, in his blistering message to Roosevelt, Stalin wrote, "You insist that there have been no real negotiations yet. One must assume that you have not been fully informed."

On Wednesday, April 4, Roosevelt sent back an indignant reply.[3] It said that Stalin's accusation had "astounded" him: "It would be one of the great tragedies of history if, at the very moment of the victory now within our grasp, such distrust, such lack of faith should prejudice the entire undertaking after the colossal losses of life, materiel and treasure involved. Frankly I cannot avoid a feeling of bitter resentment toward your informers for such vile misrepresentations of my actions or those of my trusted subordinates."

Stalin's written reply insisted that he had "never doubted" the President's integrity. Churchill advised Roosevelt that this was "as near as they can get to an apology." In his reply to Stalin, Roosevelt agreed to dismiss the whole matter as a "minor incident."

But the President could see that the shadows over postwar cooperation with Moscow were lengthening. In the next-to-last message he ever sent Winston Churchill, drafted by himself, Roosevelt wrote, "I would minimize the general Soviet problem as much as possible because these problems, in one form or another, seem to arise every day, and most of them straighten out. . . . We must be firm, however, and our course thus far is correct."

ON FRIDAY, April 6, the President read a report that Stalin might no longer be so interested in seeing Germany dismembered. In London, Ambassador Winant had warned his Soviet counterpart, Feodor Gusev, that partition might make it harder for the Soviets to get their requested ten billion dollars in reparations. While professing "no connection" between the subjects, Gusev replied that dismemberment was merely an instrument to "pressure" Germany and render it "harmless," in case "other means" did not work.

Roosevelt wrote Stettinius, "Our attitude should be one of study and postponement of final decision." He said he was more concerned with eliminating "the word Reich," which would "deeply affect the problem of what Germany will be ten or twenty years from now."

Among the intimates of the Little White House, Roosevelt spoke of quitting the Presidency to return to Hyde Park, just as he had to Morgenthau

3. The reply had been mainly drafted by General Marshall, Admiral Leahy, Bohlen and others in Washington.

the previous summer. Margaret Suckley wrote in her diary that Franklin "thinks he can retire by next year, after he gets the peace organization"—the United Nations—"well started. I don't believe he thinks he will be *able* to carry on." She recorded that when the President said he might quit, his cousin Laura Delano "reacted to his statement very much as I did the first time he mentioned it to me: that he couldn't do such a thing—it had never been done. I remarked that no one had ever before had a fourth term, either!"

Suckley told her diary that "if he cannot, physically, carry on, he will *have* to resign. There is no possible sense in his killing himself by slow degrees . . . while not filling his job. Far better to hand it over, and avoid the period of his possible illness, when he wouldn't be *able* to function. From a personal point of view, he can then take care of himself and have perhaps years of a peaceful, happy life, when his influence for good can continue—perhaps on the peace organization."

BY NOW, American forces had surrounded a hundred fifty thousand Germans in the Ruhr. At the Pentagon, Stimson asked his men, "Should we clean the pocket up now, or should we bypass it and let it starve into submission, using the rest of our troops to conquer the rest of Germany?"

To clean up the Ruhr pocket, Stimson noted, they would have to "smash practically everything in it" and "wipe out the most important industrial areas in Europe." Even the mines would be destroyed, "perhaps into irreparable ruin." Nevertheless, containing the pocket would "endanger quick success in the rest of Germany" by tying down American troops around the Ruhr's perimeter.

If there ever was an opportunity to enact the Morgenthau Plan, this was it. But Marshall cabled Eisenhower to make his decision without regard to the debates "in high government circles" about a "postwar pastoral Germany." Eisenhower told Stimson that cleaning up the Ruhr pocket would not leave him "troops enough" for the rest of his mission in Germany. He planned to inflict no "useless or unnecessary damage" on the Ruhr. With this decision, the German industrial engine that Morgenthau so dreaded was left largely intact.[4]

4. Stimson was also worried about Germany's efforts to build an atomic bomb. As he wrote in his diary, the Pentagon had "discovered" that these were "probably concentrated in southwestern Germany," which was "going to be under French occupation." He found Marshall "a little staggered by it."

• • •

DURING HIS VACATION in Daytona Beach, Morgenthau received a call from Lucius Clay, whom Roosevelt had now approved as his future American military governor in Germany. The shrewdly political Clay needed to hire an economic aide and was calling for advice. Not surprisingly, Morgenthau nominated his old aide Bernard Bernstein. Warned in advance by Pentagon friends to whom Bernstein was anathema for passing Morgenthau the *Handbook,* Clay quickly replied, "I know about Colonel Bernstein, but we need somebody with more authority."[5]

Just in case McCloy had not done enough to give the Pentagon the upper hand in running the American zone in Germany, he made sure that Clay's financial adviser would not be some Morgenthau man, but McCloy's brother-in-law, the Phelps-Dodge copper heir Lewis Douglas.

Douglas had served as Roosevelt's first budget director before quitting in 1934 over the President's fiscal liberalism. Privately Douglas complained that "most of the bad things" the New Deal had done could be "traced" to its "Hebraic influence." He carped that, "as a race," Jews "seem to lack the quality of facing an issue squarely." In a 1933 letter to his father Douglas lambasted Morgenthau's "Hebraic arrogance and conceit."

DURING THEIR VACATION, Morgenthau's wife, Elinor, suffered a heart attack. Eleanor Roosevelt wrote her husband in Warm Springs, "Henry has been terribly worried. I think Elinor can't stand the war strain and trying not to show it has had an effect on her circulation." She wrote Mrs. Morgenthau, "You must just rest and get well and then perhaps we can all have a quiet summer in the country! I'll promise to hoard my gas and come and stay."

With victory over Germany in the offing, Morgenthau did not want to be away from Washington too long. After a week of Army hospital care, Elinor's doctors told him that she was sufficiently out of danger for him to go to the capital. He arranged to stop at Warm Springs for a visit with the President.

By now, Morgenthau had received a cool reply from Roosevelt to his request to publish a book on postwar Germany. "I find it difficult to know

5. In his usual bulldog manner, Harry Dexter White told Morgenthau he should push for Bernstein, whether Clay liked him or not.

just what to say," the President had written. The "spirit of the Nation" required "articulate expression," but it was hard "to say when the Nation will or can speak" and "timing will be of the very essence. We must all remember Job's lament that his enemy had not written a book."

Morgenthau wanted to change the President's mind. He could not know that he would be sharing the last dinner of Roosevelt's life.

ON WEDNESDAY, April 11, Morgenthau flew by military plane to Fort Benning, Georgia, and motored to Warm Springs, arriving at 7:30 P.M. At the Secret Service sentry gate, he was waved into the Little White House.

In the open space that was both parlor and dining room, Roosevelt was sitting before the fieldstone fireplace in his armless wheelchair, his legs up on a wood-and-rattan footstool. Over his lap was a folding table on which he performed the nightly ritual he called "the children's hour," reaching for a cocktail shaker and chunks of ice.

"I was terribly shocked when I saw him," Morgenthau recorded in his diary. "He had aged terrifically and looked very haggard."

Roosevelt's hands shook so violently that he nearly knocked over the glasses. Morgenthau helped his host by holding each glass as he poured. He noticed a large bowl of black Russian caviar, presented by Stalin at Yalta: "If I remember correctly, Mr. President, you like it plain."

Eschewing the eggs and onion, Morgenthau spread a dollop of caviar on white toast and handed it to the President. He noticed that Roosevelt "seemed to feel a little bit better" after two drinks, but that his memory was bad "and he was constantly confusing names." Morgenthau had never seen him have such trouble moving from wheelchair to armchair for dinner: "I was in agony watching him."

Morgenthau recorded that Roosevelt was "very solicitous" about his sick wife. The President "let it slip" that he was in touch with "some heart doctor—I think he said at the Presbyterian Hospital in New York."[6]

Over dry meatballs and noodles, they were joined by Margaret Suckley, his blue-haired cousin Laura Delano, called "Polly," the Russian émigré portrait painter Elizabeth Shoumatoff ("Amazon type," recorded Hassett, "gut-

6. A reference to Dr. Bruenn, who was affiliated with Columbia Presbyterian.

tural voice—altogether too aggressive") and Roosevelt's old paramour, the now-widowed Lucy Mercer Rutherfurd, whom he had reluctantly given up to stay with Eleanor.

Unbeknownst to the First Lady, with Anna as his accessory, Roosevelt had quietly begun seeing the now-widowed Lucy again during the war. On Labor Day weekend 1944, his train had made a covert stop at her New Jersey estate. Before Christmas, as Suckley wrote in her diary, she and Lucy had wept "on each other's shoulder" and "kissed each other"—"just because we each felt thankful that the other understood and wants to help Franklin!"

During his voyage to Yalta, Roosevelt had opened a birthday package from Lucy and Margaret with presents for the trip—pocket combs, room thermometers and a cigarette lighter for use in the ocean wind. Lucy had commissioned Mrs. Shoumatoff to come to Warm Springs and paint the President's portrait. In the course of the visit, the White Russian Shoumatoff had asked Roosevelt if he had liked Stalin. Roosevelt replied that he did, "but I am convinced he poisoned his wife!"

During dinner, Polly's Irish setter vomited, and she used her handkerchief to clean the mess. Undisturbed, Roosevelt and Morgenthau reminisced about adventures with Churchill and joked about the cottage's "early Val-Kill" decor, referring to the furniture made in the workshop that Eleanor established with several woman friends in the 1920s near her Hyde Park cottage.

Roosevelt mentioned the United Nations opening session a fortnight hence in San Francisco: "I will appear on the stage in my wheelchair, and I will make the speech." With a circus frown, he clapped his hands and said, "They will applaud me . . . and I will be back in Hyde Park on May first."

When the ladies left the room, Morgenthau turned serious: "Mr. President, I am doing a lot of things in regard to Germany. . . . We are having lots of troubles, and I don't want to be doing these things if it isn't agreeable to you." He reminded Roosevelt of "what happened" with the Draft Directive on Germany.

"Oh, wasn't that terrible?" Roosevelt replied. "I had to rewrite the whole thing."

Morgenthau said that "the War Department seems to want to work with me," but General Clay had told him that Robert Murphy was one of his "headaches."

Roosevelt asked, "What's the matter with Murphy?" Morgenthau recalled that Hull had "forced him down your throat" and installed him on Eisenhower's staff in London. As long as Murphy was around, they were "just never going to have a good working group" on Germany.

Morgenthau claimed that Murphy was eager to "build up a central Germany." (He later confessed to his diary that "I was sort of drawing on my imagination.") Echoing what Eleanor had said at Hyde Park in September, Roosevelt said that it might be a "mistake" to "send a Catholic to Germany." Abruptly he asked, "What have you got on your mind?"

"To break the State Department crowd headed by Jimmy Dunn," said Morgenthau. "Just the way you broke the admirals when you were Assistant Secretary of the Navy."[7] Roosevelt retorted that Dunn's performance had been "good" at the time of his last Quebec meeting with Churchill. Morgenthau stood firm: "I think Dunn is terrible."

Morgenthau pulled out a photostatic copy of Roosevelt's letter asking him to postpone his book on Germany. "Where did you get that from?" asked Roosevelt. "I have never seen it before. . . . Hassett or somebody told me you wanted to get a book out right away, and I thought it was a mistake."

"No, what I want to do is get out a textbook after VE-Day," said Morgenthau. "For example, I would like to write a chapter on how sixty million Germans can feed themselves." He reported that the publisher, Harper and Brothers, was "ready to gamble five thousand dollars" on the project. He promised to show it to Roosevelt before publication, and hoped that the President would write the preface.

"You go ahead and do it," said Roosevelt. "I think it is a grand idea. I have a lot of ideas of my own." He hoped Morgenthau would "put something in there" about his talks with the old German finance minister Hjalmar Schacht, who in the 1930s had "wept" on Roosevelt's desk about his "poor country."

Morgenthau had heard the story more than once, but as usual did not interrupt. Offhandedly he mentioned that McCloy was visiting the European battlefront. Roosevelt replied that McCloy had been "all wrong about de Gaulle," but was "all right now."[8]

Now that he was in common cause with McCloy against the State Depart-

7. While at the Navy under President Wilson, Roosevelt and his superior, Josephus Daniels, fought back efforts by admirals to encroach upon their authority.

8. McCloy had pressed Roosevelt to be more friendly toward the Free French leader, whom the President disliked and distrusted.

ment, Morgenthau wrote in his diary that he was "glad" to hear Roosevelt praise him because "some people around town have been trying to poison him against McCloy."

Shifting the President back to the subject, Morgenthau asked him point-blank if he wanted him to "interest myself in the future treatment of Germany." Roosevelt gave no direct answer.

Morgenthau forged ahead: "Look, Mr. President, I am going to fight hard, and this is what I am fighting for. A weak economy for Germany means that she will be weak politically. . . . I want to help win the peace."

In a reply that almost certainly meant less than met the ear, Roosevelt said, "Henry, I am with you one hundred percent." Morgenthau said, "You may have heard things, because I am going to fight for this." In his diary, he later wrote, "I certainly put him on notice as to what I was going to do."

Then, perhaps prompted by Roosevelt beforehand, Polly Delano popped in: "Are you gentlemen through talking?"

Before leaving for a midnight military flight to Washington, Morgenthau left the room and called Daytona Beach to inquire about his wife. "I came back and said goodbye to the President and his company," he later told his diary. "When I left them, they were sitting around laughing and chatting, and I must say the President seemed to be happy and enjoying himself."

A FEW HOURS LATER, while Roosevelt slept in Warm Springs, it was Thursday morning, April 12, 1945, in Germany. Generals Eisenhower, Bradley and George Patton were shown a concentration camp, Ohrdruf Nord, near Gotha, discovered the previous week by the Allies.

Before this day, as Eisenhower later recalled, he had known about the Nazi death camps "only generally or through secondary sources." Demanding to be shown every corner of Ohrdruf Nord, the old soldier later wrote that he had never before "experienced an equal sense of shock." He wrote to his wife, "I never dreamed that such cruelty, bestiality and savagery could really exist in this world!"

Ike later told General Marshall that he wanted to be able to provide "*first-hand* evidence" of the camps in case anyone ever claimed that they had never existed. As he left Ohrdruf Nord, he asked a U.S. Army sentry, "Still having trouble hating them?"

• • •

ON THURSDAY MORNING in Washington, Morgenthau returned home at dawn and caught a few hours of sleep. When he opened his morning *Washington Post,* he was staggered to read an acerbic column by Marquis Childs revealing that he was once again pushing himself into planning for postwar Germany. Using information clearly leaked by State, Childs reported that Morgenthau, who had tried to "convert Germany into a vast kitchen garden," had now pressured Roosevelt to withdraw a crucial State Department directive.

Morgenthau feared he was about to be dragged into another humiliating Cabinet furor that would jeopardize his relationship with the President. Arriving at his Treasury office that afternoon, he barked at his aides that Childs had penned a "dirty story." Josiah DuBois said, "It obviously came from Stettinius."

Stettinius called Morgenthau and said he was "shocked and embarrassed": "Henry, I've had the whole crowd here this afternoon and I have read the riot act. . . . I just don't believe it came from this place."

"Certainly it wouldn't come out of *Treasury!*" cried Morgenthau. "I'm not going to take it lying down, Ed! . . . I'm not looking for any fights, but I'm not going to go through what I did after Quebec!"

Morgenthau felt stung that Stettinius did so little to mollify him. He later told Henrietta Klotz, "He didn't say, 'Wait a minute, Henry, let's see if we can get together.' " Referring to Stettinius, she bitterly replied, "*He* will sleep well tonight!"

Morgenthau's aides advised him to leak his own version of the Draft Directive struggle to the press. Morgenthau agreed. He told them, "Make it a lovely story—that Stettinius was so tired that he didn't read the document that he gave the President of the United States and didn't know what was in it. It was up to me. When I showed it to him, the President was shocked and ordered the thing rewritten. . . . You plan a little campaign, and we will just teach the State Department people a few little things."

Morgenthau said that Childs's column showed why he must publish a book on Germany: "I have clearance from the President. . . . I am going full steam ahead."

Morgenthau decided to plant a story of his own with a friendly columnist, Samuel Grafton of the *New York Post*:[9] "I'll call him up. . . . Samuel, isn't it?"

He told Grafton that he had been "reading Marquis Childs's article today." His enemies were "trying to pull a Quebec on me, see? . . . Somebody's been whining to Childs and giving him a false picture." He had "just got through telling Stettinius that this time, I am not going to take it lying down."

IN WARM SPRINGS THAT MORNING, Roosevelt had awoken with a headache and stiff neck, which Dr. Bruenn rubbed. By noon, dressed in a double-breasted gray suit and crimson tie, he began studying papers. Margaret Suckley and Lucy Rutherfurd sat on a nearby sofa.

Dipping into her water colors, Shoumatoff said, "Mr. President, you look so much better than yesterday." She found that his "gray look" had disappeared and that he had "exceptionally good color."[10]

Roosevelt had told her that the war against Germany might end "at any time." While she painted, he pulled his draft card from his wallet and threw it into the wastebasket.

Suddenly the President's head pitched forward. Margaret Suckley asked, "Have you dropped your cigarette?" He said, "I have a terrific pain in the back of my head." Someone cried, "Call the doctor, quick!" As Roosevelt was carried to bed, he murmured, "Be careful!"

FROM THE WHITE HOUSE at 5:43 P.M., Eleanor Roosevelt called Morgenthau at the Treasury and told him that the President was dead. She asked him to "come over quickly to the White House," so they could call Elinor in Daytona Beach and tell her the news before she heard it on the radio and risked another heart attack.

Morgenthau wrote his sons, "It was one of the most considerate and kind acts I've known anyone to do." After he and Mrs. Roosevelt called Elinor in

9. In 1944, Grafton had written a series of articles that encouraged American free ports for refugees like the one Morgenthau helped to establish at Oswego.

10. Doctors later explained that Roosevelt's flushness was a warning sign of his onrushing cerebral hemorrhage.

her sickbed, he issued a statement to the press: "I have lost my best friend." He wrote his sons that Roosevelt's death had "depressed me terrifically" and he felt "in a sort of daze."

In the cottage at Warm Springs, before the undertakers removed the body of the thirty-second President of the United States, a weeping Grace Tully found in Roosevelt's desk basket a cable from Allen Dulles in Bern. It reported new demands from General Wolff on the Italian front in exchange for the unconditional surrender of Germany.

CHAPTER TWENTY

"What Will We Make of It?"

So Franklin Roosevelt was dead, and the presidency had fallen to a man who had no deep experience in foreign or military affairs or diplomacy. Roosevelt had never had an extended talk with his Vice President on Germany or on any other aspect of the postwar world. For all but twenty-five of Harry Truman's eighty-two days as number two, the President had been away on his trips to Yalta, Hyde Park and Warm Springs.

Roosevelt had loved William Henley's "Invictus" ("I am the master of my fate: / I am the captain of my soul"). It is a measure of his hubris and his American conviction that he could master events—even his own life and death—that he made no serious effort to prepare Truman for the very real prospect that Truman might suddenly become, at a crossroads in history, the most powerful man in the world.

Just after Roosevelt's death, Anna Boettiger told Morgenthau that her father had known that he was seriously ill and "what was wrong with him." She explained that he had "had an enlarged heart for some time."

Still, even if, as Truman recalled, Roosevelt had told him under the Jackson magnolia in August 1944 that he wished to be succeeded by someone "slightly right of center," we have no evidence that the fading President ever admitted to himself that he might die in office. As always, Roosevelt expected to be in the driver's seat. If he were to leave the presidency before 1949, he did not expect it to happen by sudden death, while sitting in Warm Springs with his paramour and a hundred crucial presidential decisions to make before World War II was won.

If Roosevelt planned to relinquish the job—which is difficult to imagine in light of how much he relished it and how indispensable he seemed to consider himself—he would do it on his own schedule. As he had hinted to Morgenthau at Fishkill Farms the previous September, it was possible that he and Henry might have retired before the fourth term was over to become "country gentlemen" in Dutchess County and assume some leadership role in the fledgling new United Nations.

For four and a half years, while fighting a world war, the President had kept the strings of leadership under his tight control. If he alienated a Stimson, Hull or Morgenthau, he was always certain that he could bring them back into the fold. If he cavalierly signed a Quebec memorandum or Draft Directive on Germany that gave him trouble, he could deny recalling that he ever signed it. And if there were complaints in Dewey's speeches or Stimson's diary about Roosevelt's "chaotic" administrative methods and his mercurial indecision, no matter. From Roosevelt's point of view, he knew, while concealing his motives and actions, exactly what he wanted to do. As he had once boasted to Morgenthau, "I am a juggler, and I never let my right hand know what my left hand does."

But now the juggler had fallen dead, and with his sudden absence, just before the climax of World War II, the whirling bowling pins, canes and china plates were in danger of crashing down. As the historian Robert Ferrell has written, Roosevelt had "created a Rube Goldberg machine," and when he died, he had left his successor no "operator's manual."

Thus on Friday morning, April 13, 1945, when Harry Truman sat down behind Roosevelt's maple Oval Office desk, he was befuddled. He had no idea what Roosevelt, Churchill and Stalin had said or agreed to at Yalta. He had not been allowed to read a single one of the cables that had flowed into Warm Springs, informing Roosevelt about the race for Berlin, the Ruhr pocket and Stalin's anger over the talks with General Wolff.

Surrounded by Roosevelt's naval prints and ship models, Truman asked an aide to put away the ornaments that littered the massive desk. Then he called in the man who was now his own Secretary of State.

Truman once wrote his cousin Nellie Noland that after he came to Washington, "F.D.R. and nearly everybody else" had thought of him as "the representative of the devil, in the person of Tom Pendergast," the Kansas City political boss who had furthered Truman's career. Even the polished Stettinius, who so prided himself on getting along with everyone, privately thought of his new boss as a small-time courthouse politician, like the rapscallions who surrounded the scandalous Warren Harding.

While briefing Truman on the war, Stettinius told the new President about the decree that Roosevelt had approved in late March to replace the Draft Directive on Germany.[1] The Big Three, he said, had yet finally to agree on Germany's treatment under occupation. He warned Truman that since Yalta, the Soviets had taken "a firm and uncompromising position on nearly every major question."

After Stettinius departed, Truman saw Stimson and the Chiefs of Staff. Truman privately considered Stimson the best member of Roosevelt's Cabinet. When the Truman Committee had begun to scrutinize the mysterious new defense installation at Oak Ridge, Tennessee, where, unbeknownst to Truman, an atomic bomb was being created, Stimson had told the Senator that it was "one of the most important things" in the "history of the world" and persuaded him to "call off your dogs."

Now Truman's visitors warned of alarming last-ditch German resistance and the danger that Hitler and his forces might retreat to a mountain redoubt, which might postpone victory in Europe for six months. The new President praised the War Department's performance and told Stimson to keep it up.

Riding back to the Pentagon from the White House, General Marshall told Stimson that they wouldn't know what Truman was "really like until the pressure begins to be felt." But Stimson later heaved a sigh of "wonderful relief" into his diary. After five years serving Roosevelt, he appreciated the "promptness and snappiness" with which Truman operated: "No long, drawn-out soliloquies."

• • •

1. "Destruction of National Socialist organizations and influence, punishment of war criminals, disbandment of the German military establishment . . . political decentralization, reparation from existing wealth and future production, prevention of the manufacture of arms . . . and controls over the German economy to secure these objectives."

MORGENTHAU WROTE HIS SONS that Roosevelt's death had "hit" him "awfully hard." Exhausted from sleepless nights worrying about his wife, deprived of her shrewd advice on Washington personalities, on Saturday morning, April 14, he strode into Truman's Oval Office with the condescending air of someone there to assess a man who was his new boss only in title.

During the years when Truman was an obscure, backbench provincial Senator, known largely for his origins in the Pendergast machine, Morgenthau had been the President's chief crony in the Cabinet and one of the lions of the New Deal. He presumed that the new President respected and needed him as much or more than Roosevelt had. In this he was badly mistaken. Truman had resented him since an incident about which Morgenthau may never have even known, but which the new President remembered with lingering bitterness.

After Truman's first election to the Senate in 1934, his senior Missouri colleague, Bennett Clark, took him for a courtesy call on the Secretary of the Treasury. The two men were told by a Morgenthau aide that the Secretary was not in. Hypersensitive about his ties to Pendergast, Truman was certain that Morgenthau had snubbed him.[2] Despite the surface civility he showed almost everyone, Truman, like many in Washington, saw Morgenthau as a Roosevelt errand boy who had exploited the presidential friendship to wander into areas beyond his domain, intellect and expertise, such as the treatment of postwar Germany.

Truman understood Roosevelt's greatness in leading the nation through depression and world war. He knew that Roosevelt's confidence in him had made him President, and in public, he revered the fallen President's memory. But privately he was no Roosevelt acolyte. He was appalled by Roosevelt's disloyalty to people, which to Truman was a major political sin.

Truman could never forget that in 1940 Roosevelt had almost ended his career by refusing to lift a finger when Truman faced a tough Democratic primary challenge. In his diary, Truman wrote in 1948 that Roosevelt had been a "fakir." Late in life, he complained that the old President was "the coldest man I ever met. He didn't give a damn personally for me or you or anyone else in the world, as far as I could see."[3]

2. Truman may have also resented Morgenthau's role in the Treasury investigation that culminated when Pendergast went to prison in 1939 for income-tax evasion.

3. As Robert Ferrell has noted, Truman said this in old age, when his mind had begun to fog, but his comment is consistent with evidence from earlier in his life of his private attitudes toward Roosevelt.

Thus Morgenthau's friendship with Roosevelt counted for little with Truman. It probably damaged him. From reading the newspapers and while chatting over bourbon and branch water with old congressional friends like Sam Rayburn and Jimmy Byrnes, Truman had been appalled by the public tempest over the Morgenthau Plan. He blamed Morgenthau for overstepping his bounds and Roosevelt for his favoritism and sloppy administrative methods.

Truman's approach to administration was as crisp as his double-breasted suits. He had disapproved of Roosevelt's frequent resort to special envoys and troubleshooters, who had undermined the late President's Secretaries of State and War, and the messy public struggles of all-against-all that, Truman believed, had afflicted too much of Roosevelt's war leadership. Years later Truman recalled that "Roosevelt wasn't an administrator. Oh, he liked to play one outfit against the other." Truman was determined to make sure that the chief Cabinet posts were held by people he trusted enough to grant considerable autonomy. Roosevelt's fear that a Harry Hopkins or Jimmy Byrnes might threaten his dominance had moved him to cut them off at the knees when they seemed to grow too powerful.

Truman later complained in his diary about "Mr. Roosevelt's inability to pass on responsibility. . . . He was always careful to see that no credit went to anyone else for accomplishment." By contrast, Truman's sense of political self was not threatened but enhanced by the prospect of having strong people in his Cabinet. "I am willing and want to pass the credit around," he wrote. "The objective is the thing, not personal aggrandizement."

Knowing none of Truman's private feelings and intentions, taken in by his self-deprecating manner, Morgenthau treated his new boss as if the purpose of their first conversation in the Oval Office was for Truman to convince Morgenthau that he was up to Morgenthau's exacting standards. As Morgenthau wrote in his diary, on that Saturday morning, he found it difficult to address Truman as "Mr. President." Morgenthau was never very good at concealing his emotions, and Truman almost certainly sensed that Morgenthau was patronizing him.

The new President declared, "I think I admired Mr. Roosevelt as much as you did."

"I don't think that's possible," Morgenthau replied. "I feel this war very strongly. I have one son with General Patton, and another in the Pacific, and his ship has just been torpedoed for the second time." Using the same words he had spoken to Roosevelt just two nights earlier in Warm Springs, he added, "My first idea is to win the war, and then I want to win the peace."

Claiming his turf, Morgenthau told Truman he had been doing "a lot of things which Mr. Roosevelt has encouraged me to do that aren't strictly Treasury business." He wished to "talk to you sometime about Germany" and "explain the Morgenthau Plan."

Politely Truman replied, "I would like to know about it." Then, remembering Morgenthau's public wrestling matches over Germany, he added sourly, "I don't want any fussing between you and Stettinius."

Defensively Morgenthau replied, "I get along with *all* members of the Cabinet." He said there were "no problems with Stettinius and me," only with "the people under him." Truman should know that many at State "were there in Hoover's time, and they aren't in sympathy with the New Deal and Mr. Roosevelt."[4]

"I will get rid of them if they give us any trouble," the President said.

Morgenthau warned him that the "big financiers" would want to "get rid of me," and unless the President of the United States stood "right behind me," he "wouldn't last two minutes."

"I want you to stay with me," said Truman. Morgenthau promised to remain "just as long as I think I can serve you."

Truman said, "When the time comes that you can't, you will hear from me first. Direct."

Morgenthau wrote his sons that his encounter with the new President had been "very good. . . . Truman is very snappy, wants quick answers, and I think he is going to give some of the Cabinet members heart failure because they have been accustomed to taking things pretty easy." He reported that Truman "seems to want to give you all the authority that you want, and then if you don't make any good, he believes in firing people." His own "frame of mind" was that Truman "has to woo me and be nice to me." In his diary, he confided that Truman "has a lot of nervous energy, and seems to be inclined to make very quick decisions. . . . But after all, he is a politician, and what is going on in his head, time will only tell."

4. Morgenthau did not know that Truman did not share Roosevelt's deep hostility to Herbert Hoover. In fact, Truman felt that Roosevelt's rebuffs to Hoover had been shameful. One of the first things Truman did as President was to restore Hoover to political society as an informal presidential adviser.

• • •

AT HYDE PARK ON SUNDAY MORNING, April 15, a bugler played "Taps" as Franklin Roosevelt's coffin was lowered into the garden beside the Big House.

"It was a brilliant, clear spring day, and the flowers around the grave stood out like so many jewels," Morgenthau wrote his sons. "They had the West Point cadets, and they had the Marines, and when they finally blew 'Taps,' it got me." He reported that their sister Joan had "cried like a baby."[5]

The following afternoon, Monday, April 16, Truman addressed a Joint Session of Congress and reaffirmed Roosevelt's war policies: "Our demand has been, and it remains unconditional surrender!"

Privately, the new President was skeptical even of this keystone of Roosevelt's war leadership. According to transcripts of private conversations Truman had with aides in 1954 while writing his presidential memoirs, he thought "it probably would have been better had there been no policy of unconditional surrender."[6] Without Roosevelt's unflinching demand, Truman argued in retrospect, the Germans might have surrendered when they felt "certain to be defeated"—after Stalingrad and the D-Day landings. This would have saved lives and allowed "a much easier recovery for all of Europe and especially Germany."

ON WEDNESDAY, April 18, the hundreds of thousands of German troops in the Ruhr pocket threw up their hands, the largest such surrender of the European war. Crossing the Elbe River at Magdeburg, the Ninth U.S. Army had pushed within fifty miles of Berlin. With American forces so close, General George Patton reopened the question of racing the Soviets to the capital. "We had better take Berlin," he told Eisenhower, "and quick!"

Eisenhower refused, noting that the fifty thousand Ninth Army soldiers beyond the Elbe were outside the range of fighter-plane support: "We'd get all coiled up for something that in all probability would never come off."

5. After leaving the White House, Eleanor Roosevelt moved temporarily to the Morgenthaus' new apartment on Connecticut Avenue in Washington, "which makes Mother and me very happy," as Morgenthau wrote his sons. "I told her that our home was her home."

6. The transcripts were closed by the Truman Library until 1982.

More worried about Stalin's motives every hour, Churchill agreed with Patton. On Truman's behalf, Eisenhower calmed the Prime Minister down. But Churchill had larger stakes in mind.

Almost seventy American divisions had rushed into Germany faster than the Red Army, which often moved on foot and by primitive horsedrawn vehicles. American forces had thrust one hundred fifty miles into the Soviet occupation zone. Many Germans, afraid of the Soviets and their armies, were straining to surrender to the Americans. Churchill considered this vital leverage that the Anglo-Americans should not give up without some reciprocal concessions from Stalin.

On the day of the Ruhr pocket surrender, Churchill cabled Truman that when Roosevelt and he had drawn up occupation zones "rather hastily at Quebec," they had "not foreseen that General Eisenhower's armies would make such a mighty inroad into Germany." Churchill was "quite prepared" to keep the deal with Stalin on zones. But Anglo-American troops should not "be hustled back" by "some crude assertion of a local Russian general."

Churchill noted that the land in the Soviet zone produced most of Germany's food. He and Truman should insist that the Soviets consent to a "fair" distribution of food among all the zones. Only then should the Anglo-Americans "retire with dignity from the much greater gains which the Allied troops have acquired by their audacity and vigor."

Truman did not buy Churchill's proposal. As he recalled years later, he felt that if he and Churchill started breaking their promises, they wouldn't "get anywhere with Stalin." He wrote Churchill that the "only practical thing to do" was to "try our best to make the Russians carry out their agreements." Truman and Churchill told Stalin that their troops should retreat to their assigned zones "as soon as the military situation permits."

THAT WEEK, the entire world was discovering the hell of the concentration camps. As British tanks crashed through the gates of Belsen, the first large death mill to be liberated, skeletal women and men staggered to their feet as British soldiers cried through bullhorns, "You are free! You are free! You are free!"

From another liberated camp, Edward R. Murrow told Americans over CBS Radio, "I pray you believe what I have said about Buchenwald."

Harold Ickes predicted in his diary that American public opinion would now "really assert itself" against the Germans: "The pictures and the descriptions that have appeared in the newspapers are simply horrifying. . . . Since the Germans have been guilty of these atrocities, I am in favor of their disclosure because otherwise we can't possibly have the state of mind that we ought to have in agreeing upon terms for Germany."

Even now, however, Stimson could not comprehend the historic enormity of the death camps. In his diary, he persisted in referring to the "so-called atrocities." After receiving a congressional delegation just back from touring Buchenwald, Dachau and Nordhausen, he wrote that his visitors had "unanimously" concluded that Hitler's government had made a "deliberate and concerted attempt" to "eliminate by murder, starvation and other methods of death large numbers of Russians, Poles, Jews and other classes of people whom they did not wish to have survive."

Rabbi Stephen Wise hoped that the shock and outrage that Americans were feeling could be harnessed on behalf of the age-old dream of a Jewish state in Palestine. On Friday morning, April 20, in the Oval Office, Wise told the new President, "I'm not sure if you're aware of the reasons underlying the wish of the Jewish people for a homeland."

Truman told Wise he would try to help. On his desk was a stiff memo from the State Department warning that the Palestine question was "highly complex." Years later Truman recalled that the memo "from the striped pants boys" was "in effect telling me to watch my step, that I didn't really understand what was going on over there and that I ought to leave it to the experts." By Truman's account, his attitude was that "as long as I was President, I'd see to it that *I* made policy." Still, after a later visit from Wise, Truman scrawled in his diary that the rabbi's purpose was "to put me on the spot with the Jews."

NIGHT AFTER NIGHT, Truman stayed up late in Roosevelt's old Map Room in the White House basement, wearing his eyes out while poring over the secret diplomatic documents that Roosevelt had never allowed him to see. "I had to be in an intelligent position to make these decisions," Truman told his aides in 1954. "I had never seen the Map Room before I became President. I didn't know it existed." Truman was startled by the growing hostility of

Stalin's messages to Roosevelt in Warm Springs. He recalled that Stalin "accused us of everything under the sun—that we were trying to make a separate peace with Germany."

On Sunday evening, April 22, 1945, Stalin's Foreign Minister, Vyacheslav Molotov, came to the White House. Truman recalled in 1954 that Molotov had "a Cro-Magnon head, like an apple." By Truman's account, when Molotov "began to tell me what the Russians had to have," he replied that there were "two sides to the question." Molotov said, "I have never been talked to like that in my life." Truman retorted, "Carry out your agreements, and you won't get talked to like that."

In Moscow, Ambassador Harriman regretted that Truman "went at it so hard, because his behavior gave Molotov an excuse to tell Stalin that the Roosevelt policy was being abandoned."

WITH HITLER IN HIS BUNKER and Allied bombs raining down on Berlin, Heinrich Himmler was furtively offering Truman and Churchill a separate peace. As Truman later wrote, "The German idea, of course, was to split the three great powers." On Wednesday afternoon, April 25, the President was driven to the Pentagon to discuss Himmler's offer with Churchill on a secure transatlantic communication line.

As Truman recalled in 1954, Churchill was "very anxious for a surrender" and "very much afraid that the Russians would make a separate peace with Hitler." But Truman insisted that Himmler "be forced to surrender to all three governments." Churchill consented.

Stalin cabled Truman and Churchill that their reply to Himmler's peace feeler had been "absolutely sound, and as for us Russians, we pledge to continue our attacks on the Germans."

Stimson wrote in his diary that victory in Europe would soon be here: "It is hard to think of it—all the toil, energy and strain—all the blood and tears. The world has been brought to the very brink of ruin, and now complete victory. What will we make of it?"

CHAPTER TWENTY-ONE

"I Was Never in Favor of That Crazy Plan"

Before dawn on Sunday, April 29, 1945, Soviet tanks rumbled near Hitler's bunker. Soviet shells made the ceiling tremble. Inside the catacomb, the Führer perfunctorily married his mistress, Eva Braun. Then he called in a secretary to dictate his last political testament: "I will not fall into the hands of an enemy that requires a new spectacle, exhibited by the Jews, to divert its hysterical masses. My wife and I choose to die in order to escape the shame of overthrow or capitulation."

The next day, the Führer of the thousand-year Reich shot himself in the head and his new wife swallowed poison. By Hitler's orders, the two bodies were taken upstairs into the garden, doused with gasoline and set afire, with the Führer's shinbones suddenly visible through the flames.

At the White House, Truman was surprised to learn that Hitler had killed himself. He had expected "many high German officers" to "take this way out," but Hitler, "in his fanaticism," to "resist to the very end."

Accustomed to mistrust what they heard from Nazi Germany, sixty-eight percent of American respondents to a Gallup poll questioned whether Hitler was really dead. A Michigan animal trainer named Spikehorn Meyer wired Truman, "I am offering $50,000, cash American money, for the capture of Adolf Hitler, delivered to me. . . . I want to make Hitler a sideline attraction with my bear show, and I will tour Russia, England and other Allied countries."

On Sunday, May 6, Eisenhower cabled the President that General Alfred Jodl, operations chief of the German high command, and Admiral Hans von Friedeburg, supreme German Navy commander, had arrived at his headquarters in Reims, France. Jodl and Friedeburg were trying to strike a separate peace with the Anglo-Americans. Eisenhower informed Truman that the Germans had been warned that "unless they agreed to my terms of surrender," he would "break off all negotiations and seal the Western front."

On Monday, May 7, Jodl signed the surrender instrument, followed by General Walter Bedell Smith for the Anglo-Americans and General Ivan Susloparov for the Soviet high command. Jodl declared, "With this signature, the German people and armed forces are, for better or worse, delivered into the victors' hands." He hoped "that the victors will treat them with generosity."

Jodl was taken into Eisenhower's office, where the Supreme Commander warned him that he would be held responsible if surrender terms were violated. After having Jodl dismissed, Eisenhower declared that the "formula of unconditional surrender" pronounced by Roosevelt and Churchill in January 1943 "has now been fulfilled."

The next morning, Tuesday, May 8, was Truman's sixty-first birthday. He told the nation by radio that "our rejoicing" over victory in Europe was "sobered" by the "terrible price we have paid to rid the world of Hitler and his evil band."

Truman said to his aides in 1954, "It's a pity that Roosevelt could not have survived the German surrender in his former physical and mental condition. . . . The entire settlement would have been made much easier. He had world opinion with him. . . . No one else had that glamour in all the countries that he had. . . . I didn't know whether I could pick up the threads where he left them."

Unlike Roosevelt, Truman could cite no boyhood memories of Germany. But unlike Roosevelt, he had actually fought the Germans. Although past draft age when Congress declared war in 1917, stirred by Wilson's pledge to make the world safe for democracy, the thirty-three-year-old Truman faked his vision test to join the Army. Before training at Camp Doniphan, Oklahoma, he wrote his fiancée, Bess Wallace, "If we are ordered to go to Berlin, go we must, or be buried on the way. . . . I'd like to be present when Berlin falls. . . . If the war ends happily and I can steal the Russian or German crown jewels, just think what a grand military wedding you can have."

As a field artillery captain in Alsace in the summer of 1918, Truman wrote Bess from "somewhere in Parlez-Vous," "Have fired five hundred rounds at the Germans at my command, been shelled, didn't run away, thank the Lord, and never lost a man." He thought the Germans deserved "a bayonet peace" for "what they've done to France."

After the November armistice, Truman wrote Bess that he might have to join the occupation: "There are rumors rife that we will go to Germany to do police and rioting duty. . . . Shall I bring you some German spoons and tableware or just some plain loot in the form of graft money? I hope they give me Coblenz or Cologne to hold down. There should be a good opportunity for a rising young captain with an itching palm, shouldn't there?"

When President Wilson came to Paris to make the peace, Truman saw him climb into his car in front of the Hotel Crillon. But like other American servicemen, Truman was dreaming of home. "I don't give a whoop (to put it mildly) whether there's a League of Nations or whether Russia has a Red government or a Purple one," he wrote Bess, "and if the President of the Czecho-Slovaks wants to pry the throne from under the King of Bohemia, let him pry but send us home."

In the mid-1930s, mainly in deference to his isolationist Missouri constituency, Senator Truman voted for neutrality laws that kept the United States from aiding European democracies against fascism. But, serving as an Army reservist between the wars, he responded to Roosevelt's calls for preparedness. In the fall of 1940, he went to General Marshall and said he wished to enlist. "You're too damned old," said the Army Chief of Staff. "You'd better stay home and work in the Senate."[1]

After Hitler's invasion of Poland, Truman wrote his wife that he was "mighty blue" because he doubted "that England and France can lick the Germans and Russians": "If Germany can organize Russia and make England give up her fleet, look out—we'll have a Nazi or nasty world." He was less willing than Roosevelt to draw moral distinctions between the Nazis and the Stalinists. Even when the United States joined forces with the Soviets

1. When Marshall was later asked whether he would have given Truman the same reply had he known he would be President, Marshall said, "I would be a little more diplomatic about it!"

after Pearl Harbor, Truman wrote Bess that the Russians were "as untrustworthy as Hitler and Al Capone."

Like Churchill, Truman was more inclined than Roosevelt to view both the Germans and Russians through the lens of balance-of-power politics. After Hitler invaded the Soviet Union in 1941, the Missouri Senator told the *New York Times,* "If we see that Germany is winning, we ought to help Russia, and if Russia is winning, we ought to help Germany, and that way let them kill as many as possible—although I don't want to see Hitler victorious under any circumstances."

THROUGHOUT HIS LIFE, Truman was prone in private to use crude anti-Semitic language that belied his growth as a national figure. To the private Truman, New York City was a "Kike town" and greedy poker players "screamed like a Jewish merchant"—although one such merchant, Eddie Jacobson, was his old haberdashery partner in Kansas City and a lifelong friend.[2]

Despite his social anti-Semitism, Senator Truman was ahead of Roosevelt in speaking out against Hitler's war on the Jews. In April 1943, he told a Chicago rally chaired by Rabbi Wise, "We must do all that is humanly possible to provide a haven and place of safety for all those who can be grasped from the hands of the Nazi butchers." He declared that Hitler's war against the Jews was "not a Jewish problem" but "an American problem."

During World War II, Truman made his national reputation when his Senate investigation of the U.S. defense effort revealed how prewar collaboration between Big Business and German cartels may have undermined American preparedness. Deals between the German behemoth I.G. Farben and companies such as Standard Oil and Alcoa were charged with threatening dangerous wartime shortfalls in magnesium and synthetic rubber.

As a President with Confederate ancestors, Truman privately compared the job to be done in defeated Germany to the Reconstruction that had been so hard on the American South: "You can't be vindictive after a war." In 1963 he said, "I know what it means to lose. My own family had been on the losing side in the Civil War. I remember my grandmother telling me stories about the Yankee redlegs who raided her farm and shot her chickens and butchered

2. Nevertheless Bess Truman apparently never invited Jacobson or his wife to their home in Independence.

her pigs and set fire to the hay and the barns. . . . My mother hated the Yankees till she died, and I didn't want hate to be this war's gift to the future."

AS TRUMAN PRESIDED over Germany's surrender, Morgenthau and his Cabinet colleagues haggled over the final version of JCS 1067. McCloy had flown to Germany in April to find German cities standing out "like so many decayed teeth." Soon Germany would be starving. He told Stimson that "slaves from the surrounding nations," whom Germans had been "working to death," were being "released by our armies" and "running riot through the country."

Stimson wrote in his diary, "I had anticipated the chaos, but the details of it were appalling. It represents the ruin of a most powerful and efficient nation which has wrecked itself by its own failure in morals and is now suffering the terrific penance that goes with terrific cruelty."

Fortified by McCloy's bleak report, Stimson and his men defended the loopholes that McCloy had sewn into JCS 1067. Assistant Secretary of War Robert Lovett argued that plants, equipment and other industrial treasure should not be taken from Germany unless the American commander attested that they were not needed "for the support and protection of the occupying forces."

Morgenthau did not want JCS 1067 to let the Allied Control Council allow wages and prices to be managed by German authorities. He noted that Roosevelt had been "very clear" in saying that the German economy should "seek its own level."

Assistant Secretary of State Will Clayton rejoined that if inflation raced out of control, it would exhaust the German food supply and the U.S. Army "would have to act."

"We don't think we are going to stop inflation in Germany," said McCloy. But Americans would be blamed for whatever inflation took place: "We'll be blamed for *everything* that takes place." He demanded, "Give the zone commander the authority to do what he feels he may have to do." He wrote Truman that Germany was in desperate need of food, fuel and transportation: "There is complete economic, social and political collapse going on in Central Europe, the extent of which is unparalleled in history, unless one goes back to the collapse of the Roman Empire, and even that may not have been as great an economic upheaval."

When McCloy gave the President a draft of JCS 1067 at the end of April, Truman promised to "read every word of it": "I have read a million words since I became President, and I am ready to read another million."

Truman agreed with Stimson and McCloy that crippling German industry and therefore food production would penalize the other Europeans who had been Hitler's victims. He wanted Europe to be "rehabilitated by the people" who had "destroyed it."

McCloy told Morgenthau that the Army was now using German synthetic oil and rubber plants "to very great advantage." He wished to keep them operating for "our occupation" to provide heat for the French and other Europeans next winter.

Morgenthau complained, "I don't see why they just pick on oil. . . . Let's just start rebuilding the whole of Germany!" He asked Stimson and McCloy whether they were going to destroy Germany's war-making enterprises or "find excuses not to destroy them."

Stimson replied that no one disagreed about removing the German synthetic oil industry as an "integral part" of "Germany's war potential." The only question was "timing." With Eisenhower's "tremendous problems," they shouldn't "deprive him" of "temporary production of a critical material."

The Secretary of War took the matter to the President, who backed him up. Stimson wrote in his diary that Morgenthau "is afraid that the least little bit of the 'scorched earth' policy toward Germany will be relaxed. I foresee hideous results from his influence in the near future. In the face of an appalling shortage of everything needed for civilization in central Europe, it seems to me purblind to carry out such a policy indiscriminately."

THROUGH DEFEAT AFTER DEFEAT, Morgenthau still imagined that Truman might endorse his plan for Germany. In the Oval Office, he gave the President an article he had written for newspaper publication after VE-Day. He asked him to write "something I could use in connection with the release, to show that President Truman had approved it."

Truman was noncommittal: "I have complete confidence in you, and if I ever haven't, I will tell you." Morgenthau said, "I hope that day will never come." Truman said, "I am sure it never will."

The next morning, as in days of old, Morgenthau anxiously called the

President's appointments secretary, Matthew Connelly, about his article: "I don't know if he got to it last night or not." After the next Cabinet meeting, Truman told Morgenthau that he had read his piece the night before, and that his portrait of a dangerous, resurgent Germany had kept him from sleeping for two hours. He noted that he, Stalin and Churchill "haven't yet agreed" about Germany. Of Morgenthau's article Truman said, "I like everything that's in there, but it's up to me to say that."

Morgenthau brightened: "You can have it and put your name to it!"

"No, that isn't what I mean," said Truman. "You have to give me time. I am new at this thing. I wish you wouldn't do anything about it. . . . This is strictly between you and me."

ON WEDNESDAY MORNING, May 9, one day after victory in Europe, Morgenthau complained to the President that Stimson's people were "holding up" JCS 1067. He said it was "important to get out 1067 now" while Americans were "aroused over the German atrocities."

"I will stick a pin into them," said Truman. Anxious to avoid another public war with the Pentagon, Morgenthau asked him to keep their conversation in confidence: "You have to protect me on this." The President pledged, "I will."

Morgenthau gave Truman the sequel to the article on postwar Germany that the President had asked him to quash: "I realize you don't want me to publish this thing. . . . I have accepted your decision."

"I couldn't explain it to you fully," said Truman, "but you put all your cards on the table and I will put all my cards on the table. I have got to see Stalin and Churchill, and when I do, I want all the bargaining power—all the cards in my hand—and the plan on Germany is one of them." Pulling out a map of German food production and population, Truman said, "I just wanted to show you that I am studying this myself."

"I got the impression that you liked my plan," said Morgenthau. With a politician's studied imprecision, Truman said, "By and large, I am for it."

Leafing through his typescript, Morgenthau said, "Here is the part on agriculture." He showed the President a chart showing that Germany was not crucial to feeding Europe. Truman said, "That's contrary to what everybody has told me."[3]

3. In fact, Germany had had serious trouble feeding itself even before 1939.

Morgenthau had another idea. Perhaps the President might wish to "use me on the Russian situation." He explained that he had bargained on Roosevelt's behalf in the 1933 talks that led to American recognition of the Soviet Union. Disinclined to offend Morgenthau by turning him down flat, Truman replied carefully, "I will use all the tools I can lay my hands on."

Wearing rose-colored glasses, Morgenthau wrote in his diary of his "distinct feeling that the man likes me and has confidence in me, and I must say that my confidence in him continues to grow." He wrote his sons that Truman seemed "a very direct and sincere person": "Each time I see him, I come away with a good feeling."

THE NEXT DAY, Thursday, May 10, Truman signed JCS 1067, which ordered the commander of the American zone to show the conquered Germans that their "ruthless warfare" and "fanatical Nazi resistance" had "made chaos and suffering inevitable." The Germans could not "escape responsibility for what they have brought upon themselves." They must be denazified, demilitarized and reeducated.

The President also approved the recommendation of the Informal Policy Committee on Germany, appointed by Roosevelt in March, that reparations not "promote or require the building up of German economic capacity." They should be taken as much as possible from German national wealth at the time of surrender and fall equitably on each of the occupation zones.

Eisenhower pleaded with Truman not to make JCS 1067 public. He warned that publication would cause "considerable confusion and embarrassment" with the British, who thought it was much too harsh.

Truman agreed. He was also wary of alienating the defeated Germans by releasing the militant directive at a time when the Anglo-Americans and Russians were already competing for their allegiance.[4]

Choosing to overlook the loopholes that McCloy had inserted in JCS 1067, Morgenthau told his staff that Truman's endorsement was "a big day for the Treasury." He just hoped that "somebody doesn't recognize it as the Morgenthau Plan." He wrote his sons that the directive to Eisenhower was "plenty tough, and if carried out at all in the spirit in which it is conceived, I don't see how Germany can rise to make war again for at least another fifty years."

4. JCS 1067 was finally made public in October 1945.

• • •

ON FRIDAY, May 11, Churchill renewed his demand that Truman not withdraw American troops from the Soviet zone until they were "satisfied" with Soviet behavior—especially on Poland. The "character of the Russian occupation of Germany" and Soviet domination of Eastern Europe would be without "parallel" in the continent's history.

He told Truman that "terrible things have happened during the Russian advance through Germany to the Elbe." There were numerous reports of Red Army brutality, including the pillage of German houses and the rape of German women *("Frau, komm!")*.[5] Anglo-American bargaining power would be "greatly diminished" when the two countries took their armies and "war machines" out of Europe: "Every minute counts.... In these next two months, the gravest matters in the world will be decided." Churchill recommended that they invite Stalin "to meet us" that summer at some "unshattered town in Germany."

In a later message to Truman, Churchill disparaged JCS 1067. If the Anglo-Americans were distracted by "inflicting severities upon Germany, which is ruined and prostrate," they might give the Soviet Union the opening "to advance, if they chose, to the waters of the North Sea and the Atlantic. Surely it is vital now to come to an understanding with Russia, or see where we are with her, before we weaken our armies mortally or return to the zones of occupation." He implored Eisenhower not to dissolve the joint British-American command, which would remove another constraint against the Soviets. Nor should the planned four-power Allied Control Commission in Berlin be activated until the West had solved some of its differences with Moscow.

But Stimson advised Truman that this was "the time to put up with a good bit of ill-mannered behavior with the Russians" in a "sincere attempt" to maintain a "relationship." Truman agreed to send Eisenhower to Berlin, where the four powers would sign a formal declaration of victory and work out plans for the Control Council.

• • •

5. We now know that Soviet soldiers raped as many as two million German women around the end of the war, which did little to endear the Soviet way of life to postwar Germans.

· GERMANY in 1945 ·

ON WEDNESDAY MORNING, May 16, in the Oval Office, Truman told Morgenthau that he had read his second article on Germany and was asking Eisenhower to advise him as to whether it should be published. (He knew that Eisenhower would say no.)

Morgenthau reported that the French had invited him to open a War Bonds exhibit in Paris in early July. He wanted to "go up the Ruhr and Saar and see what is going on."

Truman was no doubt horrified by the idea of Morgenthau performing an encore of the previous summer's now well-known trip to Europe, which had started the public convulsion over the Morgenthau Plan. By now, thanks to Nazi propaganda, Morgenthau was perhaps the most hated American in Germany.

The President handled Morgenthau's request carefully. Rather than turn him down, he told him he did not object to the trip, knowing that he could get someone else to quash it later. Morgenthau said, "When I made these trips previously, President Roosevelt always gave me a plane." Truman pledged to "do the same."

Morgenthau was disappointed that JCS 1067 had not been made public. He told the President that there had been "so many false rumors" about how Germany would be treated that a "clear-cut" presidential statement would "ease the minds of many people in this country." He said he could have "a draft of a speech to you within twenty-four hours." Truman quickly declined.

An hour later, Stimson arrived to warn the President that the likely "pestilence and famine in central Europe next winter" might be followed by "political revolution and Communistic infiltration." Stimson hoped that the President would send Herbert Hoover, whom he had served as Secretary of State, to Europe. The former President, known for his post–World War I work on European food relief, could assess the current problem.

Stimson anticipated that Hoover would return demanding that Germany's economy be rehabilitated for the benefit of all of Europe. The previous Sunday, the War Secretary had lunched with Hoover at Highhold and found that Hoover's views "follow very much the line which McCloy and I had been fighting for since last September and the issue with Morgenthau over a pastoral Germany."

With Roosevelt gone, the resentments Stimson had been suppressing for years were rushing to the surface. Writing in his diary about Hoover, Stimson deprecated Roosevelt and Morgenthau: "It was a great pleasure to talk with a master of a subject after the amateurs that I have been running in contact with in the New Deal."

Worried that Truman might be under Morgenthau's spell, Stimson told the President it would be a "grave mistake" to let "emotional thinking" push Germany "near the margin of hunger" for "past misdeeds." Destroying German industry would drive the Germans "by stress of hardship into a non-democratic and necessarily predatory way of life." Stimson warned that Germany had about thirty million people "beyond what can be supported by agriculture alone": "Russia will occupy most of the good food lands of central Europe, while we have the industrial portions." If there were no German industrial products to trade with the Russians, the West would not get that food. "We must find some way of persuading Russia to play ball."

Truman told Stimson not to worry. He later recalled that "even when I was in the Senate," he had opposed the Morgenthau Plan. Since entering the White House, he had "come to feel even more strongly about it." He told his aides in 1954, "I never was in favor of that crazy plan."

CHAPTER TWENTY-TWO

"You and I Will Have to Bear Great Responsibility"

In Moscow on Saturday evening, May 26, 1945, Harry Hopkins met with Stalin. The Soviet leader recalled Roosevelt's Yalta toast just three months earlier to their next meeting "in Berlin." He said that, according to his commanders, Hitler's capital was so devastated that the meeting would have to be "in the region of Berlin."

Hopkins said he hoped that the Russians would find Hitler's corpse. Stalin speculated that the Führer was not really dead but "hiding somewhere." He had heard that German submarines were taking king's ransoms of gold to Japan. He wondered whether Hitler, Goebbels and other Nazi chieftains were among the passengers.[1]

1. Actually, Stalin almost certainly knew that Hitler was dead. According to Soviet evidence released in the 1990s, the Russians had discovered the charred corpses of Hitler and Eva Braun on May 4, 1945. Unbeknownst to the rest of the world, under orders from a Soviet counterintelligence officer, the remains were wrapped in blankets, packed in wooden ammunition crates and taken to the Berlin suburb of Buch, where they were autopsied by a Soviet forensic physician, who hurried the job in order to join in VE-Day celebrations. Then the bodies were reburied, along with those of the Goebbels family, which had killed itself along with Hitler, in Buch. (The jaws and teeth were sent to Moscow, examined and warehoused in a Soviet archive.) Hitler and Braun were reburied at Finow, thirty miles from Berlin, moved on June 3, 1945, to a forest near Ratenow, in the Soviet zone, then, on February 23, 1946, reburied once again under an asphalt courtyard at a Soviet counterintelligence base in Magdeburg. That same year in Berlin, much of Hitler's skull was discovered in his chancellery garden and sent to Moscow. The Soviets could not establish whether Hitler had shot himself in the temple or through the mouth. In March 1970, before ceding their Magdeburg base to their East German client state, the Soviets worried that if Germans discovered that Hitler was buried there, it might become a neo-Nazi shrine. Without telling the East Germans, by orders of the KGB chief Yuri Andropov, the Soviets secretly opened the grave after dark on April 4, 1970. The bones of Hitler, Braun and others who had died with them, including the dogs, were intermingled, taken to a garbage dump, burned and the ashes thrown into a river.

During their week of talks, Hopkins asked whether Stalin still felt, as at Yalta, that Germany should be dismembered. Stalin claimed that the Americans and British at Yalta had considered partition of Germany merely "a threat to hold over the Germans' head in the event of bad behavior," to which the Soviet Union had "finally agreed."

Hopkins reported that Truman was "inclined" toward putting the Ruhr, Saar and west bank of the Rhine under international control. Stalin predicted that Churchill would never agree. He recalled that Roosevelt had spoken at Tehran of five new German states. He noted that during Churchill's trip to Moscow in October 1944, the Prime Minister had reduced the number to two. He told Hopkins that he himself had an "open mind," but the three powers must orchestrate their approach. Otherwise the Germans would "play one off against the other" and "pretend that they were receiving better treatment from one or the other."

Ambassador Harriman asked Stalin whether food from the Soviet zone might be traded for coal from the British and American zones. Puckishly Stalin replied that such a deal would be "most difficult" because the Germans in his zone had "all fled" to Berlin, hoping to find "better conditions." Instead, they should all help the Germans reestablish farming and light industry in order to "live by their own means."

Hopkins proposed a Big Three conference "in the suburbs of Berlin" for mid-July 1945. He cabled Truman that Stalin was "very anxious to meet you at any time you wished."

Alarmed by more Soviet advances, Churchill cabled Truman that mid-July would be "much too late for the urgent questions that demand attention between us." He noted that he himself was "in the midst of a hotly contested election"[2] but would put the Big Three meeting first. Citing the demands of Congress, Truman replied that July 15 was the earliest date he could manage to leave Washington.

Once again Churchill begged Truman not to withdraw the U.S. Army from "the whole center and heart of Germany." He warned that such an action would bring "Soviet power into the heart of Western Europe and the descent of an iron curtain between us and everything to the eastward." He reminded the President that "you and I will have to bear great responsibility for the future."

2. On May 25, 1945, British elections had been announced for July 5.

At the White House on Friday morning, June 1, Morgenthau told Truman, "I don't know if you want to hear some gossip." But "the talk around town is that you are going to put Stettinius out." He said he had heard that the new Secretary of State would be James Byrnes: "So that you completely understand me, I can't get along with him. If the other people around you were honest, they would tell you the same thing."

Morgenthau had heard correctly, but Truman was not ready to announce Byrnes's appointment. To throw Morgenthau off the trail, the President said, "Oh, I know Mr. Byrnes. He is a conniver. . . . I'm just studying the situation." Truman did concede that leading Democrats thought it dangerous, "in case anything should happen to me," for the President to be succeeded by a Republican like Stettinius.[3]

Later that day, without reference to Morgenthau, Truman wrote in his diary, "The Jews claim God Almighty picked 'em out for special privilege. Well, I'm sure He had better judgment."

ON TUESDAY MORNING, June 5, Eisenhower and his three Allied counterparts—Field Marshal Sir Bernard Law Montgomery of Britain, Maréchal Jean de Lattre de Tassigny of France and Marshal Georgi Zhukov—met at the Berlin Yacht Club, which had somehow survived Allied bombing, to sign papers creating the Allied Control Council as the supreme governing authority in Germany. By surprise, Zhukov insisted that they wait until each power withdrew its armed forces to its own zone and the Soviets were "acquainted firsthand" with problems in the Soviet zone. Zhukov added that until those troop withdrawals began, the Red Army would deny the other Allies access to their assigned sectors of Berlin.

Eisenhower and his newly installed deputy, General Lucius Clay, were astounded by Zhukov's obstinance. Clay cautioned Washington that if Zhukov's display was any harbinger, the Control Council might wind up as nothing more than a "negotiating agency."

Amid the growing chill, the Americans nervously noted that Berlin was one hundred ten miles inside the Soviet zone, and that the Russians had

3. In 1945, before passage of the Twenty-second Amendment, the Secretary of State was next in the line of presidential succession if the vice presidency was vacant. After that came the Secretary of the Treasury and other Cabinet members, in order of the dates their departments had been established.

still offered no formal guarantee of access. If the growing uneasiness with Moscow ever exploded into full-fledged crisis, Stalin could twist the Anglo-American tail by blocking access to the city. Marshall and Eisenhower took the position that access was implicitly guaranteed by four-power arrangements for Berlin. But they knew that such an assumption lacked the force of an ironclad guarantee.

On his way home from Moscow, Hopkins stopped to see Eisenhower at his new headquarters in Frankfurt. After their talk, he cabled Truman that American withdrawal from the Soviet zone should be linked to a Soviet guarantee of "unrestricted access" to Berlin over "agreed routes."

Truman did suggest to Stalin by cable that withdrawal coincide with movement of Allied garrisons into Berlin and "provision of free access for United States forces by air, road and rail from Frankfurt and Bremen." But, unwilling to renege on what he considered a U.S. commitment, the President would go no further. He reminded Churchill that prompt withdrawal was required by the Quebec agreement that was "approved by President Roosevelt and you after long consideration and detailed discussion with you." Postponement to "pressure" the Soviets would be "highly disadvantageous" to our relations.

Disgruntled, Churchill replied, "Obviously we are obliged to conform to your decision." Querulously he explained to the President that the Quebec talks had been "brief and concerned only the Anglo-American arrangements which the President did not wish to raise by correspondence beforehand." Pessimistically he wrote Truman, "I sincerely hope that your action will, in the long run, make for a lasting peace in Europe."

Churchill and Truman pledged to Stalin that the troop withdrawal would start on June 21. Stalin asked them to defer the starting date to July 1. Until then, Zhukov would be gone from Berlin, leading a victory parade in Moscow. Also "not all the districts of Berlin have been cleared of mines." He proposed that their Big Three meeting be in mid-July and convene at "the palace of the German crown prince in Potsdam." Potsdam was in the Soviet zone, just outside Berlin. Churchill and Truman agreed.

It was a month after victory in Europe, and Americans in Germany were gathering the spoils of war. General Alexander Patch, commander of the Seventh Army, gave his commander in chief his own war trophy—Hermann Göring's baton. "I always get those dirty Nazis mixed up," Truman wrote his mother and sister Mary, "but it makes no difference. Anyway it's the fat

Marshal's insignia of office. It is about a foot and a half long, made of ivory inlaid with gold eagles and iron crosses, with diamond-studded end caps and platinum rings around it for engraving. Must have cost several thousand dollars—maybe forty—to make. Can you imagine a fat pig like that strutting around with a forty-thousand-dollar bauble—at the poor taxpayers' expense—and making 'em like it?"[4]

MORGENTHAU WAS STILL EAGER to make his victory tour of liberated Europe. But as he sadly wrote in his diary, he was confronting a "stone wall" in Truman. Still he did not retreat. On Wednesday, June 13, when he renewed his request, he recorded that "the President seemed very much distracted and fidgety, and sort of jumped around the room and paced up and down."

Truman told him, "I just haven't had time to think this thing through." Artlessly Morgenthau reminded him that while visiting Europe "for President Roosevelt last August," he had "found that the Army was for building up a strong Germany." He wanted to "see what they are doing now." Doubtless hoping that Morgenthau would take a hint, Truman gave him no answer.

Morgenthau wrote in his diary that Truman "knew about the trouble I had gotten into over the Morgenthau Plan, and he may just not want me to start something again." He suspected that Truman "may think that my going two weeks in advance of his going might steal some of his thunder, or that I may mess things up."

On Monday, June 18, Truman told aides that Morgenthau had no business being in Europe "with the Big Three conference coming on." He knew that the Treasury Secretary would be "mad as hell, but he'll just have to be." He called in Morgenthau and said, "You know, I feel like a brother to you, and I wish you could feel that way towards me." After thinking about Morgenthau's proposed trip "all day Sunday," he had concluded that since Morgenthau was the next-ranking Cabinet member after the Secretary of State, he shouldn't be out of Washington while the President and Secretary of State were in Europe.

Morgenthau informed Truman that when "Mr. Roosevelt" went to Yalta,

4. Göring's baton is now displayed at Fort Benning, Georgia.

he had told the Cabinet that "if any emergency arose, I should call the Cabinet together."

"That's so," said Truman. "I want you to be here. You're the ranking man by law." He said that when he returned from his conference with Churchill and Stalin, Morgenthau could go "anyplace" he wanted: "I will not go to France. I will leave that to you."

Morgenthau wrote his sons, "Naturally I was disappointed, but I think his request was a reasonable one, and he asked me in such a direct manner that I could only answer directly that I would do what he wished." Unable or unwilling to detect Truman's unease with him, Morgenthau proudly reported Truman's comment that he felt like a "brother" to him: "That gives you some idea as to how we are getting along."

During a long country weekend at Highhold, Stimson was preparing his crowning assault on the Morgenthau Plan. McCloy's brother-in-law Lewis Douglas, now working as a financial adviser to General Clay in Frankfurt, had sent him a somber description of the dangers posed by the German coal shortage.

Stimson wrote in his diary that Douglas's report "boiled down exactly" to his own arguments against Morgenthau the previous autumn, when he had advised Roosevelt that keeping the Ruhr in operation was essential not only for Germany but "the whole of Europe." Stimson recalled how Roosevelt had "yielded" to Morgenthau's "flood of hysteria. . . . Now we are going to suffer for it." He wrote that on the German question, he was confronting "the zeal of the Jewish American statesman seeking for vengeance."

Bernard Baruch, the Wall Street tycoon, self-styled "adviser to Presidents" and a nonpracticing Jew, was also demanding a more punitive approach to Germany. Baruch, who had advised Woodrow Wilson on German reparations after World War I, had written a memo on Germany to Roosevelt and then Truman, urging that Germany's economy be held down in order to deny it "the wherewithal to make future war" and also to expand "industrial opportunities for the rest of the world."

Baruch's demand "disappointed me sadly," Stimson wrote. "His influence is so great in all our Cabinet circle that I fear for the consequences." He felt consoled that so far Truman seemed to be "trying hard to keep the balance."

• • •

McCLOY WAS EMBARRASSED that Truman had invited him to Potsdam but not Stimson. Noting his boss's hurt feelings, he asked Harry Hopkins to ask Truman to bring Stimson as an informal counsel: "I know he would like to feel that his services and his advice were sought after." Stimson "would not need to attend" all the meetings.

Still Truman offered no invitation. He may have feared that, since Churchill and Stalin were not bringing their war ministers to Potsdam, it might strike Stalin as unduly militant or even anti-Soviet to include Stimson.

Finally, on Monday morning, July 2, the usually diffident Stimson raised the matter himself with Truman, who was scheduled to leave for Potsdam in four days. Stimson asked bluntly whether the President was worried that his War Secretary could not physically stand the trip.

Chuckling, Truman said he had indeed wished to save Stimson from "overexertion." Stimson replied that the Surgeon General had assured him that he was strong enough to travel. He said he didn't want to "push" himself on Truman, but with the war still being fought against Japan, the President "ought to be able to get advice from people on the Secretarial level" of the War Department who were "civilian."[5] Truman promised to "think about it."

THE NEXT DAY, on Tuesday, July 3, the President watched James Byrnes sworn in as his new Secretary of State in the White House Rose Garden.

The previous summer, before the Chicago Democratic convention, Truman had agreed to Byrnes's request that he nominate the South Carolinian for Vice President. But when told that Roosevelt's choice was not Byrnes but himself, a red-faced Truman had had to ask Byrnes to release him from his promise. The turn of events was so sudden that when Truman delivered his acceptance speech to the delegates, the draft of his Byrnes nominating address was still in his coat pocket.

Ever since Chicago, by his own political rulebook, Truman had felt that he owed it to Byrnes to "balance things up." Thus, on the evening Truman became President, he asked an aide to "find Jimmy Byrnes for me" and fly

5. A reference to the fact that Truman had already invited McCloy and a host of generals to Potsdam.

him by military plane from his South Carolina political retirement to Washington. On the presidential train returning from Franklin Roosevelt's burial on the Hudson, Truman had confided to Byrnes that he would ask Stettinius to quit as Secretary of State when the opening session of the United Nations was over. Then Byrnes would get the job.

Himself kept in the dark by Roosevelt about Yalta, Truman was impressed that the late President had seemed to take Byrnes into his confidence by including him in his party at his final Big Three conference. Byrnes had made the most of his presence at Yalta. Trained to take shorthand during his youth as a court reporter, he had made careful notes of those Yalta conversations he had witnessed. After Truman became President, Byrnes had the notes transcribed and bound in leather and presented the volumes to the new President.

When people later complained about Byrnes's lack of foreign-policy experience, Truman brought them up short by noting that Byrnes had "been to Yalta." What Truman did not understand was that Roosevelt had taken Byrnes to Yalta as a consolation prize for refusing him the vice presidency and that, to Byrnes's surly annoyance, he had banned Byrnes from more than one meeting with Churchill and Stalin.

Truman had a soft spot for Byrnes. He recalled that when, as a young Senator, he was shunned by some colleagues as the "Senator from Pendergast," Byrnes had embraced him. But he also knew that, despite Byrnes's large reputation in Washington and his influence on Capitol Hill, appointing the flamboyant and willful South Carolinian was a high-risk venture.

Later that week, Truman wrote in his diary, "Had a long talk with my able and conniving Secretary of State. My, but he has a keen mind! And he is an honest man. But all country politicians are alike. They are sure all politicians are circuitous in their dealings. When they are told the straight truth, unvarnished, it is never believed—an asset sometimes."

Stimson was delighted that Byrnes would now be Secretary of State. Byrnes's views on Germany "clicked entirely" with his own. He could rely on Byrnes to help him exclude Morgenthau, whom they both disdained, from future deliberations over the defeated nation.

Byrnes had heard that Morgenthau was prodding Truman to let him go to Europe. He warned Stimson and other officials that Morgenthau was "on the prowl" again, machinating to "turn up in Germany just on the chance that he might be needed."

• • •

IN THE OVAL OFFICE on Tuesday afternoon, after Byrnes's swearing-in, Stimson had a heart-to-heart talk with Truman about Germany. He warned that Germany would be the "biggest occupation" and the "biggest rehabilitation problem" America had ever faced: "It must go right." Of course, Nazi war criminals must be punished, but Americans must avoid "vengeance": "When you punish your dog, you don't keep souring on him all day after the punishment is over." Truman said he felt "exactly" the same way.

Stimson carped about "the problem of our Jewish people here." He described Morgenthau's interventions with Roosevelt and Churchill in Quebec. Chuckling, Truman said he had "heard about it."

Referring to Hull, Stimson recalled "poor old Cordell being left out" at Quebec and how Morgenthau's scheme had later "blown up in the press through the exuberance of the Treasury over their victory." He warned Truman against Baruch's demand for harsher treatment of Germany. The "danger" was "not yet over."

Truman remarked that the Jews were "all alike." They couldn't keep themselves from "meddling" in the German question.

Stimson said that from now on, Truman should ignore the Treasury on Germany. Let the new Secretary of State refine the policy and implement it.

Truman agreed. He invited Stimson to the Big Three conference and, by at least one account, made him a promise: "Don't worry. Neither Morgenthau, nor Baruch, nor any of the Jew boys will be going to Potsdam."

CHAPTER TWENTY-THREE

"How I Hate This Trip!"

On Thursday morning, July 5, 1945, the day before Truman's departure for Potsdam, Morgenthau went to the Oval Office in an angry mood. Indignant about Byrnes's appointment, he was anxious about rumors that he would be the next Cabinet member sacked. "The last time I was here, you said you felt like a brother to me," he said. "I would like to reciprocate that feeling and have an official family talk. You are leaving, and there is all this gossip about my being through."

Truman said, "Oh, I am going to say you are the man in charge while I am gone."

Morgenthau drew the line in the sand: "I would like to know now whether you want me to stay until VJ-Day."

"I don't know," said Truman. "I may want a new Secretary of the Treasury."

Staggered and hurt, Morgenthau replied, "Well, Mr. President, if you have any doubts in your mind—after my record of twelve years here, and after several months with you, when I have given my loyal support—you ought to know your mind now. And if you don't know it, I want to get out now."

"Let me think this thing over," said Truman.

Morgenthau refused: "Either you want me to stay until VJ-Day or you don't! . . . I don't think it is conceited to say that I am at least as good or better as some of the five new people you appointed in the Cabinet, and on some of them, I think you definitely made a mistake.[1] . . . I am going to write you a letter of resignation. Would you like me to stay while you are abroad, or would you like to have it take effect immediately?"

Truman said, "You are rushing it." The President suggested that, for now, he tell the public that Morgenthau was staying. Then after Potsdam, he could announce his resignation. Truman wanted Morgenthau to remain at his post until after the Big Three meeting because his preferred candidate as Morgenthau's successor, former Congressman Fred Vinson of Kentucky, was going to Potsdam.

Morgenthau agreed to stay at Treasury until Truman was back in Washington. But he wanted his resignation announced that very evening. Otherwise "I will be forced to give it out tomorrow—and I wouldn't like to do it while you are on the high seas."

Truman consented.

Morgenthau lamented that no one from Treasury was going to Potsdam "because we have information nobody else has." Would the President like a copy of the Morgenthau Plan to take with him? Truman said he knew "everything that is in it." With no conviction, he added, "I think it is very good."

THUNDERSTRUCK BY HIS CONFRONTATION with Truman, Morgenthau returned to the Treasury. He told Harry Dexter White and his staff, "I couldn't hold my head up and have this man say to me he was uncertain about me. . . . It has been a good twelve years, and we've worked hard."

In 1954, Truman privately gave his own boastful version of his confrontation with Morgenthau: "When the trip to Potsdam was being arranged, Morgenthau came to see me and said he had to go along. I said, 'I don't need you and it's not your business.' . . . He said, 'If I can't go to Potsdam, what's going to happen to the Morgenthau Plan?' I said they could throw it out the window. He pouted and said he would quit. 'All right,' I said, 'I accept your resignation right now.' "

Truman went on to recall that Morgenthau's plan "wasn't worth a hoot": "Hitler's treatment of the Jews is what pushed Morgenthau forward. . . .

1. A reference not only to Byrnes but also to the fact that Truman had already removed Roosevelt's Attorney General, Postmaster General and Secretaries of Labor and Agriculture.

There's not enough land in all of central Europe to feed Germany's eighty million people in a first-class manner. Half of them would starve to death. . . . I don't think Roosevelt was ever sold on the Morgenthau Plan, which was really to enslave the German people. . . . Morgenthau wanted to put an iron heel on Germany's neck."

In the years after Morgenthau's departure, Truman privately told cronies that Roosevelt's old friend was a "nut" and a "blockhead" who didn't "know shit from apple butter."

ON THURSDAY AFTERNOON, Truman told reporters that Morgenthau would leave the Treasury after Potsdam. But the next day he heard complaints that if his boat sank in the Atlantic with himself and Byrnes aboard, he would be succeeded by an unelected Jewish President, poised to enact his vindictive plan against Germany.

Truman turned to Sam Rosenman, a Roosevelt holdover and now his highest-ranking Jewish aide. He told Rosenman he had been "under pressure all day" to immediately remove Morgenthau from the line of presidential succession. Vinson would be pulled off the boat to Potsdam so that his name could be sent at once to the Senate. (Vinson's luggage was already on its way to Germany.) Rosenman must give the bad news to Morgenthau.[2]

The following Monday, Rosenman told Morgenthau he was "embarrassed" by his mission. But the President had realized that it would be "quite a while" until he returned from Potsdam and found people "very much worried" about the succession. He said he didn't know whether Morgenthau wished to remain in Truman's "good graces," but "it would make the President very happy" if Morgenthau departed the Treasury immediately. Rosenman added, "wholly on my own," that if Morgenthau went quietly, Truman might appoint him as governor of the new World Bank and International Monetary Fund.

Harry Dexter White and other aides urged their boss to accept Rosenman's offer. Morgenthau promised to think about it, but shrewdly predicted that Byrnes and Vinson would oppose him. He drafted three letters for

2. From a conversation years later with Rosenman's widow, Dorothy, Henry Morgenthau III deduced that Truman had asked Rosenman to speak to Morgenthau "as Jew to Jew."

Truman's signature and sent them for approval to the President, who was on his trip to Potsdam. The first was his request to resign immediately. The second was Truman's reply, lauding Morgenthau's "keen sense of public responsibility." The third, designed to "smoke the President out," would be Truman's offer of the Fund and Bank. As Morgenthau had foreseen, the President approved only the first two letters. Not too convincingly, Morgenthau insisted that he hadn't really wanted the Bank-Fund job but had wanted to be asked.

He wrote his sons that soon he would "no longer be Secretary of the Treasury" and asked them to "destroy this letter."[3] In it, he described Truman's anxieties about the presidential succession—"not very complimentary to your old man." He wrote that because he was so "very, very definitely a part of the Roosevelt era," Truman didn't want "to have me around. . . . Once you get a message from the President that you're not wanted, the quicker you act on it, the better." At least now he knew where he stood: "I am a free agent, and I am beginning to like it. . . . Well, boys, write me soon, and address it to Henry Morgenthau, Jr., Private First Class."

MORGENTHAU LEFT OFFICE as the longest-serving Treasury Secretary since Albert Gallatin's thirteen years under Presidents Jefferson and Madison. Despite his forced bravado, he felt publicly humiliated by how Truman had aborted his public service. His aide Henrietta Klotz recounted that when Vinson was sworn in, her "very unhappy" old boss "stood alone in the corner" and "nobody went over" to him. Klotz recalled that Morgenthau looked like "a lost sheep," adding, "It broke my heart."

U.S. Treasury trucks took Morgenthau's hundreds of boxes of papers and belongings north to Fishkill Farms. That fall the former Secretary published his volume on the Morgenthau Plan as *Germany Is Our Problem.*[4] While completing the book, he asked Churchill for permission to publish the still-secret memo endorsing a "pastoral" Germany that Churchill had dictated at Quebec and initialed, along with Roosevelt. But Churchill pleaded with Morgenthau by cable not to reveal the memo, noting that the world situation

3. Morgenthau kept his own copy.

4. Harper and Brothers, 1945.

had "changed in many respects." He did not add that it would also be politically embarrassing to him.

Morgenthau was chagrined to receive almost none of the job offers that would normally come to a newly resigned Treasury Secretary. He had always been a loner, and few on Wall Street wanted any part of the New Deal maverick. The once-indifferent Jew was asked to be general chairman of the United Jewish Appeal. "Don't have anything to do with the Jews," Morgenthau's father warned him, just before his death at ninety. "They'll stab you in the back." But Morgenthau accepted. As his son Henry III recalled, it was a perfect match: "He needed the respect and love that the Jewish community was ready to offer him, and they in turn needed his stamp of ecumenical respectability."

In his new role, Morgenthau sought instruction in the vast areas of Jewish ritual that were foreign to him. At one fund-raising dinner with Jewish cuisine, Morgenthau asked what he was eating, only to be told that if he knew, he wouldn't eat it. Henrietta Klotz recalled that after a while, her old boss "became kind of a little Jewish."

By then, Klotz felt free to tell him about a ruse she had abetted in 1943 while trying to prod him to save Jews from Hitler. During a Treasury meeting, Morgenthau was deeply upset when Rabbi Abraham Kalmanowitz, pleading with him to help the Jews, fell to the floor in a faint. Klotz, who understood Yiddish, heard the rabbi mutter in Yiddish to his translator, "Well, did I cry well?" Klotz had never revealed to her boss that Kalmanowitz's collapse was feigned, fearing that "if I told it to him, he'd never let another rabbi in."

BY 1948, THE OLD "one hundred percent American" was a Zionist. With tears in his eyes, Morgenthau toured the new state of Israel as it fought for independence. Braving mortar shells and small-arms fire, he declared that "without a Jewish Jerusalem," Israel would be "like the Jewish people without its history." He praised Israeli troops for showing the world "that the Jew is a fighting man." Later the Israeli Finance Minister, Levi Eshkol, clearly ignorant of the Morgenthau Plan and its reception in Germany, noted that since Morgenthau was Jewish and "of German extraction," he must be well suited to help Israel win $120 million in reparations from Germany.

Morgenthau gently explained that his influence would not exactly be helpful in Germany: "The seeds that Goebbels sowed about Roosevelt and me are still fresh in the minds of the Germans." Besides, he said, he was resolved never to set foot in that country.

After Elinor Morgenthau's death in 1949, Henrietta Klotz, who had quietly set her cap on Morgenthau decades earlier, evidently hoped that the distraught widower might finally marry her. Henry III suspected that in the months that followed, his father may have had a brief affair with the woman he once called his "watchdog" at the Treasury. Mrs. Klotz was stung when Morgenthau instead married Marcelle Puthon Hirsch, a French Catholic divorced from a prosperous French Jew. The jealous Klotz referred to the new wife as "that thing" and compared her to Madame Bovary.

With thick glasses and bleached blond hair, the new Mrs. Morgenthau garishly redecorated his New York apartment and nudged her husband away from Jewish charities. The austere Morgenthau's old friends were appalled to hear him joke, "Now that I married a Frenchwoman, I have to come home in the afternoon!" Soberly, Eleanor Roosevelt explained to Henry III, "Your father could never have a mistress. He had to marry his mistress."

With sadness, Henry III recalled that, at the end of his life, troubled by his misalliance, "my father cut himself off from almost everybody." "He was so unhappy," recalled Klotz, no impartial witness. "She was cruel. Common and cruel."

A more joyous moment was his elder son's marriage in 1962 to Ruth Schachter, a Jewish refugee from Vienna. The former Treasury Secretary told his new daughter-in-law that she should have known him when he "was somebody." He was not entirely joking.

Until his death in 1967, Morgenthau never relaxed his intense faith in his tough plan for postwar Germany. While working on Morgenthau's authorized biography, the young Yale historian John Morton Blum told Morgenthau he thought the plan had been a mistake.

"You're too young to know whether the Morgenthau Plan was a mistake," retorted the old man. "And I'll bet you—though I won't be around to collect—that you're going to have to fight Germany again before you die."

IN WASHINGTON ON FRIDAY EVENING, July 6, 1945, Harry Truman boarded the presidential train for Newport News, where the heavy cruiser

Augusta waited to take him and his party across the Atlantic. Launched on his first trial in high-stakes diplomacy, Truman lacked Roosevelt's self-confidence. Harold Ickes found the President so "dreading" the trip that he felt "it might be better if Truman stayed home." Truman wrote his wife, Bess, that he felt "as blue as indigo" about seeing "Mr. Russia and Mr. Great Britain." He told his diary, "How I hate this trip! But I have to make it."

During the eight-day voyage, Truman's spirits brightened. During the day, he took early-morning constitutionals down the *Augusta*'s deck, carried a metal tray through chow lines, watched sailors in firing practice and gazed through binoculars at the ocean. At night he dined to the music of "a fine band," played poker with his aides and watched films, including *Something for the Boys,* starring the fruit-adorned Carmen Miranda. "A most restful and satisfactory trip," Truman wrote Bess. "Haven't been sick a minute!"

Under balmy skies, Truman sat in deck chairs with Byrnes, Admiral Leahy, the Soviet expert Charles Bohlen and others who had advised Roosevelt at Casablanca, Tehran, Quebec and Yalta. As Leahy recalled, the President "squeezed facts and opinions" out of his people all day long.

Truman recalled in 1954 that after reading Stalin's final cables to Roosevelt, he had been "on guard" but still had "the kindliest feelings in the world toward Russia. . . . They had lost seven million men in the field, besides all the civilians the Germans had killed. . . . I hoped all the time that the Russians would live up to their agreements." Presuming that Roosevelt had committed the United States to dismembering Germany in some way, Truman told his advisers that he would listen to any suggestion made at Potsdam for a partition of the defeated nation[5]—but not Morgenthau's proposals. Those, he said, were "out."

When the *Augusta* reached Antwerp, Belgium, on Sunday, July 15, General Eisenhower was waiting. Referring to Clay, he told Truman and Byrnes that "civilian authority" should take over the American zone as soon as possible. The Army would "obviously have to stay in control" until there was order, but "military responsibility" did not include the "government of individuals in their daily lives." Eisenhower also recommended early rehabilita-

5. By 1955 and 1956, when Truman published his presidential memoirs, eager to show himself a friend of postwar Germans and the Soviets as the offending party, Truman claimed that he had not wished to partition the country: "My aim was a unified Germany with a centralized government in Berlin." But contemporaneous records show, for example, that he liked Roosevelt's old proposal for a south German confederation.

tion of the Ruhr. Let Germany export consumer products unrelated to the "banned war industries," he said. If the Germans did not have the money to import food, they would "soon be starving."

From Brussels, Truman and his party boarded Roosevelt's old *Sacred Cow* and two other C-54s for Berlin. From his window seat, Truman had his first glimpse of the defeated nation. He was told that in the Soviet zone, Red Army soldiers had "torn" up the factories and taken "everything out of them."

Truman recalled in 1954 what the Russians did to German private homes: "They would take big grandfather clocks and put them in the bottom of a Russian truck or wagon and then throw other things on top of them. . . . The Russian soldier had never seen a comfortable bed and they didn't know how to handle it. . . . They destroyed everything they could get their hands on. . . . That was what Stalin called booty. The Tatar definition of booty was taking everything that is loose and giving nothing for it."

The presidential party was driven to the Babelsberg neighborhood of Potsdam, once a summer retreat for German film stars and producers. There Truman was lodged in a yellow stucco villa by a lake, which he found so gloomy that he called it the "nightmare house." In his diary, he noted that the Red Army had stripped the villa—"not even a tin spoon left."

The American delegation was told by the Russians that the mansion had belonged to a German film mogul who had been sent to a Siberian labor battalion. But after Truman issued his memoirs in 1955, Gustav Müller-Grote, son of the owner, wrote the former President that the Russians had lied: "Ten weeks before you entered this house, its tenants were living in constant fright and fear. By day and by night, plundering Russian soldiers went in and out, raping my sisters before their own parents and children, beating up my old parents." During Truman's residence in their house, the Müller-Grote family was, unbeknownst to the Americans, under Soviet detention in a building just five hundred yards away.

TRUMAN HAD NEVER MET CHURCHILL before Potsdam. He recorded that when the Prime Minister called on him at his villa on Monday morning, July 16, Churchill "gave me a lot of hooey about how great my country is and how he loved Roosevelt and how he intended to love me." As he recalled in

1954, "I liked him from the start. . . . I think he was surprised and pleased when he met me. Of course, he had been informed of what an inadequate chief of state he had to deal with. But I think he changed his mind."

Truman was told that Stalin would be late reaching Potsdam. With time on his hands, the President decided to tour Berlin.

Conquerors like Genghis Khan and Julius Caesar, whom Truman had read about so voraciously as a boy, staged vast pageants in which they viewed their vanquished lands on horseback. Had Franklin Roosevelt achieved his dream of touring conquered Berlin, he would almost certainly have arrived in Hitler's capital with theater and ceremony.

But Truman was more modest. For his impromptu tour, he simply climbed, along with Byrnes and Leahy, into the backseat of his Chrysler convertible adorned on each side by a huge white star, and had his driver start up the Autobahn into Zero-Hour Berlin. Along the roadside he saw "a long, never-ending procession" of men, women and children, all staring straight ahead." Ejected by the Russians, they were "carrying what they could of their belongings to nowhere in particular."

The sight of defeated Germans and their victims reminded Truman once again of his Confederate grandmother and her family after the Civil War: "Forced off the farm by Yankee laws," they had wandered for weeks "along the hot Missouri roads until they found a safe place to stay." Truman thought of the "millions of people who were like her in Europe now."

Touring Berlin's ruins, Truman smelled the stench of rotting corpses and saw what was left of the blackened Reichstag. "It is a terrible thing," he said, "but they brought it on themselves." He imagined what a victorious Hitler might have done to Washington, D.C. He felt "thankful" that Americans had been "spared the devastation."

They pulled up at Hitler's chancellery, near the underground bunker. Truman refused to go in, saying that he wouldn't want any of "those unfortunate people" to think he was "gloating over them." But he muttered acidly to Byrnes that he wasn't sure the Germans had "learned anything" from the Nazis' miserable end.

Truman returned to his villa that evening deeply depressed. He wrote Bess, "This is a hell of a place—ruined, dirty, smelly, forlorn people, bedraggled hangdog look about them. You never saw as completely ruined a city." In his diary, he wrote that the "absolute ruin" of Berlin was "Hitler's folly. He overreached himself by trying to take in too much territory. He had no morals and his people backed him up."

ON TUESDAY, July 17, at noon, the President was working in his study when, as he later recorded, "I looked up from the desk and there stood Stalin in the doorway. . . . We had lunch, talked socially, put on a real show drinking toasts to everyone, then had pictures made in the backyard. I can deal with Stalin. He is honest, but smart as hell."

Over lunch, Byrnes described their visit to Hitler's headquarters and asked Stalin how he thought Hitler had died. The Marshal speculated that the Führer was still alive—"in Spain or Argentina."[6]

Truman told Stalin that he was "very anxious to get the German setup in operation" so that the Allied Control Council could "govern" Germany "as a whole."

THE FIRST FORMAL CONFERENCE session was at 5:00 P.M. at the Cecilienhof Palace, built in 1917 before the last German defeat. To demonstrate their equality, in a great-power minuet, Truman, Stalin and Churchill entered the room simultaneously through separate doors.

Seated with his allies at a burgundy-draped round table, Truman recalled the tragedy of Versailles 1919. This time, any final German peace conference should be "prepared beforehand by the victor powers." He proposed that the groundwork be laid by a Council of Foreign Ministers, composed of the Big Three plus France and China.

Stalin complained that the French were U.S. lackeys and that the Chinese should not be involved in "European problems." Truman and Churchill compromised by excluding the Chinese.

Stalin joked that if foreign ministers were to do the work, "we will have nothing to do." Truman said, "I don't want to discuss. I want to decide." He hoped they could start early tomorrow morning. Churchill jovially promised to "obey your orders."

Stalin said that since Churchill was in "such an obedient mood," he

6. Stalin may have been pretending that Hitler was still alive and dangerous in order to license harsher measures against Germany and, as the historian Alonzo Hamby notes, perhaps to deflect attention from his own aggressive ambitions.

wished to know whether the British would "share the German fleet with us." Churchill said that perhaps the armada should be destroyed. Weapons of war were horrible things.

"Let's divide it," said Stalin. "If Mr. Churchill wishes, he can sink his share."

Truman proposed that the Allied Control Council start working immediately. On "questions affecting Germany as a whole," the Control Council should be "paramount." On matters affecting each zone, the zonal commander should reign supreme.

On Wednesday afternoon, July 18, Churchill noted that his partners kept using the word *Germany*. He asked them, "What is now the meaning of 'Germany'? Is it to be understood in the same sense as before the war?"

Debate on postwar Germany's borders began. At Yalta, the Big Three had agreed that the Curzon Line, drawn after World War I, would be Poland's eastern border with the Soviet Union. They had also decided that Poland should be compensated with "substantial" German territory to its west.

Stalin felt that Poland deserved all of Germany east of the Oder and Neisse Rivers. This would force millions of Germans westward and strip Germany of some of its richest farmland. As far as Stalin was concerned, this was already a fait accompli: "Germany is what she has become after the war."

But Truman refused to consider the matter settled: "Why not say Germany as she was *before* the war, in 1937?" Stalin replied, "As she *is*—in 1945." Truman reminded Stalin that Germany had "lost everything in 1945," and that at Yalta, the Big Three had agreed to defer such questions until there was a final peace conference on Germany.

Impatient, Truman wrote in his diary, "I'm not going to stay around this terrible place all summer just to listen to speeches. I'll go home to the Senate for that."

ON FRIDAY, July 20, Truman joined Generals Eisenhower and Bradley to watch the official raising of the Stars and Stripes over the American sector of Berlin. Speaking without notes, Truman told the crowd of American soldiers, "We are not fighting for conquest. There is not one piece of territory or one thing of a monetary nature that we want out of this war."

Exactly one year had passed since Claus von Stauffenberg's failed plot against Adolf Hitler. If any of the Americans remembered the anniversary, they did not mention it in public. At a moment when they were trying to establish collective guilt for Hitler's horrors, they did not wish to confuse the issue by reminding the world that some Germans had risked their lives, however belatedly and for whatever reasons, to stop the Führer.

The next day, Saturday, July 21, Stimson brought the President an urgent message. The plutonium implosion bomb tested in Alamogordo, New Mexico, five days earlier had been "successful beyond the most optimistic expectations of everyone."

Truman told Stimson that the news gave him "an entirely new feeling of confidence." He knew that if the United States were sole owner of a successful atomic bomb, it would be poised to end the Japanese war fast, without Soviet or British help, and exercise American will on the postwar world.

That afternoon, Truman complained to Stalin that the Poles had been effectively assigned a zone of Germany "without consultation with us."[7] Were they going to "give away Germany piecemeal?" Truman warned Stalin that it would be hard to agree on reparations and other problems "if Germany is divided up before the peace conference."

Stalin replied, "We are concerned about reparations, but we will take that risk." He insisted that giving German land to Poland should be no problem because no Germans were left in the region.

"Of course not," Leahy whispered to Truman. "The Bolshies have killed all of them!"

Churchill noted that "two or three million Germans remain" in the area Stalin wanted to give Poland. Removing it from Germany would remove a quarter of Germany's farmland, "from which German food and reparations must come."

"France wants the Saar and the Ruhr," said Truman. "What will be left?" Churchill warned that if Germany lacked enough food, "we may be confronted with conditions like those in the German concentration camps—even on a vaster scale." Stalin said, "Let the Germans buy more bread from Poland!"

7. Actually, as the historian Warren Kimball has noted, since 1941 the United States and Britain had "never seriously opposed Soviet demands that East Prussia be ceded to either Poland or Russia, or both," and that "given early Soviet demands for a westward adjustment of the Russo-Polish border," the British and Americans had come to "accept some kind of westward shift in the Polish-German border."

Churchill demanded that the food supply of all Germany, according to its 1937 borders, be available to all Germans, "irrespective of the zones of occupation." He complained that Poland was already selling German coal to Sweden, while the British people faced "a bitter, fireless winter, worse than that experienced during the war."

Stalin retorted that the coal was being mined by Polish labor. As for the Germans, "we have little sympathy for these scoundrels and war criminals."

Churchill noted that Stalin had earlier said that "past bitterness" should not "color our decisions." Sounding like Morgenthau at Quebec, Stalin reminded him that "the less industry we leave in Germany, the more markets there will be for your goods."

Truman warned that he could not approve eastern Germany's removal from "contributing to the economy of the whole of Germany." He later wrote Bess, "Russia and Poland have gobbled up a big hunk of Germany and want Britain and us to agree. I have flatly refused."

Churchill attributed the President's new boldness to the bracing news from Alamogordo. "When he got to the meeting after having read this report, he was a changed man," the Prime Minister informed Stimson. "He told the Russians just where they got on and off and generally bossed the whole meeting."

CHAPTER TWENTY-FOUR

"We Are Drifting Toward a Line Down the Center of Germany"

As THE SOLE PROPRIETOR OF THE ATOMIC BOMB, President Truman had just become the most powerful man the human race had ever known. Even before the success at Alamogordo, he had longed to get back home to America and his wife. Still smoldering over Stalin's defense of his "Bolsheviki land grab," Truman wanted his counterparts to approve a plan that would punish the Germans, quash the German ability and yearning to start another global war, and still feed and warm all Europeans. Now, with the atomic weapon in his arsenal, Truman asked Jimmy Byrnes to put on the pressure to wind the Potsdam meeting up fast.

The new Secretary of State was no hidebound Cordell Hull or silken Edward Stettinius. Byrnes felt he should be President instead of Truman. Truman knew that, but he expected that if Byrnes could be made to defer to presidential authority, he would be a tough diplomatic bargainer and a powerful congressional champion for Truman's postwar programs.

Born Catholic in Charleston, South Carolina, in 1882, Byrnes was the son of an Irish immigrant father who had died before his birth. His mother supported the young Byrnes and his sister by making dresses. At fourteen, he quit parochial school to become first an office boy for a law firm, then a court reporter in Spartanburg, home of the agrarian populist and white supremacist Senator "Pitchfork Ben" Tillman.

Byrnes read the law to pass the bar exam and at twenty-six was elected district prosecutor. He went to Congress in 1920 as a Tillmanite, supporting the League of Nations. Four years later, he was defeated for the Senate after refusing to join the Ku Klux Klan. Since his wife, Maude, was an Episcopalian, Byrnes had become a Protestant, but he refused to join any anti-Catholic organization like the Klan while his mother was still alive.

In 1930, Byrnes became a Senator with financial help from his fellow South Carolinian Bernard Baruch. He built influence with fellow Senators by advising Baruch as to which of them he should "play Santa Claus."[1] One such beneficiary was Truman himself, during his difficult Senate primary in 1940. An early Roosevelt supporter, Byrnes was one of the President's Senate stalwarts, despite his growing doubts about centralized power in Washington.

As America was drawn into World War II, Byrnes helped Roosevelt push through Lend-Lease and other aid to Britain. The President repaid him with a seat on the Supreme Court, where Byrnes predictably felt chained and miserable. After Pearl Harbor, Roosevelt took him off the Court to be his chief war mobilizer. Given the press sobriquet of "assistant President," which annoyed Roosevelt, Byrnes harnessed American business behind the war effort.

Suspecting that Roosevelt might not serve out a fourth term, eager to be his successor, Byrnes schemed in 1944 to become Vice President. Roosevelt admired Byrnes's brains, wiliness and gumption but was also wary of him. He knew that black, Catholic, union and liberal voters would never accept Byrnes as Vice President. Early in his career, Byrnes had advocated the forced emigration of African-Americans.

With customary duplicity, Roosevelt told Byrnes in July 1944 that he was "the best qualified man in the whole outfit": "You must not get out of the race. If you stay in, you are sure to win."

Told by others that Roosevelt was really for Truman or Supreme Court Justice William O. Douglas, Byrnes forced a showdown with the President in a telephone call to Hyde Park. As Roosevelt spoke, Byrnes took shorthand notes to protect himself in case the President later distorted what he said. Roosevelt insisted he was not pushing for Truman or Douglas: "Jimmy, that

1. In the 1930s, Byrnes's close friend Joseph Kennedy also used his pocketbook to enhance his standing in the Senate. Kennedy privately told his friend Thomas Corcoran, "It doesn't surprise me that Senators are for sale. What surprises me is that the price is so low!" Alonzo Hamby believes that the Byrnes-Baruch financial largesse made Truman later veer between gratitude and resentment that he owed the two men favors.

is all wrong. . . . I told you I would have no preference. . . . Will you go on and run? After all, Jimmy, you are close to me personally. . . . I hardly know Truman."

After Truman's nomination, Byrnes was furious at Roosevelt's "hypocrisy." When the President addressed the Chicago convention from San Diego by radio, the delegates gave him a standing ovation. The tightlipped Byrnes remained in his seat. Nevertheless, after Roosevelt's fourth-term victory, Byrnes wired him a good-humored rebuff to Dewey's campaign charges: "For a tired, quarrelsome, sick old man, you sure can run."

Byrnes was being magnanimous because he hoped that Roosevelt would appoint him to succeed Hull as Secretary of State. Nervous about Byrnes's willfulness, Roosevelt opted instead for the docile Stettinius.

To salve Byrnes's wounded pride, the President took him to Yalta, but when Byrnes realized that he was being kept out of vital meetings, he complained, "I did not come along for the ride." Roosevelt caved in. When Stalin spotted Byrnes at the conference table, he thought him "the most honest-looking horse thief" he had ever met.

Returning to Washington, Byrnes dutifully held a press conference praising the Yalta agreements. Then he quit government, assuring Roosevelt that he was "not mad at anybody" about Chicago. The President replied that Byrnes's resignation had "knocked" him "off my feet" and that he would "miss you and Maude more than I can tell you." But privately Roosevelt complained, "It's a shame some people are so prima-donnish."

After Truman became President, overimpressed by Byrnes's presence at Yalta and mindful of his prestige in the Senate, he appointed Byrnes to his secret "Interim Committee" on how a successful atomic bomb should be used. Exhilarated by the new weapon, Byrnes advised the President that it "might well put us in a position to dictate our own terms at the end of the war."

ON MONDAY, July 23, backed by Truman, Byrnes told Molotov he was "deeply concerned" about reparations. By abruptly handing German territory to Poland, the Soviets had exposed the British and Americans to "serious dangers." He suggested that each occupying power simply take reparations from its own zone. The Anglo-Americans would want to give their share to France, Belgium, Holland and other Nazi victims.

Byrnes insisted that this approach would not harm the Soviet Union, noting that the Soviet zone held about half of Germany's existing wealth.[2] Under this plan, if the Soviets wanted certain equipment or materials from other zones, for example, they could trade coal for them. On matters such as currency and transportation, the Allied Control Council would still govern Germany as "an economic whole."

Shocked by the sudden danger that the Anglo-Americans might offer no reparations at all, Molotov warned that Stalin "strongly" favored an overall reparations plan. He offered to reduce Soviet demands from $10 billion to $8 billion—as long as the Soviet Union could claim $2 billion from the Ruhr.

The next day, Tuesday, July 24, Byrnes noted that for days the Big Three had been nattering away about a grand final German "peace conference." He said that the President and he now believed that such a meeting, with "delegates from fifty-odd nations" having no direct interest in Europe, would only produce "endless discussions." Why not refer European problems, as they arose, to a regular conference of the American, Soviet, British and French foreign ministers?

On Wednesday, July 25, Stalin told Truman and Churchill that "if the Ruhr remains a part of Germany, it must supply the whole of Germany."

The Americans blanched. Charles Bohlen of the U.S. delegation privately warned that Stalin would use such a privilege to "paralyze the German economy" and push the defeated nation "toward communism."

THE POTSDAM CONFERENCE RECESSED while Churchill returned to London to await announcement of the results of the British election.[3]

Truman flew to Frankfurt to visit Eisenhower at the former headquarters of I.G. Farben, one of the German warmaking enterprises investigated by Senator Truman during the war. "The big towns like Frankfurt and Darmstadt were destroyed," Truman wrote his mother and sister Mary, "but the small ones are intact. It is awful to see what the bombs did to the towns, railroads and bridges. To think that millions of Russians, Poles, English and

2. Byrnes was exaggerating. His aides had actually advised him that the Soviet zone held 31 percent of movable manufacturing facilities, 35 to 39 percent of prewar Germany's total manufacturing and mining and 48 percent of German agriculture.

3. The balloting had occurred three weeks earlier, but the verdict was delayed by the counting of the military vote.

Americans were slaughtered all for the folly of one crazy egotist by the name of Hitler. I hope it won't happen again."

In London, Churchill learned that despite his triumphant role in ending the European war, British voters, focused now on domestic problems, had turned out the Conservative party. The Prime Minister's aides complained of their people's "ingratitude." Despondent, Churchill replied paternally, "I wouldn't call it that. They have had a very hard time."

ON SATURDAY, July 28, Molotov pressed Byrnes about his proposal that each power take reparations from its own zone and barter for needed goods. Would that mean that "each country would have a free hand in its own zone" and "act entirely independently of the others?" Byrnes replied, "In substance."

Molotov reminded Byrnes that at Yalta, the Americans had agreed with the Soviets that they should take "as much reparations as possible from Germany."

Byrnes rejoined that much had changed since Yalta. They had not known the "extent of the destruction of Germany" or that the Soviets would give Poland such "a large and productive part of former Germany."

On Sunday, July 29, Truman wrote his wife that if he could make a "reasonably sound" deal on reparations and the Polish-German border, he could "wind up this brawl" and head home.

At noon, Molotov told Byrnes that his reparations proposal was "acceptable in principle." But contrary to Byrnes's claim, he said, the Soviet zone contained only about forty-two percent of German wealth. Therefore the Soviet Union deserved about eight percent from other zones, including $2 billion worth of industrial equipment from the Ruhr.

Byrnes replied that his experts thought it was "impossible to put any specific dollar value" on potential reparations. Therefore the Soviets should have twenty-five percent of all equipment "available for reparations" from the Ruhr. But the Soviets should pay for those machines with coal and other goods from their zone.

On Monday afternoon, July 30, Byrnes told Molotov that "as a concession," the United States would tolerate for now the Soviet grant of German territory beyond the Oder-Neisse Line to Poland. Responding to another

Soviet demand, he agreed to bestow diplomatic recognition "to the extent possible" on Kremlin-dominated governments in Romania, Hungary, Bulgaria and Finland.

Having made two concessions, Byrnes raised "the most difficult of all the questions": reparations. He suggested that they discard a fixed dollar amount and agree instead on percentages of German wealth.

After consulting Stalin, who suspected that a percentage formula might ultimately bring the Soviets a share of nothing, Molotov asked for $800 million worth of reparations. But Byrnes again rejected the notion of a fixed sum.

Molotov asked who, under Byrnes's plan, would decide which plants and equipment in each Western zone would be "available" for reparations. Byrnes replied, "The zone commander."

Molotov noted that a commander might well say that nothing in his zone was available for reparations. But Byrnes would not budge. He insisted that his offer on Poland was "a greater concession on our part than the one from the Russians." Molotov claimed that this was "a concession to Poland," not the Soviet Union.

That night, Truman wrote in his diary that the talks were at an "impasse." He wrote Bess, "The whole difficulty is reparations. Of course, the Russians are naturally looters and they have been thoroughly looted by the Germans over and over again and you can hardly blame them for their attitude. The thing I have to watch is to keep our skirts clean and make no other commitments."

On Tuesday morning, July 31, Byrnes told Molotov that his proposals on diplomatic relations for Eastern Europe, the German land for Poland and German reparations were a package: "We would agree to all three or none." As soon as the Soviets replied, "the President and I will leave for the United States the next day."

Stalin made his own reparations proposal. Each of their governments would take from its own zone lump withdrawals for two years and annual deliveries from current production for ten. From the Western zones the Soviet Union would also receive fifteen percent of basic industrial equipment, for which the Soviets would offer a similar amount in "foodstuffs, coal, potassium, timber, ceramic goods and oil products." He said that the Soviets should also get shares worth $500 million in factories and other enterprises in the Western zones, as well as thirty percent of German gold and investments abroad. The Allied Control Council could decide the "volume of withdrawals" from the Western zones.

The Marshal said he hoped that Britain and America would "meet us halfway." The Soviet Union had lost a "terrible amount" of equipment in the war: "At least twenty percent of it should be restored."

Byrnes complained that Stalin's demand for shares in German industry in the Western zones and German wealth abroad went far beyond the American proposal.

Stalin replied that if denied these, the percentage of German wealth due the Soviet Union would have to be increased.

THAT EVENING, Truman secretly scrawled out formal approval for the first atomic bomb to be dropped on Japan. Three days after learning of the successful Alamogordo test, the President had quietly told Stalin that the United States now had an unusually destructive new weapon. Truman did not know that Soviet intelligence had already briefed Stalin on the Manhattan Project and the test. Stalin simply replied to Truman that he hoped the Americans would use the weapon well against Japan.[4]

Now, in his written order, Truman specified that the thunderous event should unfold only after he and his party were safely gone from Potsdam: "Release when ready but not sooner than August 2."

ON WEDNESDAY AFTERNOON, August 1, while discussing German assets abroad, Stalin made a fateful suggestion. To Truman and Britain's new Labour Prime Minister, Clement Attlee, who now took Churchill's place at Potsdam, Stalin proposed that the Soviet Union "regard the whole of western Germany as falling within your sphere and eastern Germany as within ours."

Truman asked whether Stalin meant to establish a "line" down Europe, "running from the Baltic to the Adriatic."

Stalin said yes. "As to the German investments in Europe, they remain with us, and the rest with you." Truman asked, "Does this apply only to German investments in Europe or in other countries as well?"

ß4. In June 1942, Soviet agents in New York, London and Berlin were informed that the Roosevelt White House had "reportedly" decided to "allocate a large sum to a secret atomic development project."

"Let me put it more specifically," said Stalin. "The German investments in Romania, Bulgaria, Hungary and Finland go to us, and all the rest to you. . . . In all other countries—South America, Canada and the like—all this is yours."

The lawyerly Byrnes asked what would happen if a German firm was headquartered in Berlin, but the business itself was elsewhere. "If the business is in the West," Stalin replied, "we will make no claim to it."

Byrnes asked, "If the enterprise is not in Eastern Europe but in Western Europe or in other parts of the world, that enterprise remains ours?" Stalin replied, "In the United States, Norway, Switzerland, Sweden, Argentina—all that is yours!" Everyone laughed.

Stalin went on, "We are not fighting Great Britain or the United States."

They moved on to war crimes. No doubt suspicious that the United States would try to carry favor with the Germans—especially big German capitalists—Stalin complained that the Americans were unwilling to publish long lists of German criminals: "Aren't we going to act against any German industrialists? I think we should." As one example, Stalin mentioned the Krupp dynasty, long known for making German arms: "If they will not do, let's name others."

Truman said, "I don't like *any* of them!" His colleagues laughed. The President argued that if they mentioned some names but omitted others, "people may think that we have no intention of putting those others on trial."

As at Yalta, Stalin tweaked the British by mentioning Hitler's old underling Rudolf Hess, still imprisoned in the Tower of London: "It is surprising that Hess is in Britain, all provided for, and is not being put on trial."

Ernest Bevin, the new British Foreign Secretary, replied, "If there is any doubt about Hess, I will give an understanding that Hess will be handed over—and we will also be sending a bill for his keep!"

Stalin said he would be satisfied by listing "just three names" of German war criminals. Briefed on Stalin's view that Hitler might still be alive, Attlee suggested that they start with Hitler. Stalin said they did not have Hitler "at our disposition," but he would be willing to name him. The Big Three finally agreed to publish a list of top German war criminals within a month.

THAT EVENING AT 10:40, Truman, Stalin and Attlee signed the Potsdam Declaration. "The German people," it said, "have begun to atone for the terrible crimes committed under the leadership of those whom, in the hour of their success, they openly approved and blindly obeyed."

The victors did not wish to "destroy or enslave" the Germans, but to help them "prepare for the eventual reconstruction of their life on a peaceful and democratic basis." Allied policies toward the Germans would be uniform, "so far as is practicable." During occupation, "Germany shall be treated as a single economic unit." Each occupying power would take reparations from its own zones. Beyond that, the Soviets would take fifteen percent of industrial equipment that was "unnecessary for the German peace economy," in exchange for food, coal and other goods. They would also receive an additional ten percent for free. The Council of Foreign Ministers would draft a peace treaty "to be accepted by the government of Germany when a government adequate for that purpose is established."

After the document was signed by all three leaders, Truman pronounced the conference "adjourned until our next meeting, which I hope will be in Washington." Stalin smiled and said, "God willing!"

Truman wrote his mother, "You never saw such pig-headed people as are the Russians. I hope I never have to hold another conference with them. But of course I will."

He was wrong. Because of the deepening Cold War, Truman never saw Stalin again.

ON MONDAY, August 6, Truman was recrossing the Atlantic aboard the *Augusta* when handed a message over luncheon. An atomic bomb had been dropped on Hiroshima and was "successful in all respects." The war against Japan would soon be won. The President said, "This is the greatest thing in history." After a second report, declaring "complete success," Truman leapt to his feet and told Byrnes, "It's time for us to get home!"

THREE DAYS LATER, on Thursday, August 9, the United States closed its victory over Japan with a second atomic bomb, dropped, under existing orders, on Nagasaki. Emperor Hirohito secretly decided to "bear the unbearable" and meet the Allies' demand for unconditional surrender.

But Truman did not know that yet. That evening, he addressed Americans by radio on his European trip: "I have just returned from Berlin, the city from which the Germans intended to rule the world." He reported that Hitler's capital was now a "ghost city. . . . How glad I am to be home again—and how grateful to Almighty God that this land of ours has been spared!"

He reported that the declaration signed at Potsdam was "intended to eliminate Naziism, armaments, war industries, the German General Staff and all its military tradition." It hoped to "rebuild democracy by control of German education, by reorganizing local government and the judiciary, by encouraging free speech, free press, freedom of religion and the right of labor to organize." German industry would be "decentralized in order to do away with concentration of economic power in cartels and monopolies." Germans would be granted no higher standard of living than their former victims.

Truman said that the wartime allies were resolved to "do what we can to make Germany over into a decent nation" and "eventually work its way" back into the "civilized world."

Truman's speech largely obscured the unresolved questions and harsh compromises that were the legacy of Potsdam. The Soviets would get reparations, but the victors had still to agree on what. Germany would be treated as an "economic whole," but in each zone, the commander would have paramount authority. The defeated nation would not be partitioned; the shift of land to Poland was merely "provisional."

As the American diplomat and scholar W. R. Smyser wrote in 1999, at Potsdam "each side paid what it had to pay to get what it wanted most." Stalin got almost one quarter of pre–World War II German territory for Poland. Britain and America, by demanding that each victor seize reparations from its own zone, spared postwar Germany the staggering reparations and debt that in the 1920s had brought inflation, unemployment and Hitler. They had also prepared a means, if necessary, to protect western Germany from Soviet encroachment.

John McCloy knew that if Soviet-American relations deteriorated, the slash between the Soviet and Western zones would become much more than an abstraction. He wrote in his diary, "We are drifting toward a line down the middle of Germany."

• • •

WITH HIS TAKE-CHARGE MANNER, Byrnes had so forced Henry Stimson to the side that before the Potsdam conference ended, the old Secretary of War had asked Truman's permission to return to America early. He felt wounded when the President agreed. On the way home, Stimson stopped in Frankfurt to lunch on a sunny terrace with Eisenhower and Lucius Clay, who as zone commander would soon be charged with carrying out JCS 1067 and the Potsdam Agreement.

Eisenhower nudged Clay to express "some of your concerns" to Stimson. Clay told the War Secretary it was "self-evident" that Americans would not allow mass starvation and death in their zone. The cost would be "terrific" if his military government did nothing to help the Germans back on their feet.

Stimson agreed. He told Clay that the arrest and trial of Nazi war criminals was essential to peace, but not deliberate destruction of Germany's economy. He warned that "no matter how vindictive" Americans felt now, unless Clay restored "an economic life" to the Germans, he would be "repudiated by the very people who have given you these instructions."

Stimson advised Clay, "Sure, you've got to live with 1067." But they mustn't "let this country starve to death."

CHAPTER TWENTY-FIVE

"The Spirit and Soul of a People Reborn"

For the three years after the conference at Potsdam, the story of Americans in Germany was not chiefly Harry Truman's but Lucius Clay's. As with General Douglas MacArthur, his viceroy in Japan, Truman did little to interfere with General Clay's autonomy over the American zone.[1]

Like Truman, General Clay had ancestral reasons to compare the German occupation with the American Reconstruction. Born in 1898, he was the son of a Democratic Senator from Georgia, Alexander Stephens Clay, named for the Confederate Vice President. After his graduation from West Point, the young Clay resented his assignment to the seemingly peripheral Army Corps of Engineers. But after mapping the jungles of Panama and surveying dam construction near Pittsburgh, he went to Washington in 1933 as the number-two man for rivers and harbors, haggling with New Deal figures such as Harold Ickes and Harry Hopkins over jobs in public works.

During World War II, as Army materiel chief, Clay whipped up production of 88,000 tanks, 2 million trucks and 178,000 artillery pieces. Fearing his career would be "a failure without combat experience," he was chagrined to be told that he would succeed Eisenhower as U.S. commander in Germany. But he realized that his wartime service had taught him about the "entire economy of a nation."

1. Since this book is concerned with Roosevelt's and Truman's wartime statecraft on postwar Germany, this chapter offers a synoptical treatment of the four years that followed.

Clay first read JCS 1067 while flying to Europe in April 1945. He agreed with its premise that Germans bore collective guilt for Hitler's crimes. He wrote McCloy that he was "unwilling to concede that Germany became what it was" just because Germans were inclined to "follow the leader." Clay approved of the measures to punish German war criminals, arrest high officials and restrict factories that might make war. But like Stimson and McCloy, he felt that Americans were "not a vindictive people."

Clay objected most of all to the part of JCS 1067 that was its direct legacy from the Morgenthau Plan. He later recalled that "technically our instructions prevented us from doing anything to help the Germans financially or economically." But once he realized that there was no functioning administration in Germany, he began thinking "in terms of reconstruction—in a period when even to talk about reconstructing Germany would have been enough to get you [hanged] on the Ellipse in Washington."

Just before VE-Day, Clay assured McCloy that "destruction of Germany's war potential" was no longer a serious problem: "The progress of war has accomplished that." He asked for "sufficient freedom here to bring industries back into production" to let Germans survive, adding, "I hope you won't think . . . I am getting soft." After surveying the vast destruction across Germany, Clay wrote McCloy that some hunger was necessary to make Germans "realize the consequences of a war which they caused," but not "to the point where it results in mass starvation and sickness."

IN AUGUST 1945, Clay moved from Frankfurt to Berlin. Anxious not to strike the Germans as a hedonistic potentate, he took a modest, ivy-adorned house in the suburb of Dahlem.

One of his first problems with JCS 1067 was the ban against American fraternization with Germans, which he found "unenforceable." Clay wrote McCloy, "The only fraternization that really interests the soldiers is going with the pretty German girl, who is very much in evidence."[2] Backed by Marshall and Eisenhower, Clay lifted the ban, declaring that Americans could converse "with adult Germans on the streets and in public places."

2. Saul Padover, a U.S. Army intelligence analyst who had followed the Army into Germany, told Harold Ickes that "German women are crazy for men" and that "sexual intercourse" was "widespread." Ickes noted in his diary that "after all, they have been without men for a long time."

With the food shortage growing worse, Clay reminded his aides of the JCS 1067 loophole on "disease and unrest." In time, he warned Washington that larger food supplies were essential to avoid disorder, adding that they would help all of Western Europe: "There is no choice between becoming a Communist on 1500 calories and a believer in democracy on 1000 calories." Doing less could "pave the road to Communist Germany." Clay ordered his military government to pursue "the four D's"—demilitarization, decartelization, democratization, denazification.

As American troops had thrust into Germany, military organizations were disbanded, arms and ammunition seized. Breaking up cartels would have to be done in concert with the other occupying powers. Clay began his campaign for democracy by ordering that all Nazi textbooks and literature be destroyed, but noted that "you cannot build real democracy in an atmosphere of distress and hunger."

As for denazification, Clay advised Washington in July 1945 that he had not yet seen any "general feeling of war guilt or repugnance for Nazi doctrine and regime." The Germans "blame Nazis for losing the war, protest ignorance of the regime's crimes and shrug off their own support or silence as incidental and unavoidable."

In September, General George Patton, military governor of Bavaria, told reporters that "more than half the German people were Nazis and we would be in a hell of a fix if we removed all Nazi party members from office. The way I see it, this Nazi thing is very much like a Democratic and Republican election fight." Patton claimed he had been misquoted, but when he criticized Clay's efforts to rout his zone of Nazis, Eisenhower relieved him. Responding to the uproar back in the United States, Eisenhower and Clay issued a new decree that ex-Nazis be used as nothing more than manual laborers.

Some Germans feared that the new law was the spearhead of a revival of the Morgenthau Plan. By October 1945, Clay informed McCloy that about seventy-five thousand Germans had been removed from their jobs. Told by an aide that he was too rough on the Germans, Clay said, "The best way to get a bad order changed is to carry it out vigorously." Clay complained to the Pentagon that even if he were given ten thousand Americans to help rid his zone of Nazis, he could not finish the job.

Clay's denazification program faltered under the immensity of the task, his meager resources, his eagerness to keep the economy running by keeping many local Nazis employed and to win the contest against the Soviets for German sympathies. Even with its limitations, the American denazification program was more thorough than that of the British or French—and certainly more than the Soviet. Ultimately about three million Germans were charged, two million put on trial and almost one million punished in some fashion.

Later Clay said that his program had been too strict: "I think we carried it too far. The British and French didn't have the same feeling toward the Nazis that we did. Neither one had a huge Jewish population that had developed a hatred you can well understand. . . . We were being constantly attacked by our press, which had the unerring ability to find some Nazi that we had put in military government."

Worried about such press criticism, Truman asked Byron Price, a former wire-service editor and Roosevelt's wartime censorship chief, to visit the U.S. zone and report on Clay's performance. Price warned that many Germans "who at first greeted the Americans as liberators" were showing "surprise and depression at our stern policies" of denazification and industrial dismantling.

Price argued that the U.S. daily food ration of 1,550 calories for Germans was not enough: "If starvation comes, as now seems likely, epidemics and rioting will not be far behind."[3] He also reported "widespread surprise among Germans" that the Allies had not yet fulfilled their promise to try the highest Nazi leaders by international tribunal. This did not "improve relations with a German people who traditionally respect only firm and swift authority."

THE INTERNATIONAL TRIBUNAL that Roosevelt and Churchill had once argued about convened at Nuremberg in November 1945. Starting with Martin Bormann—in absentia[4]—and Hermann Göring, twenty-two high

3. In reply, Assistant Secretary of War Robert Patterson agreed that 1,550 daily calories was inadequate: "The difficulty here has been that the level in Poland and Austria is no higher . . . and under the Potsdam Declaration, the Germans are not to be fed better than the people in the surrounding countries."

4. Hitler's private secretary, whom he named political chief of civil defense in the last months of the war, was rumored to have escaped the Allies, perhaps to Latin America. In fact, after Hitler's death, Bormann committed suicide or was killed in Berlin. What remained of his corpse was discovered and identified in 1972.

Nazi leaders were indicted for conspiracy to commit war crimes, crimes against the peace and crimes against humanity.

Echoing Stimson's wartime arguments, Truman recalled in 1963 that he wanted "a just, swift and public trial" to show Germans "the ineradicable stain their leaders had put on their name among nations" and "to make it impossible for anyone ever to say in times to come, 'Oh, it never happened—just a lot of propaganda—a pack of lies.'"

Truman agreed with the U.S. prosecutor, Supreme Court Justice Robert Jackson, that the tribunal must convene in Germany. Clay recommended Nuremberg, site of Hitler's notorious party rallies, and provided fifteen thousand German prisoners of war to clean up the streets. He later insisted that without the record compiled during Nuremberg trials, "it would have been impossible" to convince the German people "how terrible their government really was."[5]

At the same time he had to punish the Germans in his zone, Clay was also charged with attracting them to American-style democracy. To start democratic processes and cut occupation costs, he moved faster than the other occupiers to hand local responsibility to "good" Germans. He trisected the American zone, appointed three minister-presidents—Germans who had not been Nazis—and asked them, under his guidance, to draft policies on food, denazification and other problems for the period until there was a central German government.

During a November visit to Washington after succeeding Eisenhower as zone commander, Clay was relieved to find that asking to rebuild the German economy no longer risked getting him hanged on the Washington Monument. Under JCS 1067's "disease and unrest" loophole, Clay won approval for letting his Germans use their own coal to prevent starvation and speed the rehabilitation of Western Europe.

THE PROVISIONAL FRENCH PRESIDENT, Charles de Gaulle, threw sand into the gears of the Allied Control Council. Truman felt that de Gaulle's "desire to return France to world power" was "fascist or Napoleonic." He had

5. After the international tribunal closed down in October 1946, the United States conducted a dozen trials at Nuremberg against lower-level Germans. The United States also conducted military trials at Dachau.

had to threaten de Gaulle with a halt in financial aid to France simply to evict French troops from Stuttgart, which was in the American zone. Despite Truman's assurance that the atomic bomb would "give pause" to Germany and other possible aggressors, the French leader demanded the Rhineland for France. Like the Russians, he wanted the Ruhr internationalized.

Troubled by new conflicts with the Soviets, eager to protect France and the Ruhr from communism, Truman grew impatient with Clay's soldierly collaboration with the Russians and his insistence on pursuing the Potsdam agreement to treat Germany as an economic whole.

At the second meeting of the Potsdam-mandated Council of Foreign Ministers, held in Moscow at the end of 1945, the President was furious when Jimmy Byrnes independently offered possible recognition of Soviet-backed regimes in Romania and Bulgaria and issued a public statement on his diplomacy before reporting to the President. By Truman's later account, he read aloud to Byrnes from a complaint he had written him about Byrnes's insubordination, which also warned, "Unless Russia is faced with an iron fist and strong language, another war is in the making. I'm tired babying the Soviets."[6]

In the Allied Control Council, Clay told the Soviets and French that he could not keep depleting the American zone for reparations without reaping the gains from economic unification agreed upon at Potsdam. When he halted industrial dismantling and reparations deliveries, the Soviets thundered against the "illegal General Clay."

In May 1946, Clay cabled Washington that after a year of occupation, the four German zones had become almost airtight territories. With a "deteriorating German economy," failure to achieve economic unity would make the next winter "almost unbearable." The following month, Assistant Secretary of War Robert Patterson wrote Byrnes that U.S. "national security" required economic revival of the Ruhr and Rhineland and use of German resources to buttress Western Europe against "engulfment" by the Soviet Union.

At the latest foreign ministers meeting, which began in April in Paris, Byrnes had rejected Molotov's renewed reparations demand, complaining that the United States and Britain had to pay half a billion dollars a year to feed Germans in their zones because the Soviet zone had reneged on food

6. Byrnes later said that had Truman read him such a letter, he would have quit immediately.

deliveries. When Molotov refused the Secretary of State's proposal that the four powers keep Germany demilitarized for twenty-five years, Byrnes concluded that Stalin was waiting for the Americans to depart Europe. Then the Soviets would move against Germany.

Clay warned Byrnes of the Germans' anxiety that U.S. forces would leave them to confront the Red Army alone. In September 1946, the Secretary of State came to Germany and spoke at the Stuttgart Opera House to an audience including dozens of the Germans Clay had appointed in the experiment of self-government. Millions of Germans listened by radio to a simultaneous German translation of the speech.

Byrnes declared that as long as there were any occupation soldiers in Germany, Americans would stay: "We will not shirk our duty. We are not withdrawing." He said, "The American people want to help the German people to win their way back to an honorable place among the free and peace-loving nations of the world."

As Clay later recalled, there was "enormous enthusiasm. It was unbelievable to me. Here was an American Secretary of State out there signing autographs for the Germans, little over one year after the end of the war."

THAT WINTER, at Clay's request, Truman sent Herbert Hoover to tour western Germany, using Göring's old private train. The former President soon warned that the economy of the defeated land had "sunk to the lowest level in a hundred years."

The Joint Chiefs of Staff resolved that the "complete revival of German industry, particularly coal mining" was now of "primary importance" to American security. To ease the economic hardship, the British and Americans created a single Anglo-American zone with the Gilbert and Sullivan–sounding name of Bizonia, whose capital would be Frankfurt.

Truman fired the maverick Byrnes in January 1947 and replaced him with General George Marshall, who scrapped JCS 1067 and supplanted it with a more generous JCS 1779, which decreed that "an orderly and prosperous Europe requires the economic contributions of a stable and productive Germany." The United States gave Army food rations to more than three million German children.

After another deadlocked foreign ministers' meeting, in the spring of

1947 in Moscow, Marshall concluded that more bargaining with the Russians about a united Germany might only open the way for Soviet power while the western zones were convulsed by chaos and riot. He warned that "the patient is sinking while the doctors deliberate." Clay told Washington that he had never seen the Germans more dispirited.

In June 1947, at the Harvard commencement, the Secretary of State unveiled what became known as the Marshall Plan, offering munificent U.S. aid for European recovery. For inspiration while it was being drafted, Marshall had sent for Henry Stimson's private 1944 memos to Roosevelt lambasting the Morgenthau Plan and demanding the postwar reconstruction of Germany. With Marshall's proposal, Morgenthau's plan for Germany was dead once and for all. Molotov denounced Marshall's offer as a scheme to extend American influence into Eastern Europe, but he could not derail it.

SOVIET DOCUMENTS OPENED after the Cold War suggest that Stalin hoped for a united Germany, but only so long as there remained the chance of lavish reparations, Soviet influence over the Ruhr and Western Europe and one day, after the Americans departed, his old dream of an all-socialist Germany under the aegis of the Kremlin. In the spring of 1946, Stalin told Yugoslav visitors that "all of Germany must be ours—that is, Soviet, Communist."

By 1947, those hopes were dying, thanks to the Soviet Union's growing confrontation with the West, Stalin's own ambivalence about what to do with Germany and Molotov's clumsy brokerage. Years later Molotov conceded that he had tried to "expand Soviet frontiers as far as possible," adding that there could be no "peaceloving" Germany unless it followed the "path of socialism."

Stalin also undermined the possibility of a unified Germany by entrusting the Soviet zone to the old German Communist Walter Ulbricht. An alumnus of Stalin's wartime Free Germany Committee, the rigid Ulbricht clearly felt that his best path to power was by turning the zone into a highly militarized Soviet client state. Only when it was much too late did Stalin call Ulbricht to Moscow and attack him for fighting "like your ancestors, the Teutons, with an open visor," which "may be brave" but was "often very stupid."

After the failure of the London foreign ministers' meeting in early 1948, Truman concluded that "the Russians were not going to carry out their agreement for a four-power commission on Germany." The historian Carolyn Woods Eisenberg wondered whether the United States gave up too fast on the chance for a unified Germany that would be genuinely neutral. She wrote in 1996 that "for all their alarms about Russian aggression, U.S. policy-makers saw the Soviets as weak both economically and militarily," eschewing "potentially favorable bargains" with the Soviets because they expected "a complete collapse down the road."

But gambling on a united Germany in the late 1940s might have opened the way to a Soviet Europe—or a German nation that was eager for another Hitler. The historian Thomas Alan Schwartz notes that at a time "when the German population looked back with longing to the power and economic success of the Nazi regime, it would have been the height of irresponsibility for an American leader to trust such an 'independent' Germany." Schwartz points out that surveys made a decade after the German defeat revealed that most Germans still thought that "Germany's best time in recent history had been during the first years of the Nazis." A large minority was still insisting that "Nazism was a good idea badly carried out" and that "Hitler was a great German leader."

THROUGH ALL THE BIG THREE BARGAINING over Germany during World War II, Stalin had retained a potent weapon—his ability to block access routes to Berlin, one hundred ten miles deep in the Soviet zone. In April 1948, complaining that the West was moving toward a divided Germany, the Soviets declared that no train should move in or out of Berlin without Soviet inspection and permission. Two months later, the Americans, British and French announced a step toward merger of their three zones—creation of a uniform currency that would thwart Soviet policies that caused inflation and stalled economic recovery in western Germany.

The Soviets responded by walking out of the Allied Control Commission and claiming all of Berlin. Rail and motor routes from the Western zones were shut down. From Moscow, Stalin demanded a "provisional, democratic, peaceloving" government and a peace treaty with Germany, adding that all occupation forces must be gone within a year.

Fearing a confrontation, the U.S. Army refused Clay's request to test the Soviet blockade of West Berlin by armored convoy. Instead, the British and Americans launched the Berlin Airlift, supplying the citizens of the Western sectors with up to eight thousand tons of food, coal and other provisions per day. Truman wrote in his diary, "We'll stay in Berlin—come what may."

Clay and his British and French cohorts also imposed a counterblockade of steel, equipment and coal shipments from Western Germany. Of the tenacious West Berliners, the city's U.S. commandant, Colonel Frank Howley, said, "It was their Valley Forge. They bought their right as a people willing to suffer and die for democracy."

BY THE FOLLOWING SPRING, the Berlin Blockade had failed. Seeing little chance for a united, unthreatening Germany soon, the British and Americans prepared for a Western alliance—NATO—and a West German state that would shield Western Europe against the Soviet Union and anchor the West Germans in democracy.

Under the chairmanship of Konrad Adenauer, the pre-Hitler mayor of Cologne, who was imprisoned in 1944 after Stauffenberg's plot to kill the Führer, German minister-presidents were asked to write a charter for a new West German government. Resisting any endorsement for the lasting division of Germany, they convened at Bonn, a city so provincial that it was unlikely to permanently supplant Berlin. For the same reason they called their charter not a constitution but a "Basic Law." In contrast to the shaky edifice of Weimar Germany that Hitler had pulled down, the Basic Law barred from the new parliament paralyzing no-confidence votes and splinter parties. To prevent another Führer, it placed severe limits on the new chief of state.[7]

On May 23, 1949, the Federal Republic of Germany was born. Five months later, Stalin established his own "provisional" German Democratic Republic, dominated by the brutal security service later known as the "Stasi." The new West German state was modeled on the old pre-Bismarck tradition of small, semiautonomous lands. The drafters of the Basic Law did not know it, but they had created a decentralized system resembling Franklin Roose-

7. The Western occupying powers retained control over West German reparations, industry, military and foreign affairs. They could overrule parliamentary laws that conflicted with occupation policy and maintained their authority over West Berlin.

velt's old fantasies of a postwar Germany like the peaceful, localized states he nostalgically remembered from his boyhood.

When Clay finished his job in Berlin, Eleanor Roosevelt wrote him that he had done "a wonderful piece of work." Clay reminded her that "President Roosevelt started me on my task in Germany." He hoped that the late President "would not have been disappointed."[8]

Back in Washington, Clay addressed the House and Senate, whose members cheered him for supervising the defeat of the Berlin Blockade. "One has only to revisit Buchenwald or Dachau to remember the extreme cruelty of the Nazi regime," he declared. "I saw in Berlin the spirit and soul of a people reborn."

FOR THE NEXT FORTY YEARS, the border between East and West Germany was a principal battlefront of the Cold War. In 1961 the East Germans erected the Berlin Wall and a hundred-mile-long "death strip" to stop the flow of millions of refugees to Western freedom and prosperity.

Then, in 1989, a new kind of Soviet leader, Mikhail Gorbachev, turned his back on Stalin and tore down the Wall. A year later, the victors of World War II formally gave up their rights over the land they had once conquered.

On October 3, 1990, the battle-scarred nation was unified at the heart of a Europe that was, for the first time since before Adolf Hitler, "whole and free."[9] Over Berlin, an old DC-3, once part of the Berlin Airlift, circled in celebration. At midnight, there were fireworks over the blackened old nineteenth-century Reichstag, still pockmarked from the Allied conquest of Berlin in 1945. A large red, black and gold German flag was raised to the sound of clanging by a replica of the American Liberty Bell.

The German parliament gathered in the Reichstag for the first time since 1933. Helmut Kohl, now no longer the Chancellor of the West but of all Germany, declared, "We must never forget, suppress or play down the crimes committed in this century by Germans. . . . Above all we owe this to the victims of the Holocaust, the unparalleled genocide of European Jews." Kohl

8. Appropriately, the first U.S. High Commissioner to West Germany would be John McCloy.

9. All parties carefully avoided using the term reunification of Germany. Part of the agreement to unify the country ordained that the Soviet annexation of the land east of the Oder-Neisse Line that Truman had once denounced as the "Bolsheviki land grab" should be made permanent. It was President George H. W. Bush who held out in Mainz in 1989 the prospect of a Europe "whole and free."

sent written pledges to the world's leaders that "in the future, only peace will emanate from German soil."

Presiding over the new Germany's first state ceremony at Philharmonic Hall was President Richard von Weizsäcker, whose father, one of Hitler's chief diplomats, had been convicted of war crimes. He noted that were it not for the war started "under Hitler," their country would never have been divided. He demanded that Germans reflect on the Holocaust, "that most awful of all crimes," adding, "History is giving us the chance. We want to use it—with confidence and trust."

CHAPTER TWENTY-SIX

The Conquerors

BEFORE LEAVING GERMANY as American commander in October 1945, Dwight Eisenhower told his staff, "The success of this occupation can only be judged fifty years from now. If the Germans at that time have a stable, prosperous democracy, then we shall have succeeded."

More than a half-century later, the Germany of our own time is not an ideal state. Nor can anyone be certain that it will have a perfect future. But in its democratic system, its grounding in Western institutions and its abstention from expansionist ambitions, war and dictatorship, it resembles the Germany that Franklin Roosevelt and Harry Truman once imagined far more than either man could probably have ever dreamt.

During the forty-five years after World War II, the cost was high for both Germans and Americans. To keep the peace against the Soviet Union while West Germans proved their commitment to democracy, East Germans were effectively sentenced to what John Kennedy called a Soviet "jail." The long confrontation over divided Germany, on the front line of the Cold War in Europe, required a monumental contribution of American money, soldiers and other resources, and it could have spiraled quickly into general nuclear war.

Nevertheless, in the early 1990s, when Germany was unified and the Cold War ended, Americans did not stop to fully realize the importance of their accomplishment. Thanks to their tenacity and generosity, their sense of justice without vindictiveness and their belief in Thomas Jefferson's ideas, they had done something that few in 1945 had thought possible. Working with Germans, Americans had helped to transform Europe's largest power into a democracy and rid the world of a danger that, as Churchill once warned, had afflicted humankind with three major wars.

Those who praise America's help in creating a democratic Germany usually point to the Marshall Plan, the Berlin Airlift, NATO and the long, expensive commitment to defending Western Europe against the Soviets. What is too often overlooked is the contribution before World War II ended. Had Roosevelt and Truman not been so insistent not merely on conquering Germany but ensuring that it never again threatened the world, that nation might be more dangerous today.

ROOSEVELT'S WARTIME LEADERSHIP on postwar Germany was scarcely impeccable. He should have been far bolder during what Morgenthau called "those terrible eighteen months" in 1942 and 1943 after the U.S. government began learning about Hitler's death camps. At a time when Roosevelt's administration was showing Americans "why we fight" by exposing and dramatizing other German atrocities, the President should not have been in the business of concealing what Washington knew about Hitler's murder machinery.

Roosevelt possibly believed that by singling out the murder of the Jews as a special American concern, he might provoke Hitler to pursue them more ferociously. During those eighteen months, he may have feared that issuing a specific public protest might fuel old suspicions among American anti-Semites that the United States was waging this war for the Jews. He no doubt believed that identifying any war aim other than simply winning the war would open the floodgates to all sorts of demands by domestic special interests.

But by tacitly suggesting that the United States did not know about the genocide or care enough to issue a specific protest, Roosevelt's silence may have emboldened Nazis to pursue the Jews of Europe with greater vigor, presuming that they would have to pay no special postwar penalty for their offense in case the Allies won. With almost sixty years of hindsight, Roosevelt's silence seems a strange lapse in the record of a President who normally spoke to Americans on grave world issues with courage, candor and foresight. That lapse is underscored by Roosevelt's lateness in pushing his officials to save Jewish refugees and his reluctance to seriously entertain whether bombing Auschwitz might save some of Hitler's intended victims without postponing victory in Europe.

Roosevelt's tendency to shunt Hitler's war against the Jews to a separate compartment of his mind compromised his planning for postwar Germany. Today, any scholar trying to explain why Hitlerite Germany was uniquely evil would naturally start with Hitler's zeal, shared by many Germans, to murder an entire people.

Instead, when Roosevelt privately spoke of the problem with Germany, he indulged in silly rants about Prussians, military uniforms and marching and did not mention genocide at all—even though he had privately learned more about the Holocaust than most Americans of the time. No one should expect a President to understand such a problem with the sophistication of a scholar who has twenty-twenty hindsight. But Roosevelt's failure to note the biggest thing wrong with Hitler's Germany had serious consequences.

It encouraged officials such as Hull and Stimson to think of postwar Germany mainly as a problem of reconstruction, similar to that of Mexico in 1848, after which the Americans might get out without pursuing a program such as the four "D's," and leave the future of postwar Germany to fate. Although he displayed genuine anger at the Germans, the President never instructed his top people that, unlike the nineteenth-century Mexicans, the principal offense of Hitler's Germans was not something so bland as seizure of American property but an unprecedented, criminal program of genocide.

In early 1944, Henry Morgenthau introduced an element of reality that had been missing from the internal U.S. government debate by saying that the biggest reason to dread the Germans was not the penchant for uniforms that Roosevelt harped on but for murdering an entire people. Combined with Germany's warlike history, this meant that postwar treatment of the defeated nation must be uniquely strict if the world never wished to see it again.

Such a worthy aim did not require a plan so brutal and vindictive as Morgenthau's. If enacted, the Morgenthau Plan might have fueled German bitterness that could have created another Hitler and, as the Cold War accelerated, opened the way to Soviet power in Western Europe. Yet it was Roosevelt's failure to come to grips with the most basic issue of German character that drove the understandably distraught Morgenthau to propose a plan so extreme.

Roosevelt's diplomacy on postwar Germany was also endangered by his chaotic approach to governing—letting his people struggle over policy and prominence and then reining them in when they got too powerful, defied his purposes or embarrassed him in the newspapers. The President believed that such methods let him squeeze the best out of strong-willed, independent people. The problem was that in the meantime, they could often do serious damage. It should not have required a Morgenthau to blow the whistle on disgraceful State Department efforts to stop the rescue of Jewish refugees. Had Roosevelt been more on top of the issue and more insistent that his high officials shared his values, many of Hitler's victims might have been saved.

Another example was Roosevelt's willingness to let State and War Department planners on postwar Germany go off on tangents that contradicted his private intentions, always confident that at the proper moment, he could snap them back into line. As the President grew more tired and ill, he was less able to referee public quarrels among Hull, Morgenthau and Stimson or keep a Jimmy Dunn from tricking him into unwittingly endorsing a lenient policy on Germany.

SUCH FLAWS, however, are overshadowed by the greatness in Roosevelt's leadership on Germany. In 1939 and 1940, against the advice of hard-boiled advisers who warned that most Americans were isolationist, the President risked his career by campaigning for military preparedness and aid to Britain. Had Roosevelt been more meek or shortsighted, Hitler might have won World War II.

During the war, the President benefited from his experience in Wilson's Navy Department and as the 1920 Democratic vice presidential candidate, when he had had to defend the flawed peace of Versailles. A President without this life history might not have been so determined to avoid repeating the mistakes of 1918 and 1919—the shaky German political system, the "stab-in-the-back" legend, the punishing reparations and other obligations that impoverished the country and sowed the seeds for a Hitler.

Thus Roosevelt demanded that this time the Allies should conquer, occupy and remake all of Germany. Along with his eagerness to avoid a separate Soviet-German peace, this was why he insisted on unconditional surrender. Had he bent to the reluctance of Churchill and many of his own officials about fighting the European war to ultimate victory, Germany might not be peaceful and democratic today.

Roosevelt knew that his appetite for remaking postwar Germany from the ground up placed him in opposition to many who were working for him. It affronted Hull's commitment to world peace through free trade. To the Republicans Stimson and McCloy, many of Roosevelt's ideas for postwar Germany, like the old liberal impulse to shatter cartels, almost certainly sounded like quixotic New Deal social reforms. When Morgenthau proposed his punitive plan, as James MacGregor Burns might have said, Roosevelt had the ingenuity to use the methods of the fox to serve the purposes of the lion. He used his tactical, temporary support of the Morgenthau Plan as a blunt instrument to show Hull, Stimson and Churchill that he meant business about transforming Germany—and to reassure Stalin that he did not intend to go soft on the Germans at the Soviet Union's expense.

Roosevelt also deserves credit for playing it surprisingly straight with the wartime Soviet Union. He knew that the war could only be won if Stalin remained convinced that the United States would not abruptly make a separate peace with Hitler and pull out. Upholding his unconditional surrender doctrine, Roosevelt managed to keep the Soviets fighting against Germany and, whether misguided or not, honestly tried to encourage Soviet-American cooperation in governing the conquered Germany, vetoing Churchill's demands to race the Soviets for Berlin.

Knowing that such cooperation might also fail, Roosevelt was also prepared. During the war, when it seemed that the Germans might surrender at any moment, he was poised to fly U.S. troops to Berlin to ensure that the Russian conquerors could not suddenly try to freeze their allies out of the German capital. During Roosevelt's last days, when Stalin turned more truculent, the President replied with justified firmness.

For the event of a rupture in Soviet-American relations, Roosevelt's plan to divide Germany into zones constituted his fallback option, allowing each power to seize a portion of postwar Germany, using military force to restrain the postwar Germans and keep the Russians out of Western Europe. Although Roosevelt is often remembered—and reviled—for his dreams of postwar friendship with the Soviet Union, he was the one who devised the strategy that ultimately let the West hold the line in Germany against Soviet domination of Europe.

At the dawn of the twenty-first century, it is now clear that Franklin Roosevelt had more influence than any other non-German on what Hitler's nation has now become. The democratic, decentralized Germany is largely the country that Roosevelt imagined and worked for. Of the many things that Roosevelt and his generation of Americans made possible during World War II, today's Germany is one of the most important. Despite wartime arguments that Germans were "incurable," Roosevelt and the Americans he led responded in the best American tradition, demonstrating that warlike people can become peaceable if encouraged to accept the right kind of political system. They and later generations of Americans showed that they were willing to make the sacrifices required to do that in Germany.

HARRY TRUMAN'S IMPACT on the Germany of today was exerted mainly after the World War II period treated in this book, but during the four months from his assumption of power through Potsdam, the neophyte President's instincts were usually sound.

Especially when revelation of the concentration camps was shocking most of the world, Truman, despite his deep reading of history, showed a startling lack of comprehension of what Hitler's war against the Jews had meant. Although Truman's public relationships with Jews were largeminded, his private, petty anti-Semitic comments did not abate for even a moment.

From the instant, in Potsdam, when Truman was told that the United States had a working atomic bomb, he may have been, for better or worse, more aggressive in pressing his new advantage than Roosevelt, with his eagerness to cooperate, might have been. Still, Truman did not exploit the new American hegemony in an effort to renege on Roosevelt's promise to give the Russians a large role in postwar Germany.[1]

With his fresh, open mind, Truman was probably quicker than his late predecessor might have been to respond to the rapidly changing geopolitical events in Europe and the rest of the world. He realized by the time of Potsdam that much had happened to make the Morgenthau Plan obsolete. With

1. However, in his retirement, near the height of the Cold War, Truman said he regretted that he had not used America's new power to rule Germany more singlehandedly.

the atomic bomb at his disposal, he did not need to devote immediate worry to German military power. Truman knew that Stalin's "land grab" had robbed Germany of much of its richest farmland, quashing Morgenthau's questionable argument that Germany could feed itself. And Germany's division into zones forestalled discussion of the kind of permanent dismemberment that Morgenthau had demanded.

By the summer of 1945, Truman was contending with new imperatives. He knew that with the Cold War accelerating, a weak, inert Germany might open the way to Soviet force in Europe. Destruction in Germany was so much greater than expected that Morgenthau's desire to dismantle German industry seemed to be obsolete. With Germans and so many other Europeans homeless and starving, letting Germany collapse would have had vastly more grievous consequences than Morgenthau had predicted.

In negotiating the Potsdam agreement, Truman, like Roosevelt, benefited from the mistakes of World War I. The pact forestalled the danger of vast German reparations to the Soviet Union that the United States would effectively have to finance. While preserving the ultimate chance for a unified Germany, it created the opportunity for the United States, Great Britain and France in the meantime to create, at least in part of Germany, a democratic state whose system, as Truman hoped and believed, would one day spread to the East.

Truman wanted to enforce Roosevelt's insistence that Germans know they had lost the war, but he also had to compete with Moscow for German sympathies. As General Lucius Clay warned him, Germans were unlikely to turn toward democracy if Americans treated them too much more harshly than the Soviets did. Unlike Roosevelt, who had once imagined himself as American commander in postwar Germany, Truman was content to give Clay extraordinary discretion.[2] He diverted the blame to Clay for sometimes ugly decisions, such as employing well-known former Nazis, that strengthened the position of the United States but undercut the American determination to reform the Germans.[3]

2. The historian examining Truman's public utterances during the three years after Postdam is astonished by how rarely the President spoke or answered questions about U.S. occupation policies in Germany.

3. Carolyn Woods Eisenberg notes how "inaccurately" Truman's government explained its German policy to Americans: "For the first two years after the war, little was said about the effort to rebuild the country. As far as most Americans knew, the main goal was to punish the Nazis and reform the society."

Above all, Truman proved himself able to keep opposing objectives in his mind at the same time. He wished to reform the Germans, but not so much that it scared them away from democracy. He wanted to revive the defeated country, so that starvation and chaos would not drive Europe toward communism and anarchy, but not if that would allow Germans to live better than their World War II victims. He wished to try to get along with the Soviets in Germany, but not if the price was Soviet mastery of that country or all of Europe.

LEADERS AT WAR sometimes imagine what might occur if the unthinkable happens. Lunching at Quebec in September 1944, Roosevelt and Churchill wondered aloud what Hitler would have done had he conquered Britain. Gazing at the ruins of Berlin during the Potsdam conference, Truman sank into depression as he envisaged how a victorious, vengeful Führer might have remolded Washington, D.C.

Hitler left little evidence of how he might have transformed Washington or the rest of America had he managed to win the war and turn part or all of the country into a satellite state. The Capitol and White House, housing Hitler's puppet parliament and puppet President, might have been plastered with swastikas. Washington would probably have a World War II memorial, but the soldiers honored would be Luftwaffe, SS and Gestapo.

There would, of course, be no monuments to Franklin Roosevelt or Harry Truman. In a Nazified America, a land of unspeakable cruelty, Goebbels's propagandists might have rushed to portray the last pre-Nazi Presidents as arch-criminals from whom Hitler had rescued the American people. The Nazi victors might have demolished FDR's Hyde Park mansion and Truman's white clapboard house in Independence to stop them from becoming rallying points against Hitler's domination of the United States. And it need not be added that Nazified America would be bereft of synagogues or Jews.

As for Berlin, Hitler planned, after winning World War II, to remake the capital by 1950 into "Germania," whose grandiosity would be worthy of the triumphant "Teutonic Empire of the German Nation." He ordered his court architect, Albert Speer, to ensure that future visitors to Berlin would be "stunned" by the "power of the Reich."

Dominating the city would have been a thousand-foot-tall Great Hall with a dome crowned by a gold German eagle clutching a swastika. In Hitler's "megalomania," Speer records, the Führer was "obsessed" by the structure.[4] Modeled after the Roman Pantheon, the Great Hall would be so cavernous that it could hold a number of U.S. Capitols. Its central chamber would be so huge that a hundred fifty thousand Germans could crowd in to cheer themselves hoarse at Hitler's tirades.

Down a central avenue wider than the Champs d'Elysees would loom an Arch of Triumph, forty-nine times as large as the French version, and an air ministry featuring the "greatest staircase in the world." Hitler warned Speer to equip the buildings with heavy steel shutters and doors. Someday he might "be forced to take unpopular measures" that might "lead to riots." He would have to "defend the center of the Reich like a fortress."

The new Berlin's most important landmark, of course, would be the Palace of the Führer. As Hitler willed it, his palace would be adorned by stone pillars, red mosaics and bronze lions, whose "decadence" reminded Speer of "a Cecil B. DeMille set" and the "show palaces of Oriental despots."

Hitler's palace would be grander than the ancient headquarters of Nero, a hundred fifty times the size of the house from which Bismarck ruled his own German empire. The palace would be constructed, block by block, from red granite mined by concentration-camp prisoners.[5] By Hitler's order, state visitors would have to trek a quarter-mile through its halls in order to reach his throne room.

Hitler exulted to Speer that after Germany won the war, "the whole world will come to Berlin to see our buildings." The defeated Americans would be "wild to see the most expensive building in the world." Hitler said, "My only wish, Speer, is to live to see these buildings. In 1950, we'll organize a world's fair. . . . We'll invite the entire world."

Instead, the skyscrapers, parks and plazas of today's Berlin are as original and interesting as Hitler's imaginings were banal. To be sure, there are World

4. Speer later reported that before World War II, Hitler felt "deeply irked" and "cheated" when he heard that Stalin was building the world's tallest monumental edifice in Moscow. When Germany went to war against the Soviets, the Führer was delighted that Stalin's project had to stop. He told Speer, "Now this will be the end of their building for good and all."

5. Speer recalled that because of the "incredible ignorance" of the SS officers who ran the camps, the granite blocks were produced in such a way that they developed cracks and the SS had to bow out. Hitler carped that the inmates had better return to "making felt slippers and paper bags."

War II monuments in the new city, but not to Hitler. If you search, you can probably find the site of the underground bunker where he fired a pistol into his head. But first you will probably see a columned memorial to the victims of Hitler's atrocities, which the world now calls the Holocaust.

World War II Germans are honored in present-day Berlin, but not Hitler, Goebbels or Göring. Instead, there are monuments to those who tried to assassinate them. If you go to Bendler Street, you will find that Hitler's old military headquarters, where Claus von Stauffenberg was executed on the evening of July 20, 1944, has been remade into a museum honoring the German resistance. But the street is not called Bendler anymore. Now it is named for Stauffenberg.

AUTHOR'S NOTE AND ACKNOWLEDGMENTS

I DECIDED TO WRITE THIS BOOK in early December 1991, while standing in Red Square in Moscow, shortly before midnight. It was two weeks before Mikhail Gorbachev declared the Soviet Union dead, just before the West finally won the Cold War.

As I watched Soviet soldiers marching in front of Lenin's tomb, I wondered what that scene would look like fifty years hence. If the Soviet collapse provoked some kind of authoritarian backlash, it probably would look much the same. If democracy took root in Russia, I presumed, the future Red Square would probably look more like Times Square or Piccadilly Circus.

My mind turned to the last chief American adversary. Just before victory in 1945, I wondered, how did Franklin Roosevelt and Harry Truman envision Germany fifty years after the bombs stopped falling? Did they presume that Germans, humiliated by their defeat, would soon turn to another Adolf Hitler—or had they fought World War II with the belief that German history could be diverted in the direction of a lasting democracy?

When I returned to Washington and began to read deeply in the historical literature on the period, I found that while much had been written about the American role in postwar Germany, there was little about what FDR and Truman did during wartime to ensure that Germany might ultimately be transformed into a democracy. Thus I happily returned to the period of Roosevelt and World War II, about which I wrote my first book in my early twenties.

I did not imagine that more than a decade would pass before *The Conquerors* was completed. After almost four years of research and writing, I realized that archives crucial to understanding wartime Presidential decision-making on Germany were still being opened. From the former Soviet Union, scholars were obtaining important documents on Big Three diplomacy and the early Cold War that few in the West had ever expected to see. Winston Churchill's private papers were being opened for general research. The British government was poised to release documents on such matters as British intelligence efforts to murder Hitler and his lieutenants.

The U.S. government was opening many of its thousands of wartime intercepts of messages among Soviet intelligence officers in Moscow, Washington, New York and elsewhere, providing new answers to the abiding controversy, which burned at the heart of American domestic politics for a decade after the war, over whether Harry Dexter White and other U.S. officials had worked illicitly and covertly with Soviet intelligence to bend FDR's wartime diplomacy to Soviet interests. Additionally, the FBI had yet to act on a list of Freedom of Information requests I submitted in 1992. I therefore put the basic draft of this book aside and, while writing *Taking Charge* and *Reaching for Glory*, on the Johnson White House tapes, waited for these archives to be opened.

During the course of almost eleven years, I have incurred many debts. At the Franklin D. Roosevelt Library in Hyde Park, Verne Newton gave excellent advice and shared his own work on FDR and the Holocaust. I renewed my old acquaintance with the Library's chief archivist, Raymond Teichman, always a superb guide to the documentary record of FDR's diplomacy. In the latter stages of research and writing, I benefited from the help of the capable Bob Clark, as well as Alycia Vivona, Karen Anson, Mark Renovitch and Robert Parks, and the Library's new director, Cynthia Koch. At the Harry S. Truman Library in Independence, I was aided by Larry Hackman, George Curtis, Michael Devine, Philip Lagerquist, Dennis Bilger, Pauline Testerman and Elizabeth Safly. At the National Archives, I thank the Archivist of the United States, John Carlin, and the redoubtable John Taylor.

I am happy to be an advisory board member of the Cold War International History Project of the Woodrow Wilson International Center for Scholars in Washington, D.C., which has done so much to encourage the Russian and other governments to preserve and open important Cold War documents. I have gained from the advice of the Project's first director, James Hershberg, and thank him and his successor Christian Ostermann and their excellent staffs.

I am grateful for the kindness of Henry Morgenthau III, the elder son of FDR's Secretary of the Treasury, who in 1991 published his fastidious and penetrating family history, *Mostly Morgenthaus.* With no conditions or assurance about what I would write, he turned over to me thousands of pages of notes and interviews produced for that volume, including transcripts of taped conversations with many men and women whom I would have been eager to interview were they still alive when I started this book, as well as private Morgenthau family letters and documents that remain in his possession.

This archive supplemented the vast number of transcripts of Henry Morgenthau, Jr.'s private conversations during his eleven years as Secretary of the Treasury, which now reside in the Roosevelt Library. While the original recordings have evidently disappeared, these transcripts allow the historian to describe the role of Morgenthau and other key officials in FDR and Truman's wartime statecraft on Germany with the verisimilitude that the secret taping systems of Presidents Kennedy, Johnson and Nixon allow us for the history of the 1960s. In using them, as well as other records of spoken conversations in this book, I have very occasionally altered punctuation or added italics for greater clarity, but not where this might change meaning.

For access to other restricted materials I am grateful to former Senator Claiborne Pell, who showed me his father's unpublished account of his service as an FDR appointee to the United Nations War Crimes Commission, and Senator Edward Kennedy, who in 1978 gave me permission to see portions of the diplomatic papers of his father, Joseph Kennedy.

As with my earlier books, I have imposed on other historians to read the manuscript of *The Conquerors* for accuracy of fact and interpretation. For such aid I thank my old teacher and friend Professor James MacGregor Burns of Williams College, biographer of FDR; Professor Warren Kimball of Rutgers University, scholar of Roosevelt and Churchill as well as the Morgenthau Plan; Professor Thomas Alan Schwartz of Vanderbilt University, historian of American relations with Germany and Europe; Professor Alonzo Hamby of Ohio University, biographer of Harry Truman; Professors Richard Breitman and Alan Kraut of American University, historians of FDR's approach to Jewish refugees and the Holocaust; and Dr. Bruce Craig of the National Coordinating Committee for the Promotion of History, author of a forthcoming book on the Harry Dexter White case. For additional readings I am grateful to my friends Mary Graham of the Kennedy School of Government at Harvard and Jon Meacham, who is completing his work on FDR and Churchill. I hasten to add that none of these readers is responsible for any errors that may survive in the finished book. Should any further reader find one, I would be grateful to be told of it in care of my publisher and will, of course, make appropriate corrections in future editions.

At the start of this project, Maryam Mashayekhi helped me to gather articles from scholarly journals and newspapers. During the last five months of writing, the able and resourceful Michael Hill helped me to check facts, assisted at the end by Jack Bales. My friend and literary agent Esther Newberg was, as always, an amiable Rock of Gibraltar, aided by Andi Barzvi, Chris Bauch, John DeLaney and other colleagues at ICM.

This is my third book to be published by Simon & Schuster, and by Alice Mayhew. A decade ago, she understood the potential importance of a history of the wartime Roosevelt-Truman diplomacy on postwar Germany, and she patiently waited for it to be finished. I am grateful for her intense professionalism, her command of history and her friendship, to her associate Roger Labrie for his editorial suggestions and assistance of all kinds, and also to Jack Romanos, Carolyn Reidy, David Rosenthal, Victoria Meyer, Aileen Boyle, Jackie Seow, Amy Hill, Isolde Sauer, Jonathan Jao and their colleagues at Simon & Schuster, as well as Jane Herman, who copyedited the manuscript.

Above all I thank my sons, Alexander and Cyrus, eight and six this year, and my wife Afsaneh. I began research on this book two months after we were married and am seeing it published just after our eleventh anniversary. For her support throughout this long project and for countless other reasons, it is dedicated to her.

GENERAL SOURCES

ABBREVIATIONS

COHP	Columbia University Oral History Project
CWIHP	Cold War International History Project Archives
FDRL	Franklin D. Roosevelt Library, Hyde Park, New York
FRUS	*Foreign Relations of the United States*
HSTL	Harry S. Truman Library, Independence, Missouri
HMPA	Henry Morgenthau III Private Archive, Cambridge, Massachusetts
LC	Library of Congress, Washington, D.C.
MD	Henry Morgenthau, Jr., Diaries, Franklin D. Roosevelt Library
Memcon	Memorandum of conversation
MM	Henry Morgenthau III, *Mostly Morgenthaus: A Family History*
NA	National Archives, Washington, D.C.
NYT	*The New York Times*
PRO	Public Record Office, Kew Gardens, Surrey, England
SD	Henry Stimson Diary, Yale University

MANUSCRIPT COLLECTIONS

Dean Acheson Papers, HSTL
Joseph and Stewart Alsop Papers, LC
Eben Ayers Diary, HSTL
Bernard Baruch Papers, Princeton University
John Boettiger Papers, FDRL
Charles Bohlen Papers, LC
Howard Bruenn Diary and Papers, FDRL
James Byrnes Papers, Clemson University

Winston Churchill Papers, Churchill College, Cambridge University
William Clayton Papers, HSTL
Columbia University Oral History Project
Father Charles Coughlin Papers, Northwestern University
Thomas Dewey Papers, University of Rochester
Allen Dulles Papers, Princeton University
John Foster Dulles Papers, Princeton University
Dwight Eisenhower Papers, Dwight D. Eisenhower Library
George Elsey Papers, HSTL
James Forrestal Papers, Princeton University
Felix Frankfurter Diaries and Papers, LC
Anna Roosevelt Halsted Papers, FDRL
W. Averell Harriman Papers, LC
William Hassett Diary and Papers, FDRL
Harry Hopkins Papers, FDRL
Cordell Hull Papers, LC
Harold Ickes Diary and Papers, LC
Joseph Kennedy Papers, John F. Kennedy Library (by courtesy of Senator Edward Kennedy)
Harley Kilgore Papers, FDRL
Arthur Krock Papers, Princeton University
Joseph Lash Papers, FDRL
William Leahy Papers, LC
Herbert Lehman Papers, Columbia University
Walter Lippmann Papers, Yale University
Breckinridge Long Diary and Papers, LC
Isador Lubin Papers, FDRL
George Marshall Papers, George C. Marshall Library
John McCloy Diary and Papers, Amherst College
Henry Morgenthau, Jr., Diaries and Papers, FDRL
Henry Morgenthau III Private Archive, Cambridge, Massachusetts (by courtesy of Henry Morgenthau III)
Drew Pearson Papers, Lyndon B. Johnson Library
Claiborne Pell Private Papers, Washington, D.C. (by courtesy of Claiborne Pell)
Franklin Roosevelt Papers, FDRL
Samuel Rosenman Papers, FDRL and HSTL
Walter Bedell Smith Papers, Eisenhower Library
Edward Stettinius Diary and Papers, University of Virginia
Henry Stimson Diary and Papers, Yale University
Margaret Suckley Diary, Wilderstein Preservation, Rhinebeck, New York
Kay Summersby Diary, Eisenhower Library
Time Archives, New York, New York
Harry Truman Papers, HSTL

Henry Wallace Diary and Papers, University of Iowa
Sumner Welles Papers, FDRL
Harry Dexter White Papers, Princeton University

National Archives, Washington, D.C.
Modern Military Branch Records
Assistant Secretary of War (RG 107)
Department of War (RG 165)
Joint Chiefs of Staff (RG 218)
Combined Chiefs of Staff (RG 226)
Office of Strategic Services (RG 226)
Diplomatic Branch Records
World War II Conferences (RG 43)
Department of State (RG 59)
Central European Division
European Advisory Commission
Policy Planning Staff
Records of the Postwar Planning Committees

Federal Bureau of Investigation (Freedom of Information Act Releases)
Henry Morgenthau, Jr.
Eleanor Roosevelt
Franklin Roosevelt
Henry Stimson
Harry Dexter White
Duke and Duchess of Windsor
VENONA Project

Central Intelligence Agency
VENONA Project (Declassified Army Signal Intelligence Service intercepts of Soviet diplomatic and intelligence messages, released 1995–1996)

Public Record Office, Kew Gardens, Surrey, England
War Cabinet Minutes (CAB 65)
War Cabinet Memoranda (CAB 66-68)
Foreign Office General Correspondence (FO 371)
Foreign Office Private Papers (FO 938)
Foreign Office Records on Germany (FO 943-1049)
Prime Minister's Office (PREM 3 and 4)

Cold War International History Project Archives, Woodrow Wilson International Center for Scholars, Washington, D.C.
Soviet government documents released by the Russian government since 1991

ORAL HISTORIES AND INTERVIEWS

Joseph Baldwin, COHP
Bernard Bernstein, HSTL, July 23, 1975
Edward Bernstein, HMPA, January 27, 1979
John Morton Blum, HMPA, May 15, 1984
Jonathan Daniels, HSTL, October 4, 1963
Josiah DuBois, HSTL
Josiah DuBois, HMPA, February 26, 1981
George Elsey, HSTL, April 9 and July 7, 1970
Charles Kindleberger, HSTL, July 16, 1973
Henrietta Stein Klotz, HMPA, September 19, 1978
John McCloy, HMPA, October 8, 1986
Henry Morgenthau III, by author, February 18, 2002
Randolph Paul, HMPA
John Pehle, HMPA, January 29, 1979
Claiborne Pell, by author, June 9, 1993
Sylvia Porter, HMPA
James Riddleberger, HSTL, April 6 and June 24, 1971
Gerhart Riegner, HMPA, June 1994
Samuel Rosenman, HSTL, October 15, 1968, and April 23, 1969
Henry Stimson, COHP
Harry Truman, HSTL, January and February 1954
Harry Vaughan, HSTL

PUBLISHED UNITED STATES GOVERNMENT DOCUMENTS

Foreign Relations of the United States (Washington, D.C.: U.S. Government Printing Office):
1941 (1958–1959)
1942 (1960–1962)
The Conferences at Washington, 1941–1942, and Casablanca (1968), hereafter referred to as FRUS Casablanca
1943 (1963), hereafter referred to as FRUS 1943
The Conferences at Cairo and Tehran (1961), hereafter referred to as FRUS Tehran
1944 (1966)
The Conference at Quebec (1972), hereafter referred to as FRUS Quebec
1945 (1967–1968)
The Conferences at Malta and Yalta (1955), hereafter referred to as FRUS Yalta
The Conference of Berlin (The Potsdam Conference) (1960), hereafter referred to as FRUS Potsdam
U.S. Senate, Committee on the Judiciary, *Morgenthau Diary (Germany)*, 2 vols. (Washington, D.C.: U.S. Government Printing Office, 1967), hereafter referred to as MD Senate

BASIC BOOK LIST

Acheson, Dean. *Present at the Creation: My Years at the State Department.* New York: Norton, 1969.

Alperovitz, Gar. *The Decision to Use the Atomic Bomb: And the Architecture of an American Myth.* New York: Knopf, 1995.

Ambrose, Stephen. *Citizen Soldiers: The U.S. Army from the Normandy Beaches to the Bulge to the Surrender of Germany: June 7, 1944–May 7, 1945.* New York: Simon & Schuster, 1997.

———. *D-Day: June 6, 1944: The Climactic Battle of World War II.* New York: Simon & Schuster, 1994.

———. *Eisenhower and Berlin, 1945: The Decision to Halt at the Elbe.* New York: Norton, 1967.

———. *Eisenhower: Soldier, General of the Army, President-Elect, 1890–1952.* New York: Simon & Schuster, 1983.

———. *The Supreme Commander: The War Years of General Dwight D. Eisenhower.* New York: Doubleday, 1970.

Andrew, Christopher, and Vasili Mitrokhin. *The Sword and the Shield: The Mitrokhin Archive and the Secret History of the KGB.* New York: Basic Books, 1999.

Annan, Noel. *Changing Enemies: The Defeat and Regeneration of Germany.* New York: Norton, 1995.

Armstrong, Anne. *Unconditional Surrender: The Impact of the Casablanca Policy on World War II.* New Brunswick, N.J.: Rutgers University Press, 1961.

Asbell, Bernard, ed. *Mother & Daughter: The Letters of Eleanor and Anna Roosevelt.* New York: Coward, McCann & Geoghegan, 1982.

Backer, John. *The Decision to Divide Germany: American Foreign Policy in Transition.* Durham, N.C.: Duke University Press, 1978.

———. *Priming the German Economy: American Occupation Politics, 1945–1948.* Durham, N.C.: Duke University Press, 1971.

———. *Winds of History: The German Years of Lucius Clay.* New York: Van Nostrand Reinhold, 1983.

Bagger, H. S., ed. *Eisenhower Speaks.* New York: Inter-Allied, 1946.

Beevor, Antony. *The Fall of Berlin, 1945.* New York: Viking, 2002.

Bellush, Bernard. *He Walked Alone: A Biography of John Gilbert Winant.* The Hague: Mouton, 1968.

Bentley, Elizabeth. *Out of Bondage.* New York: Devin-Adair, 1951.

Berezhkov, Valentin. *At Stalin's Side: His Interpreter's Memoirs from the October Revolution to the Fall of the Dictator's Empire.* New York: Birch Lane, 1994.

Bernstein, Barton. *Politics and Policies of the Truman Administration.* Chicago: Quadrangle, 1970.

Beschloss, Michael. *The Crisis Years: Kennedy and Khrushchev, 1960–1963.* New York: HarperCollins, 1991.

———. *Kennedy and Roosevelt: The Uneasy Alliance.* New York: Norton, 1980.

Beschloss, Michael, and Strobe Talbott. *At the Highest Levels: The Inside Story of the End of the Cold War.* New York: Little, Brown, 1993.

Bird, Kai. *The Chairman: John J. McCloy and the Making of the American Establishment.* New York: Simon & Schuster, 1992.

Birkenhead, Earl of. *The Prof in Two Worlds: The Official Life of Professor F. A. Lindemann, Viscount Cherwell.* London: Collins, 1961.

Bischof, Günter, and Stephen Ambrose, eds. *Eisenhower: A Centenary Assessment.* Baton Rouge: Louisiana State University Press, 1998.

Bishop, Jim. *FDR's Last Year.* New York: Morrow, 1974.

Blum, John Morton. *From the Morgenthau Diaries,* 3 vols. Boston: Houghton Mifflin, 1959, 1965, 1967.

———. *Roosevelt and Morgenthau.* Boston: Houghton Mifflin, 1970.

———. *V Was for Victory.* New York: Harcourt, 1976.

Boettiger, John. *A Love in Shadow.* New York: Norton, 1978.

Bohlen, Charles. *Witness to History: 1929–1969.* New York: Norton, 1973.

Botting, Douglas. *From the Ruins of the Reich: Germany, 1945–1949.* New York: Crown, 1985.

Bradley, Omar, and Clay Blair. *A General's Life.* New York: Simon & Schuster, 1983.

Brands, H. W. *Cold Warriors: Eisenhower's Generation and American Foreign Policy.* New York: Columbia University Press, 1988.

Breitman, Richard. *Official Secrets: What the Nazis Planned, What the British and Americans Knew.* New York: Hill and Wang, 1998.

Breitman, Richard, and Alan Kraut. *American Refugee Policy and European Jewry, 1933–1945.* Bloomington: Indiana University Press, 1987.

Bridgman, Jon. *The End of the Holocaust: Liberation of the Camps.* Portland, Ore.: Areopagitica, 1990.

Brinkley, David. *Washington Goes to War.* New York: Knopf, 1988.

Brinkley, Douglas, ed. *Dean Acheson and the Making of U.S. Foreign Policy.* New York: St. Martin's, 1993.

Browder, Robert Paul, and Thomas Smith. *Independent: A Biography of Lewis W. Douglas.* New York: Knopf, 1986.

Buhite, Russell. *Decisions at Yalta: An Appraisal of Summit Diplomacy.* Wilmington, Del.: Scholarly Resources, 1986.

Bullock, Alan. *Hitler and Stalin: Parallel Lives.* New York: Knopf, 1992.

Burns, James MacGregor. *Roosevelt: The Lion and the Fox.* New York: Harcourt, 1956.

———. *Roosevelt: The Soldier of Freedom.* New York: Harcourt, 1970.

Butcher, Harry. *My Three Years with Eisenhower.* New York: Simon & Schuster, 1946.

Byrnes, James. *All in One Lifetime.* New York: Harper, 1958.

———. *Speaking Frankly.* New York: Harper, 1947.

Campbell, Thomas, and George Herring. *The Diaries of Edward R. Stettinius, Jr., 1943–1946.* New York: New Viewpoints, 1975.

Cantril, Hadley, ed. *Public Opinion 1935–1946.* Princeton, N.J.: Princeton University Press, 1951.

Chace, James. *Acheson: The Secretary of State Who Created the American World.* New York: Simon & Schuster, 1998.

Chambers, Whittaker. *Witness.* Chicago: Regnery Gateway, 1984.

Chandler, Alfred, and Louis Galambos, eds. *The Papers of Dwight David Eisenhower,* vols. 4, 5, 6 and 9. Baltimore: Johns Hopkins University Press, 1970, 1978.

Charmley, John. *Churchill: The End of Glory.* New York: Harcourt, 1993.

Chuev, Felix, and Albert Resis, eds. *Molotov Remembers.* Chicago: Ivan Dee, 1993.

Churchill, Winston. *The Second World War,* 6 vols. Boston: Houghton Mifflin, 1948–1953. *The Gathering Storm* (1948). *Their Finest Hour* (1949). *The Grand Alliance* (1950). *The Hinge of Fate* (1950). *Closing the Ring* (1951). *Triumph and Tragedy* (1953).

Clay, Lucius. *Decision in Germany.* New York: Doubleday, 1950.

Clemens, Diane Shaver. *Yalta.* New York: Oxford University Press, 1970.

Cohen, Michael. *Churchill and the Jews.* London: Cass, 1985.

Coles, Harry, and Albert Weinberg. *Civil Affairs: Soldiers Become Governors.* Washington, D.C.: U.S. Government Printing Office, 1964.

Colville, Sir John Rupert. *Fringes of Power: 10 Downing Street Diaries, 1939–1955.* New York: Norton, 1985.

———. *Complete Press Conferences of Franklin D. Roosevelt.* New York: Da Capo, 1972.

———. *Winston Churchill and His Inner Circle.* New York: Wyndham, 1981.

Conquest, Robert. *Stalin: Breaker of Nations.* New York: Viking, 1991.

Craig, Gordon. *The Germans.* New York: Putnam, 1982.

———. *Germany: 1866–1945.* New York: Oxford University Press, 1978.

Cray, Ed. *General of the Army: George C. Marshall: Soldier and Statesman.* New York: Simon & Schuster, 1990.

Culver, John, and John Hyde. *American Dreamer: The Life and Times of Henry A. Wallace.* New York: Norton, 2000.

Dallek, Robert. *Franklin D. Roosevelt and American Foreign Policy, 1932–1945.* New York: Oxford University Press, 1979.

Daniels, Jonathan. *White House Witness.* Garden City, N.Y.: Doubleday, 1975.

Davidson, Eugene. *The Death and Life of Germany.* New York: Knopf, 1959.

Davis, Franklin, Jr. *Come as a Conqueror: The U.S. Army's Occupation of Germany, 1945–1949.* New York: Macmillan, 1967.

Davis, Kenneth. *FDR: The Beckoning of Destiny, 1882–1928.* New York: Putnam, 1972.

———. *FDR: The War President, 1940–1943.* New York: Random House, 2000.

Dawidowicz, Lucy. *The War Against the Jews.* New York: Holt, 1975.

Deutsch, Harold. *The Conspiracy Against Hitler in the Twilight War.* Minneapolis: University of Minnesota Press, 1968.

Divine, Robert A. *Roosevelt and World War II.* Baltimore: Johns Hopkins University Press, 1969.

Dockrill, Michael K. *The Cold War, 1945–1963.* Atlantic Highlands, N.J.: Humanities Press, 1988.

Donovan, Robert. *Conflict and Crisis: The Presidency of Harry S. Truman, 1945–1948.* New York: Norton, 1977.

Dulles, Allen. *The Secret Surrender.* New York: Harper and Row, 1966.

Dutton, David. *Anthony Eden: A Life and Reputation.* London: Arnold, 1997.

Eden, Anthony. *The Eden Memoirs: The Reckoning.* London: Cassell, 1965.

Edmonds, Robin. *The Big Three: Churchill, Roosevelt and Stalin in Peace and War.* New York: Norton, 1991.

Egan, Clifford, ed. *Essays in Twentieth-Century American Diplomatic History.* Washington, D.C.: University Press of America, 1982.

Eisenberg, Carolyn Woods. *Drawing the Line: The American Decision to Divide Germany, 1944–1949.* New York: Cambridge University Press, 1996.

Eisenhower, David. *Eisenhower at War, 1943–1945.* New York: Random House, 1986.

Eisenhower, Dwight. *Crusade in Europe.* New York: Doubleday, 1948.

Erickson, John. *Road to Berlin: Continuing the History of Stalin's War with Germany.* Boulder, Colo.: Westview Press, 1983.

Eubank, Keith. *Summit at Tehran.* New York: Morrow, 1985.

Feingold, Henry. *The Politics of Rescue: The Roosevelt Administration and the Holocaust, 1938–1945.* New York: Holocaust Library, 1970.

Feis, Herbert. *Between War and Peace: The Potsdam Conference.* Princeton, N.J.: Princeton University Press, 1960.

Fenno, Richard. *The Yalta Conference.* Boston: Heath, 1955.

Ferrell, Robert H. *Choosing Truman: The Democratic Convention of 1944.* Columbia: University of Missouri Press, 1994.

———. *Dear Bess: The Letters from Harry to Bess Truman, 1910–1959.* New York: Norton, 1983.

———. *The Dying President: Franklin D. Roosevelt, 1944–1945.* Columbia: University of Missouri Press, 1998.

———. *Harry S. Truman.* Columbia: University of Missouri Press, 1994.

Fest, Joachim. *The Face of the Third Reich: Portraits of the Nazi Leadership.* New York: Pantheon, 1970.

———. *Hitler.* New York: Harcourt, 1974.

———. *Plotting Hitler's Death.* New York: Holt, 1996.

Fisher, Marc. *After the Wall: Germany, the Germans and the Burdens of History.* New York: Simon & Schuster, 1995.

Fleming, Thomas. *The New Dealers' War: Franklin D. Roosevelt and the War Within World War II.* New York: Basic Books, 2001.

Freidel, Frank. *F.D.R.: The Apprenticeship.* Boston: Little, Brown, 1952.

———. *Franklin D. Roosevelt: A Rendezvous with Destiny.* Boston: Little, Brown, 1990.

Gaddis, John Lewis. *The Long Peace: Inquiries into the History of the Cold War, 1941–1947.* New York: Columbia University Press, 1987.

———. *Strategies of Containment.* New York: Oxford University Press, 1982.

———. *The United States and the Origins of the Cold War, 1941–1947.* New York: Columbia University Press, 1972.

———. *We Now Know: Rethinking Cold War History.* New York: Oxford University Press, 1997.

Gellman, Irwin. *Secret Affairs: Franklin Roosevelt, Cordell Hull and Sumner Welles.* Baltimore: Johns Hopkins University Press, 1995.

Gietz, Axel. *Die neue alte Welt: Roosevelt, Churchill und die europäische Nachkriegsordnung.* Munich: Fink, 1986.

Gilbert, Martin. *Auschwitz and the Allies.* New York, Holt: 1981.

———. *Churchill: A Life.* London: Heinemann, 1991.

———. *The Day the War Ended: May 8, 1945—Victory in Europe.* New York: Holt, 1995.

———. *The Holocaust.* New York: Holt, 1985.

———. *The Second World War.* New York: Holt, 1991.

———. *Winston S. Churchill: Never Despair, 1945–1965.* Boston: Houghton Mifflin, 1988.

———. *Winston S. Churchill: Road to Victory, 1941–1945.* Boston: Houghton Mifflin, 1986.

Gill, Anton. *An Honourable Defeat: A History of German Resistance to Hitler, 1933–1945.* New York: Holt, 1994.

Gimbel, John. *The American Occupation of Germany: Politics and the Military, 1945–1949.* Stanford, Calif.: Stanford University Press, 1968.

———. *Origins of the Marshall Plan.* Stanford, Calif.: Stanford University Press, 1976.

Goldhagen, Daniel. *Hitler's Willing Executioners: Ordinary Germans and the Holocaust.* New York: Knopf, 1996.

Goodwin, Doris Kearns. *No Ordinary Time: Franklin and Eleanor Roosevelt: The Home Front in World War II.* New York: Simon & Schuster, 1994.

Gormly, James L. *The Collapse of the Grand Alliance, 1945–1948.* Baton Rouge: Louisiana State University Press, 1987.

———. *From Potsdam to the Cold War: Big Three Diplomacy, 1945–1947.* Wilmington, Del.: SR Books, 1990.

Graebner, Norman A. *Roosevelt and the Search for a European Policy, 1937–1939.* Baton Rouge: Louisiana University Press, 1987.

Graml, Hermann. *Die Alliierten und die Teilung Deutschlands: Konflikte und Entscheidungen, 1941–1948.* Frankfurt: Fischer, 1985.

Greiner, Bernd. *Die Morgenthau-Legende.* Hamburg: Hamburger Edition, 1995.

Gromyko, Andrei. *Memoirs.* New York: Doubleday, 1989.

Grose, Peter. *Gentleman Spy: The Life of Allen Dulles.* Boston: Houghton Mifflin, 1994.

Gurewitsch, Edna. *Kindred Souls: The Friendship of Eleanor Roosevelt and David Gurewitsch.* New York: St. Martin's, 2002.

Hamby, Alonzo. *Man of the People: A Life of Harry S. Truman.* New York: Oxford University Press, 1995.

Hamerow, Theodore. *On the Road to the Wolf's Lair: German Resistance to Hitler.* Cambridge, Mass.: Belknap Press, 1999.

Hanrieder, Wolfram. *Germany, America, Europe: Forty Years of German Foreign Policy.* New Haven: Yale University Press, 1989.

Harbutt, Fraser J. *The Iron Curtain: Churchill, America, and the Origins of the Cold War.* New York: Oxford University Press, 1986.

Harriman, W. Averell, and Elie Abel. *Special Envoy to Churchill and Stalin, 1941–1946.* New York: Random House, 1975.

Harrod, Roy. *The Prof: A Personal Memoir of Lord Cherwell.* London: Macmillan, 1959.

Hassett, William D. *Off the Record with F.D.R.: 1942–1945.* New Brunswick, N.J.: Rutgers University Press, 1958.

Haynes, John Earl, and Harvey Klehr. *Venona: Decoding Soviet Espionage in America.* New Haven: Yale University Press, 1999.

Herf, Jeffrey. *Divided Memory: The Nazi Past in the Two Germanys.* Cambridge: Harvard University Press, 1999.

Herken, Gregg. *The Winning Weapon: The Atomic Bomb in the Cold War.* New York: Knopf, 1980.

Hirsch, H. N. *The Enigma of Felix Frankfurter.* New York: Basic Books, 1981.

Hodgson, Godfrey. *The Colonel.* New York: Knopf, 1990.

Hoffmann, Peter. *Stauffenberg: A Family History.* Cambridge, Eng.: Cambridge University Press, 1995.

Hogan, Michael. *A Cross of Iron: Harry S. Truman and the Origins of the National Security State, 1945–1954.* New York: Cambridge University Press, 1998.

———. *The Marshall Plan: America, Britain and the Reconstruction of Western Europe, 1947–1952.* New York: Cambridge University Press, 1987.

Holloway, David. *Stalin and the Bomb: The Soviet Union and Atomic Energy, 1939–1956.* New Haven: Yale University Press, 1994.

Hoopes, Townsend, and Douglas Brinkley. *FDR and the Creation of the UN.* New Haven: Yale University Press, 1997.

Hull, Cordell. *The Memoirs of Cordell Hull,* 2 vols. New York: Macmillan, 1948.

Isaacson, Walter, and Evan Thomas. *The Wise Men: Six Friends and the World They Made.* New York: Simon & Schuster, 1986.

Israel, Fred, ed. *The War Diary of Breckinridge Long.* Lincoln: University of Nebraska Press, 1966.

Issraeljan, Victor. *The Anti-Hitler Coalition.* Moscow: Progress, 1971.

Kennan, George. *Memoirs, 1925–1950.* Boston: Little, Brown, 1967.

Kennedy, David M. *Freedom from Fear: The American People in Depression and War, 1929–1945.* New York: Oxford University Press, 1999.

Kershaw, Ian. *Hitler, 1936–1945: Nemesis.* New York: Norton, 2000.

Kimball, Warren F. *Forged in War: Roosevelt, Churchill and the Second World War.* New York: Morrow, 1997.

———. *The Juggler: Franklin Roosevelt as Wartime Statesman.* Princeton, N.J.: Princeton University Press, 1991.

———. *Swords or Ploughshares?* Philadelphia: Lippincott, 1976.

———, ed. *Churchill & Roosevelt: Their Complete Correspondence,* 3 vols. Princeton, N.J.: Princeton University Press, 1984.

Kissinger, Henry. *Diplomacy.* New York: Simon & Schuster, 1994.

Klehr, Harvey, John Earl Haynes, and Fridrikh Igorevich Firsov. *The Secret World of American Communism.* New Haven: Yale University Press, 1995.

Koskoff, David. *Joseph P. Kennedy: A Life and Times.* Englewood Cliffs, N.J.: Prentice-Hall, 1974.

Krock, Arthur. *Memoirs: Sixty Years on the Firing Line.* New York: Funk and Wagnalls, 1968.

Kuklick, Bruce. *American Policy and the Division of Germany: The Clash with Russia over Reparations.* Ithaca, N.Y.: Cornell University Press, 1972.

LaFeber, Walter. *America, Russia and the Cold War.* New York: John Wiley, 1976.

Laloy, Jean. *Yalta: Yesterday, Today, Tomorrow.* New York: Harper, 1988.

Lamb, Richard. *Churchill as War Leader.* New York: Carroll and Graf, 1991.

Laqueur. Walter. *Russia and Germany: A Century of Conflict.* Boston: Little, Brown, 1965.

———. *The Terrible Secret: An Investigation into the Suppression of Information About Hitler's "Final Solution."* London: Weidenfeld and Nicolson, 1980.

Larrabee, Eric. *Commander-in-Chief: Franklin Delano Roosevelt, His Lieutenants and Their War.* New York: Harper and Row, 1987.

Lash, Joseph. *Eleanor and Franklin: The Story of a Relationship.* New York: Norton, 1971.

———. *Love, Eleanor: Eleanor Roosevelt to Her Friends.* New York: Doubleday, 1982.

———. *A World of Love: Eleanor Roosevelt and Her Friends, 1943–1962.* New York: Doubleday, 1984.

Leahy, William. *I Was There.* New York: Whittlesey House, 1950.

Leffler, Melvyn. *A Preponderance of Power: National Security, the Truman Administration and the Cold War.* Stanford, Calif.: Stanford University Press, 1992.

Leffler, Melvyn, and David Painter, eds. *Origins of the Cold War: An International History.* London: Routledge, 1994.

Leighton, Isabel, and Gabrielle Forbush. *My Boy Franklin.* New York: Ray Long and Richard Smith, 1933.

LeTissier, Tony. *Battle of Berlin.* New York: St. Martin's, 1988.

Lukacs, John. *1945: Year Zero.* New York: Doubleday, 1978.

Lyon, Peter. *Eisenhower: Portrait of the Hero.* Boston: Little, Brown, 1974.

Macmillan, Harold. *War Diaries: Politics and War in the Mediterranean: January 1943–May 1945.* London, Macmillan, 1984.

Maier, Charles S., ed. *The Marshall Plan and Germany: West German Development Within the Framework of the European Recovery Program.* Providence, R.I.: Berg, 1991.

———. *The Origins of the Cold War and Contemporary Europe.* New York: Franklin Watts, 1978.

Maisky, Ivan. *Memoirs of a Soviet Ambassador, 1939–1943.* London: Hutchinson, 1967.

Marcus, Sheldon. *Father Coughlin: The Tumultuous Life of the Priest of the Little Flower.* Boston: Little, Brown, 1973.

Marks, Frederick W., III. *Wind over Sand: The Diplomacy of Franklin Roosevelt.* Athens: University of Georgia Press, 1988.

Mastny, Vojtech. *The Cold War and Soviet Insecurity: The Stalin Years.* New York: Oxford University Press, 1996.

———. *Russia's Road to the Cold War: Diplomacy, Warfare, and the Politics of Communism, 1941–1945.* New York: Columbia University Press, 1979.

May, Ernest R., ed. *Knowing One's Enemies: Intelligence Assessment Before the Two World Wars.* Princeton, N.J.: Princeton University Press, 1984.

Mayle, Paul D. *Eureka Summit: Agreement in Principle and the Big Three at Tehran, 1943.* Newark: University of Delaware Press, 1987.

McAllister, James. *No Exit: America and the German Problem, 1943–1954.* Ithaca, N.Y.: Cornell University Press, 2002.

McCoy, Donald R. *The Presidency of Harry S. Truman.* Lawrence: University Press of Kansas, 1984.

McCullough, David. *Truman.* New York: Simon & Schuster, 1991.

McElvoy, Anne. *The Saddled Cow.* London: Faber, 1992.

McJimsey, George. *Harry Hopkins: Ally of the Poor and Defender of Democracy.* Cambridge, Mass.: Harvard University Press, 1987.

Mee, Charles. *Meeting at Potsdam.* New York: M. Evans, 1975.

Messer, Robert. *The End of an Alliance: James F. Byrnes, Roosevelt, Truman and the Origins of the Cold War.* Chapel Hill: University of North Carolina Press, 1980.

Miller, Merle. *Plain Speaking: An Oral Biography of Harry S. Truman.* New York: Putnam, 1973.

Miller, Nathan. *FDR: An Intimate History.* New York: Doubleday, 1983.

Moran, Lord. *Churchill Taken from the Diaries of Lord Moran: The Struggle for Survival, 1940–1965.* Boston: Houghton Mifflin, 1966.

Morgan, Ted. *FDR: A Biography.* New York: Simon & Schuster, 1985.

Morgenthau, Henry, Jr. *Germany Is Our Problem: A Plan for Germany.* New York: Harper, 1945.

Morgenthau, Henry, Sr. *All in a Life-Time.* New York: Doubleday, 1926.

Morgenthau, Henry, III. *Mostly Morgenthaus: A Family History.* Boston: Ticknor and Fields, 1991.

Morison, Elting. *Turmoil and Tradition: A Study of the Life and Times of Henry L. Stimson.* New York: Atheneum, 1964.

Morrison, David. *Heroes, Antiheroes and the Holocaust: American Jewry and Historical Choice.* Jerusalem: Gefen, 1999.

Mortimer, Edward. *The World That FDR Built: Vision and Reality.* New York: Scribner, 1988.

Murphy, Bruce Allen. *The Brandeis-Frankfurter Connection: The Secret Political Activities of Two Supreme Court Justices.* New York: Oxford University Press, 1982.

Murphy, Robert. *Diplomat Among Warriors.* London: Collins, 1964.

Nadeau, Remi. *Stalin, Churchill and Roosevelt Divide Europe.* New York: Praeger, 1990.

Naimark, Norman. *The Russians in Germany: A History of the Soviet Zone of Occupation, 1945–1949.* Cambridge, Mass.: Belknap, 1995.

Nelson, Daniel J. *Wartime Origins of the Berlin Dilemma: A Study in Alliance Diplomacy.* Tuscaloosa: University of Alabama Press, 1978.

Neufeld, Michael, and Michael Berenbaum. *The Bombing of Auschwitz: Should the Allies Have Attempted It?* New York: St. Martin's, 2000.

Newton, Verne, ed. *FDR and the Holocaust.* New York: Oxford University Press, 1996.

Nisbet, Robert. *Roosevelt and Stalin: The Failed Courtship.* Washington, D.C.: Regnery, 1988.

Notter, Harley. *Post-War Policy Preparation, 1939–1945.* Washington, D.C.: U.S. Government Printing Office, 1950.

O'Connor, Raymond. *Diplomacy for Victory: Franklin Roosevelt and Unconditional Surrender.* New York: Norton, 1971.

Offner, Arnold. *Another Such Victory: President Truman and the Cold War, 1945–1953.* Stanford, Calif.: Stanford University Press, 2002.

Parrish, Michael, *Felix Frankfurter and His Times.* New York: Free Press, 1982.

Parrish, Thomas. *Berlin in the Balance: 1945–1949.* Reading, Mass.: Addison-Wesley, 1998.

Paterson, Thomas. *On Every Front: The Making of the Cold War.* New York: Norton, 1979.

———. *Soviet-American Confrontation: Postwar Reconstruction and the Origins of the Cold War.* Baltimore: Johns Hopkins University Press, 1973.

Pearson, John. *The Private Lives of Winston Churchill.* New York: Simon & Schuster, 1991.

Penkower, Monty Noam. *The Jews Were Expendable: Free World Diplomacy and the Holocaust.* Detroit: Wayne State University Press, 1983.

Penrose, E. F. *Economic Planning for the Peace.* Princeton, N.J.: Princeton University Press, 1953.

Perlmutter, Amos. *FDR and Stalin: A Not So Grand Alliance, 1943–1945.* Columbia: University of Missouri Press, 1993.

Persico, Joseph. *Nuremberg: Infamy on Trial.* New York: Penguin, 1995.

———. *Piercing the Reich: The Penetration of Nazi Germany by American Secret Agents During World War II.* New York: Viking, 1979.

———. *Roosevelt's Secret War: FDR and World War II Espionage.* New York: Random House, 2001.

Peterson, Edward. *The American Occupation of Germany.* Detroit: Wayne State University Press, 1977.

Petrova, Ada, and Peter Watson. *The Death of Hitler: The Full Story with New Evidence from Secret Russian Archives.* New York: Norton, 1995.

Pogue, Forrest. *George C. Marshall: Organizer of Victory, 1943–1945.* New York: Viking, 1973.

———. *George C. Marshall: Statesman, 1945–1949.* New York: Viking, 1987.

———. *The Supreme Command.* Washington, D.C.: Department of the Army, 1954.

Public Record Office. *Operation Foxley: The British Plan to Kill Hitler.* London: Her Majesty's Stationery Office, 2001.

Radzinsky, Edvard. *Stalin.* New York: Doubleday, 1996.

Read, Anthony, and David Fisher. *The Fall of Berlin.* New York: Norton, 1992.

Rees, David. *Harry Dexter White: A Study in Paradox.* New York: Coward, McCann & Geoghegan, 1973.

Rhodes, Richard. *The Making of the Atomic Bomb.* New York: Simon & Schuster, 1986.

Rigdon, William. *White House Sailor.* New York: Doubleday, 1962.

Robertson, David. *Sly and Able: A Political Biography of James F. Byrnes.* New York: Norton, 1994.

Romerstein, Herbert, and Eric Breindel. *The Venona Secrets: Exposing Soviet Espionage and America's Traitors.* Washington, D.C.: Regnery, 2000.

Roosevelt, Eleanor. *This I Remember.* New York: Harper, 1949.

Roosevelt, Elliott. *As He Saw It.* New York: Duell, Sloan and Pearce, 1946.

———, ed. *F.D.R.: His Personal Letters,* 2 vols. New York: Duell, Sloan and Pearce, 1947, 1948.

Roosevelt, Elliott, and James Brough. *A Rendezvous with Destiny: The Roosevelts of the White House.* New York: Putnam, 1975.

———. *An Untold Story: The Roosevelts of Hyde Park.* New York: Putnam, 1973.

Roosevelt, James. *My Parents: A Differing View.* Chicago: Playboy Press, 1976.

Roosevelt, James, and Sidney Shalett. *Affectionately, F.D.R.: A Son's Story of a Lonely Man.* New York: Harcourt, 1959.

Roosevelt, Sara Delano (as told to Isabel Leighton and Gabriel Forbush). *My Boy Franklin.* New York: Crown, 1933.

Rosenman, Samuel. *Working with Roosevelt.* New York: Harper, 1952.

Ross, Graham, ed. *The Foreign Office and the Kremlin: British Documents on Anglo-Soviet Relations, 1941–1945.* Cambridge: Cambridge University Press, 1984.

Rubinstein, William. *The Myth of Rescue.* New York: Routledge, 1997.

Ruddy, T. Michael. *The Cautious Diplomat: Charles E. Bohlen and the Soviet Union, 1929–1969.* Kent, Ohio: Kent State University Press, 1980.

Rzheshevsky, Oleg A., ed. *War and Diplomacy: The Making of the Grand Alliance: Documents from Stalin's Archives.* Amsterdam: Harwood, 1996.

Sainsbury, Keith. *The Turning Point: Roosevelt, Stalin, Churchill, and Chiang Kai-Shek, 1943: The Moscow, Cairo, and Teheran Conferences.* Oxford, Eng.: Oxford University Press, 1985.

Schlesinger, Arthur M., Jr. *The Age of Roosevelt,* 3 vols. Boston: Houghton Mifflin, 1957, 1959, 1960.

———. *Robert Kennedy and His Times.* Boston: Houghton Mifflin, 1978.

Schmädeke, Jürgen, and Peter Steinbach, eds. *Der Widerstand gegen den Nationalsozialismus: Die deutsche Gesellschaft und der Widerstand gegen Hitler.* Munich: Piper, 1985.

Schwartz, Thomas Alan. *America's Germany: John J. McCloy and the Federal Republic of Germany.* Cambridge: Harvard University Press, 1991.

Seaton, Albert. *Stalin as Warlord.* London: Batsford, 1976.

Sharp, T. *Wartime Alliance and the Zonal Division of Germany.* Oxford: Clarendon, 1975.

Sherwin, Martin. *A World Destroyed: The Atomic Bomb and the Grand Alliance.* New York: Knopf, 1975.

Sherwood, Robert. *Roosevelt and Hopkins: An Intimate History.* New York: Harper, 1948.

Shirer, William. *The Rise and Fall of the Third Reich.* New York: Simon & Schuster, 1960.

Shoumatoff, Elizabeth. *FDR's Unfinished Portrait: A Memoir.* Pittsburgh: University of Pittsburgh Press, 1990.

Skidelsky, Robert. *John Maynard Keynes: Fighting for Freedom, 1937–1946.* New York: Viking, 2001.

Smith, Gaddis. *Dean Acheson.* New York: Cooper Square, 1972.

Smith, Bradley F. *The American Road to Nuremberg: The Documentary Record, 1944–1945.* Stanford, Calif.: Hoover Institution Press, 1982.

———. *Sharing Secrets with Stalin: How the Allies Traded Intelligence, 1941–1945.* Lawrence: University Press of Kansas, 1996.

Smith, Jean Edward. *Lucius D. Clay: An American Life.* New York: Holt, 1990.

———, ed. *The Papers of General Lucius D. Clay: Germany, 1945–1949,* 2 vols. Bloomington: Indiana University Press, 1974.

Smith, Richard Norton. *Thomas E. Dewey and His Times.* New York: Simon & Schuster, 1982.

Smyser, W. R. *From Yalta to Berlin: The Cold War Struggle over Germany.* New York: St. Martin's, 1999.

Snell, John L. *Wartime Origins of the East-West Dilemma over Germany.* New Orleans: Hauser Press, 1959.

Snow, C. P. *Science and Government.* Cambridge, Mass.: Harvard University Press, 1961.

Soames, Mary, ed. *Winston and Clemmie: The Personal Letters of the Churchills.* Boston: Houghton Mifflin, 1999.

Stein, Harold, ed. *American Civil-Military Decisions: A Book of Case Studies.* Birmingham: University of Alabama Press, 1963.

Stettinius, Edward. *Roosevelt and the Russians: The Yalta Conference.* Garden City, N.Y.: Doubleday, 1949.

Stimson, Henry, and McGeorge Bundy. *On Active Service in Peace and War.* New York: Harper, 1947.

Strang, Lord. *Home and Abroad.* London: Andre Deutsch, 1956.

Tanenhaus, Sam. *Whittaker Chambers: A Biography.* New York: Random House, 1997.

Taubman, William. *Stalin's American Policy: From Entente to Détente to Cold War.* New York: Norton, 1982.

Taylor, A. J. P. *Course of German History.* London: Hamish Hamilton, 1945.
Taylor, Telford. *Anatomy of the Nuremberg Trials.* New York: Knopf, 1992.
Tent, James F. *Mission on the Rhine: Re-education and Denazification in American-Occupied Germany.* Chicago: University of Chicago Press, 1982.
Theoharis, Athan G. *The Yalta Myths: An Issue in U.S. Politics, 1945–1955.* Columbia: University of Missouri Press, 1970.
Thomas, Hugh. *Armed Truce: The Beginning of the Cold War, 1945–1946.* New York: Atheneum, 1987.
———. *The Murder of Adolf Hitler: The Truth About the Bodies in the Berlin Bunker.* New York: St. Martin's, 1995.
Toland, John. *Adolf Hitler.* New York: Doubleday, 1976.
Trachtenberg, Marc. *A Constructed Peace: The Making of the European Settlement, 1945–1963.* Princeton, N.J.: Princeton University Press, 1999.
Trefousse, Hans, ed. *Germany and America: Essays on Problems of International Relations and Immigration.* New York: Brooklyn College, 1981.
Trevor-Roper, H. R. *The Last Days of Hitler.* New York: Macmillan, 1947.
Truman, Harry. *Memoirs: 1945, Year of Decisions.* New York: Doubleday, 1955.
———. *Memoirs: Years of Trial and Hope, 1946–1952.* New York: Doubleday, 1956.
Truman, Margaret. *Harry S. Truman.* New York: Morrow, 1973.
Tully, Grace. *F.D.R.: My Boss.* New York: Scribner, 1949.
Ulam, Adam. *Expansion and Coexistence: Soviet Foreign Policy, 1917–1973.* New York: Praeger, 1974.
———. *The Rivals: America and Russia Since World War II.* New York: Viking, 1971.
———. *Stalin: The Man and His Era.* New York: Viking, 1973.
U.S. Department of State. *Documents on Germany, 1944–1959.* Washington, D.C.: U.S. Government Printing Office, 1959.
———. *Documents on Germany, 1944–1970.* Washington, D.C.: U.S. Government Printing Office, 1971.
———. *Documents on Germany, 1944–1985.* Washington, D.C.: U.S. Government Printing Office, 1985.
———. *Foreign Relations of the United States.* Washington, D.C.: U.S. Government Printing Office.
U.S.S.R. Ministry of Foreign Affairs. *The Tehran, Yalta and Potsdam Conferences.* Moscow: Progress, 1969.
Volkogonov, Dmitri. *Stalin: Triumph and Tragedy.* Rocklin, Calif.: Prima, 1992.
Walker, R. *Edward R. Stettinius.* New York: Cooper Square, 1956.
Ward, Geoffrey. *Before the Trumpet: Young Franklin Roosevelt, 1882–1905.* New York: Harper and Row, 1985.
———. *A First-Class Temperament: The Emergence of Franklin Roosevelt.* New York: Harper and Row, 1989.
———, ed. *Closest Companion: The Unknown Story of the Intimate Friendship Between Franklin Roosevelt and Margaret Suckley.* Boston: Houghton Mifflin, 1995.

Weil, Martin. *A Pretty Good Club: The Founding Fathers of the U.S. Foreign Service.* New York: Norton, 1978.

Weinberg, Gerhard. *A World at Arms: A Global History of World War II.* New York: Cambridge University Press, 1994.

Weinstein, Allen. *Perjury: The Hiss-Chambers Case.* New York: Knopf, 1978.

Weinstein, Allen, and Alexander Vassiliev. *The Haunted Wood: Soviet Espionage in America—The Stalin Era.* New York: Random House, 1999.

Welles, Benjamin. *Summer Welles: FDR's Global Strategist.* New York: St. Martin's, 1997.

Werth, Alexander. *Russia at War, 1941–1945.* London: Pan, 1965.

West, Nigel. *Venona: The Greatest Secret of the Cold War.* London: HarperCollins, 1999.

Wolfe, Robert, ed. *Americans as Proconsuls: United States Military Government in Germany and Japan, 1944–1952.* Carbondale: Southern Illinois University Press, 1984.

Wood, E. Thomas, and Stanislaw Jankowski. *Karski: How One Man Tried to Stop the Holocaust.* New York: John Wiley, 1994.

Woods, Randall, and Howard Jones. *Dawning of the Cold War.* Athens: University of Georgia Press, 1991.

Woolner, David, ed. *The Second Quebec Conference Revisited: Waging War, Formulating Peace: Canada, Great Britain and the United States in 1944–1945.* New York: St. Martin's, 1998.

Wyden, Peter. *Wall: The Inside Story of Divided Berlin.* New York: Simon & Schuster, 1989.

Wyman, David. *The Abandonment of the Jews: America and the Holocaust, 1941–1945.* New York: Pantheon, 1984.

Yergin, Daniel. *Shattered Peace: The Origins of the Cold War and the National Security State.* Boston: Houghton Mifflin, 1977.

Zelikow, Philip, and Condoleezza Rice. *Germany United and Europe Transformed: A Study in Statecraft.* Cambridge, Mass.: Harvard University Press, 1995.

Zeller, Eberhard. *The Flame of Freedom: The German Struggle Against Hitler.* Boulder, Colo.: Westview Press, 1994.

Ziemke, Earl. *The U.S. Army in the Occupation of Germany, 1944–1946.* Washington, D.C.: Center of Military History, 1975.

Zink, Harold. *American Military Government in Germany.* New York: Macmillan, 1947.

———. *The U.S. in Germany, 1944–1945.* Princeton, N.J.: D. Van Nostrand, 1957.

Zubok, Vladislav, and Constantine Pleshakov. *Inside the Kremlin's Cold War: From Stalin to Khrushchev.* Cambridge, Mass.: Harvard University Press, 1996.

BASIC ARTICLES, MONOGRAPHS AND DISSERTATIONS

Chase, John. "The Development of the Morgenthau Plan through the Quebec Conference." *The Journal of Politics* 16 (1954).

Craig, Bruce. "Treasonable Doubt: The Harry Dexter White Case, 1948–1953." Ph.D. diss., American University, 1999.

Feingold, Henry. "Courage First and Intelligence Second: The American Jewish Secular Elite, Roosevelt and the Failure to Rescue." *American Jewish History* 72 (June 1983).

Franklin, William. "Zonal Boundaries and Access to Berlin." *World Politics* 16 (1963–1964).

Kimball, Warren. "U.S. Wartime Planning for Postwar Germany, or Germany Is Our Problem, Russia Is Our Problem, the Economy Is Our Problem," in Gerhard Krebs and Christian Oberländer, eds., *1945 in Europe and Asia.* Munich: Iudicium, 1997.

Laufer, Jochen. "The Soviet Union and the Zonal Division of Germany." Center for Contemporary Historical Studies, Potsdam, Germany.

Mark, Eduard. "Revolution by Degrees: Stalin's National Front Strategy for Europe, 1941–1947." Cold War International History Project.

Mosely, Philip. "Dismemberment of Germany: The Allied Negotiations from Yalta to Potsdam." *Foreign Affairs* 28 (1949–1950).

Naimark, Norman. "The Soviet Occupations: Moscow's Man in (East) Berlin." *Cold War International History Project Bulletin.*

Parrish, Scott, and Mikhail Narinsky. "The Turn Toward Confrontation: The Soviet Reaction to the Marshall Plan, 1947." Cold War International History Project.

Pechatnov, Vladimir. "The Big Three After World War II: New Documents on Soviet Thinking About Postwar Relations Between the United States and Great Britain." Cold War International History Project.

Schlaim, Avi. "The Partition of Germany and the Origins of the Cold War." *Review of International Studies* 11 (April 1985).

Van Everen, Brooks. "Franklin D. Roosevelt and the German Problem: 1914–1945." Ph.D. diss., Boston University, 1970.

Wagner, R. Harrison. "The Decision to Divide Germany and the Origins of the Cold War." *International Studies Quarterly* 24 (June 1980).

NOTES

PREFACE

April 1944 survey is in Cantril, p. 784.

EPIGRAPH PAGE

"We come as conquerors": Proclamation Number One, Eisenhower Library. "The success of this occupation": Bagger, p. 28.

CHAPTER ONE

The Plot to Murder Hitler

On the July 20, 1944, plotters, the assassination attempt and the aftermath, see Fest, *Plotting Hitler's Death,* Hamerow, Gill, Zeller, Bullock, pp. 826–827, 835–850, Kershaw, pp. 655–705, Fest, *Hitler,* pp. 697–723, Weinberg, pp. 753–755, Toland, pp. 790–818, Simon Finch, "I Agreed to Kill Hitler," in *Sunday Telegraph* (London), July 16, 2000. Now that East Prussia is part of Poland, Rastenburg is called Kętrzyn, and the Wolf's Lair is a tourist attraction. (See Simon Calder, "Europe's Killing Forest," in *The Independent* [London], November 1, 1997.) "Victory or death!": Zeller, p. 276. The German military adopted Hitler's comment as one of their slogans. On plotters' attitudes toward Hitler's war against Jews, see Gill, p. 169, Fest, *Plotting Hitler's Death,* pp. 283, 309, 326–327, and Grose, who believes (p. 202) that "the only Nazi crime that did not seem to generate their outrage was the extermination of the Jews." According to Hoffmann (pp. 115–116, 132–133, 151) and Kershaw (p. 668), Stauffenberg opposed Hitler's anti-Semitism and, as Kershaw writes, "turned irredeemably against Hitler" in 1942, responding to "eye-witness reports of massacres of Ukrainian Jews by SS men." For the range of attitudes toward the Jews among resistance members, see also

Christoph Dipper, "Der Widerstand und die Juden," in Schmädeke and Steinbach, pp. 598–616, and Kershaw, p. 1000. Placement of bomb in briefcase: Shirer, p. 1048.

"I myself saw": Toland, p. 803. There is a slightly different English translation of Stauffenberg's comment in Shirer, p. 1060. "Once again everything turned": Toland, p. 799. "Look at my uniform": Ibid., p. 801. Uniform sent to Eva Braun: Ibid., p. 812. "Traitors in the bosom": Shirer, p. 1057, Toland, p. 802. "Look me in the eyes, Blondi": Toland, p. 814. "Long live eternal Germany!": Zeller, p. 394. Fest's *Plotting Hitler's Death* (p. 278) translates the last two words of Stauffenberg's cry as "sacred Germany." Text of Hitler's radio speech is in NYT, July 21, 1944. Fest's *Hitler* (p. 710) and other volumes offer slightly different English translations. "Strung up like butchered cattle": Fest, *Plotting Hitler's Death,* p. 296. Hitler and Goebbels watching film of plotters' execution: Shirer, p. 1071. Goebbels on "ice-cold determination" is in Fest, *The Face of the Third Reich,* p. 91.

Text of Roosevelt's Democratic acceptance speech is in NYT, July 21, 1944, which identifies the location as a "Pacific coast" base. Roosevelt's train trip and its revelation by Fala is in Rigdon, pp. 111–112, and in William Rigdon's daily journal, "The Log of the Trip," July 15 to August 17, 1944, in FDRL. "Kill time" is in Rigdon's daily journal. Allen Dulles's operation in Bern is in Grose, pp. 148–256, and Persico, *Roosevelt's Secret War,* pp. 250–252, 322–326. "The next few weeks" and "a dramatic event": Grose, pp. 198–199. "Did not come as a great surprise": Donovan to FDR, July 22, 1944, in FDRL. On Roosevelt and unconditional surrender, see Chapter 2 below. "To prevent central Europe from coming": Grose, pp. 195–196. Roosevelt's refusal to comment on failed plot is documented by a thorough search of the records of his public utterances from July 20 to July 29, 1944, in FDRL. Privately he told his aide Samuel Rosenman, "If we can get rid of Hitler this way and still get unconditional surrender from any responsible German government, it would be fine because it would save many lives. I don't think we will" (Rosenman, p. 407). "We have just received news": Roosevelt to Stalin, July 21, 1944, in FDRL. "Dearest Babs": FDR to Eleanor, July 21, 1944, in FDRL.

Roosevelt's San Diego departure, voyage and arrival in Honolulu are documented in William Rigdon's daily journal, "The Log of the Trip," and Samuel Rosenman's daily journal, "Trip with President Roosevelt to Pacific Coast and Hawaii," both in FDRL. Sailors snipping Fala is in Rosenman's daily journal, in which Rosenman also describes FDR's lodgings in the mansion of the late Chris Holmes, whom he calls a "drunk who finally committed suicide." Intelligence reports on Hitler's "blood purge": Donovan to FDR, August 3 and September 22, 1944, FDRL, Charles Cheston to FDR, September 4, 1944, and February 1, 1945, "Summary of Telegrams" by Secretary of State, September 14, 1944, all in FDRL. Scene of FDR's July 29, 1944, press conference is in the Rigdon and Rosenman journals. "I don't think I know anything": FDR press conference text, July 29, 1944, FDRL.

"Murdering one another": Gilbert, *Road to Victory,* p. 868. Churchill's Foreign Secretary, Anthony Eden, wrote him a memorandum about the failed plot, but the British government has declared it secret until the year 2018 (British Foreign Office Papers, 371/30912, C 5202/48/18, in PRO). Eden's friend John Wheeler-Bennett frankly advised him on July 25, 1944, that the Allies were "better off" than they would have been had the plotters deposed Hitler because the German generals who would have assumed power would have sued "for terms other than those of Unconditional Surrender." Wheeler-Bennett added that Hitler's post–July 20 purge was "presumably removing from the scene numerous individuals who might have caused us difficulty, not only had the plot succeeded, but also after the defeat of Nazi Germany" (British Foreign Office Papers, 371/39062, C. 9896, in PRO).

"Hitlerite Germany" is in NYT, July 24, 1944. Churchill "misled" and "these men fought without help": is in Lamb, p. 292. On Operation Foxley, see newly declassified files of the Special Operations Executive in PRO, Public Record Office, *Operation Foxley,* John Keegan in *Daily Telegraph,* London, July 24, 1998, and *The Scotsman,* July 23, 1998. On specific plots against Goebbels and Himmler, see Public Record Office, *Operation Foxley,* pp. 24–28. One sign of how close Anglo-American commanders thought victory to be in August 1944 is General Omar Bradley's expectation that World War II in Europe would be over by the end of September 1944: Bradley, p. 296. FDR on waiting until arrival in Germany is in FDR to Cordell Hull, October 29, 1944, FDRL, and James Riddleberger oral history, HSTL.

CHAPTER TWO
"Unconditional Surrender"

For Roosevelt's boyhood visits to Germany and, perhaps more important, what he later remembered about them, see Ward, *Before the Trumpet,* pp. 146–150, Davis, *FDR: The Beckoning of Destiny,* pp. 89–93, FDR to Muriel and Warren Robbins, May 30, 1891, FDR Diary of July 30, 1918, FDR to Arthur Murray, March 3, 1940, all in FDRL, as well as *Public Papers of the Presidents: Franklin D. Roosevelt: 1943* (Washington, D.C.: U.S. Government Printing Office, 1944), p. 559, Robert Murphy memo, September 9, 1944, in FRUS Quebec, pp. 144–145, and Hull, vol. 2, p. 1265. "Rather amusing, but I doubt": Ward, *Before the Trumpet,* p. 149. "German swine": Ibid, p. 147. On Germany of the 1890s, see Gordon Craig, *Germany, 1866–1945,* pp. 180–324.

Roosevelt's meeting with Kaiser Wilhelm II is in FDR Diary, July 28, 1901, in FDRL, and Sara Delano Roosevelt, p. 59. FDR's recollections about "the inevitable war" and Germany "not a military nation": FDR to Arthur Murray, March 3, 1940, and FDR press conference transcript, February 23, 1945, in FDRL. "By a show of severity": Ward, *A First-Class Temperament,* p. 29. "A certain animosity": FDR to Sara Delano Roosevelt, September 7, 1905, FDRL. "Thought Franklin would burst": Eleanor

Roosevelt to Sara Delano Roosevelt, July 25, 1905, FDRL. FDR's memories of his arrests in Germany are in James Roosevelt and Sidney Shalett, *Affectionately, F.D.R.*, p. 21. His remembered confrontation with the Prussian is in Shoumatoff, p. 84.

"I hope England will join in": FDR to Eleanor, August 2, 1914, FDRL. Roosevelt's speeches against "Kaiserism" and "Prussianism" are in clippings from *Springfield Union,* May 19, 1918, and *Bridgeport Telegram,* May 21, 1918, both in FDRL. "Stolid, stupid" prisoners: FDR Diary, July 16 to August 16, 1918, FDRL. "No desire to march triumphantly": Klaus Schwabe, *Woodrow Wilson: Revolutionary Germany and Peacemaking, 1918–1919* (Chapel Hill: University of North Carolina Press, 1985), p. 19. Roosevelt's wartime views on post–World War I Germany are noted in FDR to Josephus Daniels, July 29, 1918, in FDRL. "Cut down and purged": FDR Diary, July 11, 1918, FDRL. FDR on "lesson of defeat": FDR Diary, July 11, 1918, FDRL. FDR notes his 1919 visit to Ehrenbreitstein in FDR memo, May 23, 1942, FDRL. Also see Ward, *A First-Class Temperament,* p. 427. On softness of the peace, see Schwartz, p. 297. Pershing on Germans knowing "they were beaten:" Frank Vandiver, *Black Jack: The Life and Times of John J. Pershing,* vol. 2 (College Station: Texas A & M University Press, 1977), p. 1075. For FDR attitude toward Versailles and regret about outcome of World War I, see Van Everen, pp. 27–28, Kimball, "U.S. Planning for Postwar Germany," p. 25, and John Maynard Keynes, *The Economic Consequences of the Peace* (New York: Harcourt, Brace and Howe, 1920). See also memcon of FDR's January 24, 1943, talk with General Henri Giraud: FRUS Casablanca, pp. 724, 825–828. FDR Pearl Harbor speech: NYT, December 10, 1941. "Must not allow the seeds": FDR to Daniel Marsh, March 6, 1944, FDRL.

On FDR's Casablanca meeting with Churchill, resulting in issuance of the unconditional surrender demand, see "The President's Log at Casablanca," January 14 to 23, 1943, in FDRL, FRUS Casablanca, p. 521, Churchill, *Hinge of Fate,* pp. 674–695, Eden, pp. 419–421, Gilbert, *Road to Victory,* pp. 300–310, Freidel, *Franklin D. Roosevelt,* pp. 458–467, Dallek, pp. 373–376, Edmonds, pp. 318–324, Kimball, *Forged in War,* pp. 189–195, Armstrong, pp. 5–15, 40–45, Sherwood, pp. 667–697, Burns, *The Soldier of Freedom,* pp. 314–330, Lamb, pp. 286–296. See also Warren Kimball, "Stalingrad: A Chance for Choices," *The Journal of Military History,* January 1996. Stalin complaints about second front and Soviet suspicions about Anglo-American motives: Volkogonov, pp. 484–486, Radzinsky, pp. 445–446, Perlmutter, pp. 101–103, 110–112, Burns, *The Soldier of Freedom,* pp. 229–238, Bullock, pp. 784–786. Roosevelt on not "settling everything between ourselves": Kimball, *Forged in War,* p. 182. FDR and Churchill are "resolved to pursue the war": January 18, 1943, in FRUS Casablanca, p. 635. FDR over luncheon suggests "unconditional surrender" and Churchill response: Elliott Roosevelt and James Brough, *Rendezvous with Destiny,* p. 333. Churchill claim of surprise and consultation with War Cabinet on unconditional surrender: Kimball, *Forged in War,* p. 188. Roosevelt-Churchill final press conference at Casablanca, January 24, 1943, is in *Complete Press Conferences,* January 24, 1943, vols. 21–22, pp. 86–96.

"Twice within our lifetime": Churchill to House of Commons, February 11, 1943, in Gilbert, *Road to Victory,* p. 337. Churchill ambivalence about unconditional surrender: Churchill, *Hinge of Fate,* pp. 690–691. "Nothing in the world": Churchill to Clement Attlee, PREM 3/420/3, in PRO. Churchill's private interpretation of unconditional surrender: Churchill, *Hinge of Fate,* pp. 690–691. Stalin reaction to unconditional surrender declaration: Ulam, *Stalin,* p. 584, and Bullock, p. 797. For Stalin's attitudes toward Germany, see Ulam, *Stalin,* pp. 584–585. "Communism fits Germany": McElvoy, p. 2. Stalin's semi-shock over Hitler's invasion: Volkogonov, pp. 405–414. "Hitlers come and go": Stalin speech, February 23, 1942, is in *Information Bulletin of the Embassy of the U.S.S.R.,* Washington, D.C., and Ulam, *Stalin,* pp. 584–585.

On Stalin's formation of the Free Germany Committee and American reaction to it, see Ulam, *Expansion and Coexistence,* pp. 349–350, Eisenberg, pp. 21–22, Werth, pp. 732–737, Bullock, p. 798, Mastny, *Russia's Road to the Cold War,* pp. 80–83, Gill, pp. 219–223, *Daily Worker,* July 21, 1943, and Cordell Hull to William Standley, July 30, 1943, in FDRL. Bullitt to FDR, January 29, 1943, is in FDRL. Stalin's December 1941 meeting with Eden: Eden, pp. 350–352. "Rally all Germans": Gilbert, *Road to Victory,* p. 16. Eden's March 1943 meeting with Roosevelt is in Harry Hopkins memcon, March 15, 1943, in FRUS 1943, and Mosely, pp. 487–498. "Deep-seated mistrust": Hopkins memcon, March 15, 1943, in FRUS 1943, vol. 3, pp. 16–17. "We would not use the methods": Ibid. "The Prussians cannot be permitted": Ibid. Eden's frustration on leaving Roosevelt is in Eden, p. 433.

CHAPTER THREE
"Fifty Thousand Germans Must Be Shot!"

Stalin's growing impatience over second front: Bullock, p. 785. Stalin's outrage about Anglo-American peace with Italy: Bullock, pp. 817–818. Roosevelt invitation for Hull to go to Moscow and Hull's reaction: Hull, vol. 2, p. 1255, and Gellman, pp. 363–364. Hull-FDR relationship: Gellman, pp. 363–364. "I just don't know." MD, July 9, 1943. "Jesus Chwist!" and "all-American thun": Daniels, p. 193. Welles's role and his banishment: Gellman, pp. 308–317. Hull's exclusion from Casablanca and reaction to the result: Hull, vol. 2, pp. 1570–1582, and Gellman, p. 310. FDR and State Department planning for postwar Germany: Eisenberg, pp. 15–21, Notter, pp. 69–78, 92–93, 96–97, Warren Kimball, "Anglo-American War Aims, 1941–1943," in Ann Lane and Howard Temporley, eds., *The Rise and Fall of the Grand Alliance, 1941–1945* (London: Macmillan, 1995), pp. 7–8. U.S. Department of State, *Post–World War II Foreign Policy Planning,* 2 vols. (Bethesda, Md., 1987). Swope's letter is in NYT, September 3, 1943. FDR sends letter to Hull: Hull to FDR, September 1, 1943, Hull Papers. Hull-FDR conversation: Hull-FDR October 5, 1943, memcon, in FRUS 1943, and Hull, vol. 2, pp. 1265–1266. Hull coughs up blood: Gellman, p. 336. On Moscow foreign ministers conference and Hull conversations, see State Department, Interdivisional Country

Committee on Germany, "The Political Reorganization of Germany," September 23, 1943, in NA, Hull, vol. 2, pp. 1255–1256, 1274–1291, Gellman, pp. 337–338, Eisenberg, pp. 22–24, and Weinberg, pp. 620–622. Text of Moscow Declaration: November 2, 1943, in FDRL. Eleanor Roosevelt on Hull after Moscow: Eleanor Roosevelt to Joseph Lash, November 11, 1943, FDRL.

"Looking forward to his meeting": Hull, vol. 2, p. 1313. Stalin insistence on Tehran and Roosevelt response: Dallek, pp. 423–426, FDR to Stalin, October 5 and 21 and November 9, 1943, FDR to Churchill, November 11, 1943, FDR to Stalin, November 8, 1943, all in FDRL. Roosevelt leaves Hull home: Hull, vol. 2, p. 1110. "It's a lovely day" and "I much wonder": FDR Diary, November 13, 1943, FDRL. "I revel in an old pair": FDR Diary, November 15, 1943, FDRL. Roosevelt shipboard conversation with Chiefs: November 19, 1943, memcon in FRUS 1943, Sherwood, pp. 762–763, and Wilson Brown memo, August 31, 1944, in FDRL. For Tehran Big Three summit, see FRUS Tehran, pp. 459–651, John Boettiger Diary in FDRL, Mayle, Berezhkov, pp. 236–264, Gromyko, pp. 79–80, Churchill, *Closing the Ring,* pp. 342–407, Eden, pp. 491–497, Chuev and Resis, p. 302, Bohlen, pp. 134–154, Kimball, *Forged in War,* pp. 237–261, Sherwood, pp. 776–799, Eisenberg, pp. 24–25, Gilbert, *Churchill,* pp. 759–762, Gilbert, *Road to Victory,* pp. 570–593, Bullock, pp. 818–823, Dallek, pp. 423–441, Burns, *The Soldier of Freedom,* pp. 406–417.

"The doctors don't allow it": Berezhkov, p. 238. First FDR-Stalin-Churchill session, November 28, 1943, at 4 P.M., is in Bohlen memcon and Combined Chief of Staff minutes in FRUS Tehran, pp. 487–508. First dinner, November 28, 1943, at 8:30 P.M., is documented in Bohlen memcon in FRUS Tehran, pp. 509–514. FDR's sudden illness: John Boettiger Diary, FDRL, Bohlen, pp. 143–144, and Elliott Roosevelt and James Brough, *Rendezvous with Destiny,* p. 354. "We've got to hurry": John Boettiger Diary, FDRL. Stalin-Churchill after-dinner conversation, November 28, 1943, is in Gilbert, *Road to Victory,* pp. 574–577, and FRUS Tehran, p. 571. Monday afternoon session, November 29, 1943, at 2:45 P.M., is in Bohlen memcon in FRUS Tehran, pp. 529–533. Monday dinner, November 29, 1943, at 8:30 P.M., is in Bohlen memcon in FRUS Tehran, pp. 552–555. "Stalin the Great": FRUS Tehran, p. 583. Stalin's comments that Churchill is "pro-German" and proposing liquidation of Germans: Moran, p. 152, John Boettiger Diary, FDRL. "As usual, it seems to be": Elliott Roosevelt, *As He Saw It,* p. 191. Elliott's intervention and Churchill's response: Ibid, p. 190, Churchill, *Closing the Ring,* pp. 373–374, John Boettiger Diary, FDRL. Lord Moran-Churchill encounter after dinner: Moran, pp. 136–141, Gilbert, *Road to Victory,* p. 581, and Dallek, p. 439. "Forget it": Elliott Roosevelt, *As He Saw It,* p. 191. Churchill punishes Elliott: Ibid. Wednesday evening session, December 1, 1943, 6 P.M., is in Bohlen memcon in FRUS Tehran, pp. 596–604.

CHAPTER FOUR

"On the Back of an Envelope"

Roosevelt's January 12, 1944, meeting with Eisenhower is in Dwight Eisenhower, *Crusade in Europe*, p. 218, Ambrose, *Eisenhower: 1890–1952*, pp. 279–280, Pogue, *The Supreme Command*, p. 109–110. FDR-Stalin Tehran conversation about Operation Overlord and FDR naming of Eisenhower: Churchill, *Closing the Ring*, pp. 418–419, Sherwood, pp. 802–803. "The most obscure places": Dwight Eisenhower, *Crusade in Europe*, p. 218. Eisenhower's reminiscence on Roosevelt as "almost an egomaniac" appears in a January 7, 1955, conversation with Senator Walter George he secretly recorded while President, in Eisenhower Library.

On the European Advisory Commission, see John McCloy memo, November 22, 1943, in FRUS Tehran, pp. 420–422, Department of State, "Germany: Occupation Period: Proposed Control Machinery for the Administration of Military Government in Germany," January 27, 1944, in NA, McCloy to James Dunn, April 5, 1944, in NA, memcon of John Winant–Henry Morgenthau, Jr., meeting, August 1944, in Morgenthau Papers, FDRL, William M. Franklin, "Zonal Boundaries and Access to Berlin," Lord Strang, pp. 199–225, Snell, pp. 54–63, Kuklick, pp. 36–37, Blum, *From the Morgenthau Diaries*, vol. 3, pp. 329–330, 338–339, Kimball, *Swords or Ploughshares*, pp. 17–23, Nelson, pp. 10, 13, 21–23, Gaddis, *The United States and the Origins of the Cold War*, pp. 105–114, Eisenberg, pp. 15–29. Roosevelt gives postwar planning on Germany to the State Department: Eisenberg, pp. 15–21, Kennan, pp. 164–165. Winant's role in EAC: Bellush, pp. 192–210. Winant and Sarah Churchill: Pearson, pp. 319, 338–339, 347–348. State Department proposals for postwar Germany, "General Objectives of U.S. Economic Policy with Respect to Germany," April 10, 1944, and "The Treatment of Germany," April 21, 1944, are in NA.

Stalin's more generous unsubmitted proposal is revealed in newly opened Soviet archives in Moscow, including "The Occupation of Germany," January 5, 1944, and "Protocol," January 11, 1944, and Ivan Maisky to Vyacheslav Molotov, February 4, 1944, and Maisky's reply, February 8, 1944, noted in Jochen Laufer, "The Soviet Union and the Zonal Division of Germany." See also Maisky to Molotov, January 10, 1944, and Vladimir Pechatnov, "The Big Three After World War II," both in CWIHP. Roosevelt on zones conforming "with what I decided": FDR to Edward Stettinius, February 18, 1944, FDRL. State Department request to see Tehran records and FDR refusal: Stettinius to FDR, February 19, 1944, and FDR reply, February 21, 1944, in FDRL. Kennan tells of his meeting with FDR in Kennan, pp. 170–171. Winant effort to correct Berlin problem, Eisenhower's proposal and Washington's refusal are in Bellush, pp. 200–202.

Stalin presses FDR to narrow unconditional surrender demand: Rosenman, p. 407. Molotov to Harriman on what would happen unless Germans told what to expect after defeat: Memo to Roosevelt, January 14, 1944, FDRL. Eisenhower on "German Badoglio" and eagerness to narrow unconditional surrender demand: Harry Butcher Diary, April 14, 1944, in Butcher, p. 518, and Ambrose, *Eisenhower: 1890–1952,* p. 255. "Fishing expedition" and "no intention to enslave": FDR to Churchill, January 6, 1944, FDRL. "I must say I think it is all wrong": PREM 3/197/2, in PRO, and Lamb, p. 295. Churchill to Eisenhower on Tehran and "frank statement": FO 371/39024, in PRO, and Lamb, p. 294. FDR complains to Hull and speaks of Grant and Lee: FDR to Hull, January 17, 1944, FDRL. Grant's unconditional surrender demand at Fort Donelson: Patricia Faust, ed., *Historical Times Illustrated Encyclopedia of the Civil War* (New York: Harper Perennial, 1986), p. 272. Chiefs request pledge to destroy only German "military aggression": William Leahy to FDR, March 25, 1944, in FDRL. FDR reply, April 1, 1944, is in FDRL. "What would you think of a statement": FDR to Churchill, Kimball, *Churchill & Roosevelt,* vol. 3, p. 134. Churchill's reply: Ibid., pp. 142–143. Churchill's aide Brendan Bracken told him that Roosevelt's suggested language was "sloppy and silly" (Lamb, p. 295). Anthony Eden told the War Cabinet that it was "better to be silent before battle" (CAB 65/46, in PRO).

On Allen Dulles's wartime operation in Bern, see Grose, pp. 26–36, 193–205, Dulles, pp. 45–59, 54–66, Persico, *Roosevelt's Secret War,* pp. 250–252, 416–426. "Ideal gift": Grose, p. 175. Dulles on Free Germany Committee: Ibid., p. 203. Dulles warning that "Moscow has been the only source of hope": Ibid. "I do not understand what our policy is": Ibid., p. 202. Dulles on conspirators in April 1944: Ibid., pp. 195–196. "The old predicament": Ibid., p. 196. Dulles learns of July 20 plot failure: Ibid., p. 199. Dulles reported on Gisevius intelligence about Stauffenberg and possible "workers and peasants" government in a radiotelephone call, a transcript of which appears in Charles Cheston to FDR, January 27, 1945, in FDRL. Dulles gave his warnings on "stubborn resistance," the need to find the "right kind of Germans" and a "Bolshevized Germany" in other radiotelephone calls, included in Cheston to FDR, September 4, 1944, and January 27, 1945, in FDRL. Sherwood's D-Day draft and accompanying memoranda are in FDRL. FDR to Hull on insufficient "Allied progress on all the fronts": Hull, vol. 2, p. 1581.

CHAPTER FIVE
The Terrible Silence

On the information available to FDR and the American government about the war against the Jews, see Feingold, "Courage First and Intelligence Second," Newton, pp. 32–34, 72–76, 116–121, 156–158, 160–161, 170, 180–181, Wyman, pp. 72–73, Neufeld and Berenbaum, pp. 137–138, 191–192, Gilbert, *The Second World War,* p. 307, Breitman and Kraut, pp. 244–249, Feingold, p. 248, Breitman, *Official Secrets,* pp. 88–233. Richard Breitman wrote in 1996, "There is little question that the President was aware of the Final Solution by November 1942, if not earlier" (Newton, p. 116, similarly in Breitman and Kraut, p. 242). On Roosevelt not mentioning Hitler's war against the Jews at Tehran, in Churchill correspondence or explicitly in public, see FRUS Tehran, pp. 475–604, Kimball, *Churchill & Roosevelt,* vols. 1–3, and *Public Papers of the Presidents: Franklin D. Roosevelt: 1942, 1943* (Washington, D.C.: U.S. Government Printing Office, 1943, 1944). "Annihilate the Jewish race": Hitler speeches, January 31, 1939, in *Trials of War Criminals Before the Nuremberg Military Tribunals* (Washington, D.C.: U.S. Government Printing Office, 1949–1953), and January 30, 1942, in Gilbert, *The Holocaust,* p. 285.

Wise request for FDR Madison Square Garden statement: Memo to Stephen Early, July 15, 1942, Wise to FDR, July 17, 1942, FDRL, Newton, p. 116. FDR reply and statement as issued: Newton, p. 116. Wise and Jewish leaders ask to give FDR details on "most overwhelming disaster": Wyman, p. 71. FDR's effort to refer to State Department: Newton, p. 117. FDR's meeting with Wise and other Jewish leaders, December 8, 1942, is documented in Penkower, pp. 83–86, *Bulletin of the World Jewish Congress,* January 1943, and Breitman, "Roosevelt and the Holocaust," in Newton, pp. 117–118. On December 17, 1942, declaration, see Gilbert, *Auschwitz and the Allies,* pp. 102–104, and Breitman and Kraut, p. 171. On FDR-Karski meeting, July 28, 1943, see Wood and Jankowski, pp. 196–202, Breitman, *Official Secrets,* p. 195, and Breitman, "Roosevelt and the Holocaust," in Newton, pp. 119–120. Breitman on FDR not matching Hitler's "frenzy" with "corresponding determination": "Roosevelt and the Holocaust," in Newton, p. 123. On restraint of U.S. propaganda organs on killing of Jews, see Breitman, *Official Secrets,* pp. 134–136, 157–158, 231–232.

FDR on World War I atrocities and demands translation of German book: Freidel, *Rendezvous with Destiny,* p. 333. FDR's incomprehension of war against Jews: Newton, p. 116. Laqueur on information not knowledge is in Neufeld and Berenbaum, p. xii. "Refugee matters ranked way down": Newton, p. 7. Anti-Semitic aspersions against FDR and New Deal: Wyman, p. 107, MM, p. 321. "If there was a demagogue around here": Joseph Kennedy unpublished diplomatic memoir, Joseph Kennedy Papers, and Beschloss, *Kennedy and Roosevelt,* p. 180. On FDR and American Jews, see Newton, pp. 51–58, and Feingold, *Politics of Rescue,* p. 8. Jewish support for FDR in 1932, 1936 and 1940: Newton, p. 55, and Feingold, *Politics of Rescue,* p. 8.

Unwillingness of many American Jews to look like special pleaders in wartime: Newton, p. 57. On the Katyn massacre, see *The Oxford Companion to World War II* (Oxford: Oxford University Press, 1995), pp. 644–646. Churchill's sporadic willingness to take risks to help Jews: Breitman, *Official Secrets,* pp. 152–153, 228–229, Newton, p. 16, Bird, pp. 217–218, and Gilbert, *Auschwitz and the Allies,* pp. 24–25, 103, 141, 276–277. Stalin and genocide: Volkogonov, p. 166. Stalin's history toward the Jews: Ulam, *Stalin,* p. 266. Churchill efforts to halt German atrocities: Bird, pp. 217–218, Gilbert, *Road to Victory,* pp. 245, 287, 846–847. Churchill role in Moscow Declaration: Gilbert,

Churchill, p. 737. Churchill to Eden on making "some of these villains shy": PREM, 4/100/9, PRO. Churchill renounces responsibility: Breitman, *Official Secrets,* pp. 215–216. Three million Jews perished by November 1943: Wyman, p. 5. Hitler speeds up death mills: Feingold, pp. 249–250, 254–255. Possibility of no Jews left to save: Newton, p. 17, and Neufeld and Berenbaum, p. 26.

Morgenthau never had attended seder before 1945: Morgenthau to Robert and Henry Morgenthau III, March 25, 1945, HMPA, and MM, p. 412. FDR jokes about Morgenthau as "Leader in Zion": Felix Frankfurter Diary, October 31, 1942, LC. Morgenthau avoidance of Jewish matters at Treasury: MM, pp. 321–323. Rabbi Wise informs Morgenthau about death camps: Gerhart Riegner interview, HMPA, Henrietta Klotz interview, HMPA, Herman Klotz to Henry Morgenthau III, October 16, 1985, in HMPA, and MM, p. 323.

CHAPTER SIX
The "One Hundred Percent American"

Morgenthau's relationship with FDR as "most important thing": John Pehle interview, HMPA. Henry Morgenthau III on father as "one hundred percent American": MM, p. 211. Among published sources on family background, life and career of Henry Morgenthau, Jr., see especially his official biographer John Morton Blum's three-volume *From the Morgenthau Diaries,* Blum's revision and condensation *Roosevelt and Morgenthau* and Henry Morgenthau III's family memoir-history *Mostly Morgenthaus.* "Very ambitious for himself" and "my father was really an extension": Henry Morgenthau III interview with author. "Centered around his business": John Morton Blum interview, HMPA.

"Fight every inch of the way" and "his theory for me": Blum, *Roosevelt and Morgenthau,* p. 6. "Desperate move to get out from under": Henry Morgenthau III interview with author, Klotz interview, John Morton Blum interview, *Time* Archives notes, in HMPA. On Morgenthau Sr.'s support for Woodrow Wilson and as ambassador to Turkey, see MM, pp. 98–134. On Fishkill Farms, see March 16, 1934, memo in Henry Morgenthau, Jr., file in *Time* Archives, *Fortune,* May 1934, *Time,* January 25, 1943, and MM, pp. 217–218, 244–245. Morgenthau suggested to journalists in the 1930s that he bought the farm with profits made from family money he had invested (see March 16, 1934, and January 25, 1943, memos in *Time* Archives). But Henry Morgenthau III writes that actually Henry Sr. bought the farm for his son (MM, p. 218). "Tried to regulate his life": Blum, *Roosevelt and Morgenthau,* p. 5.

Henry Morgenthau III on his parents and Judaism: MM, pp. viii, and interview with author. "Early in life, I sensed" and "a kind of birth defect": MM, p. xiii. "Firmly assimilationist": Henry Morgenthau III interview with author. "Just tell them you're an

American": MM, p. xiv. "Tended to avoid": Ibid., p. xvi. "Almost all of my parents' friends": Henry Morgenthau III interview and notes in HMPA. Elinor's deliberate distance from Augusta Jewish community is in MM, pp. 253, and Henry Morgenthau III interview with author. Henry Morgenthau, Sr., and Zionism: MM, pp. 193–194, 206–208, "Zionism a Surrender, not a Solution," in Morgenthau Sr., *All in a Life-Time,* pp. 385–405. "We Jews of America": MM, p. 208. "Young Morgenthau was easy": Ibid., p. 247, Ward, *A First-Class Temperament,* p. 253.

On the origins of the FDR-Morgenthau friendship, see Blum, *From the Morgenthau Diaries,* vol. 1, pp. 12–15, MM, pp. 245–265. "Henry the Morgue" as gibe at Morgenthau's doleful countenance: Henry Morgenthau III comment in Sylvia Porter interview, HMPA. Relationship between FDR and Morgenthau wives is described in MM, pp. 242–253. Blum on "bond of affection": John Morton Blum interview, HMPA. "You are worse than Elinor": Eleanor Roosevelt to Elinor Morgenthau, November 13, 1928, FDRL. Eleanor Roosevelt Colony Club resignation: MM, p. 274. Joan Morgenthau debutante party and "I am sorry": Ibid., pp. 293–296, Herman Klotz to Henry Morgenthau III, October 16, 1985, HMPA. "I have always felt": Eleanor Roosevelt to Elinor Morgenthau, November 13, 1928, FDRL.

Morgenthau and *American Agriculturalist:* MM, pp. 239, 252, 256. "Fabled success": MM, p. 245. Shyness with Dutchess County farmers: Ibid., p. 247. "While you are moving on in your work": Elinor Morgenthau to FDR, December 14, 1930, FDRL. "From one of two of a kind": Blum, *Roosevelt and Morgenthau,* p. 25. Morgenthau hopes for Agriculture and rebuff: John Morton Blum interview, HMPA, MM, pp. 267–268, 271–272. Morgenthau lobbying for Treasury is described by Henrietta Klotz's husband, Herman, in a letter to Henry Morgenthau III, September 7, 1982, in HMPA. "Broke out in a cold sweat": MM, p. 272. *Fortune* on Morgenthau is in May 1934 issue. Gladys Straus's wisecrack is in Richard Norton Smith, p. 356. Morgenthau Sr. on son's appointment and Klotz reaction is in Klotz interview, HMPA. Louis Howe on Morgenthau earning job is in John Morton Blum interview and Blum, *From the Morgenthau Diaries,* vol. 1, p. 77. FDR, Acheson resignation and need for loyalty: Blum, *Roosevelt and Morgenthau,* pp. 43–53, MM, pp. 272–273.

Morgenthau's recording system: Klotz interview, HMPA, Blum interview, HMPA, Henry Morgenthau III interview, memo by Bob Clark, FDRL Archivist, May 8, 2002. The transcripts are included in what the FDRL has catalogued as the Morgenthau Diaries. Morgenthau once wrote his sons that he dictated letters into an Ediphone, which recorded human voices onto cylinders: Morgenthau to sons, January 5, 1945, HMPA. Joseph Kennedy and Morgenthau taping: Koskoff, p. 569. "Would come back and dictate": Klotz interview, HMPA. "All the New Dealers were scared": Blum interview, HMPA. Morgenthau standing Monday lunch is in Morgenthau file in *Time* Archives. FDR and Morgenthau notes on Frances Perkins's new hat are in HMPA, undated.

Farley on Morgenthau and organized Jews: Harold Ickes Diary, April 21, 1936, LC. Morgenthau on FDR playing "one person against another" and "insecurity": Morgenthau memcon, July 26, 1946, FDRL. Morgenthau furnished residences: MM, p. 273, Henry Morgenthau interview, and Jim McConaughy to Mike Griffin, January 18, 1943, in *Time* Archives. Morgenthau to Eleanor on FDR "bullying me": MD, May 18, 1939. "You and I will run this war": MD, August 25, 1944, FDRL. "You know this is a Protestant country": MD, January 27, 1942. On Jews around FDR, see Ward, *A First-Class Temperament,* pp. 253–255, Newton, pp. 56–70, MM, 321–322. FDR and Morgenthau on Guiana and Paraguay as refugee havens: Blum, *Roosevelt and Morgenthau,* pp. 518–519. Rabbi Wise to Morgenthau on refugees in French ports and Morgenthau reply: November 20 and December 12, 1939, FDRL.

On Morgenthau and pre–World War II preparedness, see Blum, *From the Morgenthau Diaries,* vol. 2, pp. 86–93, and MM, pp. 318–320. "If we don't stop Hitler now": Blum, *Roosevelt and Morgenthau,* p. 237. Hull on "second Secretary of State": Hull, vol. 2, p. 1073. Morgenthau complaint to Stimson about Darlan: Blum, *From the Morgenthau Diaries,* vol. 3, p. 149. Morgenthau early belief in German collective guilt: Blum, *From the Morgenthau Diaries,* vol. 3, pp. 332–333. Morgenthau agrees to change Carnegie Hall speech: Fred Smith memo in Morgenthau papers, FDRL. Morgenthau headaches and nausea: Morgenthau to Klotz, June 9, October 5 and November 22, 1944, and MM, pp. 240–241, 243. Klotz background and relationship to Morgenthau: Klotz interview, HMPA, and Henry Morgenthau III interview. Klotz prods Morgenthau with "pressure and unpleasantness": Herman Klotz to Henry Morgenthau III, October 16, 1985, HMPA. Treasury lawyers discover State Department refugee obstruction: Josiah DuBois and John Pehle interviews, HMPA, Morgenthau unpublished draft, September 10, 1946, in FDRL, MM, pp. 324–327, Blum, *From the Morgenthau Diaries,* vol. 3, pp. 220–222, Rubinstein, pp. 113.

"Breck, we might be a little frank": Morgenthau unpublished draft, September 10, 1946, in FDRL, Blum, *Roosevelt and Morgenthau,* p. 529, and MM, p. 326. Morgenthau on if Hull "were a member of the Cabinet": MD, December 18, 1943, and Gellman, p. 347. Hull's avoidance of refugee issue, worry about wife's Jewish heritage and public attacks on wife are in Gellman, pp. x, 25–26, 97–99, 209, 286 and 347. "I once told the President": MD, January 12, 1944, FDRL. Morgenthau on Eisenhower attitude toward refugees and White reply: MD, January 13, 1944, FDRL. "Valued above everything," "he didn't want to stand out" and Morgenthau "unshirted hell" when Pehle spoke to President: John Pehle interview, HMPA. Roosevelt "not the greatest" on Jewish problem: Josiah DuBois interview, HMPA.

Morgenthau quiet help to refugees early in war: MM, pp. 324–326, Henry Morgenthau III interview with author. Henry Morgenthau III on Henry Sr. and Elinor aversion to his involvement in Jewish affairs, Klotz influence and "delayed rebellion": Henry Morgenthau III interview, Klotz interview, HMPA. "Didn't need [Elinor] as much": Henry

Morgenthau III in Henrietta Klotz interview, HMPA. Morgenthau compares activism for Jews to his father's efforts for Armenians: Blum, *Roosevelt and Morgenthau,* p. 8. "Taking his political life": Randolph Paul undated reminiscence in Morgenthau Papers, FDRL. Morgenthau resumes Jewish practice: Blum interviews, HMPA. "So this is the fellow": Riegner interview, HMPA. "Report to the Secretary," January 13, 1944, and toned down version are both in FDRL. "If it means anything": Josiah DuBois interview, HMPA. Hull "known as a killer": Randolph Paul undated reminiscence in Morgenthau Papers, FDRL.

CHAPTER SEVEN

"Oppressor of the Jews"

Morgenthau January 16, 1944, meeting with FDR: MD, January 16, 1944, Morgenthau unpublished draft, September 10, 1946, in FDRL, Josiah DuBois interview, HMPA, Randolph Paul undated reminiscence in Morgenthau Papers, HMPA, Blum, *Roosevelt and Morgenthau,* pp. 531–532, "FDR Day by Day—The Pare Lorentz Chronology," January 16, 1944, FDRL. "I was very serious" and later telephone call to FDR: MD, January 17, 1944, FDRL. Roosevelt's previous Jewish voter support is described in Newton, p. 55. FDR establishes War Refugee Board: Feingold, *Politics of Rescue,* pp. 243–245, Blum, *From the Morgenthau Diaries,* vol. 3, pp. 221–227. Seven Treasury aides to Morgenthau on his "courage and statesmanship," February 2, 1944, is in FDRL. "But the tragic thing is": MD, December 20, 1943. "Whatever credit I deserve": Morgenthau to Klotz, August 5, 1945, in HMPA. FDR wants "big name" and Morgenthau suggests Willkie, then Pehle: Morgenthau memo, 1946, in Morgenthau Papers, FDRL. The figure of two hundred thousand Jews saved is the War Refugee Board's own estimate (see Newton, p. 154, and MM, p. 335). Eden cavils about "large Jewish vote": Gilbert, *Auschwitz and the Allies,* p. 173. Stimson worries about War Refugee Board: Bird, p. 203. Morgenthau asks McCloy to send FDR directive: Ibid., p. 205. McCloy "very chary of getting the Army involved": Ibid.

On danger to Hungarian Jews, see Newton, p. 221, Gilbert, *Auschwitz and the Allies,* pp. 181–189. Morgenthau asks FDR for declaration: MD, March 7, 1944. Weakening of Roosevelt statement and Allied reaction: Wyman, pp. 256–257, Breitman and Kraut, pp. 193–196, Gilbert, *Auschwitz and the Allies,* pp. 184–186. Text of statement and FDR questioning is in FDR press conference transcript, March 24, 1944, in FDRL. McCloy finds Morgenthau "vindictive" and "irate": John McCloy interview, HMPA. On McCloy's background and career, see Bird, Schwartz, pp. 1–17, and Isaacson and Thomas, pp. 65–71, 119–125, 182–183, and 192–202. "We were all very European": Bird, p. 70. McCloy meets Stimson: Isaacson and Thomas, p. 182. "I got to know him very closely": John McCloy interview, HMPA. Kai Bird on McCloy sharing "some of the same prejudices": Bird, p. 206. McCloy skeptical of World War I atrocity and World War II death camp stories: Ibid., pp. 205.

McCloy "bothered generally" by Jewish requests: Neufeld and Berenbaum, pp. 68–69. Stimson and McCloy insist that refugee help must be "direct result" of military operations: Wyman, p. 291. February 1944 directive: Ibid., p. 292. June 1, 1944, Cabinet meeting, Morgenthau's June 2, 1944, meeting with McCloy and his reactions afterward are in MD, June 2, 1944, McCloy Diary, June 2, 1944, and Bird, p. 223. "Remote possibility of saving lives": Bird, p. 218. Anthony Eden's response: Gilbert, *Auschwitz and the Allies,* p. 260. Soviet reaction: Feingold, *Politics of Rescue,* p. 274. On Eichmann's "goods for blood" proposal, see Gilbert, *Auschwitz and the Allies,* pp. 201–202, Wyman, p. 244. "Surely we cannot negotiate": Gilbert, *Auschwitz and the Allies,* pp. 260.

On requests to bomb Auschwitz and railway lines generally, see Neufeld and Berenbaum, pp. 6–7, 48, 65–73, 121–126, Wyman, pp. 288–297, Rubinstein, pp. 157–181. Rosenheim appeals: Rosenheim to Morgenthau, June 18, 1944, FDRL, Neufeld and Berenbaum, p. 48, 65–68. Eden suggests to Churchill that Auschwitz might be bombed, July 3 and 6, 1944, and Churchill's July 7, 1944, reply: PM 44/501 and M 800/4, PREM 4/51/10, 1368–1369 and 1365–1366, FO 371/42809, 164, in PRO, Gilbert, *Auschwitz and the Allies,* p. 270, and Neufeld and Berenbaum, pp. 262–267. Churchill on "greatest and most horrible crime": Churchill to Eden, July 11, 1944, FO 371/42809, WR27, PRO, Gilbert, *Road to Victory,* p. 847. Potential missions as "costly and hazardous": Sir Archibald Sinclair to Eden, July 15, 1944, FO 371/42809, 178–179, PRO, and Gilbert, *Auschwitz and the Allies,* pp. 284–285.

Pehle asks McCloy to consider bombing: Pehle memcon, June 24, 1944, FDRL. Henry Morgenthau III on father's acquiescence is from interview with author. Pehle letter to McCloy enclosing cablegram from Switzerland: Pehle to McCloy, June 29, 1944, FDRL. Pehle on "we pretty well ran" War Refugee Board: Pehle interview, HMPA. Gerhardt on McCloy instruction to "kill" Rosenheim request: Harrison Gerhardt to McCloy, July 3, 1944, NA. McCloy to Pehle on "doubtful efficacy": July 4, 1944, FDRL. McCloy turned down a later bombing suggestion, among others, in McCloy to Pehle, November 18, 1944, in FDRL.

Schlesinger gives FDR credit for destroying "Nazi barbarism" in "Did FDR Betray the Jews?" in *Newsweek,* April 18, 1994. For retrospective arguments for and against bombing Auschwitz and rail lines, see Neufeld and Berenbaum, pp. 61–226, Newton, pp. 169–272, Rubinstein, pp. 157–181. Elie Wiesel on failure to bomb Auschwitz and "we were no longer afraid of death": quoted in Neufeld and Berenbaum, p. x. "The record of the Allies would have been brighter": Gerhard Weinberg, "The Allies and the Holocaust," in Newton, p. 26. For retrospective criticism of McCloy for failure to bomb Auschwitz, see David Wyman, "Why Auschwitz Was Never Bombed," *Commentary,* May 1978, Jacob Heilbrunn review of Kai Bird, *The German,* and Thomas Alan Schwartz, *America's Germany* in *New Republic,* May 11, 1992, Morton Mintz, "Why Didn't We Bomb Auschwitz?" in *Washington Post,* April 17, 1983 (including the columnist George Will's comment that the failure to bomb was a "scandal"), Richard Cohen, "Dishonor," in *Washington Post,* May 19, 1983, PBS documentary "America and the

Holocaust: Deceit and Indifference," written and directed by Martin Ostrow, 1984, Wyman, p. 305, Bird, pp. 658–660, Breitman, *Official Secrets,* pp. 208–209, Schwartz, pp. 17–18.

McCloy "never talked" with Roosevelt about bombing Auschwitz and on Hopkins comments: Mintz in *Washington Post,* April 17, 1983. During over eleven and a half hours of conversation, McCloy told Mintz that the Auschwitz bombing appeal was "not much of an episode in my life" at the War Department, because he was as busy as "a one-armed paperhanger." Hopkins's tendency to speak in Roosevelt's name: Sherwood, p. 833. Wyman on bombing proposals "almost certainly" not reaching FDR and Levy on "if McCloy is to be faulted": Wyman, p. 410, and Richard Levy in "The Bombing of Auschwitz Revisited," in Neufeld and Berenbaum, p. 122. Almost alone, Richard Breitman speculated in 1996 that it was "likely" that the Auschwitz bombing proposals "reached" Roosevelt through McCloy ("Roosevelt and the Holocaust," in Newton, p. 122). Henry Morgenthau III's 1986 conversation with McCloy is in HMPA. McCloy's meetings with Roosevelt are noted in McCloy Diary, "FDR: Day by Day—The Pare Lorentz Chronology," as well as in the White House Usher's Diary, the Stenographer's Diary and Grace Tully's Appointment Diary, all in FDRL. The McCloy Diary provides no evidence that McCloy raised the bombing of Auschwitz with Roosevelt, nor does it document every issue McCloy ever discussed with the President. The single source for McCloy raising the matter with Roosevelt remains his 1986 interview with Henry Morgenthau III. McCloy adds new anti-bombing argument of vindictiveness: McCloy to A. Leon Kubowitzki of the World Jewish Congress, August 14, 1944, NA.

Morgenthau July 6, 1944, meeting with Roosevelt is in MD, July 6, 1944, FDRL. De Gaulle, Eisenhower and French currency problem: McCloy to FDR, June 10 and 13, 1944, Amherst College Library. FDR note to Marshall, July 6, 1944, is in FDRL. Morgenthau insists only purpose of trip request was currency problems: MM, p. 350. Morgenthau exhilaration at visiting battlefront: Henry Morgenthau III interview with author. Morgenthau proposal of Lauchlin Currie for European Advisory Commission: MD, December 21, 1943. Jews deported from Hungary by early July: Newton, p. 229. McCloy reaction to Morgenthau invitation is in McCloy Diary, July 6, 1944. Marshall to Eisenhower and Eisenhower reply on Morgenthau visit: July 10 and 14, 1944, FDRL. Frank McCarthy to Morgenthau, July 13, 1944, is in file on Morgenthau's European trip planning, Morgenthau Papers, FDRL. "Some more half-grain Nembutal": Morgenthau to Klotz, July 27, 1944, FDRL. Departure for Europe and "leaving today for England": Morgenthau to FDR, August 5, 1944, FDRL.

CHAPTER EIGHT
"We Will Have to Get Awfully Busy"

Harry Dexter White and Morgenthau on flight to England: "Trip to the European Theatre" (hereafter referred to as "Trip"), August 5 to 17, 1944, Morgenthau Papers, FDRL,

MD, August 17, 1944, FDRL, Josiah DuBois interview, HMPA, Josiah DuBois oral history, HSTL, Harry Dexter White memo, August 31, 1944, in White Papers, Fred Smith account, "The Rise and Fall of the Morgenthau Plan," in Drew Pearson Papers, Henry Morgenthau III interview, MM, pp. 352–356. "By the time we arrived": DuBois interview, HMPA. "Morgenthau was sure": Fred Smith account in Pearson Papers. The document White showed Morgenthau was Department of State, Executive Committee on Foreign Economic Policy, "Report on Reparation, Restitution and Property Rights, July 31, 1944," in NA. The later document referred to is Department of State, "General Objectives of the United States Economic Policy with Respect to Germany," August 14, 1944, in NA.

Morgenthau train trip from Prestwick and conversation with Bernard Bernstein: "Trip," August 7, 1944, FDRL, MD, August 17, 1944, Bernstein oral history, HSTL, MM, pp. 354–355. Bernstein relationship to Morgenthau: Bernstein oral history, HSTL, Henry Morgenthau III interview. Draft of SHAEF *Handbook for Military Government* is in NA, as is the April 1944 Combined Chiefs of Staff directive. "A nice WPA job": MD, August 17, 1944. Morgenthau's conversation with Eisenhower: "Trip," August 5 and 7, 1944, FDRL, Kay Summersby Diary in Eisenhower Library, August 7, 1944, Bernstein oral history, HSTL, MD, August 18, 1944, and MM, pp. 354–356. Eisenhower's German ancestry: Ambrose, *Eisenhower: 1890–1952,* p. 332. "As the months of conflict wore on": Dwight Eisenhower, *Crusade in Europe,* p. 470.

"The German is a beast": Ambrose, *Eisenhower: 1890–1952,* p. 422. "God, I hate the Germans!": Ibid, p. 332. American death and casualty toll in Europe since D-Day: MD, August 17, 1944. Eisenhower briefed on death camps: MM, p. 355. "Severest critic in the Cabinet": Butcher, p. 432. Eisenhower and Darlan: David Eisenhower, pp. 5–6. "I have been called a Fascist": Ambrose, *Eisenhower: 1890–1952,* p. 206. Morgenthau complaint to Eisenhower about Darlan: "Trip," August 5, 1944. Eisenhower reply to Morgenthau questions about Germany: Ibid. "Very positive that he was going to treat them": MD, August 17, 1944. "We may want to quote you" and "I will tell the President myself": "Trip," August 5, 1944. Morgenthau *Collier's* article is November 1947. Fred Smith account is in FDRL. Eisenhower reacts to Morgenthau article and 1947 memories of conversation: Ambrose, *Eisenhower: 1890–1952,* pp. 422, Craig Cannon memo, August 19, 1947, Eisenhower Papers. See also Chandler and Galambos, vol. 9, pp. 1877–1878. Eisenhower's published version is in *Crusade in Europe,* p. 287.

Morgenthau's visit to France: "Trip," August 8, 1944, FDRL, MM, pp. 352–356. "To hell and gone", MM, p. 359. Bedell Smith effort to restrict Morgenthau and Morgenthau reply: MD, August 17, 1944. Morgenthau's processed motion-picture film had to be cleared by U.S. censors before he was allowed to have it (Frank McCarthy to Morgenthau, September 2, 1944, FDRL). "Odor of the wounded": MD, August 17, 1944. Bradley's speculation about imminent Nazi defeat: Bradley, p. 296. Morgenthau reunion with Henry III: "Trip," August 9, 1944, FDRL, Henry Morgenthau III interview, MM, pp. 351, 360–361. Morgenthau bourbon to Bradley and Smith and Bradley reply: Morgenthau to Smith, September 4, 1944, and Bradley to Morgenthau, September 2, 1944, FDRL. German propaganda against the "Jew Morgenthau": *Daily Telegraph,* August 14, 1944, and undated news clippings in Morgenthau Papers, FDRL. Morgenthau housing at Red Rice and Smith worry: "Trip," August 7, 1944, FDRL, and Smith to Morgenthau, August 21, 1944. Morgenthau-Anderson meeting: "Trip" and MD, August 10, 1944, FDRL.

Morgenthau-Churchill meeting: "Trip" and MD, August 10, 1944, MM, p. 361. "Very glad to see me": MD, August 10, 1944, FDRL. Debate on Weizmann request for Jewish brigade and Churchill approval: Gilbert, *Auschwitz and the Allies,* p. 261. Plight of Jews in Hungary, Hungarian offer and Morgenthau efforts to help: "Trip," August 10, 1944, "Discussions Concerning Acceptance of Hungarian Offer to Release Jews," September 30, 1944, FDRL, Sidney Browne to Josiah DuBois, August 14, 1944, FDRL, Morgenthau to John Pehle, August 18, 1944, Morgenthau to John Winant, August 19, 1944, Morgenthau to Chaim Weizmann, August 23, 1944, all in FDRL, DuBois oral history, HSTL, DuBois interview, HMPA, Gilbert, *Auschwitz and the Allies,* pp. 289–298, Wyman, p. 239. Announcement of Anglo-American deal on refugees is in NYT, August 18, 1944. "They actually said in so many words": DuBois interview, HMPA. "Got very worked up": DuBois oral history, HSTL. Morgenthau complains that Churchill "doesn't want to let the Jews come into Palestine": "Trip," August 10, 1944. "How much good it did psychologically": DuBois interview, HMPA. Morgenthau on visit to Churchill War Room: "Trip," August 10, 1944.

Morgenthau-Winant meeting: "Trip" and MD, August 12, 1944. Morgenthau-Eden conversation at Eden's house: "Trip" and MD, August 13, 1944. Eden "wants to take Germany apart": MD, August 17, 1944. Morgenthau-Eden meeting at Eden's office: "Trip" and MD, August 15, 1944, and Harry Dexter White memcon, White Papers. Morgenthau tour of air-raid shelters: "Trip" and MD, August 16–17, 1944, Clementine Churchill to Morgenthau, August 14, 1944, FDRL, MM, p. 361. Morgenthau hears of Churchill jeering on streets: MD, August 19, 1944. "Funny vague old thing": Clementine to Winston Churchill, August 16, 1944, in Soames, p. 499. Churchill on opposition "not fit to run a whelk stall": Soames, p. 499.

Sherwood and Murrow help on speech: MD, August 17, 1944. Text of speech, August 15, 1944, is in FDRL. "Your voice was warm": Clementine Churchill to Morgenthau, August 21, 1944, FDRL. "Your speech was excellent": Elinor Morgenthau to Morgenthau, August 14, 1944, FDRL. Morgenthau asks Bell for appointment with FDR: Morgenthau radiogram, August 14, 1944, and Klotz memo, August 14, 1944, FDRL. "Gentleman with whom you wish appointment": Daniel Bell to Morgenthau, August 15, 1944, FDRL. Morgenthau arranges to hop ride: Morgenthau to Daniel Bell, August 13, 1944, FDRL.

On William Hassett's antipathy to Jews, see Daniels, p. 268, and Ward, *A First-Class Temperament,* pp. 254–255fn. Hassett displays gratuitous hostility toward the Morgenthaus in his diary, saying, for instance, "The President and Princess Martha to tea with the Morgenthaus this afternoon. How they must have been bored, and I don't mean the Morgenthaus" (Hassett Diary, June 25, 1942, FDRL). Hassett's drinking is noted in Daniels, p. 255. "The Morgenthaus muscled in": Hassett Diary, August 19, 1944, FDRL. Morgenthau to aides after European trip: MD, August 17, 1944. "Nose under the tent": MD, September 6, 1944. Morgenthau-Hull meeting and Morgenthau description of it to aides afterward: MD, August 18, 1944.

CHAPTER NINE
"Not Nearly as Bad as Sending Them to Gas Chambers"

FDR's August 18, 1944, lunch with Truman: *Time,* August 28, 1944, McCullough, pp. 324–327, Hamby, pp. 284–285. "Putting the finger on me": Truman to Bess Truman, August 18, 1944, HSTL. "When you have made as much progress": Baldwin's recollection appears in his oral history, COHP. Roosevelt on staying off airplanes: Harry Truman, *Year of Decisions,* p. 5. "I had no idea": Harry Vaughan oral history, HSTL. Truman exchange with Army friend: Ferrell, *Harry S. Truman,* p. 175.

On FDR's health in 1944, see Howard Bruenn, "Clinical Notes on the Illness and Death of President Franklin D. Roosevelt," FDRL, Howard Bruenn Diary, 1944, FDRL, Ferrell, *The Dying President,* pp. 1–97, 138–152. Bruenn's first examination of FDR: Bruenn Diary, March 27, 1944, FDRL. Bruenn in 1992 on fourth term: Ferrell, *The Dying President,* p. 76. "Protect him from stress": Ibid., p. 46. "His mind was unaffected": Ibid., p. 4. FDR business two to four hours: Ferrell, *The Dying President,* pp. 73–74. Dewey on "tired old men": Sherwood, p. 820. Bruenn on FDR not asking questions: Bruenn, "Clinical Notes," FDRL. "Increasingly difficult": Butcher, pp. 518–519. "Complains of getting tired": Eleanor Roosevelt to Joseph Lash, August 18, 1944, FDRL.

Morgenthau August 19, 1944, meeting with FDR and comments afterward are in MD, August 19, 1944. Morgenthaus on train to Dutchess County: Hassett, p. 266. FDR asks Hopkins to ask Stimson to talk with Morgenthau: SD, August 21, 1944. Stimson-FDR August 23, 1944, meeting: SD, August 23, 1944. On Stimson's life and career, see Stimson and Bundy, Morison, Isaacson and Thomas, pp. 180–183, and Hodgson. "Sturdy, middle-class": Hodgson, p. 26. "Disgusted by the martial swagger": Ibid., p. 171. "Devoted to the making of money": Ibid., p. 44. "I have seen and felt": Ibid., p. 84. "Probity and rationality": Ibid., p. 96.

FDR appointment of Stimson as Secretary of War: Stimson and Bundy, p. 323, Morison, p. 476, Hodgson, pp. 212–221. "The poorest administrator": Hodgson, p. 230. Stimson refusal to entertain the divorced: Ibid., pp. 13–16. "Tremendous Jewish influence": Ibid., pp. 171–172. Stimson and National Origins Act: Ibid. "Awestruck": MM, p. 320. On Stimson's early relationship with Morgenthau, see Blum, *From the Morgenthau Diaries,* vol. 2, pp. 165–169, and vol. 3, pp. 223–225, 344–350, 359–369, 381–382. Stimson and building of the Pentagon: David Brinkley, p. 282, Sidney Shalett, "Mammoth Cave, Washington, D.C.," *New York Times Magazine,* June 27, 1943. Roosevelt and War Department expectations of postwar Pentagon are in David Brinkley, p. 282. "Tires very easily": MD, August 23, 1944. Stimson-Morgenthau meeting is in SD and MD, August 23, 1944.

CHAPTER TEN
"Somebody's Got to Take the Lead"

Morgenthau meets with staff after Stimson luncheon: MD, August 23, 1944. "Obsessed": Henry Morgenthau III interview. Morgenthau-McCloy August 25, 1944, conversation is in MD, August 25, 1944. On military marks, see MD, August 24 and 25, 1944, and Blum, *From the Morgenthau Diaries,* vol. 3, p. 345. Morgenthau-FDR August 25, 1944, meeting is in MD, August 25 and 28, 1944. Morgenthau's summary of excerpts from the *Handbook,* August 25, 1944, is in FDRL. McCloy had sent the handbook to Harry Hopkins a month earlier (McCloy to Hopkins, July 24, 1944, McCloy Papers). FDR and Morgenthau musing about resignation and work with United Nations: Henry Morgenthau III interview, Suckley Diary, April 6, 1945, James Roosevelt and Sidney Shalett, *Affectionately, F.D.R.,* p. 342, Ferrell, *The Dying President,* p. 116, and Ward, *Closest Companion,* p. 412. Morgenthau on "You go see Cordell": MD, August 22, 1944.

Stimson-FDR August 25, 1944, luncheon is in SD, August 25, 1944. "Briefing for Conference with the President" and "Memorandum as to Problem of Germany," both August 25, 1944, are in Stimson Papers. FDR at August 25, 1944, Cabinet meeting and Morgenthau reaction are in SD, August 25, 1944, and MD, August 25 and 28, 1944. FDR "spanking letter": FDR to Stimson, August 25, 1944, FDRL. McCloy did not think *Handbook* "as bad": McCloy Diary, August 28, 1944. "Unduly solicitous": Stimson to FDR, undated, in McCloy Papers. Morgenthau encounter with Stimson and McCloy at airport and flight with Stimson: SD and McCloy Diary, August 25, 1944, MD, August 25 and 28, 1944. Stimson at Ausable Club and talks with McCloy: SD, August 26 to September 3, 1944, McCloy Diary, August 28, 1944.

CHAPTER ELEVEN
"Christianity and Kindness"

Morgenthau talks with aides from Malone and considers visit to Oswego: MD, August 28, 1944. DuBois on "they'll be staying here" and "magnanimously": DuBois interview,

HMPA, and DuBois oral history, HSTL. On Oswego generally, see Wyman, pp. 265, 268–276. Paul Sheehan to Truman, July 18, 1945, is in HSTL. "The people were so evidently happy": Eleanor Roosevelt to Joseph Lash, September 18 and 21, 1944, FDRL. On Oswego visit, see also Eleanor Roosevelt, "My Day," September 22, 1944, in FDRL. Morgenthau farmhouse and Morgenthau's habits there: Henry Morgenthau III interview, "Henry Morgenthau, Jr.'s Farm in Dutchess County," January 13, 1943, memorandum in *Time* Archives. Morgenthau September 2, 1944, visit with FDR is in MD, September 2 and 4, 1944. "We don't have any Naziism": MD, May 18, 1944. "I don't want Palestine": FDR Diary, November 1943, FDRL. "The nicest men": Gurewitsch, p. 186. Morgenthau's memo, "Suggested Post-Surrender Program for Germany," September 1, 1944, as handed to FDR, is in FDRL. Monnet's lunch with Stimson and McCloy is in SD, September 7, 1944.

On Robert Murphy's background and relationship to Darlan, see Weil, pp. 48–49, 52–53, 116–117, 119–125, 138–139, 148, and Robert Murphy, pp. 1–12, 53, 62–63, 112–115, 129–133, 140–143. On Carmel Offie, see Gellman, pp. 304–305. Morgenthau to Stimson on Darlan is in MD, November 17, 1942. Morgenthau visit with Eleanor is in MD, September 2 and 4, 1944. Hopkins to Stimson on interest in being military governor and FDR scotching idea: McJimsey, p. 345. Eleanor reaction to manifesto on Germany: Eleanor Roosevelt to Trude Lash in Lash, *A World of Love,* p. 123. Eleanor's reaction to Brickner is in Eleanor Roosevelt to Joseph Lash, June 5, 1943, and Eleanor Roosevelt to Esther Lape, June 6, 1943, in FDRL. Eleanor to Joseph Lash on Morgenthau visit is September 11, 1944, FDRL. Morgenthau consults source: MD, September 2, 1944. Morgenthau to aides on FDR conversation and instructs them: MD, September 4, 1944. Stimson-Morgenthau dinner is in MD and SD, September 4, 1944, Stimson and Bundy, pp. 573–574.

Cabinet Committee on Germany September 5, 1944, meeting is in Hull, vol. 2, pp. 1608–1609, SD, September 5, 1944, MD, September 5 and 6, 1944, and McCloy Diary, September 5 and 6, 1944. McCloy on Stimson depression is in MD and McCloy Diary, September 6, 1944. Stimson on "ganged up": MD, September 6, 1944. Morgenthau to staff on September 5, 1944, meeting and telephone conversation with Hopkins: MD, September 5, 1944. Hopkins-McCloy telephone call: McCloy Diary, September 5, 1944. FDR meets Cabinet Committee on Germany, September 6, 1944: Hull, vol. 2, pp. 1609–1910, SD and MD, September 6, 1944, MM, pp. 374–375. On Chic Sale, see *The Specialist* (St. Louis: Specialist Publishing, 1929). Gaston and White joke about destroying Ruhr plumbing: MD, September 6, 1944. Morgenthau on meeting to aides: Ibid.

On John Boettiger life and career, see Boettiger, pp. 153–173. Harold Ickes on Boettiger "leaning" on FDR: Harold Ickes Diary, July 16, 1944. McCloy on "distinct embarrassment": Ickes Diary, September 17, 1944. Boettiger-Morgenthau antipathy: Blum, *Roosevelt and Morgenthau,* p. 620. Boettiger-Morgenthau September 6, 1944, meeting is in MD, September 6 and 7, 1944. Morgenthau-McCloy conversation is in McCloy Diary, September 6, 1944, and MD, September 6 and 7, 1944. FDR-Morgenthau September 7, 1944, meeting is in MD, September 7, 1944. Morgenthau clash with Brand is in MD, September 7, 1944. Henry Morgenthau III on father's anger is in interview with author. Stimson-Marshall conversation: SD, September 7, 1944. Morgenthau and Watson on new meeting: MD, September 7, 1944. McCloy warns Stimson about Morgenthau "sticks to his guns": SD, September 7, 1944.

CHAPTER TWELVE

"It Is Very, Very Necessary"

Stimson horseback ride and dinner with Frankfurter is in SD, September 7, 1944. Stimson on wood thrush: Hodgson, p. 242. "Cave of Adullum": William Gentz, ed., *The Dictionary of Bible and Religion* (Nashville: Abingdon, 1986), p. 249. "Although a Jew like Morgenthau": SD, September 7, 1944. Frankfurter's dislike of Morgenthau is in Hirsch, p. 54, Newton, pp. 63–64. "Stupid bootlick": Newton, p. 64, Michael Parrish, p. 224. Morgenthau reciprocated Frankfurter's antipathy, calling him "Mr. Fixer": MD, November 17, 1942. "Flying around trying to help": SD, September 9, 1944. Morgenthau-Hull September 8, 1944, meeting: MD, September 8, 1944. FDR-Murphy meeting: Murphy memcon, September 9, 1944, is in NA.

Copy of Morgenthau Plan is in FDRL. Morgenthau instructions to staff on drafting Plan: MD, August 28 to September 9, 1944. "I am very glad": MD, September 9, 1944. FDR feeling "low": Margaret Suckley Diary, September 4, 1944. September 9, 1944, meeting of Cabinet Committee on Germany: SD, MD, September 9, 1944, Stimson and Bundy, p. 574, Stimson to Hull, September 9, 1944, Stimson Papers. "Inch by inch" and White's observations: MD, September 9, 1944. "Very discouraging": SD, September 9, 1944. Stimson flight to Long Island: SD and McCloy Diary, September 9, 1944.

Stimson's comments on the Morgenthau Plan appear scrawled in his copy, in Stimson Papers. See also Hodgson, p. 265. "Fall to the wayside": SD, September 11, 1944. Stimson sends McCloy to New York: SD and McCloy Diary, September 11, 1944. "Much troubled": SD, September 9, 1944, and Stimson and Bundy, p. 575. FDR train departure for Highland is in White House Usher's Log, September 9, 1944, FDRL. On creation of FDR Library and on Roosevelt's Wilson desk, see NYT, July 1 and November 9, 1941, and *New York Times Magazine,* February 23, 1941. Roosevelt's day at Hyde Park is in Suckley Diary, September 9, 1944. "This Canadian meeting will not be all smooth sailing": Eleanor Roosevelt to Joseph Lash, September 4, 1944, FDRL.

CHAPTER THIRTEEN
"Do You Want Me to Beg Like Fala?"

For Roosevelt-Churchill arrival at Quebec, see NYT, September 11 and 12, 1944. On Quebec conference generally, see William Rigdon and Wilson Brown, "The President's Log for the 1944 Quebec Conference, September 9–21, 1944," FDRL, Gilbert, *Road to Victory,* pp. 935–970, Kimball, *Forged in War,* pp. 270–279, Edmonds, pp. 377–380, Blum, *Roosevelt and Morgenthau,* pp. 594–600, MM, pp. 379–387, Dallek, pp. 467–478, Eisenberg, pp. 42–46, and Woolner. FDR and Churchill wonder if Hitler "got into Britain": FRUS Quebec, p. 299. "My dear Friend": Churchill to FDR, September 12, 1944, in FDRL. "PLEASE BE IN QUEBEC" and delivery to Morgenthau: FDR to Morgenthau, September 12, 1944, in FDRL, and FRUS Quebec, p. 43. Morgenthau-White flight to Quebec: MM, pp. 381–387. Roosevelt-Churchill meeting with Combined Chiefs: memcon, September 13, 1944, 11:45 A.M., and Andrew McFarland minutes, in FRUS Quebec, pp. 312–318, Churchill, *Triumph and Tragedy,* pp. 149–151.

Churchill as First Lord before World War I: Gilbert, *Churchill,* pp. 239–262. "Might have to build up": Ibid., p. 401. "Incomparably more hideous": Ibid., p. 412. "Strong and peaceful Germany": Ibid., p. 420. "Kill the Bolshie.": Ibid., p. 412. Churchill tries to relax Versailles treaty and "in permanent subjugation": Ibid., p. 464. "British policy for four hundred years": Ibid., p. 555. Churchill to Parliament after Munich: Ibid., pp. 598–600. No enemies "except the Huns": Ibid., p. 689. Churchill "wooed Joe Stalin": Ibid., p. 743. "The cause of any Russian": Ibid., p. 701. "I do not want to be left alone": Ibid., p. 743. "We musn't weaken Germany too much": Gilbert, *Road to Victory,* p. 518. "Winston never talks of Hitler" and "The advance of the Red Army": Lord Moran, p. 185.

FDR-Morgenthau September 13, 1944, meeting at Citadel: Harry Dexter White memcon, September 13, 1944, 4 P.M., based on Morgenthau's immediate reminiscences, in FDRL, and FRUS Quebec, pp. 323–324. On Eden journey to Quebec, see FRUS Quebec, pp. 3 and 46, and NYT, September 14, 1944. FDR-Churchill September 13, 1944, dinner: Harry Dexter White memcon, September 13, 1944, in FDRL, FRUS Quebec, pp. 324–328, Lord Moran, pp. 190–191. "How would you like to have the steel business": FRUS Quebec, p. 323. Churchill on chaining himself to "a dead German": Henry Morgenthau, Jr., "Our Policy Toward Germany," *New York Post,* November 28, 1947. Churchill and entourage dislike of Morgenthau: Lamb, p. 297, Skidelsky, pp. 98–99. Churchill's Foreign Office on "a starving and bankrupt Germany": Lamb, p. 296. Harriman cable to FDR: FRUS Quebec, p. 328.

Stimson on "outrageous" news and "never seen him so depressed": SD, September 13 and 14, 1944. Morgenthau will try to "beguile the British": McCloy Diary, September 14, 1944, quoting Stimson. Hull refusal to stage emergency meeting: SD, September 15, 1944. Morgenthau did not sleep: Blum, *From the Morgenthau Diaries,* vol. 3, p. 369.

"Closest friend and confidant": Gilbert, *Churchill,* p. 951. On Cherwell's life and career and friendship with Churchill, see especially Harrod, the Earl of Birkenhead, and Rhodes, pp. 371–372, 469–470, 529–530, 537–538. "To avoid exposing himself": Rhodes, pp. 222–223. "Because he was by birth": Ibid., p. 100. "Detested Germans": Colville, p. 736. Cherwell's role during World War II: Gilbert, *Road to Victory,* p. 962. Cherwell on "secret weapon": Rhodes, p. 320. "There were many touches in his deportment": Harrod, p. 108. McCloy wonders if Cherwell is Jewish: McCloy interview, HMPA. "The question of whether the Prof was a Jew": Harrod, p. 108. Charles Lindemann on non-Jewishness: Earl of Birkenhead, pp. 24–25. Cherwell to Churchill after Wednesday night dinner: Lord Moran, pp. 177–178, Gilbert, *Road to Victory,* p. 962.

Morgenthau consults Goodhart on Cherwell: MD, September 14 and 19, 1944, and MM, pp. 384. Cherwell-Morgenthau September 14, 1944, 10 A.M. meeting: Harry Dexter White memcon, September 14, 1944, FDRL, and MM, p. 384. Roosevelt-Churchill September 14, 1944, 11:30 A.M. meeting: Churchill, *Triumph and Tragedy,* pp. 156–157, memcons in FRUS Quebec, pp. 343–346. "Why shouldn't it work": Lord Moran, p. 191. FDR storytelling and "What do you want me to do?": Harry Dexter White memcon, September 14, 1944, FDRL. Hull anger at Morgenthau presence in Quebec: Hull, vol. 2, p. 1614.

Roosevelt-Churchill September 15, 1944, noon meeting: MD, September 15, 1944, FRUS Quebec, pp. 360–363, Lord Moran, p. 192. Eden-Churchill confrontation: FRUS Quebec, p. 362. Eden on tiff with Churchill: Eden Diary, September 15, 1944, Lord Avon Papers, Birmingham University, England, Dutton, pp. 171–172. FDR-Churchill memo on "agricultural and pastoral" Germany, September 15, 1944, is in FDRL. Morgenthau "terrifically happy": MD, September 15, 1944. Churchill on why he signed: Churchill, *Triumph and Tragedy,* pp. 156–157. Churchill claims "surprised to find" Morgenthau at Quebec: Ibid., p. 150. FDR-Morgenthau romanticism about democracy and farming: Blum, *Roosevelt and Morgenthau,* pp. 3–4, 648–649. On Morgenthau Plan and FDR intention to withdraw troops from Europe, see Kimball, *Forged in War,* p. 277, and McAllister, pp. 53–55. Churchill on signing Quebec memorandum: Churchill, *Triumph and Tragedy,* p. 156.

FDR-Churchill Friday afternoon meeting: FRUS Quebec, pp. 365–367. FDR on postponing until "everything else settled": Ibid., p. 370. FDR sketch on map of Germany: FRUS Quebec, pp. 369–370, and Blum, *From the Morgenthau Diaries,* vol. 3, p. 372. On history of argument over German occupation zones, see George Elsey to Wilson Brown, August 31, 1944, in FRUS Quebec, pp. 145–158, Dallek, pp. 472–477, and Kimball, *Swords or Ploughshares,* pp. 7–9. "Absolutely unwilling": FDR to Churchill, February 7, 1944, in FDRL. FDR to Hull on problems of landlocked zone: Hull, vol. 2, p. 1612. FDR "hell-bent": SD, September 14, 1944. Stimson on having "such great success with our invasion": SD, August 25, 1944. Morgenthau Friday evening visit with FDR: MD, September 15, 1944, and "The President's Log for the 1944 Quebec Conference," FDRL. Screening of *Wilson* and "By God, that's not going to happen": Ferrell, *The Dying President,* pp. 84–85.

Churchills' visit to Hyde Park: MM, pp. 387, 432, Rhodes, pp. 537–538, Churchill, *Triumph and Tragedy,* pp. 160–161, Gilbert, *Road to Victory,* pp. 968–971. "Knew Franklin rose early": Gurewitsch, p. 190. "Eleanor's here!" and Eleanor frictions with Churchill: *Washington Post,* September 22, 1944, Elliott Roosevelt and James Brough, *Rendezvous with Destiny,* p. 319, Eleanor Roosevelt to Joseph Lash, September 18, 1944, FDRL, and undated news clippings in Eleanor Roosevelt FBI file. "Having something done to her innards": Hassett Diary, September 18, 1944, FDRL. FDR orders FBI surveillance of Windsors: FBI file on Duke and Duchess of Windsor, including especially FBI reports of September 13, 1940, April 16, 1941, and May 2, 1941. Eleanor on Churchill's table talk on Spain and "picturesquely" but "stupidly": Eleanor Roosevelt to Joseph Lash, September 18, 1944, FDRL. Robert Morgenthau surprise at Churchill temperance: MM, p. 432. "Tube Alloys" and "it might perhaps": "Tube Alloys," September 18, 1944, in PREM 3/139/8A, PRO. "Under a heavy strain": Hassett, p. 272. "Good conference" but FDR wanted "to *sleep*": Suckley Diary, September 17, 1944.

CHAPTER FOURTEEN
"A Hell of a Hubbub"

"The high spot of my whole career": MD, September 19, 1944. McCloy call to Stimson and Stimson rage into diary: SD, September 15–17, 23–24, 1944. Stimson to "far-sighted and greatly humanitarian President": Stimson to FDR, in Stimson and Bundy, p. 578. McCloy recruits allies against Morgenthau: SD and McCloy Diary, September 1944. McCloy to Forrestal: Forrestal Diary, September 18, 1944. McCloy-Ickes luncheon and Ickes's comments afterward: Ickes Diary, September 17, 1944. Morgenthau September 20, 1944, meeting with Hull, Stimson, McCloy: Harry Dexter White memcon in FDRL, Freeman Matthews memcon in FRUS Yalta, pp. 134–135, SD, September 20, 1944, McCloy memcon in McCloy papers, Hull, vol. 2, pp. 1614–1615.

Stimson birthday celebration: SD, September 20–21, 1944. Drew Pearson column is in *Washington Post,* September 21, 1944. McCloy to Stimson on Pearson column: McCloy to Stimson, October 1, 1944, McCloy Papers. Harry Dexter White on leaking: MD, September 29, 1944. McCloy leak to Krock: McCloy Diary, September 21, 1944. Byrnes-Morgenthau feud: Blum, *From the Morgenthau Diaries,* vol. 3, p. 70, MM, pp. 404–405. Ickes-FDR luncheon is in Ickes Diary, September 22, 1944. Byrnes hint to Krock: Krock to Vladimir Petrov, May 13, 1963, Krock Papers, Krock, p. 208. Anna Boettiger's resentment of Morgenthau: Ickes Diary, October 6, 1944. "Treasury Plan Calls": Alfred Flynn, *Wall Street Journal,* September 23, 1944. Associated Press story is in *Washington Post,* September 24, 1944. Morgenthau reading newspapers before breakfast: Elizabeth Watkins to Jim McConaughy, January 15, 1943, *Time*

Archives. Morgenthau's failed efforts to contact FDR are in MD, September 25, 1944. Morgenthau listens to radio, Morgenthau-Hull conversation, Morgenthau talk with aides and further efforts to reach FDR are in MD, September 25–26, 1944.

Morgenthau September 26, 1944, conversations with Hopkins and FDR: MD, September 26–27, 1944. FDR-Stimson September 27, 1944, telephone talk and Stimson reaction: SD, September 27 to October 1, 1944. Morgenthau asks aides to find negative information about Stimson: MD, September 27, 1944. For Stimson and post–World War I German reparations, see Stimson and Bundy, pp. 200–219, and Hodgson, pp. 193–209. Morgenthau-Marshall September 28, 1944, luncheon: MD, September 28, 1944. American embassy in Moscow on fraternization: U.S. Embassy Moscow to Hull, September to October 1944, in NA. "There has been a hell of a hubbub": MD and McCloy Diary, September 28, 1944. "ROOSEVELT AND CHURCHILL AGREE": Armstrong, p. 76. German propaganda against Morgenthau Plan: Allen Dulles to William Donovan, December 8, 1944, Donovan to FDR, December 11, 1944, FDRL, and Lamb, p. 297.

Washington Post on Morgenthau Plan: September 26, 29 and 30, 1944. Naval officer's letter is in *Washington Post,* October 2, 1944. Coughlin on Morgenthau wish to "emasculate the German men" is in undated transcript of interview in Father Coughlin Papers, Northwestern University Library. Morgenthau's revelation of Coughlin as silver trader: Marcus, pp. 68–70. Arthur Krock on FDR "about-face": NYT, September 29, 1944. Morgenthau's vain efforts to contact FDR: MD, September 29, 1944. Morgenthau feeling tortured by charge of increasing German resistance: MM, p. 390, Blum, *From the Morgenthau Diaries,* vol. 3, p. 382. Morgenthau discusses with aides: MD, September 29, 1944. Hull talk with Krock, September 29, 1944, is in Krock memo, Krock Papers. Morgenthau headaches: Morgenthau to Henrietta Klotz, October 5, 1944, FDRL. Morgenthau walk to White House and confrontation with Anna Boettiger is in MD, September 29, 1944. FDR press conference, September 29, 1944, is in FDRL. "No one wants to make Germany a wholly agricultural nation": FDR to Hull, September 29, 1944, in FDRL. FDR-Stimson October 3, 1944, luncheon: SD, October 3, 1944, Stimson memcon, October 3, 1944, in McCloy Papers, "Notes for use in talk with the President on October 3, 1944," Stimson Papers, James Byrnes memcon of June 27, 1947, conversation with Stimson, in Byrnes Papers.

CHAPTER FIFTEEN
"As Useful as Ten Fresh German Divisions"

White-Gromyko October 5, 1944, meeting is in MD, October 5–6, 1944. On history of Soviet embassy in Washington, see *Washington Post,* May 30, 1990. On Harry Dexter White's life and career, see Rees, Bruce Craig, Harry Dexter White FBI File, *Time,* November 23, 1953, MM, pp. 310–311. A revised version of the Bruce Craig dissertation is to be published in 2003 by the University Press of Kansas as *Treasonable Doubt: The Harry Dexter White Case—A Tale of Espionage.* On White's Soviet connections, see VENONA cables, Harry Dexter White FBI file, Bruce Craig, Haynes and Klehr, pp. 125–126, 138–145, Weinstein and Vassiliev, pp. 157–158, 161–169, Romerstein and Breindel, pp. 29–30, 41–53, MM, pp. 423–427, Tanenhaus, pp. 110, 116, James M. Boughton, "The Case Against Harry Dexter White: Still Not Proven," *History of Political Economy,* 2001. White's birth and Anglicization of name: "Harry Dexter White—Espionage," FBI File, November 16, 1953. Rees, pp. 9, 20–21. White adds "Dexter": Fanny White to Morgenthau, August 27, 1948, Morgenthau Papers. "I think Harry was exposed": Edward Bernstein interview, HMPA. White tells friends learning Russian to study Soviet planning: Skidelsky, p. 240.

White included in "9:30 Group": Skidelsky, p. 241, "Harry Dexter White—Espionage," FBI file. White "in charge of foreign affairs for me" and "I want it all in one brain": Rees, p. 131. "Gadfly": McCloy interview, HMPA. "Son-of-a-bitch": Blum interview, HMPA. White's flattery: *Time,* November 23, 1953. White relationship with Klotz: Klotz interview, HMPA. On White's role in postwar economic order, see Rees, pp. 9–11, Skidelsky, pp. 337–360, and Blum, *Roosevelt and Morgenthau,* pp. 563–564. White's July 31, 1944, meeting with Kolstov: VENONA cables, New York to Moscow, August 4 and 5, 1944. White code-named "LAWYER": Weinstein and Vassiliev, p. 157. White's appearance before HUAC: August 13, 1948, transcript in NA. White's death: MM, p. 424.

Brownell on White as "Russian spy": Transcript of speech, November 6, 1953, in Harry Dexter White FBI file. Morgenthau tortured by charges against White and worries about White's pressures on him: Henry Morgenthau III interview and MM, pp. 426–427. Morgenthau met twice with Ladd, on January 21 and 24, 1952. J. Edgar Hoover, who disliked and distrusted Morgenthau, pleaded previous engagements. Morgenthau's comments to Ladd are in Ladd to Hoover, January 21 and 24, 1952, and G. A. Nease to Hoover, January 22, 1952, in Harry Dexter White FBI file. Chambers testimony on White description of Soviet monetary proposal and transmittal to Bykov are in his January 25, 1949, grand jury testimony (transcript in NA), as well as in Chambers, p. 431. See also Bruce Craig, pp. 86–100, and Boughton. Chambers receiving four pages of White notes and other information: Rees, pp. 76–97, 432–435, Chambers, p. 737, Weinstein, *Perjury,* pp. 237–240, Tanenhaus, pp. 290–317, Boughton, Chambers written statement to FBI, December 3, 1948, Harry Dexter White FBI file. Bruce Craig writes of the "inherent difficulty" in a message to the author, July 9, 2002.

Chambers to FBI on White picking him up and driving: Chambers interviews with FBI, January to April 1949, Guy Hottel to J. Edgar Hoover, July 24, 1950, Harry Dexter White FBI file. "Endlessly" and "If White's spirits were up" appear, undated, in Harry Dexter White FBI file. Chambers gives list to Berle: Chambers, pp. 466–470, Haynes and Klehr, pp. 90–91, Rees, 84–86, Weinstein, *Perjury,* pp. 64–65. Levine insistence is in grand jury testimony, February 10, 1949, transcript in NA. "I don't think White ever personally gave me": Chambers January 28, 1949, grand jury testimony, transcript in NA. Craig on Chambers's testimony: Bruce Craig, pp. 99–100, and Bruce Craig to author, July 7, 2002. Chambers said did not mention White because White had pledged to stop collaboration: Guy Hottel to J. Edgar Hoover, July 24, 1950, Harry Dexter White FBI file. Chambers on White as "member-at-large": Weinstein, *Perjury,* p. 346. Bentley offers list, November 30, 1945: Bentley, pp. 164–166, Rees, pp. 377–390, "Harry Dexter White—Espionage," FBI file. Bentley later testimony: Rees, pp. 199–201, 212.

On VENONA generally, see Central Intelligence Agency announcement and first release of materials, July 11, 1995, National Security Agency website, David Hatch, "VENONA: An Overview," *American Intelligence Journal* (1996), Haynes and Klehr, Romerstein and Breindel. Sixteen VENONA cables mention White: April 29, August 4 and 5, September 2 and 7, October 1, November 20, 1944, and January 18, March 19 and 29, April 6, May 4, 5, 13 and 26, June 8, 1945. White financial need and on "offer of assistance": New York to Moscow, November 20, 1944, VENONA files. White "data" on Wallace and loan: Boughton, Haynes and Klehr, pp. 140–142, San Francisco to Moscow, VENONA files. White's relationships with Wallace and Hull: Rees, pp. 132, 407. Morgenthau to sons on White and Wallace is January 28, 1945, HMPA.

Soviet agents among White associates are treated in Boughton, Bruce Craig, pp. 154–215, and Haynes and Klehr, p. 139. Weinstein and Vassiliev terms of access: Weinstein and Vassiliev, p. xi. White fear of exposure: Ibid., p. 158. Silvermaster's complaint: Ibid., p. 169. Silvermaster claims of Morgenthau-Klotz affair and White obstruction of his promotion are in Ibid., pp. 165–166. "To treat the Soviets exactly" and Chambers-Bykov-White connection: Boughton. White on relationships with Silvermaster, Ullman and Silverman: Harry Dexter White FBI file. On White's motives, I have benefited from correspondence with Bruce Craig, July 7, 2002, and Warren Kimball, July 16, 2002. Reasons for White's promotion: Bruce Craig to author, July 7, 2002. FDR saying White had "earned" promotion and "please clear" the nomination: MD Senate, vol. 1, pp. 760–761. Hannegan roadblock: Morgenthau to sons, January 21, 1945, HMPA. "About half of my best people": Morgenthau to Klotz, December 12, 1944, Morgenthau Papers.

For Churchill-Stalin October 1944 meetings, see memcons, October 9 to 17, 1944, in PREM 3/434/2/61–62, 92–94, in PRO, Kimball, *Swords or Ploughshares,* pp. 135–140, Gilbert, *Road to Victory,* pp. 978–1033, Churchill, *Triumph and Tragedy,* pp. 217–243, Berezhkov, pp. 307–315, Ulam, *Expansion and Coexistence,* pp. 364–365. Litvinov on postwar world is in "On the Prospects and the Basis of Soviet-British Cooperation," November 14, 1944, "On the Relationship to the U.S.A.," January 10, 1945, and "On the Question of Blocs and Spheres of Influence," January 11, 1945, in CWIHP. See also

Vladimir Pechatnov, "The Big Three After World War II," CWIHP. "This terrific drive on me": MD, October 25, 1944. Morgenthau on "coordinated attack" is in Stettinius Diary, October 26, 1944. FDR sends paper on prewar Europe's farm machinery and Morgenthau response: FDR to Morgenthau, October 9, 1944, with Morgenthau reply handwritten at bottom of page, accompanied by William Donovan to Allen Dulles, October 4, 1944, FDRL. Morgenthau on Stimson's "olive branch": MD and SD, October 21, 1944. American victory at Aachen: NYT, October 22, 1944. See also Ambrose, *Citizen Soldiers,* pp. 146–154. Morgenthau's proposal for Eisenhower proclamation and McCloy-Morgenthau discussion: MD, September 7, 1944. Text of Proclamation Number One is in Eisenhower Library. See also *Washington Post,* September 29, 1944.

"I dislike making detailed plans": FDR to Hull, October 29, 1944, FDRL. McCloy excludes Morgenthau from seeing memo: MD, November 1944. McCloy on FDR's "very much chastened approach": McCloy to Stimson, October 31, 1944, McCloy Papers. FDR to Winant on "mistake" bringing Morgenthau to Quebec: SD, October 27, 1944. Stimson on campaign "getting hot and uncertain": SD, October 18, 1944. British ambassador on possible Dewey victory: Halifax to Foreign Office, October 1944, in PRO. Dewey speech at Waldorf: NYT, October 18 and 19, 1944. Unreleased proposed statement is in FDRL. Stimson's abstention from campaign and Ickes complaint: Ickes Diary, November 20, 1944, describing October 20, 1944, luncheon with McCloy. Hopkins asks McCloy to make a speech: McCloy Diary, October 18, 1944. Stimson presence at FDR Foreign Policy Association speech: NYT, October 22, 1944. "One of the great strengths of this Administration": McCloy Diary, October 18, 1944. *Time* on Roosevelt being "wheeled" is October 30, 1944. Morgenthau worry that Germans might capture Henry III and explores possibility of giving him false identity: Henry Morgenthau III interview, MD, November 14, 1944, and McCloy Diary, March 7, 1945.

FDR October 26, 1944, conversation with Joseph Kennedy and Kennedy luncheon with Arthur Krock are in Krock memo, October 26, 1944, Krock Papers, Ickes Diary, November 15, 1944, and Beschloss, *Kennedy and Roosevelt,* pp. 257–259. Kennedy's foiled wish to be Treasury Secretary: Beschloss, ibid., pp. 78–79. "Harry, what the hell are you doing campaigning": Merle Miller, p. 186. Kennedy to son Robert on Morgenthau Plan: Schlesinger, *Robert Kennedy and His Times,* p. 59. Edward Bernstein opposition to Morgenthau Plan: Bernstein interview, HMPA. Krock report that FDR and Morgenthau had "bribed" Churchill: NYT, November 3, 1944. Morgenthau's reaction, complaint to Stettinius and Stettinius reply: MD, November 3, 1944.

Reporter's warning that Dewey will "skin" Morgenthau "alive": MD and SD, November 4, 1944. Morgenthau's failed efforts to reach FDR aides: MD, November 4, 1944. Morgenthau telephone conversation with Stimson: MD, SD, McCloy Diary, November 4, 1944. Dewey speech on Morgenthau Plan is in NYT, November 5, 1944. Stimson reaction and feels "sorry for Morgenthau": SD, November 4, 1944. McCloy-Morgenthau

November 5, 1944, conversation and Morgenthau complaint to Herbert Gaston are in MD, November 5, 1944. FDR-Morgenthau tradition of Hudson "sentimental journey": Henry Morgenthau III interview, Hassett Diary, October 23, 1944. Nineteen forty-four ride up Hudson, Election Night, Hassett on "the graceless Dewey" and "I still think he is a son-of-a-bitch" are all in Hassett Diary, November 6 and 7, 1944. Morgenthau "gloomily unsure of himself": MM, p. 398. Ickes to Anna Boettiger on Morgenthau: Ickes Diary, March 31, 1945. Ickes ponders writing a book: Ickes Diary, December 2 and 9, 1944. Morgenthau considers book on Morgenthau Plan and Klotz bet that FDR will stop him: MD, November 3, 1944, Josiah DuBois interview, HMPA. "You people have to be prepared": MD, November 3, 1944.

CHAPTER SIXTEEN
"Lord Give the President Strength"

FDR-Morgenthau postelection luncheon: MD, November 15, 1944. Kilgore report: NYT, November 13, 1944. On Kilgore and interest in cartels, see *West Virginia History,* vol. 55, pp. 127–142. Morgenthau to Kilgore: Blum, *From the Morgenthau Diaries,* vol. 3, p. 391. Hull hospital treatment, Mrs. Hull on Morgenthau episode and Hull's resignation: Gellman, pp. 358–360, Krock, pp. 209–211, Krock memo of visit with Hull, May 26, 1945, Krock Papers, Hull, vol. 2, pp. 1714–1718, NYT October 21, 25 and 31, and November 1, 9, 11, 16, 21 and 28, 1944. On Stettinius, see Blum, *From the Morgenthau Diaries,* vol. 3, pp. 392–393. FDR on Hull's "wife trouble": Ickes Diary, November 24, 1944. "About as much Secretary of State": James Riddleberger oral history, HSTL. Morgenthau on Stettinius: Morgenthau to sons, January 28, 1945, HMPA, MM, pp. 398–399. "Pretty ignorant": SD, August 3, 1944. "Make everyone feel happy": Ickes Diary, December 30, 1944. "A douche of cold water": Ickes Diary, December 2, 1944. "A backslapper": Ibid., November 14, 1944. Ickes and rumor about Hopkins and Stettinius: Ickes Diary, December 2, 1944.

Stettinius warns Morgenthau about memo: MD, November 16, 1944. McCloy and Stimson renewed irritation with Morgenthau: SD and McCloy Diary, November 1944. McCloy jokes about Morgenthau Plan and pulls out spy camera: Isaacson and Thomas, p. 236. "Just an example of how he likes to push": SD, November 27, 1944. Morgenthau to aides on Stimson and McCloy "dislike us heartily": MD Senate, vol. 1, p. 789. FDR "determined to be tough": November 15, 1944, memcon in FRUS Yalta, pp. 171–172. "We can't make Germany so weak": Stettinius to FDR, November 22, 1944, in FDRL. "We should let Germany come back": FDR to Stettinius, December 4, 1944, in FDRL. Morgenthau to Stettinius on "set me back on my heels": MD Senate, vol. 1, p. 786. Morgenthau to aides on treating Stettinius: MD Senate, vol. 1, pp. 798–799. On JCS 1067 generally, see Eisenberg, pp. 47–51. Text of JCS 1067 is in NA. On McCloy loopholes, see Eisenberg, pp. 46–51, Morgenthau insistence on presumption of Naziism: MD Senate, vol. 1, p. 854. Morgenthau and Stimson differences about governor of American zone: Backer, *Winds of History,* p. 4. On FDR's decision affecting history of Europe, see Eisenberg, p. 51.

British Foreign Office opposition to Morgenthau Plan is in Woolner, pp. 15, 33–35, 91–93. McCloy finds British military terrified of "chaos in Germany": McCloy to Colonel Chanler, October 12, 1944, McCloy Papers. Cherwell and Eden views are in PRO, November–December 1944, MD, November 1944, and Blum, *From the Morgenthau Diaries,* vol. 3, pp. 383–386. McCloy warning on British belief "they are going into a country": Blum, *From the Morgenthau Diaries,* vol. 3, p. 385. Morgenthau overlooks McCloy undermining his plan with JCS 1067: MD, November–December 1944. Stimson-McCloy October 1944 decree on "orderly process of trade" is in NA. FDR on German bomb is in Suckley Diary, December 9, 1944. Battle of the Bulge "a complete surprise": McCloy Diary, December 16, 1944. Marshall warning to Stimson: SD, December 27, 1944. Boettiger meeting with Morgenthau: MD, December 19, 1944. On Battle of Aachen and American occupation, see NYT, October 23, 1944, *Life,* November 6, 1944, Ambrose, *Citizen Soldiers,* pp. 146–154, and Klaus Schwabe, "Setting up the Right Kind of Government—American Occupation Experiences in Aachen Before Germany's Surrender," Aachen Historical Society, 2000. "If every German city": Ambrose, *Citizen Soldiers,* p. 154. "When you go up against a fellow like that": MD, December 19, 1944. "Nobody is starving": Morgenthau to sons, January 21, 1945, HMPA. Dulles on effect of Morgenthau Plan on Germans: Allen Dulles to William Donovan, December 8, 1944, and Donovan to FDR, December 11, 1944, FDRL. McCloy and Morgenthau on German counterattack: MD, December 20, 1944. Bernstein's failure to become general: Henry Morgenthau III interview.

FDR plan to fly to London after victory: Rosenman, p. 546. Stimson on the "pressure of the great battle": SD, December 1944. Stimson sees FDR on New Year's Eve: SD, December 31, 1944. Wheeler on "brutal and costly" unconditional surrender: NYT and Associated Press, January 6, 1945. British Embassy on Wheeler: British Embassy Washington to Foreign Office, January 1945, PRO. "If we negotiate a peace": Ickes Diary, January 1945. Pepper to Morgenthau on Wheeler: MD Senate, vol. 2, p. 869. "I just wasn't going to give anybody a chance": MD Senate, vol. 2, p. 869. Morgenthau pajamas to FDR: Morgenthau to Klotz, November 29, 1944, in Morgenthau Papers, and FDR to Morgenthaus, January 8, 1945, in FDRL. Morgenthau to sons on "beating back the Germans": January 21, 1945, HMPA.

"Very sumptuous luncheon": Morgenthau to sons, January 5, 1945, HMPA. Morgenthau notices that FDR is "very tired": MD Senate, vol. 2, p. 869, and MM, p. 401. "The real motive of most who oppose": Morgenthau to FDR, January 10, 1945, FDRL. January 19, 1945, Cabinet meeting is treated in SD, MD, January 19, 1945, and Morgenthau to sons, January 21, 1945, HMPA. FDR 1945 inauguration: NYT, January 21, 1945. "The President looked distinguished": McCloy Diary, January 20, 1945. "Tonight we are going to the White House": Morgenthau to sons, January 21, 1945, HMPA.

Departure for Yalta: Ferrell, *The Dying President,* pp. 103–110, and Asbell, pp. 18–19. Anna "wanted desperately" to go to Yalta: Asbell, pp. 181–182. Anna Boettiger on her departure: Anna to John Boettiger, January 23, 1945, FDRL. Hassett on FDR leaving for Yalta: Hassett Diary, January 22, 1945.

CHAPTER SEVENTEEN
"The Only Bond Is Their Common Hate"

On Yalta Big Three conversations, see "The President's Log at Yalta," FDRL, Clemens, Edmonds, pp. 409–418, Churchill, *Triumph and Tragedy,* pp. 346–394, Dallek, pp. 506–525, Bohlen, pp. 173–201, Smyser, pp. 13–18, Sherwood, pp. 850–870, Gromyko, pp. 84–93, and U.S.S.R. Ministry of Foreign Affairs, *The Tehran, Yalta and Potsdam Conferences.* FDR drive to Yalta: Anna to John Boettiger, February 4, 5 and 13, 1945, FDRL. "About two weeks ago" and "a block to the bath": Anna to John Boettiger, February 4, 1945, FDRL. "Tried to pet me" and "most sinister appearing pest": Ibid., February 9, 1945, FDRL. "Just between you and me": Ibid., February 5, 1945, FDRL. "Just sit on their fannies": Ibid., February 9, 1945, FDRL. "This is a very sad situation": Ibid., February 5, 1945, FDRL.

Stalin-FDR February 4, 1945, meeting, 4 P.M.: Bohlen memcon in FDR and FRUS Yalta, pp. 570–573, and Bohlen, p. 180. Kennan's doubts about joint government of postwar Germany: Eisenberg, p. 55, Kennan, pp. 239–240, Bohlen, pp. 174–177. Big Three February 5, 1945, meeting 4 P.M., is in FDRL and FRUS Yalta, pp. 611–633. Churchill to Eden on "much too soon for us to decide": Churchill, *Triumph and Tragedy,* pp. 350–351. Churchill "hastily repudiated" Morgenthau Plan: Isaacson and Thomas, p. 238. Bohlen on FDR's "ill health": Bohlen, pp. 182–183. Stalin-Gromyko exchange is in Gromyko, pp. 87–88. Soviet public version on Anglo-American "ruling circles" position on dismemberment: Issraeljan, p. 332. Stalin longing for reparations: MD Senate, vol. 1, p. 52, Smyser, p. 14–15. Maisky to Stalin and Molotov on reparations is in Maisky, "The Formula of Reparations from Germany" (draft), January 17, 1945, in CWIHP. See also Vladimir Pechatnov, "The Big Three After World War II," CWIHP.

Big Three February 9, 1945, meeting, 4 P.M.: Bohlen memcon, FDRL and FRUS Yalta, pp. 841–850. For background of war crimes issues, see SD, October 9 and 24, November 19, 1944, Department of the Treasury, "Trial and Punishment of War Criminals," undated, in Morgenthau Papers, and Telford Taylor, pp. 3–42. Stimson to FDR on investigating Nazi "conspiracy": SD, November 21, 1944. Herbert Pell's role is treated in his unpublished manuscript, "Commission and Omission," 1945, provided to the author by courtesy of his son, former Senator Claiborne Pell, as well as the author's interview with Senator Pell. Dunn on Pell is in McCloy Diary, November 9, 1944. Rosenman role on war crimes is in Rosenman, p. 519.

DuBois warns Rosenman: January 17, 1945, memcon in "Trial and Punishment of War Criminals," and DuBois to Morgenthau, January 29, 1945, in Morgenthau Papers. Stimson persuades FDR to insist on "state trial": SD, January 19, 1945. Stalin-Churchill exchange about Hess: FRUS Yalta. On Hess 1941 mission, see Fest, *The Face of the Third Reich,* pp. 193–194, David Stafford, ed., *Flight from Reality: Rudolf Hess and His Mission to Scotland 1941* (London: Pimlico, 2002), Martin Allen, *Hidden Agenda: How the Duke of Windsor Betrayed the Allies* (New York: Macmillan, 2000), and John Costello's speculative *Ten Days to Destiny* (New York: Morrow, 1991). Stimson and Biddle to FDR on world tribunal: Telford Taylor, p. 39. Big Three February 10, 1945, meeting, 4 P.M., is in Bohlen memcon in FDRL and FRUS Yalta, pp. 897–906. Big Three dinner, February 10, 1945, 9 P.M., is in Bohlen memcon in FDRL and FRUS Yalta, pp. 921–925. "The only bond of the victors": Gilbert, *Road to Victory,* p. 1196.

CHAPTER EIGHTEEN
"Arguing About the Future of the World"

FDR voyage back from Yalta: Sherwood, pp. 873–874. Anna worry about his health: Anna to John Boettiger, February 14, 1945, FDRL. Stimson on Eisenhower's "big offensive": SD, March 1, 1945. FDR to Congress: *Public Papers of the Presidents: Franklin D. Roosevelt: 1945,* March 1, 1945. Truman on FDR's speech: Transcript of interviews with aides, 1954, HSTL. MacLeish on "the cold spring light": Weil, p. 189. FDR March 1, 1945, Cabinet meeting: SD and MD, March 1, 1945, and Ickes Diary, March 4, 1945. "Something in him besides this revolutionist": Dallek, p. 521. Stimson-FDR luncheon, March 3, 1945, is in SD, March 3, 1945, and Stimson, "Notes After Conference with the President," March 3, 1945, Stimson Papers.

McCloy boomlet for governor of American zone: SD, August 9 and 10, 1944, Ickes Diary, August 20, 1944. Morgenthau objections: MD, September 5, 1944. Byrnes possibility: Hull to FDR, September 2, 1944, and FDR to Hull, September 3, 1944, FDRL. Patterson possibility: SD, October 13, 16 and 19, December 11, 1944, and March 5, 1945, McCloy Diary, October 18, November 14, 1944, MD, September 5, 1944. Stimson on Dresden: SD, March 5, 1945. Stimson needs Patterson at Pentagon: SD, March 3, 1945, and "Notes" on luncheon, Stimson Papers. Stimson decides on Clay and brings Clay's name to FDR: SD, March 3 and 16, 1945, "Notes" on March 3, 1945, luncheon, Stimson Papers.

McCloy-Morgenthau March 9, 1945, conversation is in MD, March 9, 1945. FDR worries about Dunn: Weil, p. 186. Stettinius on FDR not realizing breadth of Dunn's new job: Ibid., pp. 180–181. Eleanor Roosevelt's outrage about Dunn: Eleanor Roosevelt to FDR, December 4, 1944, FDRL. "He'll sabotage everything": Weil, p. 186. Dunn watching FDR deal with telegram on Poland: Ibid., p. 189. Dunn tricks Stettinius into submitting Draft Directive on Germany: Blum, *From the Morgenthau Diaries,* vol. 3, pp.

400–403, MD, March 17, 1945. "Draft Directive for the Treatment of Germany," March 10, 1945, FDRL, SD, March 29, 1945. See also Morgenthau to sons, April 13, 1945, HMPA. Dunn tells McCloy to revise JCS 1067: Memcon of State Department meeting, March 14, 1945, FDRL. McCloy warns Stimson: McCloy to Stimson, March 15, 1945, McCloy Papers. McCloy-Morgenthau conversation, March 15, 1945, is in MD, March 15, 1945. March 15, 1945, 2:45 P.M. meeting is in McCloy memcon, March 15, 1945, in McCloy Papers, and SD, March 15, 1945. McCloy-Morgenthau call afterward is in MD, March 15, 1945. Stimson asks FDR why he signed Draft Directive and FDR reply: MD, March 17, 1945, and June 27, 1947, memcon, Byrnes Papers. Ickes to Anna on Roosevelt not understanding and forgetfulness: Harold Ickes Diary, April 7, 1945. Morgenthau-McCloy March 17, 1945, conversation is in MD and McCloy Diary of same date. Boettiger to Morgenthau on Dunn's perfidy: MD, March 17, 1945.

Stettinius refuses to show Yalta records to Morgenthau and Morgenthau discussion with aides: MD, March 19, 1945. Morgenthau luncheon with FDR and Boettigers is in MD, March 20, 1945. Anna on father's "incapacity" and "regency" and Daniels reaction: Jonathan Daniels oral history, HSTL. "This is a vulgar way to put it": Ibid. Anna antipathy to Morgenthau and Ickes reply: Ickes Diary, March 31, 1945. "Who told her that?": Jonathan Daniels oral history, HSTL, and Daniels, p. 272. Morgenthau-Boettiger exchange is in MD, March 20, 1945. Morgenthau to aides on luncheon: MD, March 20, 1945. "This is sort of embarrassing": MD and McCloy Diary, March 20, 1945. Morgenthau-Grew call is in MD, March 20, 1945. FDR meeting on Draft Directive, March 22, 1945, is in McCloy Diary of same date. State Department revised version, March 22, 1945, is in McCloy Papers. IPCOG creation is in Blum, *Roosevelt and Morgenthau,* p. 616.

"*Heil McCloy*" and FDR discussion of American governor of Germany: Isaacson and Thomas, p. 202, Bird, p. 233, Jean Edward Smith, *Lucius D. Clay,* pp. 211–212. McCloy describes meeting for Morgenthau: MD, March 22, 1945. Morgenthau goes to White House with request to write book: MD, March 23, 1945. "Summary of U.S. Initial Post-Defeat Policy Relating to Germany," March 22, 1945, is in FDRL. FDR meeting and Morgenthau reactions afterward are in MD, March 23, 1945. Stimson on Roosevelt's "indecision" is in SD, March 29, 1945. Morgenthau-Tully conversation is in MD, March 24, 1945. Morgenthau warns John Boettiger: MD, March 23, 1945. Gertrude Lerner to Morgenthau on restricted hotel, undated, March or April 1945, is in Morgenthau Papers. "As you know, it is the celebration of the freedom of the Jews": Morgenthau to sons, March 29, 1945, HMPA. On Clay's life and career, see Jean Edward Smith, *Lucius D. Clay,* Backer, *Winds of History,* pp. 44–52, and *The Papers of General Lucius D. Clay,* pp. xxxi–xxxvii. On importance of Clay's expertise in reconstruction and his willingness to use McCloy JCS 1067 loopholes, see Eisenberg, pp. 67–68. FDR looks Clay over and Byrnes-Clay exchange afterward: Jean Edward Smith, *Lucius D. Clay,* pp. 215–216.

CHAPTER NINETEEN

"No Earthly Powers Can Keep Him Here"

FDR wanted to "sleep and sleep and sleep": Suckley Diary, undated, probably March 14, 1945. "He is steadily losing weight" and "He is slipping away from us": Hassett Diary, March 30, 1945, FDRL. Thunderstorm: Suckley Diary, April 2, 1945. Marshall sends Army intelligence estimate: Marshall to FDR, "Probable Developments in the German Reich," April 2, 1945, FDRL. Hitler's order to flood German mines and destroy other facilities: Kershaw, pp. 784–786. On Churchill's demand to race the Soviets to Berlin and Roosevelt's response, see Gilbert, *Road to Victory,* p. 1280, Churchill, *Triumph and Tragedy,* p. 465, Ambrose, *Eisenhower: 1890–1952,* pp. 394–397, Larrabee, pp. 505–506, Lamb, pp. 305–306. Bradley warns of "pretty stiff price": Bradley, p. 417. Eisenhower feels that Soviets deserve honor: Ambrose, *Eisenhower: 1890–1952,* p. 401. Churchill cable to FDR on "the overwhelming contributor" is April 1, 1945, in FDRL, as is FDR's refusal. "I regard the matter as closed": April 4, 1945, in FDRL.

For talks with General Wolff about surrender on the Italian front, see Dwight Eisenhower, *Crusade in Europe,* p. 423, Grose, pp. 228–247, Persico, *Roosevelt's Secret War,* pp. 421–428, Gilbert, *Road to Victory,* pp. 1261, 1273, Churchill, *Triumph and Tragedy,* pp. 440–454. Wolff involvement in Italian Jews deportation: Richard Breitman and Timothy Naftali, "Report to the IWG on Previously Classified OSS Records," National Archives, 2000. Stalin to FDR, April 3, 1945, on "a lenient truce" is in FDRL. Molotov wants two or three Soviet generals at talks and "It was a very quarrelsome letter": SD, March 17, 1945. Roosevelt and Churchill tell Moscow that meeting is only for "establishing contact": Grose, p. 235. Harriman on Soviet leader's "belief that they can force their will": Grose, p. 236. FDR to Stalin, April 4, 1945, rebutting Stalin's accusation, is in FDRL. Stalin "never doubted" Roosevelt's integrity: Stalin to FDR, April 7, 1945, FDRL. FDR agrees to dismiss "minor incident": FDR to Stalin, April 12, 1945, FDRL.

Winant report on Soviet attitude toward German dismemberment: Winant to Stettinius, March 29, 1945, FDRL. "Our attitude should be one of study": FDR to Stettinius, April 6, 1945, FDRL. FDR on retiring: Suckley Diary, April 6, 1945. On Ruhr pocket, see Ambrose, *Eisenhower: 1890–1892,* p. 383, David Eisenhower, p. 751, Larrabee, pp. 475, 503–504. "Should we clean the pocket up": SD, April 6, 1945. Marshall's advisory cable to Eisenhower, April 6, 1945, is in Eisenhower Papers. Eisenhower tells Stimson that cleaning up Ruhr pocket will not leave "enough troops": SD, April 6 to 11, 1945. Stimson worry about atomic bomb work in southwestern Germany: SD, April 3, 4 and 5, 1945.

Clay consults Morgenthau on economic aid and Harry Dexter White advice: MD, April 4, 1945. Clay appoints Lewis Douglas: Jean Edward Smith, *Lucius D. Clay,* p. 232. Douglas complaints about "Hebraic influence": Bird, p. 101. Douglas on Morgenthau's "Hebraic arrogance": Browder and Smith, p. 106. Elinor Morgenthau heart attack:

MM, p. 402, Morgenthau to sons, April 9, 1945, HMPA. Eleanor Roosevelt to FDR on "Henry has been terribly worried," April 8, 1945, is in FDRL. "You must just rest": Eleanor Roosevelt to Elinor Morgenthau, April 5, 1945, FDRL. Morgenthau reluctance to be away from Washington and decision to return: MM, p. 402, and Morgenthau to sons, April 13, 1945, HMPA. "I find it difficult to know just what to say": FDR to Morgenthau, March 23, 1945, FDRL.

Morgenthau flight to Warm Springs and evening with FDR, April 11, 1945: MD, April 11 and 12, 1945, Morgenthau to sons, April 13, 1945, HMPA, Shoumatoff, pp. 111–114, Suckley Diary, April 11, 1945. On James Dunn and Quebec, see Hull, vol. 2, pp. 1608–1610. "The children's hour": Frank Friedel, *Launching the New Deal* (Boston: Little, Brown, 1973), p. 281. FDR resumes relationship with Lucy Mercer Rutherfurd: Daniels, p. 271, Ward, *Closest Companion,* pp. 287–288, 322–324, 349, Asbell, pp. 31–32. Covert stop on Labor Day weekend 1944: Suckley Diary, September 1, 1944. Suckley and Lucy wept "on each other's shoulder": Ibid., December 3, 1944. Birthday package from Rutherfurd and Suckley on Yalta voyage: Anna to John Boettiger, January 30, 1945, FDRL. FDR convinced Stalin "poisoned his wife": Shoumatoff, p. 103. Eisenhower visit to Ohrdruf Nord: David Eisenhower, p. 763. "Only generally or through secondary sources": Dwight Eisenhower, *Crusade in Europe,* pp. 408–409. "I never dreamed that such cruelty": Eisenhower to Mamie, April 15, 1945, Eisenhower Papers. Eisenhower to Marshall on "*first-hand* evidence": Ambrose, *Supreme Commander,* p. 659. "Still having trouble": David Eisenhower, p. 763.

Morgenthau return to Washington: MD, April 11 and 12, 1945, Morgenthau to sons, April 13, 1945, HMPA. Marquis Childs column is in *Washington Post,* April 12, 1945. Morgenthau fury at column, discussions with aides, telephone conversations with Stettinius and Samuel Grafton: MD, April 12, 1945. On Grafton, see his obituary in NYT, December 15, 1997. FDR's last day is in Shoumatoff, pp. 114–118, and Suckley Diary, April 12, 1945, FDRL. FDR on war might end "at any time": Shoumatoff, p. 103. FDR throws away draft card: Burns, *The Lion and the Fox,* p. 478. Eleanor call to Morgenthau at 5:43 P.M.: MD, April 12, 1945. "It was one of the most considerate and kind acts": Morgenthau to sons, April 13, 1945, HMPA. "I have lost my best friend": statement, April 12, 1945, with Morgenthau handwritten revisions, is in Morgenthau Papers. Morgenthau "depressed": Morgenthau to sons, April 13, 1945, HMPA. Grace Tully finds report: Grace Tully memo, May 9, 1945, attached to William Donovan to FDR, April 10, 1945, FDRL.

CHAPTER TWENTY
"What Will We Make of It?"

On Truman's lack of experience in foreign or military affairs or diplomacy: Ferrell, *Harry S. Truman,* p. 198. FDR's lack of contact with Truman as Vice President: Hamby, pp. 287–289, Ferrell, *Harry S. Truman,* pp. 175–176, McCullough, pp. 333–339, Truman appointments record, January to April 1945, HSTL. FDR love of "Invictus": President's Personal File 1-A, FDRL. Anna Boettiger on FDR "knew what was wrong with him": MD, April 12, 1945. "Enlarged heart": Morgenthau to sons, April 13, 1945, HMPA. "I am a juggler": MD, May 15, 1942. Ferrell on "Rube Goldberg machine": Ferrell, *The Dying President,* p. 151. Truman in Oval Office on April 13, 1945: McCullough, pp. 351–357, Hamby, pp. 294–295. "F.D.R. and nearly everybody else": Truman to Nellie Noland, May 9, 1948, HSTL. Stettinius compares Truman to Harding: McCullough, p. 349.

Stettinius-Truman meeting: Stettinius Diary, April 13, 1945, Stettinius to Truman, April 13, 1945, HSTL, Harry Truman, *Year of Decisions,* pp. 14–18, Donovan, p. 35. Truman meeting with Stimson and Joint Chiefs, including Marshall and Stimson comments afterward: SD, April 13, 18, 1945. Morgenthau to sons on FDR death: April 21, 1945, HMPA. Truman's supposed snub by Morgenthau is in Ferrell, *Harry S. Truman,* p. 133. On the Truman-Pendergast relationship and Pendergast's demise, see Robert H. Ferrell, *Truman & Pendergast* (Columbia: University of Missouri Press, 1999), and Rudolph H. Hartmann, *The Kansas City Investigation: Pendergast's Downfall 1938–1939* (Columbia: University of Missouri Press, 1999).

Truman private view of Morgenthau: Hamby, p. 306, Ferrell, *Harry S. Truman,* p. 186. Truman resentment of FDR role in 1940 campaign: Truman to Nellie Noland, May 9, 1948, HSTL. Truman on FDR as "fakir": Truman Diary, July 16, 1948, HSTL. "The coldest man I ever met" and Ferrell's caution are in Thomas Fleming, "Eight Days with Harry Truman," *American Heritage,* July–August 1992, and Ferrell, *The Dying President,* p. 168. Truman appalled by public tempest over Morgenthau Plan: Transcript of interviews with aides, 1954, HSTL. "Roosevelt wasn't an administrator": Transcript of interviews with aides, 1954, HSTL. "He was always careful to see": Truman Diary, May 6, 1948, HSTL. "I am willing and want to pass the credit": Ibid.

Morgenthau-Truman first Oval Office meeting is in MD, April 14, 1945. Truman desire to rehabilitate Hoover: SD, May 2 and 4, 1945, McCullough, pp. 389–390. Morgenthau to sons on first Truman meeting is in April 21, 1945, letter, HMPA. "Has a lot of nervous energy": MD, April 14, 1945. "It was a brilliant, clear spring day": Morgenthau to sons, April 21, 1945, HMPA. Eleanor Roosevelt's temporary lodging with Morgenthaus is in same letter. "Our demand has been": Transcript of speech, April 15, 1945, HSTL. "It probably would have been better": Transcript of interviews with aides, 1954, HSTL. Ruhr surrender: NYT, April 19, 1945. "We had better take Berlin": Ambrose, *Eisenhower and Berlin,* p. 97. "We'd get all coiled up": Ambrose, *Eisenhower: 1890–1952,* p. 397. Churchill's worry about Soviets and Berlin: Gilbert, *Road to Victory,* pp. 1264, 1273–1276, 1280–1281, Elliott Roosevelt and James Brough, *Rendezvous with Destiny,* pp. 404–405. Eisenhower calms down Churchill: Ambrose, *Eisenhower and Berlin,* p. 96. Churchill-Truman April 18, 1945, cable is in HSTL, as is Truman's reply. See also transcript of interviews with aides, 1954, HSTL. Truman and Churchill to Stalin on retreat to zones: Harry Truman, *Year of Decisions,* p. 83.

Liberation of Belsen: NYT, April 19, 1945. Murrow on Buchenwald: *PM,* April 16, 1945. Ickes on American public opinion against Germans: Ickes Diary, April 29, 1945. Stimson on "so-called atrocities": SD, May 9, 1945. Wise-Truman April 20, 1945, meeting and Truman's later recollection: Harry Truman, *Year of Decisions,* pp. 68–69, Merle Miller, pp. 215–216, transcript of interviews with aides, 1954, HSTL. "To put me on the spot": "The President's Appointments," September 29, 1945, HSTL. Truman studying diplomatic documents is in McCullough, pp. 371–372, 382. "I had to be in an intelligent position": Transcript of interviews with aides, 1954, HSTL. Molotov-Truman April 22, 1945, meeting: Harry Truman, *Year of Decisions,* pp. 78–82, Bohlen April 22, 1945, notes in FRUS 1945, Bohlen, pp. 212–214, Donovan, pp. 39–42, transcript of interviews with aides, 1954, HSTL. Harriman regrets: Donovan, p. 42. Himmler separate peace offer and Truman's reaction: Harry Truman, *Year of Decisions,* pp. 88–94. "The German idea, of course": Truman to Eleanor Roosevelt, May 10, 1945, HSTL. Truman's later recollection is in transcript of interviews with aides, 1954, HSTL. Stalin to Truman and Churchill, April 26, 1945, is in HSTL. "It is hard to think of it": McCloy Diary, April 25, 1945.

CHAPTER TWENTY-ONE
"I Was Never in Favor of That Crazy Plan"

For Hitler's demise, see Kershaw, pp. 824–828, Fest, *Hitler,* pp. 744–750, Bullock, *Hitler and Stalin,* pp. 889–893, Petrova and Watson, "I will not fall into the hands": Kershaw, p. 822, Shirer, p. 1125. Truman's surprise at Hitler's suicide: Transcript of interviews with aides, 1954, HSTL, Harry Truman, *Year of Decisions,* p. 203. In an unreliable 1995 book, *The Murder of Adolf Hitler,* a British surgeon named Hugh Thomas used inconsistencies in the sundry accounts of Hitler's end to claim that Hitler was murdered and Eva Braun escaped the bunker. The 1945 poll was taken by the Gallup Organization, Princeton, New Jersey. Spikehorn Meyer to Truman is in HSTL. Eisenhower to Truman on German effort for separate peace, May 6, 1945, is in HSTL. German surrender: Dwight Eisenhower, *Crusade in Europe,* pp. 425–426, Ambrose, *Eisenhower: 1890–1952,* pp. 406–407, NYT, May 9, 1945. Truman on "our rejoicing": *Public Papers of the Presidents: Harry S. Truman: 1945,* May 8, 1945. "It's a pity that Roosevelt": Transcript of interviews with aides, 1954, HSTL. "If we are ordered to go": Truman to Bess, July 14, 1917, HSTL. Truman to Bess from "somewhere in Parlez-Vous," September 1, 1918, is in HSTL. "There are rumors rife": Truman to Bess, November 15, 1918, HSTL. "I don't give a whoop": Truman to Bess, January 21, 1919, HSTL.

Truman's votes on neutrality laws and preparedness: Hamby, pp. 265–271, and McCullough, pp. 242–243. Truman "mighty blue": Truman to Bess, September 22, 1939, HSTL. "If we see that Hitler is winning": NYT, June 24, 1941. Truman asks Marshall to enlist and Marshall's reply: Ferrell, *Harry S. Truman,* p. 153. "As untrustworthy as Hitler": Truman to Bess, December 30, 1941, HSTL. "Kike town" and "Screamed like a Jewish merchant": Truman to Bess, March 27, 1918, and June 30, 1935, HSTL. Alonzo

Hamby notes the Jacobson friendship and Jacobson's exclusion by Bess in a July 1, 2002, message to the author. Truman at 1943 Chicago rally: Hamby, p. 269. Truman Committee investigations of American business links to German cartels: McCullough, pp. 266–267, Hamby, pp. 258–259. "You can't be vindictive": Transcript of interviews with aides, 1954, HSTL. "I know what it means to lose": Transcript, "The Stacked Deck: The Harry S. Truman Series," Ben Gradus Films, Screen Gems, 1963, in HSTL.

Morgenthau quotes McCloy comment on German cities in MD, April 21, 1945. McCloy to Stimson on situation in Germany and "I had anticipated the chaos": SD, April 19, 1945. Lovett on not taking industrial treasure from Germany: Blum, *From the Morgenthau Diaries,* vol. 3, p. 452. Morgenthau on preventing Allied Control Council from managing German wages and prices: Ibid., p. 454. Clayton on danger of inflation: Ibid. "We don't think we are going to stop inflation": Ibid. McCloy to Truman on Germany in desperate need, April 26, 1945, is in HSTL. Truman promise to "read every word" of JCS 1067: Ibid., p. 457. Truman desire to let Germans rehabilitate Europe: Transcript of interviews with aides, 1954, HSTL, and Truman, *Year of Decisions,* pp. 235–237. Morgenthau on Army use of German synthetic oil plants and Morgenthau reply: Blum, *From the Morgenthau Diaries,* vol. 3, pp. 456–458, and MD, May 8, 1945. Stimson on Morgenthau fear that " 'scorched earth' policy will be relaxed": SD, May 8, 1945, Blum, *From the Morgenthau Diaries,* vol. 3, p. 458.

Morgenthau gives draft article to Truman: MD, May 2, 1945. Morgenthau-Connelly call: MD, May 3, 1945. Morgenthau sees Truman after Cabinet meeting: MD, May 4, 1945. Morgenthau May 9, 1945, meeting with Truman and Morgenthau's reaction to it are in MD, May 9, 1945. Morgenthau to sons on Truman is in May 10, 1945, letter, HMPA. On prewar German food crisis, see Kershaw, pp. 47–49. Truman signs JCS 1067 and approves IPCOG recommendation: Donovan, p. 77. Eisenhower to Marshall on not making JCS 1067 public: Jean Edward Smith, *The Papers of General Lucius D. Clay,* vol. 1, p. 15. Morgenthau on "big day for the Treasury": MD, May 10–12, 1945. Morgenthau on directive as "plenty tough": Morgenthau to sons, May 18, 1945, HMPA.

Churchill to Truman, May 11, 1945, is in HSTL. Churchill disparagement of JCS 1067, May 12, 1945, is in HSTL. Churchill cautions to Eisenhower: Memcon, May 16, 1945, in Cabinet papers 79/33, PRO. Red Army brutality and rape: Naimark, pp. 69–140, and Gaddis, *We Now Know,* p. 45. Stimson to Truman on tolerance of Russians is in SD, May 1945. *"Frau, komm!"*: Read and Fisher, pp. 438–440. Truman consents to send Eisenhower to Berlin: Harry Truman, *Year of Decisions,* pp. 300–301. Truman-Morgenthau May 16, 1945, meeting is in MD of the same date. Truman-Stimson meeting an hour later is in SD and Stimson to Truman, May 16, 1945, and Leffler, p. 64. Stimson lunch with Hoover and attack on New Deal "amateurs": SD, May 13, 1945. "Even when I was in the Senate": Harry Truman, *Year of Decisions,* p. 234. "I never was in favor of that crazy plan": Transcript of interviews with aides, 1954, HSTL.

CHAPTER TWENTY-TWO
"You and I Will Have to Bear Great Responsibility"

Hopkins and Harriman May 1945 conversations with Stalin in Moscow: FRUS Potsdam, vol. 1, pp. 25–30. For post–Cold War evidence on Hitler's death and disposition of his corpse, see Petrova and Watson, pp. 7–127. Hopkins to Truman on Stalin "very anxious": May 28, 1945, HSTL. Churchill to Truman on mid-July summit "much too late" and Truman reply: FRUS Potsdam, vol. 1, pp. 91, 93. Churchill begs Truman not to withdraw the U.S. Army: FRUS Potsdam, vol. 1, p. 92. Truman-Morgenthau June 1, 1945, meeting is in MD of same date. "The Jews claim God Almighty": Truman Diary, June 1, 1945, HSTL. Eisenhower and Allied counterparts June 5, 1945, meeting in Berlin: Jean Edward Smith, *Lucius D. Clay,* p. 256. American worries about no Soviet guarantee on Berlin access and Marshall-Eisenhower view: Ibid., pp. 258–259. Hopkins to Truman on U.S. withdrawal: Ibid., p. 259. Truman to Stalin on withdrawal: June 15, 1945, HSTL. Truman to Churchill on withdrawal delay: Harry Truman, *Year of Decisions,* pp. 303–305. Churchill reply: Ibid., pp. 303–304. Churchill-Truman withdrawal pledge and Stalin request for delay: June 15 and 16, 1945, HSTL. Stalin proposal of Potsdam: Harry Truman, *Year of Decisions,* pp. 332–334. "I always get those dirty Nazis mixed up": Truman to mother and sister, June 1945, in HSTL.

Morgenthau frustrations by Truman: MD, June 1945. Truman-Morgenthau June 13, 1945, meeting and Morgenthau's reaction are in MD of same date. Truman to aides on Morgenthau no business in Europe: Eben Ayers Diary, June 18, 1945, in HSTL. Truman-Morgenthau June 18, 1945, meeting, is in MD of same date. "Naturally I was disappointed": Morgenthau to sons, June 21, 1945, HMPA. Stimson on Douglas report and Baruch demands on Germany: SD, June 1945. Baruch had given Truman a copy of his March 18, 1945, memo to Roosevelt, which was reported in NYT, June 1, 1945. McCloy to Hopkins, June 29, 1945, on taking Stimson to Potsdam is in McCloy Papers. Truman-Stimson July 2, 1945, meeting is in SD, July 1945.

Truman reversal on nominating Byrnes in 1944 and desire to "balance things up": Robertson, pp. 360–363, Harry Truman, *Year of Decisions,* p. 23. Truman has Byrnes flown to Washington after becoming President and informs he will be Secretary of State: Robertson, pp. 390–391, Harry Truman, *Year of Decisions,* p. 22. Truman impressed by Byrnes presence at Yalta: Robertson, p. 389. Byrnes exploitation of presence at Yalta: Ibid., pp. 388–389. Truman embrace by Byrnes on arrival in Washington: Ibid., p. 103. "Had a long talk with my able and conniving Secretary of State": Truman Diary, July 7, 1945, HSTL. Stimson delight with Byrnes at State: SD, July 1945. Stimson warned that Morgenthau "on the prowl" again: SD, July 4, 1945. Truman-Stimson July 3, 1945, talk is in SD of July 3 and 13, 1945, Blum interview, HMPA, and MM, p. 435.

CHAPTER TWENTY-THREE
"How I Hate This Trip!"

Truman-Morgenthau July 5, 1945, meeting and Morgenthau comments about it to aides are in MD of that date and later in July 1945. "When the trip to Potsdam was being arranged": Transcript of interviews with aides, 1954, HSTL. Truman opinion of Morgenthau as "nut" and "blockhead" appears in an unsent letter to Jonathan Daniels, February 26, 1950, in HSTL. Truman on Morgenthau not knowing "shit from apple butter": Weil, p. 224. White House July 5, 1945, announcement of Morgenthau's replacement by Vinson: NYT, July 6, 1945. Complaints to Truman that Morgenthau might be successor: MD, July 11, 1945, McCullough, p. 404. Truman-Rosenman July 6, 1945, meeting: MD, July 11, 1945, and Morgenthau to sons, July 16, 1945, HMPA. Vinson pulled off boat: MM, p. 406.

"As Jew to Jew": Henry Morgenthau III in Blum interview, HMPA. Rosenman-Morgenthau meeting: MD, July 11, 1945, and Morgenthau to sons, July 16, 1945. Fate of Morgenthau's three letters to Truman and explanation to sons are in his July 16, 1945, letter, HMPA. Morgenthau at Vinson swearing-in: Klotz interview, HMPA. Churchill to Morgenthau, August 24, 1945, is in FO 371/46979, PRO. Morgenthau's lack of job offers and United Jewish Appeal offer: Klotz interview, HMPA, MM, pp. 406, 408, 411. "Don't have anything": MM, p. 411. "He needed the respect": MM, p. 411. Morgenthau learns about Jewish ritual and told about Kalmanowitz: Klotz interview, HMPA, Herman Klotz to Henry Morgenthau III, September 7, 1982, HMPA. Morgenthau 1948 visit to Israel: MM, p. 416. Eshkol request and Morgenthau reply: MD, December 9, 1953. Klotz hope to marry Morgenthau and possible affair: Henry Morgenthau III interview. "Watchdog": Morgenthau to Klotz, August 5, 1945, HMPA, NYT, December 21, 1988. Klotz comments on Morgenthau second wife: Klotz interview, HMPA. "Now that I married a Frenchwoman": Ibid. "Your father could never have": MM, p. 302. "My father cut himself off": Henry Morgenthau III in Klotz interview, HMPA. "He was so unhappy": Klotz interview. Morgenthau joke with daughter-in-law: MM, p. 436. Blum view of Morgenthau Plan and Morgenthau reply: Blum interview, HMPA.

Truman departure for Potsdam: McCullough, pp. 404–405. Ickes on Truman "dreading" trip: Ickes Diary, July 8, 1945. "As blue as indigo": Truman to Bess, July 6, 1945, HSTL. "How I hate this trip!": Truman Diary, July 7, 1945, HSTL. Truman's voyage: McCullough, pp. 405–406. "A most restful and satisfactory trip": Truman to Bess, July 12, 1945, HSTL. "Squeezed facts and opinions" and Truman sessions with advisors: McCullough, pp. 409–410. Truman feeling "on guard": Transcript of interviews with aides, 1954, HSTL. Eisenhower to Truman and Byrnes: Bohlen, p. 222, and Dwight Eisenhower, *Crusade in Europe*, p. 441. Truman briefed on situation in Germany: Transcript of interviews with aides, 1954, HSTL. "My aim was a unified Germany": Harry Truman, *Year of Decisions*, p. 306. For Truman's contemporary views, see FRUS Potsdam. "They would take big grandfather clocks": Transcript of interviews with aides, 1954, HSTL. Truman on "nightmare house": Truman Diary, July 16, 1945, HSTL. Truman's delegation told of mansion ownership: McCullough, p. 407. "Ten weeks before you entered this house": Gustav Müller-Grote to Truman, February 10, 1956, HSTL.

On Potsdam conference generally, see Mee, Leffler, pp. 37–38, McCullough, pp. 444–453, Ferrell, *Harry S. Truman,* pp. 203–210, Hamby, pp. 325–331, Donovan, pp. 80–89, Harry Truman, *Year of Decisions,* pp. 343–414, Gilbert, *Never Despair,* pp. 60–104, Eisenberg, pp. 89–120, Trachtenberg, pp. 15–33, Ulam, *Expansion and Coexistence,* pp. 391–392, 442–443, Offner, pp. 72–91. "Gave me a lot of hooey": Truman Diary, July 16, 1945, HSTL. "I liked him from the start": Transcript of interviews with aides, 1954, HSTL. Truman tour of Berlin: Donovan, p. 73. "A long, never-ending procession": Truman Diary, July 16, 1945, HSTL. "Forced off the farm": Transcript of 1963 interview, Ben Gradus Films, Screen Gems, HSTL. "It's a terrible thing": NYT, July 17, 1945.

Truman imagines Hitler conquering Washington, D.C.: Harry Truman, *Year of Decisions,* p. 341, McCullough, pp. 412–416. Berlin an "absolute ruin": Truman Diary, July 16, 1945, HSTL. Truman on "those unfortunate people": McCullough, p. 415. Truman comment to Byrnes: Donovan, p. 73. "This is a hell of a place": Truman to Bess, July 20, 1945, HSTL. "I looked up from the desk": Truman Diary, July 17, 1945, HSTL. Truman-Stalin conversation: FRUS Potsdam. Hamby on deflecting attention is in letter to the author, July 1, 2002. July 17, 1945, 5 P.M. session: FRUS Potsdam, vol. 2, pp. 52–63. July 18, 1945, afternoon session: FRUS Potsdam, vol. 2, pp. 88–98. Kimball on Soviet and Polish border changes is in his *Swords or Ploughshares,* p. 8. "I'm not going to stay around": Truman Diary, July 18, 1945, HSTL. Truman watches Stars and Stripes: FRUS Potsdam, vol. 2, p. 16. Stimson informs Truman of successful atomic test and Truman reaction: McCullough, pp. 430–432. July 21, 1945, afternoon session: FRUS Potsdam, vol. 2, pp. 203–211. "When he got to the meeting": Mee, p. 164.

CHAPTER TWENTY-FOUR
"We Are Drifting Toward a Line Down the Center of Germany"

Truman longing for home: McCullough, p. 427. "Bolsheviki land grab": Truman Diary, July 20, 1945, HSTL. Truman asks Byrnes to hasten end of meeting: McCullough, p. 455. On Byrnes life and career, see especially Robertson; Messer; and Byrnes, *Speaking Frankly* and *All in One Lifetime.* Byrnes conviction he should be President: Robertson, pp. 77–78. Byrnes relationship with Baruch: Ibid., pp. 77–78 and 118. "It doesn't surprise me that Senators are for sale": Interview by author with Thomas Corcoran, March 5, 1977. Hamby on Byrnes-Baruch largesse is in letter to the author, July 1, 2002. Byrnes relationship with Roosevelt: Robertson, pp. 289–294. "The best qualified man": Byrnes, *All in One Lifetime,* p. 222. "Jimmy, that is all wrong": Ibid., p. 224. Byrnes remains in seat at Chicago: Robertson, p. 363. "For a tired, quarrelsome": Byrnes to FDR, November 8, 1944, FDRL. "I did not come along": Robertson, p. 383. "The most honest-looking horse thief": Ibid. "Not mad at anybody": Ibid., p. 387. Resignation knocks FDR "off my feet": FDR to Byrnes, March 25, 1945, FDRL. "It's a shame some people": Robertson, p. 387. Byrnes appointment to Interim Committee and advice to Truman on new weapon: Ibid., p. 395.

Byrnes-Molotov July 23, 1945, conversation: FRUS Potsdam, vol. 2, pp. 274–275. For aides' actual advice to Byrnes, see Byrnes briefing notes in NA. Byrnes comments on July 24, 1945: FRUS Potsdam, vol. 2, pp. 354–355. Stalin on Ruhr: Ibid., p. 385. Bohlen on Stalin's intention to "paralyze the German economy": Bohlen, p. 233–234. "The big towns like Frankfurt": Truman to mother and sister Mary, July 28, 1945, HSTL. "I wouldn't call it that": Gilbert, *Never Despair,* p. 108. Byrnes-Molotov July 27, 1945, conversation: Mee, p. 243. Truman to Bess on "reasonably sound" deal, July 29, 1945, is in HSTL. Byrnes-Molotov July 30, 1945, conversation: Ibid., pp. 480–483.

Truman on "impasse": Truman Diary, July 30, 1945, HSTL. "The whole difficulty is reparations": Truman to Bess, July 31, 1945, HSTL. Byrnes-Molotov July 31, 1945, conversation: FRUS Potsdam, and Eisenberg, pp. 111–112. July 31, 1945, meeting: FRUS Potsdam, Truman informs Stalin of new weapon and scrawls approval for bomb against Japan: Rhodes, pp. 689–693, Donovan, pp. 93–96, McCullough, pp. 435–443, Hamby, pp. 333–334. Soviet intelligence on U.S. atomic program: Gaddis, *We Now Know,* pp. 93–95. August 1, 1945, meeting: FRUS Potsdam. Text of Potsdam Declaration is in HSTL. On German peace treaty, see Smyser, p. 23. Truman pronounces conference adjourned and Stalin response: Mee, p. 281. "You never saw such pigheaded people": Truman to Mary Ellen Truman, July 31, 1945, HSTL. Truman informed of Hiroshima, Nagasaki and Japanese unconditional surrender: Hamby, pp. 335–337, and McCullough, pp. 454–460. Hamby, pp. 335–336, Transcript of Truman's radio address, August 9, 1945, is in HSTL. Smyser on Potsdam is pp. 23–26. "We are drifting toward a line": Isaacson and Thomas, p. 308. Stimson departure from Potsdam: Jean Edward Smith, *Lucius D. Clay,* p. 234. Stimson meeting with Eisenhower and Clay: Ibid., pp. 234–235.

CHAPTER TWENTY-FIVE
"The Spirit and Soul of a People Reborn"

For Clay's life and career, see especially Jean Edward Smith, *Lucius D. Clay.* "A failure without combat experience": Jean Edward Smith, *Lucius D. Clay,* p. 213. Clay's attitudes to JCS 1067: Ibid., p. 233. Clay to McCloy on "unwilling to concede that Germany became what it was": Clay to McCloy, June 16, 1945, in Jean Edward Smith, *The Papers of General Lucius D. Clay,* vol. 1, pp. 23–24. "Technically our instructions prevented us": Jean Edward Smith, *Lucius D. Clay,* p. 238. Clay assures McCloy that

Germany's war potential no longer a serious problem: April 26, 1945, in Jean Edward Smith, *The Papers of General Lucius D. Clay,* vol. 1, pp. 7–9. Clay to McCloy on hunger necessary: June 16, 1945, in ibid., pp. 23–24. Padover to Ickes on German women "crazy for men" and Ickes's comment: Ickes Diary, June 9, 1945. "The only fraternization": June 29, 1945, in Jean Edward Smith, *The Papers of General Lucius D. Clay,* vol. 1, pp. 35–45, 52–53. Clay lifts ban: Jean Edward Smith, *Lucius D. Clay,* p. 238. "There is no chance": Jean Edward Smith, *Lucius D. Clay,* p. 361. "Four Ds": Smyser, p. 42.

"You cannot build real democracy": Backer, p. 59. No "general feeling of war guilt": Clay to John Hilldring, in Jean Edward Smith, *The Papers of General Lucius D. Clay,* vol. 1, pp. 46–49. "More than half the German people were Nazis": NYT, September 23, 1945. Eisenhower relieves Patton: Ambrose, *Eisenhower: 1890–1952,* pp. 423–425, Eisenberg, p. 134. New decree: Lyon, pp. 361–362. Clay to Pentagon on removals, October 13, 1945, is in Jean Edward Smith, *The Papers of General Lucius D. Clay,* vol. 1, pp. 101–105. "The best way to get a bad order changed": Jean Edward Smith, *Lucius D. Clay,* p. 233. American denazification compared to that of allies and magnitude of program: Ambrose, *Eisenhower: 1890–1952,* pp. 423–425, and Zink, *The U.S. in Germany,* pp. 150–168. "I think we carried it too far": Jean Edward Smith, *Lucius D. Clay,* p. 240. Truman sends Byron Price to Germany and Price Report: Eisenberg, pp. 175–176, and Price Report file, HSTL.

On Nuremberg trials, see Persico, *Nuremberg,* and Telford Taylor. "A just, swift and public trial": Transcript, "The Stacked Deck: The Harry S. Truman Series," Ben Gradus Films, Screen Gems, 1963, in HSTL. Clay on Nuremberg trials convincing Germans "how terrible their government really was": Jean Edward Smith, *Lucius D. Clay,* p. 297. Clay's early moves toward democracy in U.S. zone: Ibid., pp. 240–245. Clay's November 1945 visit to Washington: Ibid., p. 235.

On de Gaulle's role in occupation, see Jean Lacouture, *De Gaulle: The Ruler, 1945–1970* (New York: Norton, 1992), pp. 43–65. "Desire to return France to world power": Transcript of interviews with aides, 1954, HSTL. On foreign ministers negotiations on Germany generally, see Eisenberg, pp. 228–231, 233–240, 277–317, 487–488, Smyser, pp. 25–31, and Vladimir Pechatnov, "Foreign Policy Correspondence Between Stalin and Molotov and Other Politburo Members," September 1945–December 1946, CWIHP. Truman reprimand of Byrnes: Smyser, p. 28. Clay's halt on reparations deliveries and Soviet response: Clay, p. 120, Botting, pp. 286–287, Leffler, p. 118, and Ulam, *Expansion and Coexistence,* p. 443. Clay's May 1946 report: May 26, 1946, in Jean Edward Smith, *The Papers of General Lucius D. Clay,* vol. 1, pp. 212–217. Patterson on Ruhr-Rhineland revival: Patterson to Byrnes, June 10, 1946, NA. Paris foreign ministers meeting: Eisenberg, pp. 228–229.

Byrnes's September 1946 Stuttgart speech: Robertson, p. 456, Botting, pp. 287–288, Jean Edward Smith, *Lucius D. Clay,* vol. 1, pp. 386–389, and Smyser, pp. 44–45. Truman sends Hoover to Germany and Hoover report: Ibid., p. 50. Joint Chiefs on "complete revival": U.S. Department of State, *A Decade of American Foreign Policy* (Washington, D.C.: U.S. Government Printing Office, 1985), p. 331. Creation of Bizonia: Smyser, p. 47. Marshall and JCS 1779: Jean Edward Smith, *Lucius D. Clay,* p. 431, and text in NA. Marshall warns that "the patient is sinking": McCullough, p. 561. Clay on dispirited Germans: See Jean Edward Smith, *The Papers of General Lucius D. Clay,* vol. 1, pp. 308–367. Marshall drafts and unveils Marshall Plan: McCullough, pp. 562–565. Molotov's rejection: Ibid., p. 565, Pogue, *Organizer of Victory,* p. 469. Scott Parrish, "The Turn Toward Confrontation: The Soviet Reaction to the Marshall Plan, 1947," and Mikhail Narinsky, "The Soviet Union and The Marshall Plan," CWIHP.

Stalin's hopes for united Germany: See especially Smyser, pp. 63–67, 73–78, Gaddis, *We Now Know,* pp. 113–121, and Eisenberg, pp. 485–493. See also Novikov to Molotov, September 27, 1946, CWIHP. "All of Germany": Gaddis, *We Now Know,* p. 116. Molotov effort to "expand Soviet frontiers": Smyser, p. 69. Ulbricht's role: Eisenberg, pp. 187–188, and Smyser, p. 33. "Like your ancestors, the Teutons": Smyser, p. 99. "The Russians were not going to carry out": Transcript of interviews with aides, 1954, HSTL. "For all their alarms about Russian aggression": Eisenberg, p. 491. "When the German population looked back": Schwartz, p. 300. Schwartz on surveys is in Ambrose and Bischof, p. 221. On Berlin Blockade and Berlin Airlift, see McCullough, pp. 630–631, Leffler, pp. 217–218, Donovan, pp. 363–368, Eisenberg, pp. 379–394, 411–416, Smyser, pp. 73–87, Thomas Parrish, pp. 147–155, 233–236. "We'll stay in Berlin": Truman Diary, July 19, 1948, HSTL. "It was their Valley Forge": Smyser, p. 87.

Founding of NATO: McCullough, pp. 734–735. Smyser pp. 101–103, and Leffler, pp. 198–218. Founding of Federal Republic of Germany: NYT, May 24, 1949, and Smyser, pp. 89–96. Founding of German Democratic Republic: NYT, October 8, 1949, and Smyser, pp. 96–100. "A wonderful piece of work" and Clay's response: Jean Edward Smith, *Lucius D. Clay,* p. 550. "One has only to revisit Buchenwald": Ibid., p. 555. George H. W. Bush on Europe "whole and free": Beschloss and Talbott, pp. 80–81. For unification of Germany in 1990 and scenes in Berlin at moment of unification, see Beschloss and Talbott, p. 271, Zelikow and Rice, pp. 362–370, Smyser, p. 396, *Facts on File,* Associated Press reports, NYT, *Washington Post, Los Angeles Times, Christian Science Monitor, Financial Times, The Independent* (London), *The Daily Telegraph* (London), October 3 to 5, 1990. Kohl on "We must never forget": Associated Press, October 4, 1990. Von Weizsäcker on "the war started under Hitler": NYT, October 4, 1990.

CHAPTER TWENTY-SIX
The Conquerors

"The success of this occupation": Bagger, p. 28. John Kennedy on Soviet "jail": Beschloss, *The Crisis Years,* p. 278. "Those terrible eighteen months": Blum, *From the Morgenthau Diaries,* vol. 3, p. 207. The reference to Burns is from the subtitle of his

1956 volume on FDR, which noted Machiavelli's dictum that the prince be both lion and fox. Truman regret at not ruling Germany singlehandedly: Transcript of interviews with aides, 1954, HSTL. "For the first two years after the war": Eisenberg, p. 491. For Hitler's plans for postwar Berlin generally, see Speer, pp. 151–160. Hitler on future visitors "stunned" by "power of the Reich": Ibid., pp. 134–135. Hitler "megalomania" and "obsessed": Ibid., pp. 155–157. Speer on Hitler "deeply irked" by Stalin's Moscow project: Ibid., p. 155. "Greatest staircase in the world": Ibid., p. 137. Hitler on being "forced to take unpopular measures": Ibid., p. 158. "Decadence" of Hitler's planned palace: Ibid., pp. 159–160. Speer on SS "incredible ignorance": Ibid., p. 144. "The whole world will come to Berlin": Ibid., p. 141. For context of architecture of current-day Berlin, see Rudy Koshar, *From Monuments to Traces: Artifacts of German Memory, 1870–1990* (Berkeley: University of California Press, 2000). Bendler Street was renamed for Stauffenberg in 1955, at a time when West Germans were searching their past for nonauthoritarian antecedents.

INDEX

PHOTOGRAPHY CREDITS

© Hulton-Deutsch Collection/CORBIS: 1, 5
AKG Photo: 2, 24
© CORBIS: 3, 17, 23
© Bettmann/CORBIS: 4, 9, 14, 20, 26, 27, 28, 29
© Underwood & Underwood/CORBIS: 6
Pirie MacDonald/Library of Congress: 7
Franklin D. Roosevelt Library: 8, 12, 16
AP/Wide World Photos: 10, 11, 13, 18, 19, 21, 22, 25, 30
National Archives: 15
Harry S. Truman Library: 31

ABOUT THE AUTHOR

MICHAEL BESCHLOSS has been called by *Newsweek* "the nation's leading Presidential historian." Born in Chicago in 1955, he is the author of six previous books on the history of American Presidents and international relations. A frequent lecturer and regular commentator on ABC News and PBS's *The NewsHour with Jim Lehrer*, he is a trustee of the White House Historical Association, the National Archives Foundation, the Thomas Jefferson Foundation, the Urban Institute and the University of Virginia's Miller Center of Public Affairs. He lives with his wife and their two sons in Washington, D.C. His next book will be a history of the Abraham Lincoln assassination.